MUL.BABBAR

The White Star
Over Bethlehem

MUL.BABBAR

The White Star Over Bethlehem

A Novel of the Magi

Dwight Hutchison

Editions Signes Célestes

MUL.BABBAR: The White Star Over Bethlehem

Version Imprimée (Printed Version) : ISBN-13: 979-10-95558-13-2

PDF ebook : ISBN-13: 979-10-95558-14-9

Published by the Association «Signes Célestes» (Editions Signes Célestes) (Association Culturelle de la Loi 1901)

Association Signes Célestes
10, Allée du Luberon
26130 St. Paul-Trois-Chateaux, France

Dépôt Légal : 4ème trimestre 2018

Book Website: www.star-of-bethlehem.info
Email: association.signes.celestes@gmail.com
Printed and distributed by Createspace (USA)

Dedication

The author dedicates this book to his beloved friends and family who have encouraged him to serve the risen Messiah over almost six decades.

Thanks

The author would like to express his appreciation and gratitude to several people who have supported and encouraged at least various aspects of this project and who have given very helpful advice and needed corrections. The people include Warren Molberg, Richard Humble, Norm Wood, Kasandra McNeil, Joséphine Hutchison, Eléna Hutchison, Marie-Thérèse Plaine, Jan Simenson, Bob Causey, Andrew Kirk, Laura Avers, and Ken Elchert.

In addition, the author wants to express his appreciation for all work of the men and women who have deciphered, translated, interpreted, published, and written about the ancient Babylonian astronomical texts during the last 150 years. Without their painstaking attention to detail, the theory of the Star of Bethlehem outlined in this book would not have been possible.

Table of Contents

*M*UL.BABBAR, *The White Star Over Bethlehem* is a historical novel that recreates the account of the wise men found in Matthew's Gospel. The novel takes place in the years 4 BC through 1 BC. (See Appendix 6 concerning the dates.) The book is based on the author's unique research about the Star of Bethlehem.

The name MUL.BABBAR was used by Babylonian astronomers for the planet Jupiter. Modern linguistic specialists usually write ancient Sumerian names in all capitals. Originally the name MUL.BABBAR, meaning "the white star," was written: ⸭ ⸭ in the cuneiform texts. Planets in our solar system look like stars when observed with the naked eye. The Babylonians also designated MUL.BABBAR (Jupiter) as a "king star" (^MUL^LUGAL). The star Regulus also carried the same name. The novel includes significant insights from Babylonian astronomy. The Babylonian names of many celestial bodies have often been retained.

Many Christians have a mystical, uniquely supernatural understanding of the Magi and the Star of Bethlehem. However, from my perspective, such an understanding of Matthew's text is a mistake. I have sought to portray the wise men as real human beings who had a completely unexpected experience with a well-known royal star.

There were many supernatural aspects of the story of Jesus' birth and the visit of the wise men to Bethlehem. Even so, the star itself was a natural object, which was manifest in extraordinary circumstances. The God of Abraham established the dimensions, orbits, qualities, and movements of all the heavenly bodies at the beginning of creation. At that time, He also planned the unique circumstances of the star's appearing.

The star was a real heavenly object, but its role was to announce the Messiah's coming, not to serve as a visual guide. The star was a herald of the king, not a guiding light. The astronomical events described in this book did take place as can be verified by many computerized astronomy applications. See appendices two to five at the back of the book for further explanations.

MUL.BABBAR, The White Star Over Bethlehem covers the eastern experience of the wise men in an in-depth manner. When one understands how the wise men initially identified the messianic star, then the object's significance over Bethlehem also becomes clear.

Unfortunately, we do not know very much about the wise men. They were probably Babylonians, but the group could have had mixed origins. The novel portrays the Magi as Babylonians, a Zoroastrian, and a Greek.

The author's theory about the star has been given a detailed treatment in three books. The longest book, entitled *The Lion Led the Way (Third Edition)*, contains much of the author's original research. Two other shorter books, *A Sign Over Bethlehem*, as well as, *The Star of Bethlehem, Signs in the East and a Surprise in the West* were written to make the author's Bethlehem Star theory more accessible to a larger public.

Additional Notes:

- A list of characters has been provided in the Supplements section at the end of this book. Many of the character names will be unfamiliar to most readers.

- Some prophetic, explanatory, and historical material has been included in footnotes and appendices. These texts also partially explain the author's star theory and his choice in dating the events.

- A partial bibliography is also included which points to some of the important books and articles used in the author's research.

- The image, ⊏⊐⊦⊦⊤ which is used to separate texts in the novel, is the word "MUL" meaning "star" written in cuneiform.

- Dates are indicated by Babylonian and Jewish month names. Each month began with the first visibility of the crescent moon in the west after sunset. Jewish and Babylonian days began at sunset and ended the next evening at sunset.

Important Moments of the Jewish Calendar

Pesach (Passover)	Nisan 14
Feast of Unleavened Bread	Nisan 15-21
First Fruits Offering	Nisan 16
Counting of the Omer	Nisan 16-Sivan 5
Shavuot (Pentecost)	Sivan 6
The Day of Trumpets	Tishrei 1
Yom Kippur	Tishrei 10
Sukkot (Tabernacles)	Tishrei 15-22
The Great Day	Tishrei 22
Hanukkah	Kislev 25-Tevet 2 or 3

Months of the Babylonian and Jewish Calendars

	Babylonian	Jewish	Season
1	Nissanu	Nisan	Spring
2	Ayyaru	Iyar	Spring
3	Simānu	Sivan	Spring
4	Du'ūzu	Tammuz	Summer
5	Abu	Av	Summer
6	Ulūlu*	Elul	Summer
7	Tašrītu	Tishrei	Fall
8	Arahsamna	Marcheshvan	Fall
9	Kislīmu	Kislev	Fall
10	Tebētu	Tevet	Winter
11	Šabātu	Shevat	Winter
12	Addaru	Adar	Winter
13	Addaru II**	Adar II**	Winter/Spring

* Ulūlu II was added once every 19 years in the Babylonian calendar.

**(The second month of Addaru (Adar) was added every two or three years in both calendars.)

Cappadocia
Comma
Samosat
Limit Roman Empire and Its Allied States
Asia Minor
Roman Empire
Ephesus
Cilicia
Tarsus
Antioch
Roman Syria
Cyprus
Apamea
Tadmu
Mediterranean Sea
Beyritus
Sidon
Tyre
Ptolemais
Damascus
Caesarea
Herod's Kingdom
Jerusalem
Judaea
Pelusium
Alexandria
Limit Roman Empire
Petra
Memphis
Kingdom of Arabia
Sinai
Limit Roman Empire
Roman Egypt
Red Sea

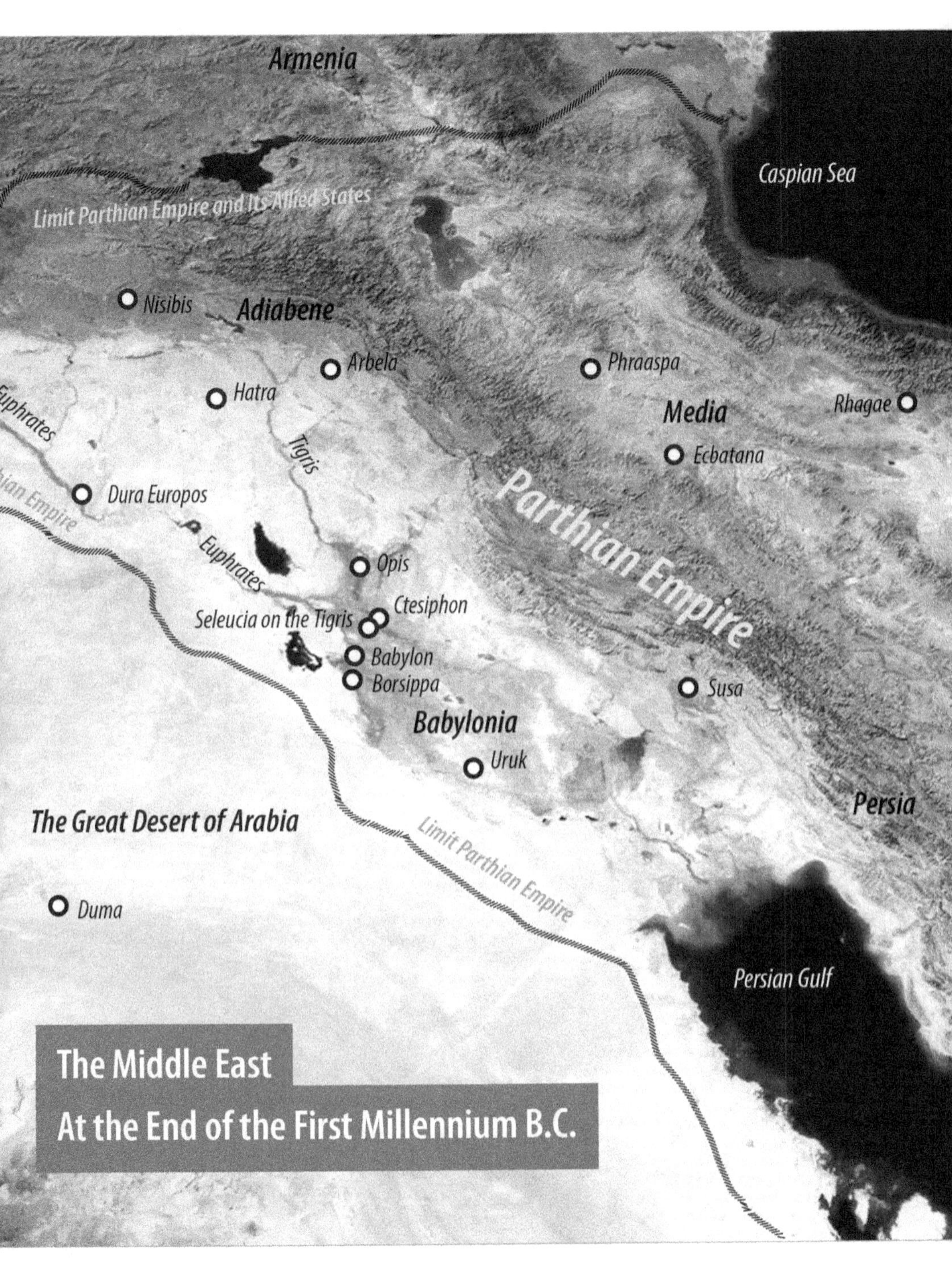

Armenia
Caspian Sea
Limit Parthian Empire and Its Allied States
Nisibis
Adiabene
Arbela
Phraaspa
Hatra
Media
Rhagae
Euphrates
Tigris
Ecbatana
Parthian Empire
Dura Europos
Euphrates
Opis
Ctesiphon
Seleucia on the Tigris
Babylon
Borsippa
Susa
Babylonia
Uruk
Persia
The Great Desert of Arabia
Limit Parthian Empire
Duma
Persian Gulf
The Middle East
At the End of the First Millennium B.C.

Part 1: The Promised Messiah

1

Prophecies of the Messiah

Chapter Contents:

The Shiloh

Egypt, toward 1900 BC

It was always the same, thirty cavalrymen preceded the prime minister's chariot, and thirty followed it. The men rode three abreast in ten ranks with marvelously crafted swords hanging from their waists. The dark brown horses contrasted well with the white and gold clothing of the horsemen, making a stunning appearance, which was the desired effect. In the middle of the procession, a chariot was pulled forward by two striking white stallions. An imposing passenger stood beside the driver dressed in regal attire. Besides Pharaoh himself, he was the most powerful man in Egypt.

On this particular day, the column was supplemented by two other chariots following the second group of cavalrymen, then a final group of thirty horsemen closed the column. Ninety horsemen and three chariots advanced up a dusty road toward an isolated residential compound. Date palms lined part of the road and green fields with some herds of sheep and goats extended to the left and right. To the east, a band of tan colored sand in the distance showed the way to the desert. To the left, the fields and palm trees filled the horizon from the north to south.

The man in the first chariot realized that very soon his father in the grand villa in the distance was very probably going to join his ancestors.

---

* The Hebrew text behind the title on this page and elsewhere in this book is from Genesis 49.

The old man was dying. The family patriarch had summoned his son, who was the prime minister, as well as his other sons, to give them his blessing before his departure. A group of soldiers could be seen at the entrance to the compound on the right, standing prepared to receive the column. Their officer saluted the cavalry commander leading the column as he passed. As the prime minister's chariot approached, the soldiers bowed. There would be no fanfare from the trumpeters today. The prime minister had sent word not to blow the trumpets upon his arrival. His father was dying.

In the vast courtyard in front of the villa, the first 30 cavalrymen veered off to the right as the principal chariot continued to advance all the way to an outdoor staircase leading to an upper terrace. The next group of cavalrymen arranged themselves on the left as the two following chariots arrived. The final group of horsemen remained at the gate since the courtyard was now full. Two young boys dressed in fine robes descended from their chariots and joined their father who was already at the base of the stairs.

Joseph, Ephraim, and Mannaseh climbed the stairs to the terrace. Arriving at the top without looking further, Joseph lifted each of his young sons in turn so they could see the view beyond the low wall surrounding the terrace. Below the lands of their grandfather stretched out in all directions. Sheep and goats ate the grass under the scattered palm trees and the late afternoon sun reflected on pools of water and a sliver of a branch of the Nile toward the west. The boys laughed as Joseph raised them high over his head to see and then brought them down almost with a crash to the ground. Afterward, the three of them turned away from the scene and saw a group of eleven men standing under a vine-covered pergola on the far side of the terrace. As soon as Joseph had turned in their direction, without a word the men bowed and remained facing the ground as Joseph and his two sons approached.

Joseph broke the silence saying calmly and in soft tones, "Brothers, let me greet you. Today is a solemn day, but I am happy to see you." He then heartily embraced each of them one by one.

Finally, Ruben, the oldest of the group, addressed his brother, "Our father has called for you first. He knows that you have arrived with your sons. He wants to see you privately."

Ruben then pointed to the doorway in the shade at the end of the pergola. Joseph breathed profoundly and moved toward the door. It was not every day that one's father steps back from death's embrace to speak to his son one last time.

A servant at the door disappeared into the interior as Joseph drew near. Entering the spacious bedroom, Joseph saw the servant speaking to his father. The old man stirred himself upon his bed. Jacob, the family patriarch also named Israel, made an effort to rise, but finally, he could only sit on the edge of his bed. He indicated to Joseph that he should approach.

When they had come to the side of his bed Jacob said to Joseph, "God Almighty appeared to me at Luz in the land of Canaan and blessed me, and He said to me, 'Behold, I will make you fruitful and numerous, and I will make you a company of peoples, and will give this land to your descendants after you for an everlasting possession.'" [2] Hearing these words Joseph remembered how his father had made him solemnly promise to bury him in the land of Canaan.

Jacob continued, "Now your two sons, who were born to you in the land of Egypt before I came to you in Egypt, are mine; Ephraim and Manasseh shall be mine, as Reuben and Simeon my oldest sons are mine. Unfortunately, my eyes are now so dim from age that I cannot see very well."

Then Jacob finally perceived the children he thought to be Joseph's sons standing a bit further away from the bed, he said, "Who are these?" Joseph said to his father, "They are my sons, whom God has given me here in Egypt." So he said, "Bring them to me, please, that I may bless them." [3] The boys were placed on Jacob's knees, and he blessed them.

Afterward, through his servant, Jacob then summoned his other sons saying, "Assemble yourselves that I may tell you what will befall you in the days to come. Gather together, you sons of Jacob and listen to Israel your father." [4]

When the men had arrived in the room near their father, Jacob began blessing each one, in turn, starting with his firstborn Ruben. Afterward,

---

2 Genesis 48:3-4

3 Genesis 48:8-9

4 Genesis 49:1

he blessed Simeon and Levi. When it came time for the fourth son Judah to receive his blessing, Jacob seemed to hesitate for a moment, and then these words came from his mouth,

> *"Judah, your brothers shall praise you; Your hand shall be on the neck of your enemies; Your father's sons shall bow down to you. Judah is a lion's whelp; From the prey, my son, you have gone up. He couches, he lies down as a lion, and as a lion, who dares rouse him up? The scepter shall not depart from Judah, nor the ruler's staff from between his feet, until Shiloh comes, and to him shall be the obedience of the peoples."* [5]

Joseph marveled at the words. It seemed that the leadership of Jacob's descendants would not follow his line. Joseph was prime minister of Egypt, second only to Pharaoh, but for some reason, the ruler's staff and authority would follow Judah's line. Joseph was surprised that Jacob had said: "And to him shall be the obedience of the peoples." Which peoples? All the peoples of the earth? It was a curious phrase.

Joseph stood by Jacob's bed, puzzled, but also content. God was foreseeing an unexpectedly brilliant future for Judah's descendants. Apparently, later this glorious future would be manifest for one person, in particular, the Shiloh. Joseph knew that the word Shiloh was a way of referring to the person who had the right to the scepter, the ruler's staff.

Who would this man be? The prophetic blessing had been pronounced. How would this happen? What would the accomplishment of the prophetic word bring? As a man who had yielded immense power in the service of Pharaoh, Joseph's thoughts were drawn to the words. Joseph had been surprised that the leadership of his family would not definitively rest with his descendants. Yes, he had been brought to a place of significant power in Egypt, but not in his own family.

Jacob continued to bless the other brothers, and toward the end of the time, he blessed Joseph also. Within hours the old man would breathe his last and lay still in his bed, but the prophetic words remained chiseled in Joseph's mind. Even more than his blessing, Joseph pondered the words, "And to the Shiloh shall be the obedience of the peoples."

---

5 Genesis 49:8-10

The Sun and Moon

Jerusalem, Possibly in the Late 920s BC

The aging psalmist, Ethan the Ezrahite, had seen the best and the worse of times in Jerusalem. As a young man, he remembered King David's reign. Despite his failings, the good king had passed the kingdom on to Solomon. The reign of David's son had been magnificent even though in his later years Solomon had turned away from the Lord. But now the kingdom was in desolation following the Egyptian invasion under Pharaoh Shishaq. This foreign intervention in Judaea had ended only weeks before. The fifth year of the reign of Rehoboam the son of Solomon had been one of the worst which Ethan had witnessed. In his old age, his grief was immense. He did not know if he would survive for very much longer.

Pharaoh Shishaq had arrived with 1,200 chariots, 60,000 horsemen, and other troops.[1] The Egyptian king had laid siege to Jerusalem. Being hard pressed, Rehoboam had emptied the treasuries of the temple in order to persuade the Egyptians to leave. Ethan could almost weep as he remembered the golden shields and other treasures stored up by David and Solomon which had left the city in dozens of carts only about three weeks earlier. But even worse the whole country around Jerusalem had been pillaged, the women were raped, and many of the young and old

---

1 See 2nd Chronicles 12:1-16. Rehoboam reigned from 931-914 BC. Shishaq conquered Judaea in 926 BC.

had been put to death with the sword. The kingdom had not been able to resist the might of Pharaoh. And now King Rehoboam was a vassal of the Egyptian king. The king and the people had forgotten that the fear of the Lord was the beginning of wisdom. Ethan knew that their situation was directly attributable to their lack of submission to the Holy One of Israel.

In recent days, Ethan had written down his thoughts:

But you have rejected, you have spurned, you have been very angry with your anointed one. You have renounced the covenant with your servant and have defiled his crown in the dust. You have broken through all his walls and reduced his strongholds to ruins. All who pass by have plundered him; he has become the scorn of his neighbors.

You have exalted the right hand of his foes; you have made all his enemies rejoice. Indeed, you have turned back the edge of his sword and have not supported him in battle. You have put an end to his splendor and cast his throne to the ground. You have cut short the days of his youth; you have covered him with a mantle of shame.

How long, Lord? Will you hide yourself forever? How long will your wrath burn like fire? Remember how fleeting is my life. ... Lord, where is your former great love, which in your faithfulness you swore to David? ...[2]

From the terrace of his home in the upper city near the king's palace, Ethan looked out toward the east in the early evening. The sun had set a while before, and stars were beginning to appear. The cool of the evening air refreshed Ethan's body and spirit. He then noticed an area of brightness on the horizon to the south and east above southern flank of the Mount of Olives. Within moments, the full moon became visible as it slid gently over the top of the opposing ridge. Darkness would not reign through this night. Ethan's heart was encouraged at the thought. Darkness would not dominate Jerusalem this night. The faithful God would not allow evil to overcome his people forever. There was still hope. Ethan began to ponder the promises that God had given to David. The word of the Lord through the prophet Nathan to David came to his mind:

"David, when your days are fulfilled and you rest with your fathers, I will set up your seed after you, who will come from your body, and I

---

2 Psalm 89:38-49

will establish his kingdom. He shall build a house for My name, and I will establish the throne of his kingdom forever. I will be his Father, and he shall be My son. If he commits iniquity, I will chasten him with the rod of men and with the blows of the sons of men. But My mercy shall not depart from him ... And your house and your kingdom shall be established forever before you. Your throne shall be established forever." [3]

The kingdom was not finished. Ethan remembered how the Rehoboam had humbled himself before God in the sight of all the people. The Lord would remember his faithfulness. Ethan began to sense a new song in his mind and spirit. Words came to his mind, and certain phrases seemed to be underlined in his thinking. Finally, as the moon filled the valley with light, Ethan called his wife to bring him a parchment and a small lamp. No, darkness would not reign forever. God had promised to David, "Your throne shall be established forever." When his wife arrived with the parchment, Ethan took it and almost as quickly began to write:

"I will sing of the mercies of the Lord forever; With my mouth will I make known Your faithfulness to all generations. For I have said, 'Mercy shall be built up forever; Your faithfulness You shall establish in the very heavens. I have made a covenant with My chosen, I have sworn to My servant David: Your seed I will establish forever, And build up your throne to all generations.'" Selah

"And the heavens will praise Your wonders, O Lord; Your faithfulness also in the assembly of the saints. For who in the heavens can be compared to the Lord? Who among the sons of the mighty can be likened to the Lord? God is greatly to be feared in the assembly of the saints, And to be held in reverence by all those around Him. O Lord God of hosts, Who is mighty like You, O Lord? Your faithfulness also surrounds You. ... The heavens are Yours, the earth also is Yours; The world and all its fullness, You have founded them. The north and the south, You have created them; Tabor and Hermon rejoice in Your name."

"You have a mighty arm; strong is Your hand, and high is Your right hand. Righteousness and justice are the foundation of Your throne; Mercy and truth go before Your face. Blessed are the people who know the joyful sound! They walk, O Lord, in the light of Your countenance. In Your name they rejoice all day long, And in Your righteousness they

---

3 2 Samuel 7:13-16

are exalted. For You are the glory of their strength, and in Your favor our horn is exalted. For our shield belongs to the Lord, and our king to the Holy One of Israel."

"Then You spoke in a vision to Your holy one, and said: "I have given help to one who is mighty; I have exalted one chosen from the people. I have found My servant David. With My holy oil I have anointed him, with whom My hand shall be established. Also My arm shall strength-en him. The enemy shall not outwit him, nor the son of wickedness afflict him. I will beat down his foes before his face, and plague those who hate him."

"But My faithfulness and My mercy shall be with him, and in My name his horn shall be exalted. Also I will set his hand over the sea, and his right hand over the rivers. He shall cry to Me, 'You are my Fa-ther, My God, and the rock of my salvation.' Also I will make him My firstborn, the highest of the kings of the earth. My mercy I will keep for him forever, and My covenant shall stand firm with him. His seed also I will make to endure forever, and his throne as the days of heaven."

"If his sons forsake My law and do not walk in My judgments, if they break My statutes and do not keep My commandments, then I will punish their transgression with the rod, and their iniquity with stripes. Nevertheless My lovingkindness I will not utterly take from him, nor allow My faithfulness to fail. My covenant I will not break, nor alter the word that has gone out of My lips. Once I have sworn by My holiness; I will not lie to David: His seed shall endure forever, and his throne as the sun before Me; It shall be established forever like the moon, even like the faithful witness in the sky." [4]

Looking up from his text, Ethan raised his eyes to the ancient object in the skies. The moon had been established of old, at the beginning of the world. It had endured as long as the sun. Ethan took courage. Indeed David's throne would also last through all generations like the sun and moon. The Lord had sworn, David's seed would endure, and his throne would be established for ages to come. Just as the witnesses in the sky had endured for thousands of years by God's design, so God would also be faithful to his covenant with David.

---

4   Psalm 89:1-37 Please note that in Hebrew "forever" is actually "olam" which means a very long time, as in the sense of ages past or ages to come.

Jeremiah - Prophecy of the Righteous King

Jerusalem, About 587 BC

For several weeks, Jeremiah had been held as a prisoner in the court of the royal guard, under the eyes of dozens of Judaean soldiers. As a believing Jew, Jeremiah had resisted the king's efforts to continue in idolatry. However, the Jewish king had imprisoned him specifically because Jeremiah had given a word from God to cease the Judaean rebellion against the king of Babylon. The king was afraid that Jeremiah would discourage the Judaean army and the population of Jerusalem. The Babylonian army was camped just outside the city walls.

Day and night, Jeremiah was in chains outside in the courtyard. Happily, a bit of shade provided by a small porch protected him from the sun and an occasional rainstorm. There were moments when the prophet wished that he was no longer alive. Thousands had died, and many had been taken captive. Starvation threatened the survivors trapped in the city under siege, and the whole land was devastated by the Babylonian army.

But this particular afternoon, Jeremiah had been able to reclaim some of his courage. He quietly sang some of the Psalms, while not wishing to attract too much attention to himself because sometimes the soldiers in the king's guard would mock him. Four of them were about thirty paces away cleaning some of their equipment. Toward sunset, as the last light of day touched the top of the fortress wall facing him, Jeremiah was reciting a passage from a prayer of David for his son Solomon.

"Endow the king with your justice, O God, the royal son with your righteousness. May he judge your people in righteousness, your afflicted ones with justice. ..."

"May he vindicate the afflicted of the people, save the children of the needy and crush the oppressor. Let them fear You while the sun endures, and as long as the moon, throughout all generations. May he come down like rain upon the mown grass, Like showers that water the earth. In his days may the righteous flourish, and abundance of peace till the moon is no more. May he also rule from sea to sea And from the River to the ends of the earth." [1]

Jeremiah pondered the words and then prayed, "Yes, may it be that the kings of your people will do all of this and more." He thought, "A day is coming when again a king of Israel 'will reign from the Euphrates to the ends of the earth.' I long to see that day. A son of David shall arise and he shall reign."

Looking around, Jeremiah noticed wisps of smoke of various cooking fires which passed above the wall above him. He thought of all the sheep, the flocks of Judaea which were being devoured day after day by the Babylonians. Occasionally the soldiers on the wall above him would lament as they saw yet another sheep being roasted. The Babylonians were well fed, while the inhabitants of Jerusalem were beginning to starve.

Jeremiah thought to himself, "I have had so many moments of significant hunger. I am a prisoner. I can go nowhere. I can not prepare the least bit of food to quench my hunger. Happily, God has given me favor with the guards. They generally do not cause me any great pain nor abuse me."

Later, as the evening began passing into night, other words started to come into his mind as well as visual images in his spirit. The prophet knew that the Lord was speaking to him, exhorting him, but also giving him hope for the future. He felt encouragement. He knew that he needed to speak out the words, to prophecy everything that God showed him:

"Praise the Lord of hosts, for the Lord is good, for His mercy endures forever" ... For I will cause the captives of the land to return as at the

---

1 Psalm 72:4-8

first,' says the Lord. "Thus says the Lord of hosts: 'In this place which is desolate, without man and without beast, and in all its cities, there shall again be a dwelling place of shepherds causing their flocks to lie down. In the cities of the mountains, in the cities of the lowland, in the cities of the South, in the land of Benjamin, in the places around Jerusalem, and in the cities of Judah, the flocks shall again pass under the hands of him who counts them,' says the Lord. 'Behold, the days are coming,' says the Lord, 'that I will perform that good thing which I have promised to the house of Israel and to the house of Judah:

'In those days and at that time, I will cause to grow up to David a branch of righteousness; He shall execute judgment and righteousness in the earth. In those days Judah will be saved, and Jerusalem will dwell safely. And this is the name by which she will be called: THE LORD OUR RIGHTEOUSNESS.'

"For thus says the Lord: 'David shall never lack a man to sit on the throne of the house of Israel; nor shall the priests, the Levites, lack a man to offer burnt offerings before Me, to kindle grain offerings, and to sacrifice continually.'" [2]

The prophet sat astonished. Now, this was the second time he had received a similar prophecy.[3] God had not forgotten. In the hours that followed, other details came to Jeremiah. However, he pondered over the words:

"In those days and at that time, I will cause to grow up to David a branch of righteousness; He shall execute judgment and righteousness in the earth. In those days Judah will be saved, and Jerusalem will dwell safely."

Jeremiah thought, "This was certainly something to rejoice about. A righteous king will arise. He will occupy David's throne doing justice and righteousness on the earth!"

But there was more. Something that he personally found very encouraging. God had not forgotten the lowly people of the land.

---

2 Jeremiah 33:10-18

3 See also Jeremiah 23:5-6.

"Thus says the Lord of hosts: 'In this place which is desolate, without man and without beast, and in all its cities, there shall again be a dwelling place of shepherds causing their flocks to lie down."

"... in the places around Jerusalem, and in the cities of Judah, the flocks shall again pass under the hands of him who counts them,' says the Lord."

Jeremiah thought, "This war has been an absolute disaster for so many people, in the villages, towns, and cities, but also even for the shepherds. God is faithful even to small details. He is concerned about the lowly people, even the shepherds who were often despised by the wealthy, but sometimes even by poor city dwellers. But God will remember them. This prophecy is a strong indication of the just dealings of God. Our leaders have led us astray into the worship of idols. How many times I warned the kings of Judah, but they would not listen. However, God has seen even the painful decimation of our flocks. He has seen the suffering of the shepherds. He will remember them."[4]

Within a few days, someone came who was able to write down the prophetic words. Within weeks, the siege would be over, the city would be devastated, and the women ravished. However, the prophetic word remained. Copies of it spread among the faithful. A few rolled copies of the text left with some of the captives who were being taken to Babylon.

Jeremiah himself stayed in the land until he was taken against his will to Egypt by some of the Jews who were in revolt against the king of Babylon.

---

4 These passages about the shepherds are remarkable when one considers Luke's account of the birth of Jesus. See Luke 2:8-20.)

Daniel - Prophecy of the Messiah

Babylon, Toward 539/538 BC

The First Year of the Reign of Darius the Mede (Cyaxares II) [1]

From Daniel's vantage point in an upper room in the palace at Babylon, the great wall of the city toward the Euphrates river was only about 140 cubits away.[2] Daniel could just see over the wall toward the western portion of the city beyond the river. The vast plain toward the northwest spread out toward the desert. Then turning slightly and looking almost due west, Daniel saw the faint light of a narrow crescent moon hanging low over the horizon. It was the beginning of a new month. Daniel found a comfortable position against the wall on several cushions piled on a massive carpet which covered much of the surface of the small room. Daniel had come to this secluded private chamber to reflect on his recent experiences. Daniel remembered one incident that had happened two weeks previously like it was yesterday.

At the time of the evening offering, in Daniel's great weariness be-

---

1 Darius the Mede was probably also called Cyaxares II, the son of Astyages of Media. Darius was the father-in-law of Cyrus, who was later named Cyrus the Great, King of Persia. See Daniel 5:29-30 and 6:28. Babylonia was conquered by Cyrus, but Darius the Mede was the senior partner in the Medo-Persian alliance at the moment when Babylon was captured. Darius the Mede apparently died within a few years following the conquest. See Steven D. Anderson, *Darius the Mede: A Reappraisal*. Grand Rapids: Steven D. Anderson, 2014.

2 A cubit was about 50 centimeters. The distance was 70 meters or 76.5 yards.

cause of several days of fasting, the angel Gabriel had appeared to him. Daniel had first sensed a presence in the room, and then slowly he saw the invisible presence become manifest. At first, the air about two yards away in front of him glowed slightly, then a long shimmering flame followed. Within a few more moments a man stood in front of him, clothed like a rich merchant. But in addition to the richness of his apparel, light shone from his face and clothing. Daniel had recognized the angel immediately. Several years before, he had seen the same angel Gabriel who had come to bring another message. There had been no hint of fear in Daniel's heart. Intuitively he had realized that the being was sent for his encouragement. In the moments that followed the angel spoke:

"O Daniel, I have now come forth to give you insight with understanding."

"At the beginning of your supplications the command was issued, and I have come to tell you, for you are highly esteemed; so give heed to the message and gain an understanding of the vision."

"Seventy periods of seven have been decreed for your people and your holy city, to finish the transgression, to make an end of sin, to make atonement for iniquity, to bring in everlasting righteousness, to seal up vision and prophecy and to anoint the most Holy One."[3]

"So you are to know and discern that from the issuing of a decree to restore and rebuild Jerusalem until Messiah the Prince there will be seven "sevens" and sixty-two "sevens;" it will be built again, with plaza and moat, even in times of distress."[4]

In the moments following these statements the angel lingered briefly and then slowly disappeared before Daniel's eyes. A type of shimmering flame replaced the man, then a glowing patch of air replaced the flame until there was no one.

Now sitting quietly in an upper room reserved for his private use, Daniel puzzled over the prophecy. The periods of "sevens" were going to be important. The phrases, "Finishing transgression, making an end

---

3 Many translations read "holy place," but the author believes that the Holy One is the center of the prophecy.
4 Daniel 9:22-25

of sin, making atonement for iniquity and bringing in everlasting righteousness," were amazing words. Every aspect of the early portion of the prophecy seemed to cause hope to surge in one's heart. The world would become a better place. Even so, all this would take time, and God's new world filled with justice and righteousness apparently was being delayed for many years in the future.

It seemed to Daniel that the "sevens" must refer to Sabbatical years. The first set of "sevens" was obviously a Jubilee period of 49 years, but the second period was less clear. Daniel puzzled over the division between the two periods. God's anointed Prince would arrive at the culmination of the 62 "sevens." If the "sevens" did indeed refer to Sabbatical years, then the anointed Prince would not come for a long time to come. How much time would be separating the seven "sevens" and the 62 "sevens"? The periods were specifically mentioned, that means that there must be some significance to the periods of time that were indicated. In all, the prophecy represented 490 years. It was divided into periods of (7 x 7) or 49 years and (62 x 7) or 434 years with one "seven" of years left over, but how much time was allotted between the separate periods? That could add decades or longer to the timeline of the anointed Prince's appearing. Apparently, the Messiah's arrival would take place the culmination of 62 "sevens" of years. That would be at the very least 483 years into the future.

Daniel also thought about the starting point of the prophecy. While Babylon had fallen to the Medes and the Persians less than one year before, there had still not been any decree to restore and rebuild Jerusalem as indicated in the prophecy. When would that take place? Would the decree be issued within months or several more years in the future?

However, there were other odd phrases that followed the main prophecy. Those words now came back to Daniel's mind:

"Then after the sixty-two "sevens" the Messiah will be cut off and have nothing, and the people of the prince who is to come will destroy the city and the sanctuary. And its end will come with a flood; even to the end there will be war; desolations are determined."[5]

What did this mean? Had Jerusalem not been several decades de-

---

5 Daniel 9:26.

stroyed earlier? With the promise of rebuilding which was indicated in the prophecy, why was there also a decreed certainty of further judgment? What did it mean for the Messiah to be "cut off and have nothing?" Was he not destined to save God's people? Why would he ever be "cut off and be reduced to nothing?" How could this be, would God forsake his people?

Daniel then thought of something else. The prophetic word did not say "sevens" of years. It simply made mention of "sevens." Were there other fulfillments that were possible? Daniel thought again of the new crescent moon which had no doubt already disappeared below the horizon. He remembered a phrase from the creation account, God had said, *"Let there be lights in the expanse of the heavens to separate the day from the night, and let them be for signs and for seasons and for days and years."*

Daniel suddenly realized: "The heavens are related to time, including years, months, weeks, and days. The prophecy must be related to the heavens." Daniel recalled his experience with Nebuchadnezzar decades previously. Had not the king lost his mind for seven lunar months? [6] He had eaten grass and crawled about like an animal. That incident also took seven periods of time. It involved seven months, marked by the lunar crescent.

Daniel thought, "Perhaps the prophecy has various aspects? Certainly, if God's anointed Prince would only arrive at the culmination of 62 "sevens," then he could not be cut off immediately after 62 "sevens." The prophecy was indeed a puzzle. While Daniel would have liked to continue to muse over the prophecy, sleep began to take hold of his aging body. His eyes closed and before he knew what had happened, he was sound asleep.

---

6 See Daniel 4:1-37 and especially verse 32. The author believes that the period was seven lunar months. Bible commentators often speculate that it was a period of seven years. It does not seem probable that even the most loyal ministers or the imperial guard would have allowed Nebuchadnezzar, in his deranged state, to continue even to have a semblance of authority for seven years. However, a period of seven months might have been possible.

2

The Men from the East

Fall 4 BC - Spring 3 BC

Chapter Contents:

The Men from the East

Jerusalem - Fall, 4 BC

Several days after the Feast of Tabernacles

Month VII - Tašrītu / Tishrei - Day 25

Eliab looked at the lines of text, which he had just copied onto a new piece of parchment on his desk.

All the lines had been well copied and were sharp. Another fifteen lines to go and then Eliab could rest for the night. The two lamps on his desk were providing abundant light, but even so, Eliab preferred to copy texts during the daytime. Eliab was a notarial scribe. He wrote up legal documents in Aramaic for clients of his employer. Eliab also sometimes earned money copying biblical texts. He was only doing this rush job at night because his cousin had promised a completed text for a friend for the next morning.

Eliab[1] pondered the passage again; he had never really noticed how this text from the Psalms spoke of David's throne. From the same text, one could also think of the Messiah concerning the heavens.

Eliab thought to himself, "It is somewhat surprising that I have not

---

1 Eliab means: God is my father, God is the father.

* The image behind the chapter titles is an original Babylonian astronomical document. (Credits in Appendix 10.)

noticed this before. My employer, Ekur-zakir, is not only a professional notary, but he is also an astronomer.[2] He might be interested in this passage. I am amazed. How did I miss the importance of these words until now?"

לא אחלל בריתי ומוצא פתי לא אשנה

אחת נשבעתי בקדשי אם־לדוד אכזב

זרעו לעולם יהיה וכסאו כשמש נגדי

כירח יכון עולם ועד בשחק נאמן סלה

He began to recite the words in a low voice, not wanting to disturb his son who had fallen asleep on a bed a few yards away.

"My covenant I will not violate, nor will I alter the utterance of My lips. Once I have sworn by My holiness; I will not lie to David. His descendants shall endure forever and his throne as the sun before Me. It shall be established forever like the moon, and the witness in the sky is faithful." [3]

He then repeated the last words, "The witness in the sky is faithful." Eliab thought, "Yes, the sun and moon have existed since ancient times. Creation was a long time ago. When the Psalmist says that the throne of David and his royal line shall endure for ages like the sun and moon, the image is certainly appropriate."[4]

As a devoted Jew, Eliab usually did not discuss his faith with his employer or his associates. The men were from old Babylonian families who had been established in Mesopotamia for well over a millennium. They worshiped the Babylonian gods. Amazingly, Eliab had been able to work in Ekur-zakir's notarial office for over two decades. He did not want to

---

2 It is known that at least some of the Babylonian astronomers also functioned as notaries. See Mathieu Ossendri-jver, "Science in Action: Networks in Babylonian Astronomy," in *Science Culture Between Orient and Occident*, (Berlin, Boston: De Gruyter, 2011), 213-221. Some of the Babylonian names used in this book also come from this text.

3 Psalm 89:34-37.

4 The witness is the combined testimony of the sun and moon together, not just the moon alone.

have lots of religious discussions which might put his job in peril.

Although Eliab had worked for a long time in the notary office, at this moment, he found himself struggling inwardly.

He thought, "I have been in that office for such a long time, and I have not really tried to turn my employer and coworkers from paganism to the true God. Certainly, I thought about it many times, but I have allowed all this time to pass. Now I find this passage about the heavens and the royal line of David. It is certainly the type of thing that the notary and his fellow astronomers could find to be interesting."

Eliab felt some tension in his shoulders and back. He laid down his reed pen beside the parchment and stretched his back, raising his arms above him. After a few moments, he let his arms fall again. He stretched out his hand, took the reed pen, looked at the next lines, and began to copy the text. Sleep would have to wait. He still had another hour of work to do.

The next morning, Eliab woke to the sound of chirping birds and a man who was yelling curses in the street. Startled, Eliab thought, "Does he not know this is only a few days after the Feast of Tabernacles? Does he not realize that he is in Jerusalem, the city of the great God?"

Eliab rose, went to the window, and opened the shutters. In the street below, a pushcart loaded with various fruits and vegetables was obviously about ready to lose a wheel, causing no little frustration to its owner. Eliab looked to the right and up the street. Being on the third floor, he could see above the rooftops of the buildings next door. About two hundred yards away, standing high above all else, were the walls of the Royal Portico of the Jerusalem temple. The massive structure filled the brightening sky to the north. It was already fairly late for Eliab, who was used to rising in the darkness well before dawn. Eliab turned and looked across the room and saw that his son Eitan was beginning to stir.

Eliab said, "Eitan, good morning. This is our last day before our departure tomorrow. We are going home. Make sure you get everything done today that you need to do, like seeing your cousins and new friends."

Eitan mumbled a reply and Eliab moved toward his desk. The parchment documents were ready. He rolled the one that had been completed the night before and gathered all the documents together in preparation to take them downstairs to his cousin's living quarters. Then he washed and got dressed.

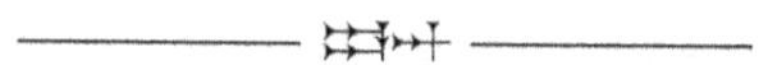

After Eliab took the documents downstairs to his cousin Joram, they ate a bit of bread and some fruit together, and then Eliab excused himself. For several days he had been stuck in the lower city of Jerusalem. He wanted to get out and breath some fresher air. He felt a great need to escape from the crowded lower city, so he decided to go to the Mount of Olives, which faced the Temple Mount across the Kidron Valley.

Coming out of the lower city of Jerusalem through the Water Gate deep in the valley, Eliab climbed a road steadily upward, arriving under the walls of the temple complex on his left. Eventually, he turned to his right and started to ascend toward the summit of the Mount of Olives.

The Feast of Tabernacles had ended just two days previously. Already in the morning light, several hundred people were on the road that hugged the lower part of the Mount of Olives. They were on their way down to Jericho, and from there they would move toward the north up the Jordan Valley.

As Eliab passed over the road, he thought to himself, "Tomorrow it will be our turn. Most of the crowd will be gone. The beginning of our trip home will be more tranquil."

A large cemetery spread out on his right as he climbed the hill blanketed with olive groves. Thousands of people had slept among the trees in tents and huts during the festival; but now most of them had departed or were preparing to go, leaving only an occasional encampment.

Arriving near the summit, Eliab found a large, broad limestone rock about 20 feet wide and five feet tall. It was shaded toward the east by some large trees. Gathering his strength, Eliab found a steep path up the back side where he could haul himself up to the top. He seated himself toward the western edge of the large rock so that he could look back toward Jerusalem on the other side of the valley.

It was still early morning, so the sun in the east was shining brightly against the gold plated eastern facade of the great temple. Large numbers of departing pilgrims continued to stream out of the city gate north of the temple. They, like the others previously, were crossing the Kidron Valley below and rounding the southern part of the Mount of Olives as they traveled toward Jericho.

As the morning progressed, the sun continued to shift in the southeastern sky causing alternating zones of brightness and shadows to fall on the city's fortified walls, houses, and monuments. Just to the lower left of the temple itself, Eliab could also see the house of hewn stone where the Sanhedrin usually met. Behind that, one could just see other temple structures such as the council house. Further south, the so-called "Royal Portico" dominated the southern part of the Temple Mount standing high over the lower city. It even blocked the view of the upper city to the west.

Facing the temple itself, Eliab could see the entrance into the inner sanctuary of the building. Against the wishes of the temple priests, and in direct violation of God's commandment not to make graven images, Herod had placed there a massive golden eagle above the main gate of the temple. However, from across the Kidron Valley, the massive metal bird deep inside the temple courts was not very impressive. As Eliab looked to the right side of the temple, there were other buildings similar to those on the south side. Further north on the other side of an extensive open area, the imposing Fortress of Antonia was a reminder of King Herod's military strength. In the west, one could see the ramparts, towers, and roofs associated with Herod's palace in the upper city.

As he watched, the long line of pilgrims moving away from the city, Eliab's mind drifted into thinking about his own return trip that would begin the next day. In about two months, Eliab would need to be back at work in Ekur-zakir's notarial office. Eliab thought briefly of the sights and sounds of the large eastern city, Borsippa, south of ancient Babylon. Working as a notarial assistant, Eliab had been able to marry and raise a family of three boys and one girl with his income. His life was full.

Over two decades he had seen his employer grow much older. Now well over sixty, Ekur-zakir was less dynamic than he had been. But his business sense was still active, and the notary office was very prosperous.

In reality, Ekur-zakir was a notary by necessity, earning most of his living through the notarial business. But Ekur-zakir was also an astronomer and a priest of Nabu, the Babylonian god of wisdom. It was rare for a practicing Jew to be in such close proximity to Babylonian priest-astronomers, but this was made possible by the circumstances of the notarial office. Even so, the business itself was well separated from the older man's other activities.

In the office, Eliab had rubbed shoulders with the astronomers in Borsippa for years, but he hardly knew anything about their celestial science. This was not because Eliab was not necessarily interested. He enjoyed looking at the starry heavens just like anyone else. However, the clannish astronomers were more or less sworn to secrecy concerning their celestial knowledge, which they regarded as the wisdom of the gods. They almost never shared any of their in-depth technical knowledge of the heavens outside their professional clans, although some foreign astronomers did enter into their confidence.[5]

Before he began working for Ekur-zakir, Eliab had been trained as a professional scribe who was capable of writing in Greek, Aramaic, and Hebrew. He had a good reputation and was in high demand for drafting legal documents and also for copying Jewish religious texts.

Eliab well remembered the day, when Ekur-zakir had come to visit his father and had offered him a job. Ekur-zakir's principal Babylonian scribe had died only days before, and the notary desperately needed help in the preparation of documents for his business. Eliab's skill in putting together texts in Aramaic was very much appreciated. Eliab was thankful to God for the opportunity to work for Ekur-zakir. He had the impression that his entry into the notarial office was somehow his destiny, but also the job certainly provided well for his family.

Thoughts of home filled Eliab's mind while he was still looking over the city of Jerusalem. However, after a few hours, the sun grew hot, and the shade on his back departed. Eliab then decided to return to his cousin Joram's home in the lower city.

---

5   The Greek astronomer Hipparchus (second-century BC) may have spent some time among the astronomers of Mesopotamia. There is substantial evidence of Babylonian astronomical concepts and specific technical information in the eastern Mediterranean astronomical literature.

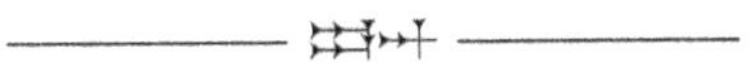

Eliab's cousin's family had moved from Babylonia to Judaea thirty years previously. Since his arrival in Jerusalem as a youth, Joram had become a Pharisee, but also he was thoroughly acquainted with the ideas circulated by the Jewish sect called the Essenes. At the end of his cousin's visit, Joram had finally decided to talk to Eliab about a subject which held great interest for him: the coming of the Messiah.

After supper, Joram broached the subject, "Eliab, I am not sure what you think about messianic thought, but in recent years I have spent plenty of time in the presence of several Essene teachers who believe that the appearing of one or more Messiah figures is imminent. Some of them speak of a priestly Messiah, while others insist that God will soon send us a righteous king as was indicated by the prophet Jeremiah. You may know the passage:

'In those days and at that time I will cause to grow up to David a Branch of righteousness; He shall execute judgment and righteousness in the earth. In those days Judah will be saved, and Jerusalem will dwell safely.[6]

"Some of the Essene teachers believe that the kingly Messiah will be manifest in the next several years, and perhaps very soon. They have sought to establish their ideas through various calculations involving Daniel's famous prophecy of the 70 'sevens.' I think you also know the passage in the latter part of the book of Daniel,

"Seventy 'sevens' are decreed upon thy people and upon thy holy city, to finish transgression, and to make an end of sins, and to make reconciliation for iniquity, and to bring in everlasting righteousness, and to seal up vision and prophecy, and to anoint the most holy.[7]*"*

Joram continued, "Many scribes and religious teachers believe that these numbers are referring to Sabbatical years. It seems to me that this

---

6 Jeremiah 33:14-16 NASB.

7 Daniel 9:24 NASB with the change of 'sevens' for 'weeks.'

is very possible. The Sabbatical years are significant in the Mosaic law."

"However, I am not very confident about all of their calculations because they use the numbers as they like and they seem to make no real appeal to history. For instance, in the prophecy, it is indicated that there will be seven 'sevens' and 62 'sevens' from the decree to restore Jerusalem until the Messiah, the prince. It is written,

> 'Know therefore and discern, that from the going forth of the commandment to restore and to build Jerusalem unto the anointed one, the prince, shall be seven 'sevens,' and 62 'sevens:' it shall be built again, with street and moat, even in troubled times.'" [8]

"However, when I ask the men when did this decree happen, they usually are not able to give me a solid answer. They do not know the history of the exile very well. This lack of historical knowledge also applies to most of the rabbis in Israel. They are very careful in copying our scriptural texts. They will not change a single letter. However, they are not well versed in other types of historical documents, and sometimes they tell a lot of tales, which may or may not be true. I think the Jewish leaders and scribes in Babylonia may be similar."

Joram looked intently at Eliab for a short moment to discern how his cousin would react.

Finally, Eliab responded, "Yes, I am aware that some of our teachers often despise anything they perceive as being 'profane, unholy' knowledge. Happily, not all the men are like that, but one finds such attitudes even among Babylonian Jews. It is true that our sacred texts should occupy first place in our hearts and minds, but even so, one can know a few other facts. I would never have made a successful career as a scribal assistant in my employer's notary office without being open to learning about their documents and methods. I also had to acquire a good knowledge of both Greek and written Babylonian Aramaic. One does need practical knowledge of many subjects to live and work."

Joram, relieved to hear his cousin's response, said, "I thought you probably valued scholarship. I am glad to hear you express yourself positively concerning learning in general."

---

8 Daniel 9:25 NASB with the change of 'sevens' for 'weeks.'

Then after a few moments of hesitation, Joram continued, "I have a favor to ask of you."

Eliab, responded with a chuckle and a smile, "Go ahead, make your request, I can only say yes, or otherwise refuse you. It might be worth trying. Sometimes I can be agreeable."

Joram grinned as well, and replied, "Well, since you live in Babylonia, could you make some inquiries for me? I would like to know exactly when the commandment to restore and to rebuild Jerusalem was issued."

Joram continued, "I think that the prophecy is referring to periods of Sabbatical years. But even so, the text is not completely straightforward because the 70 periods of time are divided into seven 'sevens', 62 'sevens', and an additional final Sabbatical period of seven years. However, there is a big problem, if one does not even know the starting point, then how can one be so sure about how to calculate the time of the Messiah's arrival? The Essenes take the entire period and are calculating 70 times seven or 490 years from their supposed date for the end of the exile, however, if you ask them they cannot historically justify their dates. Their calculations are all in the realm of theory. They are not historically based."[9]

"It seems to me that the first decree to restore and rebuild Jerusalem was issued by Cyrus the Great. That is what Isaiah and the Book of Chronicles seem to indicate.[10] However, the rebuilding process was interrupted, and aspects of it were completed later by Darius and others. King Artaxerxes I of Persia also gave Nehemiah the right and responsibility of reestablishing the walls of the city, which had not yet been rebuilt. However, the prophet Isaiah makes it clear that God gave Cyrus a role, which was comprehensive. Look here at this, I copied the following texts from the Isaiah scroll."

Joram looked around on a side shelf and found a text written on parchment, which he handed to Eliab saying, "Here is the passage:"

> *"Thus says the LORD, your Redeemer, and the one who formed you from the womb, I, the LORD, am the maker of all things, ... It is I who*

---

9 See some of the Essene speculations in Roger T. Beckwith, *Calendar and Chronology, Jewish and Christian: Biblical, Intertestamental and Patristic Studies*: (Leiden: E.J. Brill, 1996), 232, 239 and 248.

10 See 2 Chronicles 36:22 and Isaiah 44:26-28, 45:13. In addition, this seems to be the understanding of Josephus in the first century AD; see *The Antiquities of the Jews*, 11.1.1-3.

says of Jerusalem, 'She shall be inhabited!' And of the cities of Judah, 'They shall be built.' And I will raise up her ruins again. It is I who says to the depth of the sea, 'Be dried up!' And I will make your rivers dry. It is I who says of Cyrus, 'He is My shepherd! And he will perform all My desire.' And he declares of Jerusalem, 'She will be built,' and of the temple, 'Your foundation will be laid.'" [11]

Joram said, "This indicates that Cyrus probably would be implicated in rebuilding the city and the temple. Then the text that follows makes this even clearer."

"Thus says the LORD to Cyrus His anointed, ... 'I have aroused him in righteousness. And I will make all his ways smooth; He will build My city and will let My exiles go free, without any payment or reward,' says the LORD of hosts." [12]

With a bit of frustration, Joram continued, "I do not know the true dates for Cyrus' reign or those of most of the other kings who succeeded him. Here in Jerusalem, we are far from Babylonia where one might be able to get some right answers. Can you ask around in Babylonia concerning these dates? I want to get to the truth concerning the matter."

Eliab said, "I never was extremely interested in messianic speculations. However, one of the prophecies concerning the Messiah did influence me a lot. My great-grandfather built a house near Borsippa at a plantation where they produce dates. On the lintel above the door, he inscribed an ancient prophecy given by the patriarch Jacob in Egypt. You know the text about the 'One to who would be the obedience of the peoples.'[13] That text intrigued me. I will not go into the details now, but while looking at that inscription one day about 30 years ago, I was inspired to become a scribe."

Joram interrupted again, "We are possibly more interested in the messianic promises here because this is our Jewish homeland. While King Herod is favorable to our religion, he is a foreigner. He also has financed pagan temples in several other places in the Roman Empire. He even builds temples to the glory of the emperor and Rome."

---

11   Isaiah 44:24-28 NASB.

12   Isaiah 45:1-13 NASB.

13   Genesis 49:9-10.

"Several months ago he put two of his sons and heirs, Alexander and Aristobulus, to death on suspicion of treason. They were from the Hasmonean royal family. Their mother was put to death over 20 years ago on similar charges. The Hasmoneans were not from the line of David, but at least the family was Jewish. Now the Hasmonean royal house is completely decimated; and we have a foreigner, an Idumean for a ruler."

"It is rumored that Herod's son Antipater, the crown prince, actually was behind the king's suspicions, which caused our ruler to put his sons to death. Antipater seems to have always been jealous of his brothers, thinking that the king might be persuaded to make them the principal heirs. However, now the king has given Antipater significant power so that he is running much of the government.[14] Therefore, even when the king dies we will inherit a wicked man as Herod's successor."

"Do you see why the Pharisees and the Essenes, in particular, have turned their thoughts increasingly toward a deliverer, a Messiah, who could restore our national pride? And remember, the Messiah is called to reign over the nations as well, thus restoring God's reign on the earth. Some people here in Herod's kingdom are ready to take up arms against the king, and if need be, also against the empire of the Romans in hopes of restoring Israel to true obedience to God."

Eliab was giving his full attention to his cousin, trying to size up the situation. But he was still hesitant to commit himself fully. While briefly contemplating a lamp shining on a table several feet away, he pondered his cousin's statements for a few moments.

Then looking directly at Joram, Eliab responded, "Let me be clear, I want to avoid getting involved in insurrections or conspiracies against Herod or the empire of the Romans. Do you understand?"

Joram nodded his head and raised a hand slightly indicating that he certainly understood Eliab, "Yes, I completely understand your hesitation."

Then Eliab continued, "However, I am somewhat interested in understanding more about Daniel's prophecy. I guess I can ask around back in Babylonia concerning the history of the kings. The main archives of

---

14 In the last years of the king's life, Antipater was a joint ruler with his father: Josephus, *Antiquities of the Jews*, 17.1.4. Same as *AJ* 14.13.1; See also 17.5.3, 17.5.4 and 17.5.5.

these events would be in Babylon. As you know, the city is still functioning, and a few tens of thousands of people still live there, but the former vast metropolis is now largely in ruins. Some of the royal archives there have been destroyed. Even so, there remain plenty of the ancient cuneiform tablets. Some of the archives were transferred to Seleucia on the Tigris or the imperial capital at Ctesiphon across the river from Seleucia. Those documents may be beyond my reach, although perhaps I can find some help through my contacts in those cities."

Then after reflecting for a few moments, Eliab continued, "Although, there may be an easier manner to proceed. As you know, I work in a notarial office, which is connected to a Babylonian astronomical observatory. The chief notary, Ekur-zakir, is also one of the main astronomers at the Ezida temple complex, where the observatory is located. They have records, which are called 'astronomical diaries' going back hundreds of years. I have seen some of the astronomers come through our office with cuneiform tablets that go back six to seven hundred years. I know just enough cuneiform text to read some lines here and there on the tablets. I have noticed that the reigns of kings indicate the dates on the tablets."

"I am also told that the astronomical diaries contain much more information than accounts about the heavens. The diaries contain records about the weather, market prices, the river level, and significant events. Again the dates of these things are listed by the years of the reigns of various kings. For example, the tablets are often labeled 'In the third, fourth, or fifth year of king so-and-so.'"

"Through these texts, I suspect that it will be possible to get some useful dating information from the astronomers. That would be the simplest solution. I will keep you informed. It will take me a while to get back to Babylonia. After my arrival back there, give me a few months to find out something. Perhaps I can get some word to you by the beginning of the new year in the spring."

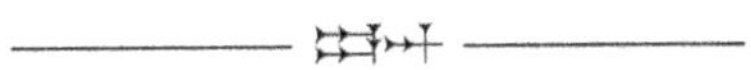

Later, during the last hours of the night, Eliab dreamed of a day about three decades early at his home on the date plantation outside Borsippa. His memory of that day seemed more detailed and precise than he could remember previously. The entire scene including the smells and sounds came back to him.

In the dream, all around the enormous mud-brick house, rows of date palms reached toward the sky. The sound of chirping crickets came from clumps of grass nearby and far away. In the distance, in busy conversation, several workers were climbing the palms as they were actively engaged in the date harvest. About one hundred yards away through the rustling of the palm branches one could just hear those who climbed to the tops of the trees shouting down to the other workmen on the ground. Female voices speaking Aramaic came through clearly in the kitchen area on one side of the building.

After almost 100 years of occupation, the house was now an ancestral home. In his dream, Eliab was staring at the doorpostss and the lintel in front of him. The Hebrew letters around the door had significantly affected his whole life and even now their message from 19 centuries before was so crucial to him. The inscription was unique, just as the lintel itself was unique.

Eliab's great-great-grandfather had bought the massive wooden lintel at great expense. The single cedar beam came from the uplands of the Median plateau. On the beam, Eliab's grandfather had hired a man to make a special inscription in Hebrew.

As the dream continued, Eliab saw himself again laying on a bench under the shaded porch at the entrance of the house as a lazy boy of eleven years. He had been well aware of his laziness, and had become ashamed of himself, as his mother and father sometimes reacted angrily to his lazy and negligent ways. Indeed, he was just a boy, but even at play, he was slothful. He seemed to have no energy. His father, Ariel,[15] was disgusted but he cared deeply for his son. However, Eliab could not be depended

---

15 The meaning of Ariel in Hebrew is "Lion of God."

upon for the smallest task. Obedient and industrious, Eliab's four older siblings were well thought of by their parents.

Eliab remembered the days before his 11th birthday when he had been laying on the bench placed below a shaded porch near the door of his home. He was observing a trail of ants marching one after another up a portion of the exterior wall of the house. The ants had done this for many months over the same path, so that their passage had left a slightly gray-brown trail on the shaded mud-brick wall.

While watching the little colony climbing up the wall, inside Eliab heard his father read words from the Proverbs of Solomon in Hebrew, which he almost immediately translated into Aramaic. Eliab was delighted to hear how the words rolled gracefully off his father's tongue,

"Go to the ant, O sluggard, observe her ways and be wise, which, having no chief, officer or ruler, prepares her food in the summer, and gathers her provision in the harvest. How long will you lie down, O sluggard? When will you arise from your sleep? A little sleep, a little slumber, A little folding of the hands to rest — Your poverty will come in like a vagabond and your need like an armed man." [16]

The words profoundly touched Eliab. He had heard them several times before, but this time it seemed like every word drove itself into his spirit. He could not erase them from his thoughts. The words came up again and again, "Go to the ant, O sluggard, Observe her ways and be wise … Your poverty will come in like a vagabond and your need like an armed man." Eliab sensed that poverty and hunger were almost there within a few feet ready to strangle him. He had the crushing feeling that a stormy black cloud threatened his whole future. Eliab did not know that his father, Ariel, in the shadows inside the house had seen his son lying on the bench watching the ants.

A few moments later, a sparrow flew under the porch and settled on the end of the wooden lintel over the doorway. Eliab noticed the bird and looked up toward the lintel and door posts of the family home.

Eliab had sometimes wondered what the inscription on the lintel and doorposts said, but he had even been too lazy to ask. He had understood

---

16 Proverbs 6:6-11.

that the phrases had been placed on there by his great-great-grandfather who had built the house. Looking up at the Hebrew text carved in the wood, it was as though the letters of the words themselves carried life inside them.

Eliab increasingly focused his attention on the carved cedar lintel above the open door where it was written in two lines:

לא יסור שבט מיהודה ומחקק מבין רגליו

עד כי יבא שילה ולו יקהת עמים

Two other short phrases dominated the tops of the doorposts on the right and left it was written:

גור אריה יהודה   יהודה אתה יודוך אחיך

As Eliab looked at the words, a certain peace and joy came over his spirit. It was an entirely new experience for Eliab. He had never been overly inquisitive, but now he wanted to know what was written on the lintel and doorposts. The threatening dark cloud associated with poverty and hunger receded from his thoughts while a piercing light, like the sun breaking through the clouds, burst into his mind. Then Eliab arose, stepped back a few feet, and looked up at the phrases written on the doorposts and the lintel. It was almost as if the sentences glowed. It was as if they were beckoning to him. However, in reality, their appearance had not changed. [17]

A yearning to understand the phrases gripped Eliab's mind. He determined that he would not ask his father the meaning of the words. He would learn to decipher the message, diligently applying himself to learning the letters and their purpose. The mysterious letters seemed to be calling Eliab to make his father and mother proud. Looking at the text on the doorposts and lintel gave Eliab new hope. A mysterious light had shown in his heart and kindled a fire. It was a hungry devouring flame of wanting to know, to understand and to do what was right.

---

17 Genesis 49:10 was in the center and the beginning words of verse 8 to the left and verse 9 to the right.

Later, Eliab came to understand the words as he studied Aramaic and the Hebrew language in a scribal school. For six years he studied hard. At the end of his efforts, he had several job propositions. However, destiny guided Eliab to work in the notary office run by Ekur-zakir.

Waking, Eliab opened his eyes and stared at the ceiling. He began asking himself, "Why is it that I have such a vivid dream of that day about 30 years ago? Why did this happen now at the end of my time in Jerusalem and after my cousin asked for my help concerning determining the time of the Messiah's arrival? The Hebrew text in the inscription on the lintel and doorposts was about the coming of the Shiloh, the expected leader from the tribe of Judah who would rule over the nations."

Borsippa in the Province of Babylonia

The Astronomers

Month VII - Tašrītu / Tishrei - Day 26 — Evening, October 17, 4 BC

The evening after Eliab had his vivid dream in lower Jerusalem, Illis-ku-tul,[18] a Babylonian of 55 years with a well-kept, relatively short, curly, salt-and-pepper beard and equally colored curly hair, walked beside the docks on a branch of the Euphrates River. He was in the Mesopotamian city of Borsippa.[19] The sun had set perhaps a half hour earlier, and darkness was falling on the city. There was a slight breeze, which caused rustling noises among the branches of the relatively abundant palm trees along the river-front. The river flowed calmly and silently to the right of Illis-kutul among the numerous bundled reed and wooden boats and rafts. Some were even small seafaring vessels that had been brought up the Euphrates.[20]

A branch of the great river split Borsippa partly in two as it traversed

---

18 The name Illis-kutul means "Look to your god." See Stol, Marten M., "Old Babylonian Personal Names." Sel 8, 1991. p. 196.

19 In a straight line Borsippa is about 875 kilometers or 544 miles east of Jerusalem. However, any Babylonian magi who eventually may have been in Bethlehem were forced to travel to the northwest along the Euphrates, then west cross the Syrian desert, and descend the Jordan Valley in order to arrive in Jerusalem.

20 Brought up from the Persian (Arabian) Gulf between Iran and the Arabian Peninsula.

the northern and northwestern areas of the city. On Illis-kutul's left several mud-brick warehouses stood silently just below a section of the city wall, itself made of tan colored mud-bricks. As he strolled, Illis-kutul did notice an occasional watchman among the storehouses. They were used to seeing him and did not attempt to discourage his evening promenade.

The thriving port activities of the day had ceased, and workmen, slaves, and trade-oriented entrepreneurs had gone off to rest at home. But some were spending their day's wages in local bars and brothels. Their merrymaking could be heard in the distance as Illis-kutul was walking in the cool evening air and the growing darkness. All through the daylight hours barley, wheat, dates, vegetables, linen, salted meat, pottery, clothing, and other goods came and went to the docks area and the nearby market. Throughout the day, the docks were filled with the grunts of men laboring under heavy loads. A variety of ox-drawn carts were employed, but much of the time the men simply carried large baskets and bundles on their heads. The docks reflected the city in a significant way: the inhabitants of Borsippa were particularly interested in commercial activities, including nearly all means of making a living. A small minority had amassed vast fortunes, but their homes were not near the working class neighborhoods near the docks on the riverfront.

Borsippa was a large city of perhaps 65,000 men, women, and children. By comparison, in the city of Babylon, just upriver on the Euphrates, perhaps only 15,000 people lived in what remained of the former capital of Mesopotamia. Babylon had largely fallen into ruin in the years following the death of Alexander the Great because of the founding of Seleucia on the Tigris about 40 miles to the north. Eventually, Seleucia on the Tigris had become a great city of 600,000 inhabitants.

As Illis-kutul arrived at a city gate on his left, he stopped and looked down the long street toward the southeast. In the distance, less than a quarter of a mile away, he could see the ancient ziggurat at the center of the city. It was in a sorry state of disrepair, the top three levels including the upper sanctuary had collapsed into a pile of rubble. However, the four lower levels of the Mesopotamian pyramid were still standing with their walls mostly intact. Illis-kutul could just see some dim lamps lit on the southern point of the pyramid where the local astronomers maintained an observatory.

Illis-Kutul was part of the team of astronomers, but he was off-duty this evening. Illis-kutul's life had changed remarkably in the previous four years. He had never dreamed of living in Borsippa. He and generations of his ancestors had been among the chief astronomers in Uruk for about 300 years. But with the rise of a certain Selebum, who had become head of the observatory in Uruk, Illis-kutul decided to leave. The two men already had been at odds for about 15 years concerning various subjects, but in more recent times Selebum had shown a marked penchant for wanting to make a lot more money through popular astrology. Notably, Selebum had been almost completely won over to the Greek horoscope ideas linked to birthdates and fate.

Illis-kutul was an old style Babylonian astronomer. He believed that the gods did sometimes indicate their will through signs in the heavens. This so-called "heavenly writing" was mainly centered on the affairs of the state. The ancient Babylonian omen collections and their commentaries like the *Enuma Anu Enlil* and *Summa Sîn ina tamartisu* were filled with texts concerning the king, the economy, military affairs, farming, rains, and various warnings for rulers. Illis-kutul was not convinced that their astronomical science could be used to predict the lives of private individuals. Babylonian astronomy and astrology had been developed and originally used for the affairs of the king and the state.

However, Selebum and many others like him saw an increasing opportunity to make small fortunes based on establishing horoscopes for just about anyone who would pay, whether a noble, a businessman or the poorest peasant. Selebum gave lip service to the ancient traditions, but his heart had gone after money. He had adopted Greek ideas about fate determining one's destiny through the influence of the heavens on one's life from birth until the grave. The old Babylonian astrological school believed that the heavens might announce various events, but evil events could often be warded off and avoided through multiple sacrifices and rituals. The Babylonians did not have a strongly deterministic vision of heavenly influences. They saw the heavens as giving messages, not creating destinies.

Illis-kutul was not comfortable with the recent Greek innovations of horoscopes. It seemed obvious to him that all the people born at a particular date and time were not destined to behave in any specific way. For Illis-kutul, the fatalism assumed by the Greeks based on the physical position of the sun, moon, and planets at the birth of any one individual could not be the source of their character, intelligence, good fortune, marriage prospects, success, or wealth. Life was much more complicated.

Eventually, Illis-kutul had contacted the astronomers in Borsippa looking for a way out of a difficult working situation. The Borsippian astronomers were still more inclined to the old-school Babylonian astronomical/astrological mentality. When Illis-kutul heard that two of the Borsippian astronomers had died and that Ekur-zakir wanted to replace them, he had jumped on the opportunity, even though it meant that he would possibly be leaving Uruk forever.

Another astronomer from Uruk who shared Illis-kutul's convictions about horoscopes had decided to accompany him. This man, named Suen-magir, was a specialist concerning lunar motion and the calendar.

Looking at the ziggurat in the distance, Illis-kutul decided to enter the gate and thus left the docks behind him. It was time to get home before some of the drunken dock workers and sailors came out of the bars. They could sometimes be a bit dangerous for isolated unlucky scholars.

Illis-kutul had been surprised with his new living arrangements in Borsippa. He had been able to buy property in a section of the city mainly populated by Jews. He had heard plenty about the Jews, but he had known very few of them in Uruk. Most Babylonian Jews seemed to be in the region of Babylon, near Borsippa or in the area from Babylon to Seleucia on the Tigris. Possibly 50,000 Jews lived in Seleucia, making up a bit less than one-tenth of the population.

Illis-kutul had been trained as a Babylonian priest of the sky god named Anu, the god who was principally worshiped in Uruk. Coming to Borsippa had liberated Illis-kutul from his priestly responsibilities. Therefore, he was able to devote his time primarily to astronomy although he did have a part-time job in the local notarial office run by several of his fellow astronomer-scholars.

Being innately curious, Illis-kutul found himself attracted to people from other religions. He had explored Greek and Roman thought and even some Indian ideas about divinities. Yet, until his arrival in Borsippa, Illis-kutul had not been exposed to Jewish doctrines about the God of Abraham. In discussing with his neighbors, he had made some interesting discoveries. Illis-kutul had become fascinated with Jewish religious literature as well. He had obtained portions of the Greek version of the Hebrew Scriptures that was translated a few hundred years before by Jewish scholars in Egypt.[21] Illis-kutul was also able to read some of the Hebrew Bible because it was related to his own Aramaic language. Besides, as he consistently observed the Jews, he saw the manner of life and began to become familiar with some of their beliefs.

Approaching his house, Illis-kutul passed under a few poplar trees on a small square in front of his house. As he passed by the tree branches, he suddenly thought of a passage he had read in the Jewish book of Psalms, and that he had even heard quoted by a few of his neighbors in Borsippa.

"By the rivers of Babylon we sat and wept when we remembered Zion. There on the poplars [22] *we hung our harps, for there our captors asked us for songs, our tormentors demanded songs of joy; they said, 'Sing us one of the songs of Zion!' How can we sing the songs of the Lord while in a foreign land? If I forget you, Jerusalem, may my right hand forget its skill. May my tongue cling to the roof of my mouth if I do not remember you, if I do not consider Jerusalem my highest joy."* [23]

Illis-kutul spoke very quietly under his breath to himself, "I wonder what life is like in Jerusalem? I wonder if I will ever know."

He had never thought about this before. He stood briefly looking at the poplar tree within ten yards of his home. Then his eye glanced around toward his neighbors' houses. The doors were shut. Although some sounds could be heard, almost everyone had gone or was going to bed.

Illis-kutul walked to his door, pushed it open, and saw the joy of his life sewing a garment in the dim lamplight across the room. Even at 50 years of age, this woman was still a delight to his eyes. His wife, Sarpanit,[24]

---

21 The Greek translation of the Old Testament is commonly called the Septuagint.

22 It seems that poplar tree is a better translation than "willows" which is found in some Bibles. Western willow trees do not grow in central Iraq.

23 Psalm 137:1-6

24 Also written: Sarpanitu, Zarpanit, Zarpandit, Zerpanitum, Zerbanitu, or Zirbanit. Sarpanit was the name of the goddess consort of the chief god, Marduk. Her Akkadian name means "the shining one." She might be somewhat equivalent to the goddess Hera/Juno in the Roman and Greek pantheon (wife of Zeus/Jupiter). By the time of Christ, Sarpanit had been assimilated with the goddess Erua, who was connected to the date harvest. In the heavens, Sarpanit (Erua) was located in the eastern portion of Virgo and the constellation Coma Berenices. (The Babylonians did not conceive of Virgo as did the Greeks. Two goddesses, Shala (Šala) and Sarpanit/Erua, were present in that region of the sky, not one. The two goddesses stood across or above the ecliptic. They did not lay on the ecliptic as

looked up and smiled. They had married quite late. Illis-kutul was excessively engaged in his scholarly pursuits in his twenties. Sarpanit had been widowed at 28 years, after several years of a previous marriage. Her two sons from her first marriage had already established families and were doing well in neighboring cities. Their only daughter together, Kallisto,[25] had a Greek name, but she was still very much a traditional Babylonian girl. She was already in her room and possibly sleeping. At 19 years, she was still at home and unmarried. Her parents simply had not found anyone whom they thought to be suitable for her as a husband.

Illis-kutul closed the front door behind him. Still looking across the room, he decided that his wife's beauty would occupy his thoughts for the rest of the evening.

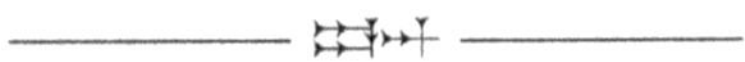

In one of the taverns in Borsippa, Suen-magir [26] looked around the room. He was disgusted with himself. Again he had gotten drunk.

He said to himself, "Imagine this! A professional astronomer with an excellent academic reputation! I am drunk again. And now I want something else, too."

These thoughts raced through his head as he struggled to concentrate. The melodious gentle tones of an eastern kettle drum floating through the tavern had a somewhat soothing effect on his mind, but not enough to encourage his best thinking.

Suen-magir had fallen into depression about six years previously when his young wife had unexpectedly died in childbirth. The child did not survive either, leaving Suen-magir in a terrible state. He had a pronounced tendency to spend time nursing his sorrow with strong drink

---

in Greek concepts of the constellation Virgo. Popular astronomy applications on computers generally only present the Greek idea of Virgo.

25 Kallisto: Greek myth name of a nymph loved by Zeus, derived from the word kallistos, meaning "most beautiful." http://monsaventinus.wikia.com/wiki/Ancient_Greek_Female_Names_(Greek_Community)

26 Suen-magir or Sîn-māgir means "Sîn upholds," referring to the lunar god Sîn. See Stol, Marten M. "Old Babylonian Personal Names." SEL 8, 1991. pp. 191-212.

and prostitutes. He had never tried to marry again. The thought of it was too painful.

Suen-magir had just lost a few coins in a game of Twenty Squares, when he decided that he had enough.[27] Rising abruptly to his feet, he signaled with his hand that he had finished and began walking across the floor.

A man behind him raised a cry saying, "But we have not finished!" However, some of his companions said, "Oh enough. He has little honor. He will not come back now, let him go." Even as Suen-magir stumbled slightly, the words, "he has no honor," entered like a dagger into his mind.

Staggering across the floor, he began to think of tomorrow when he needed to work. Arriving at the door of the tavern, Suen-magir thought of other moments when he had arrived to work in a drunken state at the astronomical archive buildings in both Uruk and Borsippa. Repeatedly his colleague Illis-kutul had to send him home because of his drinking. Illis-kutul tried to cover for him at work. Suen-magir did not want this to continue. There in the tavern, he was embarrassed even to think that he might not be able to work again tomorrow.

Suen-magir thought at times that his friend Illis-kutul perhaps wished he (Suen-magir) had stayed in Uruk. There was a good possibility that he would already be dead by now if he had not changed locations. Despite all the outward evidence of the hopelessness of his case, Illis-kutul still maintained hope that Suen-magir might change his style of living.

Passing through the tavern door, Suen-magir stepped into the street. Looking down the street to his right, in the distance, he saw the great ziggurat where he usually worked. He needed to be ready for tomorrow night. However, at the moment he just did not know how that could happen. The evening's wine had taken effect. He could kick himself. Suen-magir hoped that he would be sobered up by the next night. A few doors away, he heard some of the boatmen striking up a song. They were having a great time. They were still able to sing strong and clear; their wine had not yet taken effect.

---

27   The game "Twenty Squares" was played in the Middle East for over 2,000 years. The games is also known as "The Royal Game of Ur." Copies of the board and the instructions have been found in ancient Iraq. A YouTube video exists that explains the game and gives an example of it being played (Tom Scott vs. Irving Finkel, The Royal Game of Ur).

Looking straight ahead, Suen-magir saw some women across the street in the darkness. He thought to himself, "Perhaps one more time, and then I will stop." Even as he thought it, he said to himself, "No, you are wrong, you do not ever seem to stop."

Then, standing there a moment, he started to weep softly. Afterward, he crossed the street, and two girls ushered him into a dimly lit room a few feet away. He would not keep his newly earned wages very long. Fortunately, he had left about half of his money at home. Otherwise, he would have been reduced to absolute poverty. The women soothed his pain for an hour, and he recovered enough sobriety to get home.

That same evening, about 70 cubits[28] above the ground, Ekur-zakir looked down on Borsippa from the fourth level of the Babylonian ziggurat. The smoke from cooking fires was staying fairly low to the ground. It would not interfere with observing the horizons nor the sky above. The night was falling very strongly now. The last light of day was fading in the west where the star Dilbat [29] was very bright, although it could be slightly brighter. It would set in about an hour.

The 64-year-old Ekur-zakir,[30] whose white hair and white curly beard fell to the middle of his chest, faced toward the west. There was a little bit of noise from the local taverns far away to his right, closer to the river and the docks. It sounded like singing. He imagined that there were several drunken sailors and river-men having a good time.

He thought to himself, "They certainly do work hard, perhaps they need

28 About 35 meters or 114 feet.

29 The planet Venus. Dilbat was also referred to as the Star of Ishtar, a Babylonian god/goddess with a dual masculine and feminine nature. The planet/star was seen as being a feminine fertility goddess in the morning sky and as a masculine war god in the evening sky.

30 The meaning of Ekur-zakir: Ekur is a Sumerian term meaning "mountain house." It is the assembly of the gods in the Garden of the gods, parallel to Mount Olympus in Greek mythology. Ziggurats recalled "mountain houses." Zakir is also is known to mean "recording or recorder." Zakir may mean "to remember." Does it mean "Remember the mount house of the gods?" See: https://en.wikipedia.org/wiki/Ekur, For Zakir see: George Bertin, *Abridged Grammars of the Languages of the Cuneiform Inscriptions*, (Trubner and company, Ludgate Hill, London, 1888) p. 40.

these moments to relieve the stress. However, they use up all their wages and have to work harder later. It is not the best life."

Again looking to the south, over the wall in front of him, almost all of the massive Babylonian pyramid was behind or below him.[31] Ekur-zakir could just see the tops of several palm trees lower down at the base of the pyramid and a few lights in various homes. The streets were dark, except for a principal avenue here and there which were lit up with a few torches. It was too expensive to maintain any lighting for the entire night, so even these lights were extinguished a hour or so after dark.

From his vantage point on the southern tip of the ziggurat, Ekur-zakir then looked toward the east. There, toward the horizon, he could see that GENNA[32] was visible. It was also called "Kajamänu," meaning the "slow, steady one." A few days before it had risen visibly for the last time above the horizon in the east after sunset.[33] Now it was already present, low in the increasingly dark eastern sky. The Pleiades had now become visible several degrees above the planet.

Turning again slowly to the northeast Ekur-zakir could see the retaining wall of the fifth level of the ziggurat stretching out before him. Nearby, one could make out its yellow and gold baked-mud bricks through the light of a few small lamps positioned near the wall.[34]

Beside the wall, a couple of astronomical assistants were sitting on a mud-brick bench beside the lamps writing on wax tablets. They were seated about twenty feet away from a small door which led to a storage room used by the astronomers as a small auxiliary library. The men also used it as a place to store their instruments and writing materials. Another man was standing near the door. Ekur-zakir could see that he was

---

31 The ziggurat at Borsippa was apparently oriented so that each of the four corners was facing toward a cardinal point (north, east, south, west).

32 The planet Saturn. The planet takes 29 years to make a complete circuit around the zodiac.

33 This is called the acronycal (acronychal) rising in modern astronomical terms. Essentially Saturn was rising in the east just after sunset in the west. There is a day each year when Saturn rises in the east for the last time at sunset. After that, it is in the eastern sky and above the horizon when the sun sets.

34 Each level had a different color. The lowest level of the pyramid was the color of asphalt, black; the second level was a type of tan-orange, the third a kind of rose, the fourth and fifth were various shades of yellow and gold while the sixth level was blue. The seventh level was a white-silver; and formerly the top of the pyramid had been dominated by a small temple shrine, which itself was colored gold.

eating a piece of bread, no doubt because he had not already eaten, and he would be passing the night on the terrace keeping the regular watch of the heavens.

As Ekur-zakir followed the wall with his eyes he saw a few places where the wall had partially collapsed, leaving piles of rubble on the fourth level terrace. There was still enough room to walk despite the various piles of broken baked-mud bricks and dust. The pyramid was not in great shape. Its upkeep had been neglected for several centuries. Off in the distance, Ekur-zakir could see the white-colored star Dil-gan I-ku (Capella) burning brightly fairly high in the sky above the far end of the ziggurat terrace.

Then, Ekur-zakir turned his face toward the north and the wall directly behind him. The North Star was shining slightly over halfway to the zenith, and to its right, the five bright stars of the Babylonian Stag constellation had appeared.[35] The original seven levels of the Borsippian pyramid were no longer completely intact. The temple sanctuary of the god Nabu, atop the ziggurat, had collapsed along with two of the upper terraces. Large portions of the bricks on those levels had fallen mainly away toward the north and northwest, but the majority remained in a sea of disorder. The inhabitants below had used a lot of the bricks to enlarge or build their own constructions. The collapse of the upper levels had reduced the total height of the structure to about 120 cubits from 140 cubits.[36]

After looking again toward the west where Dilbat (Venus) had already moved lower toward the horizon, Ekur-zakir then turned and spoke to two of his assistants on the bench. He discovered that they had made all the notations concerning GENNA and Dilbat.[37] Ekur-zakir was satisfied. It was time for him to go home. The others would take care of other observations during the night. It was well after dark now, so a servant lit a small lamp and helped Ekur-zakir see his way along the terrace. Several minutes later, they arrived on the northeast side of the pyramid where the grand staircase led to the lower level. There at the beginning of

---

35 The Stag (Cassiopeia & part of Andromeda).

36 About 43 and 50 meters. It is doubtful that the entire ziggurat was completely intact in the last years of the first millennium BC. However, no one really knows about the exact state of the Babylonian pyramid at that time.

37 Saturn and Venus.

the fifth level, a small shrine had replaced the original temple sanctuary which had been on the seventh level of the ziggurat.

Standing at the top of the stairs, Ekur-zakir stopped, glanced toward his left and bowed slightly toward the dark outlines of the small shrine building. He wanted to honor the god Nabu before he began going down the stairs. Then turning toward the stairs, Ekur-zakir and the accompanying servant continued to descend. In the darkness below, one could just see the main temple of Nabu in Babylonia, named the Ezida. The astronomical library was not far away from the temple across a courtyard, and Ekur-zakir's notary office was a bit further away through a few other courtyards near a major street.

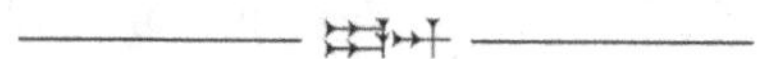

In another part of Borsippa, northeast of the partially ruined ziggurat, Ekur-zakir's son Iqisa had been listening to his twelve-year-old son, Belanum,[38] recite an ancient cuneiform text from memory. They were at home, and Belanum had since gone to bed like his two siblings before him. Iqisa's wife, Berenice, had also gone to bed in an adjoining room. She had been hard at work with the affairs of the household all day and certainly merited to have some rest. She was from a Babylonian background, but because her parents liked the Greek name Berenice, they had chosen it for their daughter. Now only Iqisa remained in the main living area of his two-story, mud-brick home.

Iqisa's heart leaped as he looked down at the baked-mud cuneiform tablet[39] on the table. He cherished the words of the text of the MUL. APIN,[40] an astronomical text written at least 1,200 years before. The passage mentioned and described portions of several constellations. The text read:

---

38 Belanum, The name was found in: Eleanor Robson, *Mathematics in Ancient Iraq: A Social History,* Princeton University Press, Princeton, N.J. 2008), p. 105.

39 Examples of cuneiform astronomical and astrological tablets can be found in Appendix 10.

40 The title means "The Plow Star," which is the first constellation mentioned in the text. For simplicity, here the English language names have been used here for the planets and constellations.

The Plough, Enlil, the lead star of the stars of Enlil (Most of Draco)
The Wolf at the seed funnel of the Plough (Head & middle of Draco)
The Old Man, Enmesharra (Perseus)
The Crook, the Crouching god (Auriga)
The Great Twins, Lugalirra and Meslamtaea (Gemini)
The Little Twins, Alammush and Ninezengud (Canis Minor)
The Crab, the seat of Anu (Cancer)
The Lion, Latarak (Leo)
The stars that stands in the breast of the Lion, the King Star, LUGAL,
(The star Regulus in Leo)
The dusky stars that stand in the tail of the Lion, the Frond of Erua,
Zarpanitu (Coma Berenices & the western part of Virgo)

Minutes before, his son Belanum had recited a passage from another part of the MUL.APIN text:

The Sun travels the path the Moon travels.
Jupiter travels the path the Moon travels.
Venus travels the path the Moon travels.
Mars travels the path the Moon travels.
Mercury, whose name is Ninurta, travels the path the Moon travels.
Saturn travels the path the Moon travels.
Total six gods whose positions are one, who touch the stars of heaven,
who keep changing their positions.

Iqisa had been so proud of his son, who had recited the words perfectly from memory. But Iqisa was particularly excited that his son's mathematical capabilities were growing. As Iqisa looked down another cuneiform tablet caught his attention:

In the first month Nisannu, on the 15th day, the daytime watch is three minas, the night-time watch is three minas.

The text referred to time measured with a water clock [41] and the length of a normal day at the time of the spring equinox. Over 1,000 years previously during the ideal month of Nisannu (Nisan)[42] the length of day

---

41 The ancients sometimes measured time by observing a measured amount of water that would flow from one recipient to another, hence the name "water clock."

42 Nisannu (Nisan) is the first month of the Jewish and Babylonian year. It was in the spring time. After about

and night were equal. A few lines higher, it was mentioned about the calculation of the 13th lunar month of the year. Adding an additional month was necessary about every two to three years to keep the lunar calendar in line with the seasons.

Iqisa was certainly going to do his best to transmit this ancient knowledge to Belanum. Hopefully, his son's future would be assured if he followed in the long line of family astronomers. Iqisa's father, Ekur-zakir, had been faithful in educating him. Now Iqisa wanted to follow in the steps of his father by passing on all his understanding of the heavens to his son. In addition, his son was receiving other training from mathematicians and professional scribes, but Iqisa was determined to do his part as well. He was so satisfied that his son was doing well even at his young age of 12 years.

Looking at the cuneiform tablet, Iqisa thought back briefly over his life. He was an eighth-generation descendant of astronomers. His son would be the ninth. Iqisa had been born on the second day of Tašrītu in the 213th year of the Arsacid Era, in the third year of the Parthian Emperor Phraates IV. [43] Iqisa's father, the astronomer Ekur-zakir, was intrigued by the birth because the star SA4 šá ABSIN [44] (Spica) rose in the east at practically the same hour as when Iqisa was born. It was the first appearance of the star in the morning sky after an absence of six weeks in the solar glare.

However, neither Iqisa, nor Ekur-zakir, put much stock in the new-style horoscopes, which supposedly charted the destiny of individuals according to the time and date of their birth, but the coincidence of the first visibility of SA4 šá ABSIN was interesting. All of Iqisa's forefathers for 300 years had studied the skies in association with their roles as priests in the temple of Nabu in Borsippa. Some of Iqisa's earliest memories were filled with his exploits of climbing the increasingly ruined ziggurat associated with the temple complex.

---

450 BC or before, among the Babylonians, Nisannu always began on or after the spring equinox. Among the Jews Nisan could begin before the equinox, but the Feast of Passover usually fell on or after the equinox.

43 October 6th, 35 BC. The date is given in terms that the ancient Babylonians would have understood.

44 This is the modern transliteration of the cuneiform name. The Babylonian name means "The bright star of the Furrow." The Babylonian "Furrow" constellation is related to, but not exactly equal with the Greek constellation Virgo. The constellation rose in the east in the fall about the time when the Babylonians planted winter barley and wheat.

After briefly thinking about these things, Iqisa decided to go to bed. His wife was already sound asleep in the next room. Iqisa covered one of the last two remaining lamps and used the other one to arrive in the bedroom. In a few moments, he joined his wife Berenice, blowing out the lamp in the process.

The Pilgrims Journey Back to Babylonia

Eliab, Eitan, and their group of Jewish pilgrims spent about two months returning to Babylonia. The trip was uneventful, but it was very long. The fall nights after the Feast of Tabernacles turned from cool to cold as the group crossed the Syrian Desert and the upper end of the Euphrates Valley. Heavy rain showers and storms met the group when they reached the Euphrates River at Dura-Europos. Then the 110 pilgrims slowly disbanded each to his own home, as they arrived in the upper Euphrates Valley and proceeded through central Babylonia. Near the ancient city of Babylon, the remaining group disbanded and dispersed into the cities and towns in the area. Eliab and Eitan returned to Borsippa with a group of seven. Arriving home, it took Eliab about three days to recover from the trip. He was delighted to be able to spend some time again with his wife as well as his other younger son and daughter.

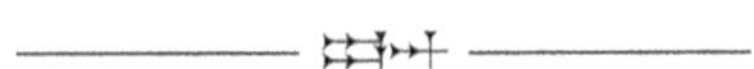

On the fifth day after their arrival back in Borsippa, Eliab and Eitan traveled out to his father's date palm plantation with the rest of the family. They walked the ten miles from their home to the gates of the estate. Several servants were busy cleaning an irrigation ditch on the right side of the entrance road. The men immediately recognized the travelers and greeted them verbally or with hand gestures. One of the slaves ran toward his master's house about 100 yards away. As Eliab arrived near the house, his father, Ariel, came out under the porch at the front entrance. Eliab's mother also made her appearance at the door. The greetings were joyful. Eliab and Eitan had completed their journey to Judaea and back. It was indeed a cause for celebration.

They all stood in the shade of the porch for several minutes. Then as they started to enter the house, Eliab looked up above at the cedar lintel and doorposts. The Hebrew words were still there, as they had been for generations, carved in the wood:

On the right: *Judah, your brothers shall praise you.*

On the left: *Judah is a lion's cub.*

And in the center:

"The scepter shall not depart from Judah, nor the ruler's staff from between his feet, until Shiloh comes, and to him shall be the obedience of the peoples." [45]

Eliab paused even as the others entered the house. He remembered the dream that he had before leaving Jerusalem. A certain sense of awe rose in his heart. The message on these pieces of wood had changed his life. The promised Messiah would come at his appointed time. Eliab knew that in the coming weeks he would try to fulfill his promise to Joram. He would ask Ekur-zakir to help him get the details on the history of the ancient kings in relation to Daniel's prophecy.

After a short moment, Ariel, standing just inside the door of the house beckoned, "Eliab, come on in, come and be refreshed. Why are you looking up at the lintel and doorposts?"

Eliab, replied back, "It is a long story," and looking at his father, he entered the house.

Eliab Arrives Back at the Notarial Office

Four days after visiting his father and mother, Eliab went back to the notarial office. There was much work to be done; many things had either been neglected or left for later during Eliab's absence. The first month was intense. Eliab worked literally from dawn until dusk six days each week to get caught up.

Even so, every few days the conversation with his cousin Joram came

---

45 Genesis 49:10.

back to mind. Eliab waited about three weeks, and then he finally decided to broach the subject with his employer. Seeing that Ekur-zakir seemed to be in a good mood and a bit unoccupied, Eliab launched into the matter, but at the same moment, Iqisa, Ekur-zakir's son, entered the office. He greeted his father and Eliab and sat down over to one side, seeing that the men were in conversation.

Eliab was saying, "Ekur-zakir, when I was in Jerusalem I stayed at my cousin's home. His family was originally from Babylonia, but they moved to Jerusalem about 30 years ago. Since he returned to Judaea as a young boy my cousin, Joram, has become particularly religious. He has also become interested in questions related to prophecy. As I think you are aware, there is an idea in Judaism that God will one day send a great deliverer who will rescue our people from foreign oppressors. Our religious teachers also believe that this man will eventually reign over the world in righteousness."

Ekur-zakir responded, "Yes, I am acquainted with these ideas. I have even read some of your ancient texts which speak about such things. So why are you speaking to me about this today?"

Iqisa also spoke up saying, "I also find these things interesting. I have briefly looked at some of the prophecies in the Greek Septuagint text of your religious writings. I remember reading some texts associated with the prophet Daniel concerning a figure who would arise to rule over the nations."

Eliab continued, "While I was in Judaea on pilgrimage some of these texts were brought to my attention. The passage that you mention is found in the book of Daniel, a man who lived during the days of Nebuchadnezzar through the time of Cyrus the Great. Do you both know about Daniel?"

Iqisa said, "No, not in any great detail," but Ekur-zakir answered, "Yes, certainly I have heard of him, I have also read the book which is attributed to him. Since a good portion of the original book is written in Aramaic, I had no trouble reading that part and a Jewish friend of your father Ariel explained the rest to me."

Eliab continued, "Well, you are probably aware of the prophecy of the 70 'sevens?'

Ekur-zakir replied, "Yes, I vaguely remember it."

Eliab replied, "In Daniel's text, it is written that the Messiah will appear at the end of a period of time which is sometimes associated with Jewish Sabbatical years. Many of our religious teachers think that the 'sevens' in the prophecy refer to a number of Sabbatical cycles."

Ekur-zakir said, "Tell us a bit more about your Sabbatical cycles. I would like to understand that."

Eliab explained, "It is written in our law that every seven years our land is to lie fallow, and there would be no planting. After a period of seven Sabbatical cycles, we have a Jubilee year, in which debts are forgiven, and slaves can receive their freedom. Since this cycle of 'sevens' is already established in our beliefs and practices, it would seem logical to conclude that the 70 'sevens' have something to do with the Sabbatical cycle."

Eliab continued, "According to the prophecy, it would appear that Daniel's Sabbatical cycles had their beginning not long after Babylon was conquered by Cyrus the Great. Daniel's text says,

"Know therefore and discern, that from the going forth of the commandment to restore and to build Jerusalem unto the anointed one, the prince, shall be seven 'sevens,' and 62 'sevens.'"

"So one must account for these seven 'sevens' and 62 'sevens" which make a total of 69 'sevens' in order to arrive at the Messiah's coming. However, there is a problem. The religious teachers in Israel are not very aware of specific matters concerning the history of our people when dealing with exact dates. No one seems to know exactly when the decree to restore and rebuild Jerusalem was given. My cousin thinks that this decree concerns Cyrus the Great who released the Jews to return to Judaea early in his reign. But when did that happen? Some of the religious teachers speculate that this happened about 490 years ago."

"However, my cousin was not at all certain concerning their calculations. He asked me to try to find out more about the real history of the period when Cyrus made his decree. I know that in your astronomical diaries you certainly have the complete list of the kings including the kings of the Babylonian Empire and the subsequent Persian Empire. It must be indicated in your astronomical diaries exactly when Cyrus reigned. If I know the dates of Cyrus' reign, it should be possible to calculate the approximate date of the Messiah's appearing with more exactitude. This would be better than the speculations which are so present in Judaea right now. If you could possibly help me to do a little bit of research concerning the dates, I will then send this information to my cousin."

Looking toward his son, Ekur-zakir said, "Well, I do not have the time nor the patience to do the research, but what about you Iqisa? It would not be a bad idea for you to be a bit more familiar with our astronomical documents from several hundred years ago. What do you think, would you be willing to do some research in the archives for Eliab?"

Smiling back, Iqisa looked at his father and said, "Of course, you know me well enough, I am a curious sort of fellow. Sure I will do it. Doing the research will be interesting. I think I would like to know more about this messianic king."

Iqisa continued saying, "Eliab, on a practical level perhaps you could help me do the research. The dates and the names of the kings will need to be noted. I could read off the dates and names, and you can write it all down. At the same time that we make the lists, you could indicate the Jewish Sabbatical years on the same copy."

Looking at Ekur-zakir, Iqisa said, "Do you think that would be alright father? I know we usually do not allow people in the archives or the observatory who are not priests or astronomers. We do have some Zoroastrian apprentices working with us at the moment. Would it be a problem for Eliab to come to the observatory library and make the notations with me?"

Iqisa continued smiling at his father, "I know we do not usually share our professional secrets with outsiders. He has worked for you for more than 20 years. He seems to be at least a bit trustworthy."

Ekur-zakir laughed heartily, "Yes, take him to the observatory library. Let him help you. You all arrange the times between yourselves."

Turning to Eliab, Ekur-zakir said, "You must have wondered what the inside of the observatory must look like?"

Eliab responded, "Yes, certainly, I have been here for over 20 years, but I have never been to the observation post on the ziggurat or seen where you all record your observations and do calculations. I would enjoy being present when you all are observing the sky sometime in the evening or early morning."

"Very well, It is agreed. You will join us in the observatory library for the research, and at least a few times we will invite you to observe a celestial event or two with us. But now we all need to get back to work!" said Ekur-zakir with a smile.

In the Archives - Winter in Late 4 BC and Early 3 BC

A few days later, Iqisa arrived at the notary office to meet Eliab, and the two went together to the astronomical archives. To get to the building, which was located at the base of the ziggurat, one had to pass through two outer courtyards. The archive building itself was a flat-roofed, mud brick structure like most other buildings in Borsippa. It stood about 14 cubits from the ground to the roof.[46]

Before passing inside the mud-brick building, Eliab stopped and looked up at the ziggurat, while saying to Iqisa, "You know I have never been so close to this structure. It seems high from a distance, but here at the base near the grand staircase, it seems even loftier."

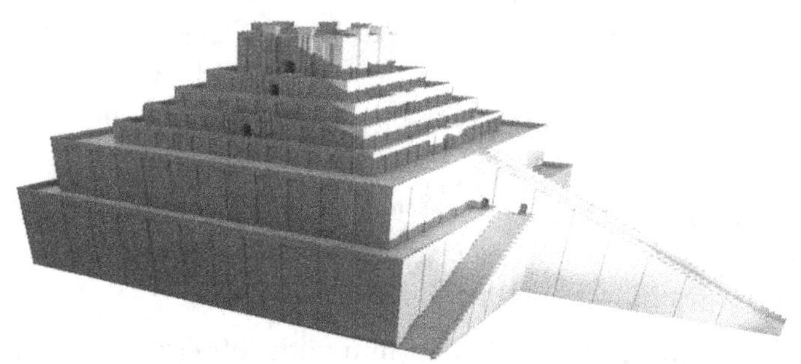

The ziggurat at Borsippa had seven levels which represented the sun, moon and the five visible planets. According to archaeologists, the building was much more rectangular than square (G. Rawlinson). Each level was decorated in various colors. Differing ideas have been proposed concerning the colors and their order. Following is one possibility; the colors are indicated from the top to bottom: Gold - Sun, Silver - Moon, Light Red - Mercury, Blue - Venus, Dark Red - Mars, Black - Saturn, and White - Jupiter.

---

46   About seven meters (yards) high. A cubit was about 50 cm.

Iqisa replied, "The other day, Ekur-zakir said that you could probably visit the observatory. We will look for a good moment. There may be an interesting event which will take place in the coming weeks or months."

Going on into the building which housed the archives, Iqisa showed the two principal rooms each of which was about 25 by 25 feet in surface area. Three other side rooms held more archives and some working tables. The rooms were relatively cool. The mud-brick walls protected the inside from both heat and cold. The structure was reasonably well-lit through several windows high up toward the ceiling.

Cuneiform documents were stocked in several dozen wooden and mud-brick shelves, each being about a foot and a half deep, which were distributed around the walls. In addition, several rows about four feet high were arranged in the center of the room. Thousands of cuneiform tablets were distributed in neat rows on the shelves in both rooms. One section held parchment rolls as well. Not all of the records or correspondence was done on cuneiform tablets. Eliab also noticed that some new shelving had been erected at the back of the second room, but it was still not filled. The men were making provision to stock other documents.

Two of the other astronomers in the building came toward Iqisa and Eliab as they found themselves in the doorway between the two main rooms. The men, whom Eliab knew a bit through their visits to the notarial office, warmly greeted Eliab.

Illis-kutul, stroking his curly white and grey beard, said, "We were informed that you would be coming. Welcome. It has been a long time since a non-astronomer has been in these rooms. We hope you have a good experience as you do your research. At noontime, we will eat a light meal together in a building on the other side of the courtyard. You are welcome to join us. I think that Ekur-zakir will be eating with us as well. Please bring your own food as you usually do. We know that you Jews have dietary restrictions."

Eliab said, "I am pleased to accept your invitation and thank you for the possibility of us doing a bit of research in your archives. I am amazed to see the extensive nature of your records. I have heard over the years that the library here was large, but I had no idea how true it was."

Iqisa then introduced the second astronomer who was about 30 years of age with a long, black beard saying, "Eliab, this is Suen-magir, who is an expert in lunar astronomy. He essentially keeps our calendar and informs us of when we should expect solar and lunar eclipses."

Eliab said, "Yes, I recognize you. Very occasionally you come by the notary office looking for Ekur-zakir."

Suen-magir greeted Eliab, but he was a bit taken aback to have a foreigner and a non-astronomer in the archives building. He welcomed Eliab but did not spend much time with the group before retiring to another section of the room.

After the initial greetings, Iqisa led Eliab into one of the three side rooms. There were plenty of wax writing boards, as well as virgin clay tablets, which were being kept moist, and unused parchment rolls. Some servants in this side room were busy copying documents. They did not seem to notice the newcomer too much.

Iqisa explained their activity to Eliab, "These men are making the initial preparations concerning next year's astronomical almanac. Since the motions of the moon and planets are cyclical, we take clues concerning the future behavior of the heavenly objects from the archives. These men are getting records from the archives according to the years which we have indicated to them. Based on the previous behavior of the objects, we can project the appearances of the wandering stars that the Greeks call planets, as well as forecast the movements of the moon. During the next month or so, we will establish the calendar and the astronomical schedule for next year."[47]

Iqisa then showed Eliab a small row of cuneiform documents stacked one beside the other on their edges.

"This morning I have already taken the liberty of getting out certain critical documents from the last 100 years. With these texts, we should be able to establish the dates of several kings. At the same time, you can

---

47   Babylonian Astronomical Diaries (daily observational records) were used to make almanacs along with what modern astronomers now call "Goal-Year Texts." These last documents were made by extracting cyclical information from the Diaries. The records were extensive and allowed the Babylonian astronomers to make predictions with significant accuracy. Several hundred pages of the "Goal-Year Texts" have survived until our day. The remaining "Goal-Year Texts" have been assembled in Volume 6 of the series *Astronomical Diaries and Related Texts from Babylonia*, edited by Abraham Sachs and Hermann Hunger. The sixth volume contains lunar and planetary data, from the 3rd to the 1st century BC. The entire series of six books done by Sachs and Hunger amounts to more than 3,000 pages of transliterations, translations and photographic plates of Babylonian astronomical documents.

mark the Jewish Sabbatical years on a parchment roll. By the end of the morning, we should finish at least 200 or 300 years of tablets. So let us get started."

Iqisa read out the information on the astronomical records concerning the dates and kingships. Eliab began making notes.

He began his list with the reigning king Phraates IV, then they looked at the years of his predecessors: Orodes II, Mithridates III, Phraates III, Sanatruces, Orodes I, Gotarzes I, Mithridates II, Artabanus II, Phraates II, and Mithridates I. Under the reign of the last king, the Parthians had been able to conquer Babylonia. Before Mithridates I, the Greek Seleucid kings reigned over Syria, Mesopotamia, and much of the Iranian plateau.

The research process took more time than Iqisa had projected, but both men were trying to be exact and not make any significant errors. Iqisa would check Eliab's notations from time to time by comparing it with several of the tablets in order just to double check the results. When Iqisa and Eliab had arrived at Mithridates I, the first Parthian king of Babylonia, they decided to stop and have something to eat as foreseen. Eliab got his own food from the nearby notary office and joined the men.

The Gods and the Messiah at the Midday Meal

Over the noon meal, the men spoke more personally asking questions about each other's families and the progress of the historical research. Eventually, the conversation shifted when Suen-magir asked a significant question. He also had heard several things about Judaism and being innately curious he led the way in the discussion, "I understand that you are doing historical research about a certain prediction concerning a prophesied king. Can you tell us more about this Messiah figure according to Judaism?"

Looking around, Eliab saw that he had everyone's full attention. He began his answer, "There are various ideas about the Messiah in Judaism. The Essenes, a sect of Judaism in my ancestral homeland, generally has the idea that there will be two Messiahs. Some think that there will be a kingly Messiah and others have the idea that the Messiah will be a priest. There are passages in our Scriptures which seem to point to both roles.

The Pharisees, another group, seems to be more concentrated on the kingly Messiah. That is the one which has most interested me."

"Judaism is, as you know, monotheistic. Essentially, we have the idea that one great God made the world. In our story of creation, God gave authority to humankind to reign over the world as God's viceroy. However, mankind fell into temptation from the ancient serpent, a spiritual being named Satan, and the world and mankind came under the domination of wicked spirits. We believe that death, injustice, and unrighteousness have come into the world, because of our disobedience and our falling under the domination of the wicked spirits. I know that in Babylonian thought wicked spirits have a role. You believe that they are associated with certain sicknesses and evil events."

"Yet in the face of all these difficulties, there is a very ancient prophecy that the seed of the first woman, Eve, will one day crush the serpent's head, setting humanity free from the domination of the evil one.[48] It seems to us that God has determined that one day the world will again be liberated from the oppression of evil through a special righteous king, who will bring God's rule to the world.[49] We sometimes use the terms 'Melech Sedeq'[50] in referring to this king. We also call him the 'Righteous One.' This king is to come forth from the line of one of our ancient kings, who was named David. If you have read any of our sacred Scriptures, you will know that King David wrote many songs in praise to God."

Suen-magir continued his questioning, "I guess there would be very little room for other gods in the kingdom of the 'Righteous One.' That might put some of us priest/astronomers out of work," he said with a smile.

Iqisa responded as well, "You do understand, don't you Eliab, having work is important to us all," he said while laughing in a good-hearted way.

Eliab spoke up smiling, "I understand your concerns. According to our belief, there is only one God. However, that does not mean that the study of the stars would necessarily be neglected entirely in the coming reign of the righteous king. Our father Abraham, the patriarch, came from

---

48 Genesis 3:15.

49 Jeremiah 23 and Jeremiah 33.

50 Sedeq can be written as Tsedeq or Tzedek.

Ur of the Chaldeans about 2,000 years ago. There is a legend that he understood Sumerian and Babylonian astronomical concepts and later he taught these ideas to the Egyptians.[51] I am not sure that the story is true since at present our people is not known for its knowledge of astronomy. Anyway, God made the sun, moon and the stars; and I would not be surprised that he might like to have some astronomers in his kingdom."

"That is good to know. I do have about 12 years of experience," said Suen-magir as he laughed. The others all chuckled as well before the subject changed slightly.

Illis-kutul spoke up, "I have been interested in knowing more about Judaism as well. I live in a district of the city where there are numerous Jews. Most of them are linen makers and merchants. I have read many of your sacred texts. I was not unaware of the prophet Daniel when it was mentioned that you were coming to do some historical research with Iqisa. I know of Daniel's prophecy concerning the 70 'sevens.' I have also heard about something concerning the resurrection of the dead. As you may have noticed, I am 55 years old. It is a joke among us astronomers that three 19 year lunar cycles is about the age limit for people in our field. If you are not familiar with our 19-year lunar cycles, the numbers add up quickly: Three times 19 years makes 57 years. I may only have a couple of years left to live."

Ekur-zakir finally spoke up, "Well, at 64 years, I have gotten well beyond the 57-year barrier."

Everyone, including Eliab, chuckled.

Eliab responded, "No, I am not familiar with the technical side of lunar cycles. However, I can assure you there is also an idea of the resurrection of the dead that is often associated with the Messiah. A group of religious teachers named the Pharisees insists on teaching about the resurrection of the dead and the judgment to come."

Ekur-zakir said, "It is good to know that this rumor about the resurrection of the dead could be true. We will need to teach you about lunar cycles so that you can participate in our jokes. Essentially 235 lunar months is equivalent to 19 solar years. We use these figures to regulate the calendar and keep it in line with the seasons. If someone adds seven

---

51 Flavius Josephus, *The Antiquities of the Jews* — Book I, Chapter 8, Section 2.

additional lunar months to the calendar in 19 years, one can keep the calendar in line with the seasons. This is one of our great trade secrets, but you may have heard about it already. Many people do not realize that if needed, we can make calendars for decades in advance.

Eliab responded, "Yes, I have some knowledge of adding months to the calendar because our Jewish calendar is based on somewhat similar concepts. However, I did not know that your calendar was so well calculated in advance. Our calendar is partly determined by the celebration of the Passover festival in the spring. The timing of the festival depends on the ripening of grain, which is given annually as an offering on the 16th day of Nisan, your Nisannu. If the grain is not ripe, then the first month and the festival are delayed for another month. We add a second month of Adar in that case. Your calendar is not dependent on such things."

Iqisa piped up, "Among some of us there have been some speculations that the details of the calendar may have been planned by the gods or a god for the benefit of mankind. Certainly having a predictable calendar and maintaining it has been a great source of revenue for my family for generations. We thank the gods for their planning every day."

Again everyone laughed, and Illis-kutul even snorted as he laughed, which caused everyone just to roar, including Eliab.

Then finally as the laughter died off, Eliab said, "Well, thank you for this time. Iqisa, I am not sure that I should continue today. There is some pressing business in the notarial office. I do know at least one person who is interested in the preparation of documents at the office."

Ekur-zakir broke into the conversation with a smile, "I am thrilled to hear that you are thinking about the office!"

It was quickly agreed that the research would continue on the same day during the next week.

Eliab thought to himself as he left the room, "That did not go too badly. I am glad we had this discussion. My needing help seems to have opened doors for me to speak of my faith in God."

About an hour later back in the notary office, Eliab remembered the passage from the Psalms, which spoke of the sun and moon bearing witness that the Messiah's throne will endure for long ages.

He said to himself, "If I had a bit more presence of mind I would have been able to tell the men about that passage from the Psalms.[52] Well, too bad, perhaps there will be another opportunity to tell them in the future."

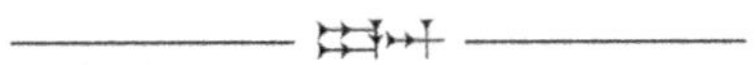

Suen-magir returned to the table in the archives where he was using several cuneiform tablets to prepare the almanac for the coming year. However, he was distracted, as he kept remembering Eliab's words, "There is a very ancient prophecy that the seed of the woman will one day crush the serpent's head ... God has determined that one day the world will again be liberated from the oppression of evil through special righteous king ..."

Suen-magir, staring at one of the tablets before him without really reading its contents, thought to himself, "I know what it is like to need to be liberated." Eventually, he snapped out of his state of near trance and decided that he needed to work.

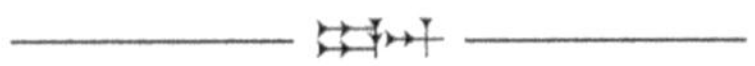

During their second encounter in the archives, Iqisa and Eliab were able to cover the Seleucid period of kings going back to the time of Alexander the Great. They noted all the kings, the dates of their reigns and the Sabbatical years.

The following week, in a third encounter, the two men went back to the Achaemenid (Persian) dynasty. They saw that the beginning of the Empire was actually the Medo-Persian[53] empire. In reality, Darius the Mede (Cyaxeres II of Media)[54] was the chief partner. It was only upon

---

52 Psalm 89:35-37. This was explored in more depth in pages 9-12 in the first chapter.

53 It is important to note that the Medes were the senior partners before the death of Darius the Mede. The Empire was known as the Medo-Persian Empire (Daniel 6:12 and 15). Cyrus the Persian afterward became the chief ruler. Later in the book of Esther the roles were reversed. (Esther 1.3, 1.14, 1.19).

54 See Steven Anderson, *Darius The Mede: A Reappraisal*, and also See James Bejon, Appendix 5C: Darius the Mede, pages 9-39.

Darius' death that Cyrus the Great [55] became the only ruler of the Empire and formally established the Achaemenid (Persian) dynasty.

As the two men explored the Persian period, Eliab became uncomfortable. His chart of dates now contained more than 70 periods of Sabbatical years. In fact, it seemed that the first period of Sabbatical years began several years after Cyrus came to power, but also a few years following his declaration that the Jews could return to their ancestral homeland and rebuild Jerusalem and the temple.

Eliab discerned that there already had been 75 Sabbatical periods from the time of Cyrus until the current ongoing Sabbatical period (the 76th Sabbatical period).[56] This last one was supposed to end soon.[57] Therefore, from the time of Cyrus' reign until the present moment there were simply too many cycles to fit the 490 years of the prophecy.

Eliab pointed this out, "You know Iqisa, I already have 75 Sabbatical cycles here, and we are currently in another one, which will make 76 periods when complete. That is a total of 532 years, which is more than the 490 years in the complete prophecy. Therefore, there seems to be some kind of problem. Should there not only be 70 or possibly just 69 Sabbatical periods?"

"The prophecy says seven 'sevens' and 62 'sevens until the coming of the Messiah. That makes a total of 69 'sevens' which amounts to 483 years (7 x 7 and 62 x 7). It is clear that we have worked hard and very methodically as we have done the research. The question is, how is it that we have many more Sabbatical cycles than allowed by the prophecy when counting from Cyrus to the present?"

Iqisa thought about this for a few moments. He said, "Well, this may be a problem. Indeed, perhaps the prophecy is simply wrong. After all, we know when Cyrus made the decree, and there are over 483 years in our list. However, there may be separation periods between the sequences

---

55 Cyrus II of Persia c. 600 – 530 BC, commonly known as Cyrus the Great. He was the founder of the Achaemenid (Persian) Empire.

56 See Appendix 8, pages 444-445, for a list of the Medo-Persian, Seleucid, and Parthian kings from Cyrus the Great up until the time of Christ.

57 The last Sabbatical period of their survey was 8/7 to 2/1 BC. This follows the Sabbatical year scheme developed by Israel ben Wacholder. Some scholars prefer the Sabbatical year scheme established by Benedict Zuckermann.

of Sabbatical years. The fact that there are too many years could also be an indication of how to solve the riddle. The 70 'sevens' are divided into three groups according to the prophecy? Isn't that right?"

Eliab responded, "Yes, there are seven Sabbatical periods, then 62 Sabbatical periods and one final Sabbatical period of seven years. We could even write it out." And taking a reed pen Eliab wrote the numbers:

$$(7 \times 7) + (62 \times 7) + (1 \times 7) = 490$$

"The prophecy also says that the Messiah will appear at the culmination of the 62 'sevens' which follows the seven 'sevens.' Therefore we are only dealing with 69 'sevens' until the coming of the Messiah. We do not need to worry about the final 'seven.' That leaves us with just two series of 'sevens.'

$$(7 \times 7) + (62 \times 7) = 483$$

Iqisa pondered the question a bit and then added, "It seems that there may be some separations between the Sabbatical periods. Perhaps they are not all to be counted together. Otherwise, why does the prophecy insist on groups of seven 'sevens' and 62 'sevens'? They are apparently unconnected periods of time. What makes the separation? We need to discover that."

Iqisa reflected, "Think about this. If one wanted to hide the mysterious numbers in a riddle, then the exact nature of the separation periods would need to be hidden. If there are separation periods between the series of Sabbatical years, they are not spelled out in the prophecy."

Iqisa continued, "Let's think about the numbers. Seven times seven is 49 years, and 62 times seven is 434 years. There seem to be two distinct periods indicated concerning the first two groups of 'sevens.' Certainly, the separation period will need to be a multiple of seven, otherwise one would fall out of the Sabbatical sequence. The Sabbatical cycle seems to be the key to the mysterious numbers. After the first 49 years, one must skip a period, then calculate the Sabbatical cycles again to arrive at the culmination of the 62 'sevens.'"

"However, think about this: If the separation period were only one Sabbatical period, then the 62 'sevens' would already be accomplished, and the Messiah should already be present. But apparently, this is not the case. Your cousin and the others in Israel do not think that the Messiah has arrived. In fact, notice that there have certainly been almost seven 'sevens' too many already. Only two years are lacking to arrive at the following sequence."

Taking the reed pen Iqisa wrote out the numbers:

7 x 7 = 49

7 x 7 = 49 (Seven extra Sabbatical Periods)

62 x 7 = 434

Eliab was a bit startled. It was like a revelation. "Yes, in the numbers we have established there are seven 'sevens' in addition to the numbers in the prophecy. In Judaism, there is the concept of the Jubilee. It is exactly the period of seven 'sevens' or 49 years which are in surplus. The Jubilee is an important concept in Judaism. It has never been practiced correctly, but it appears to have been God's design for my people. Every 49 years all debts are to be forgiven, and each person is supposed to be able to return to his own land in the 50th year when the cycle restarts, therefore a period of seven 'sevens' does have a significant place in Judaism."

Iqisa replied, "Essentially you are saying that if a period of 49 years or seven 'sevens' were introduced between the two periods of 49 years and 434 years, It would be wholly appropriate and symbolically significant considering your Jewish beliefs about the Jubilee. The Messiah has a role of more or less freeing the world from injustice, right? This may be the answer to the riddle. It would seem to be appropriate that a symbolic Sabbatical period like a Jubilee would provide the missing connection."

Iqisa continued, "If this manner of thinking is correct, it would bring us to the following result: 49 + 49 + 434 years. That makes a total of 532 years from the time of the beginning of the first Sabbatical year under Cyrus until the end of the present Sabbatical cycle. Then there would remain a single 'seven' in the prophecy to make 70, but perhaps that is not important for the present calculation. The Messiah is supposed to appear at the culmination of the 62 'sevens,' right?"

"By placing a Jubilee between the periods and calculating from the first Sabbatical cycle under Cyrus until now, there have now elapsed 530 years. We are now in the 531st year. If we are right, that would mean that the 532nd year will begin in the spring about 14 months from now. That is more or less in line with the calculations done by the Essenes, is that not right?"

Eliab said, "Yes, it is. The numbers line up. However, one could also ask the question, What does it mean for the Messiah, the Prince, to appear? The text says, 'So you are to know and discern that from the issuing of a decree to restore and rebuild Jerusalem until Messiah the Prince there will be seven 'sevens' and 62 'sevens' … Is this speaking of the Messiah's birth? Is it speaking about him becoming a public figure? I am not sure what to think about the meaning of the Scripture."

Eliab continued, "The calculations and historical research that we have done indicate that the coming of the Messiah could very well be imminent. I guess my cousin will be pleased. Of course, there probably would not be any way of knowing if all this is right before two years from now. And then perhaps one would need to wait 20-30 years before the Messiah would become manifest if the text is referring to the Messiah's birth. It would seem doubtful to me that he would be acclaimed as a public figure from the moment of his birth. Even so, perhaps God will give some other indications about the coming of the Messiah without it being necessary to wait for an additional 20 to 30 years."

Iqisa responded, "You say 'God,' but you are talking to an astronomer who works for 'the gods.'"

Eliab simply said back with a smile, "Everyone can make errors in counting the numbers of gods. I think there is only one. You count several more gods."

Eliab paused and continued with a sigh, "However, I hope we have not made big errors with our calculations of Sabbatical years. This has been a lot of work. If we did make mistakes, my cousin might be irritated. If I ever had a chance to return to Judaea, I would like to enjoy his hospitality. I do not want him to be upset with me."

Iqisa responded again, "Well, we have certainly tried hard. You can encourage your cousin to be merciful. I have read that your God is full of mercy and slow to anger. I rather like that. Your cousin should imitate his Creator."

Eliab looked at Iqisa straight in the face and lifted his hand toward him and said, "I perceive that you are a discerning young man."

Then Iqisa, looking back briefly at the prophetic text, brought up another subject, "Did you notice that according to the prophecy, the 'Anointed One' is also 'cut off and has nothing' after a period of 62 'sevens.' This is odd. Indeed, the entire text is strange. Notice how it reads,

"After the sixty-two 'sevens,' the Anointed One will be cut off or put to death and will have nothing. The people of the ruler who will come will destroy the city and the sanctuary. The end will come like a flood: War will continue until the end, and desolations have been decreed." [58]

"I wonder if this second period of 62 'sevens' is the same as the first in the previous lines? In the first, we have the arrival of the Messiah, but in the second the 'Anointed One' will be cut off and have nothing. What does this mean? Does he die? And indeed at the place of the Messiah's triumph, there is the victory of a prince who will destroy the city and the sanctuary. That is your temple, I assume. How is this possible? The Messiah arrives and is he immediately 'cut off' or 'put to death.' Or, conversely, is this second aspect of the prophecy dealing with another period of 62 'sevens' separate from the one indicated initially? I think it is a legitimate question. This prophecy is indeed a puzzle."

Then Eliab finally thought of something which he had forgotten several weeks before. He said, "Oh, I just remembered something which I observed in our Scriptures months ago in Judaea. There is a passage in the Psalms, which speaks of the line of King David, and by implication the Messiah, in relation to the sky. I am not sure how this escaped me for such a long time, but you might be interested. The passage goes like this:

"His descendants (that is King David's descendants) shall endure forever, and his throne as the sun before Me. It shall be established forever like the moon, and the witness in the sky is faithful." [59]

Iqisa replied, "Yes, that is interesting. The sun and moon have existed for a long time. If David's throne endures like the sun and moon, one can expect that his the reign of his descendants will last thousands of years. Yes, that is interesting to know." The men continued to discuss for a brief moment, and then they called it a day.

---

58 Daniel 9:27.

59 Psalm 89:36-37.

A week or so later, Eliab wrote up the findings of the research and sent a copy to his cousin in Jerusalem. He made another copy which he kept in Babylonia. He had a good feeling about the research. It seemed to him that the result could help determine the time of the Messiah's appearing.

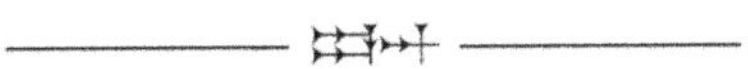

As the winter drew to a close, there was a bit more business activity in the notary office and several of the men, including Eliab, were well occupied. The first month of the new year arrived. Celestial events started to come to pass as indicated in the newly prepared almanac.

Part 2: The Star Appears

The Babylonian Almanac and Jewish Calendar

3/2 BC

The following is an example of what a Babylonian astronomical almanac would have been like in the years 3/2 BC. This almanac is modeled from copies of the still surviving Babylonian astronomical almanac from 7/6 BC. This example is given simply to familiarize readers with the form and content of the late Babylonian almanacs. The Babylonian and Jewish years always started in the spring and continued to the next spring. Many of the Jewish month names have Babylonian origins. The Jewish months had other names in the years preceding the Babylonian exile. Both Babylonian and Jewish days always began in the evening at sunset and ended at sunset the next day. The months began with the first sighting of the lunar crescent in the west at sunset.

The year 3/2 BC was equal to the year 309 of the Seleucid Era (Successors of Alexander, the Greek rulers of Syria, Mesopotamia and Iran) or the year 245 of the Arsacid Era (Parthian Era). In this year, it is probable that the Jewish month of Nisan fell one month earlier than the Babylonian month of Nisannu. The two calendars were out of synchronization once in about every two to three years. The Jewish month of Nisan could begin before the spring equinox; however, in the Babylonian calendar, the first month of the year always began on or after the spring equinox.

In the original documents the Babylonians used their own names for the sun, moon, stars, and planets. In the Babylonian Almanac the names of the planets were as follows:
Jupiter = MUL.BABBAR and also the "kakkabu pesu" both meaning "the white star." There were also other names: Sag.me.gar, Sulpae, Neberu (Nibiru), and Ud.al.tar.
Venus = Dilbat (Delebat), It was also called Na-ba-at kak-ka-bu, meaning "the brightest star."
Saturn = GENNA or Kajamänu, meaning "the steady one."
Mars = Salbatanu (unknown meaning).
Mercury = GU4 .UD or Sihtu, meaning "the jumping one" (because of its quick movements).

There may be a number of errors in this almanac. The author has not been able to verify every aspect of the events and dates.

Babylonian Almanac in 3/2 BC

Month I (April 16/17) Nīsannu
The first of which will follow the 30th of the previous month.
Jupiter in Cancer, Saturn in Taurus, Venus in Pisces, Mercury in Aries,
Mars in Capricorn

18th Venus will reach Aries (May 3/4)
27th Mercury enters Taurus (May 12/13)
On the 28th, last lunar visibility before sunrise. (May 13/14)

Month II (May 15/16) Ayyāru
The first of which will follow the 29th of the previous month.
Jupiter in Cancer, Saturn in Taurus, Venus in Aries, Mercury in Gemini,
Mars in Capricorn

11th Saturn heliacal rising (May 25/26)
14th Mercury will reach Gemini (May 28/29)
16th Venus will reach Taurus (May 30/31)
21st Mars stationary in Capricorn (June 4/5)
28th Mercury will reach Cancer (June 11/12)
On the 28th, last lunar visibility before sunrise. (June 11/28)

Month III (June 14/15) Simannu
The first of which will follow the 30th of the previous month.
Jupiter in Cancer, Saturn in Taurus, Venus in Taurus, Mercury in Cancer,
Mars in Capricorn

3rd Mercury evening visibility begins (June 15/16)
12th Venus will reach Gemini (June 24/25)
16th Mercury will reach Leo (June 28/29)
17th last visibility of Jupiter in the West (June 29/30)
19th Mars acronychal rising in Capricorn (July 1/2)
On the 27th, last lunar visibility before sunrise. (July 11/12)

Nisan

14 Passover
15 Unleavened Bread
16 First Fruits

Iyar

Sivan

5th end of Omer Count
6th Pentecost

Tammuz

Jewish Dates

Month IV (July 13/14) Du'ūzu
The first of which will follow the 29th of the previous month.
Jupiter in Cancer, Saturn in Taurus, Venus in Gemini, Mercury
in Leo, Mars in Capricorn

7th Venus will reach Cancer (July 19/20)
11th Mercury evening visibility ends (July 23/24)
17th First visibility of Jupiter in the East (July 29/30)
23rd Mars stationary in Capricorn (August 4/5)
On the 28th, last lunar visibility before sunrise. (August 9/10)

Month 5 (August 12/13) Ābu
The first of which will follow the 30th of the previous month.
Jupiter in Cancer, Saturn in Taurus,
Venus in Cancer, Mercury in Leo, Mars in Capricorn

2nd Venus will reach Leo (August 13/14)
8th Jupiter will reach Leo (August 19/20)
9th Mercury Evening visibility begins (August 20/21)
22nd Saturn Stationary in Taurus (September 2/3)
25th Mercury will reach Virgo (September 5/6)
26th Venus will reach Virgo (September 6/7)
28th Mercury morning visibility ends (September 8/9)
On the 28th, last lunar visibility before sunrise.

Month 6 (Sept 11/12) Ulūlū
The first of which will follow the 30th of the previous month.
Jupiter in the beginning of Leo, Saturn in Taurus,
Venus in Virgo, Mercury in Virgo , Mars in Capricorn

12th Mercury will reach Libra (September 22/23)
20th Venus will reach Libra (September 30/Oct. 1)
29th last visibility of Venus in the morning (October 9/10)
30th Mars will reach Aquarius (October 10/11)
On the 27th, last lunar visibility before sunrise. (7/8 October)

Av

Elul

Tishrei

1 Day of Trumpets
10 Day of Atonement
15-22
Feast of Tabernacles

Jewish Dates

Month 7 (October 11/12) Tašrītu
The first of which will follow the 30th of the previous month.
Jupiter in Leo, Saturn in Taurus, Venus in Libra,
Mercury in the end of Libra, Mars in Aquarius

1st Mercury will reach Scorpio (October 11/12)
14th Venus will reach Scorpio (October 24/25)
19th Saturn Acronychal rising (October 29/30)
21st Mercury will reach Sagittarius (October 31/Nov. 1)
24th Mercury evening visibility begins (November 3/4)
On the 27th, last lunar visibility before sunrise. (November 5/6)

Month 8 (November 10) Arahsamna
The first of which will follow the 30th of the previous month.
Jupiter in Leo, Saturn in Taurus, Venus in Scorpio,
Mercury in Sagittarius, Mars in Aquarius

3rd Mercury evening visibility ends (November 12/13)
8th Venus will reach Sagittarius (November 17/18)
18th Mars will reach Pisces (November 27/28)
18th Mercury will reach Scorpio (November 2/28)
23rd Mercury morning visibility begins (December 1/2)
On the 27th, last lunar visibility before sunrise. (December 6th)

Month 9 (December 9/10) Kisilīmu
The first of which will follow the 29th of the previous month.
Jupiter in Leo, Saturn in Taurus, Venus in Sagittarius,
Mercury in Scorpio, Mars in Pisces

2nd Venus will reach Capricorn (December 10/11)
5th Mercury will enter Sagittarius (December 13/14)
26th Venus will reach Aquarius (January 3/4)
28th Mercury reaches Capricorn (January 5/6)
On the 28th, last lunar visibility before sunrise. (January 5th)

Marheshvan

Kislev

25
Beginning of Hanukkah

Tevet (Tebet)

Jewish Dates

Month 10 (January 7/8) Tebētu
The first of which will follow the 29th of the previous month.
Jupiter in Leo, Saturn in Taurus, Venus in Aquarius,
Mercury in Capricorn, Mars in the end of Pisces

4th Mercury morning visibility ends (January 10/11)
6th Mars will reach Aries (January 12/13)
7th Saturn Stationary in Taurus (January 13/14)
14th Jupiter acronychal rising in Leo (January 20/21)
18th Mercury reaches Aquarius (January 24/25)
22nd Venus will reach Picises (January 28/29)
On the 28th, last lunar visibility before sunrise. (February 3rd)

Month 11 (February 6) Šabātu
The first of which will follow the 30th of the previous month.
Jupiter, Saturn in Taurus, Venus in Pisces, Mercury in Capricorn,
Mars in Aries

4th Mercury reaches Pisces (February 9/10)
8th Mercury evening visibility begins (February 13/14)
16th Venus will reach Aries (February 21/22)
21st Mars will reach Taurus (February 26/27)
26th Mercury reaches Aries (March 3/4)
On the 28th, last lunar visibility before sunrise (March 5th)

Month 12 (March 7/8) Addāru
The first of which will follow the 29th of the previous month.
Jupiter in the beginning of Leo, Saturn in Taurus, Venus in Aries,
Mercury in Pisces, Mars in Aries

1st Mercury evening visibility ends (March 7/8)
2nd Mercury reaches Pisces (March 8/9)
12th Venus will reach Taurus (March 18/19)
23rd Jupiter Stationary in the beginning of Leo (March 29/30)
On the 28th, last lunar visibility before sunrise. (April 3rd)

Shevat

Adar

Adar II

Jewish Dates

3

The Heavens Speak - I

Spring 3 BC through August 3 BC

Chapter Contents:

The Heavens Speak - I

Nazareth in Galilee

Months I et XIII - Nisan and Ve Addar [1]

The Days Leading to Passover

March / April 3 BC

On the 14th of the first month of the year according to the Jewish calendar, an annual event called the Passover took place. On that day, in the whole area around Jerusalem, thousands of lambs were sacrificed in the late afternoon and early evening. In a multitude of households and at the temple the memory of the Hebrew exodus out of Egypt was remembered.

In this particular year, several days previous to Passover, some unusual events took place in Galilee in the northern part of the land of Israel. Late one morning, a young woman named Mary was preparing the noon meal for herself, her mother, and some siblings at her home. Her father

---

1 March 30, 3 BC. The Jewish and Babylonian calendars were probably not in agreement during this year. The Babylonian dates are known with certainty. The Jewish dates are debatable. The Jewish and Babylonian months differed from each other about one-third of the time. The Jewish month of Nisan may have been earlier than the Babylonian one in 3 BC. Also, the beginning of the month could occasionally differ because Jerusalem is much farther west than Mesopotamia (ancient Babylonia). Sometimes the first sighting of the new moon, which signaled the beginning of a new month, would have been visible in Judaea, but not in Babylonia.

and brothers had left a day or so earlier to go to Jerusalem to celebrate the Passover, as it is written in the law of the Lord:

"The Lord's Passover begins at twilight on the fourteenth day of the first month. On the fifteenth day of that month the Lord's Festival of Unleavened Bread begins; for seven days you must eat bread made without yeast. On the first day hold a sacred assembly and do no regular work. For seven days present a food offering to the Lord. And on the seventh day hold a sacred assembly and do no regular work."[2]

Mary's father thought that he might visit some of their relatives in and around Bethlehem while they were in the Jerusalem area. Their family was from the lineage of David, the king. However, the family certainly did not appear to be from a royal background. They lived in a simple house. Mary only owned three dresses, and she considered herself fortunate.

Mary had left the back door of the house open so she could have more light as she prepared the noon meal. Although it was undoubtedly spring, and the barley was ripe for harvest, a north wind made it a bit cool outside. Often Mary would even prepare meals outside, but today she preferred to stay in the shelter of the house.

At a particular moment, Mary looked up and out the door. As she was looking out into the middle of the courtyard in the back of the house, a shimmering light appeared. It was extraordinary. Mary moved closer to the door to look. At first, she wondered if a light was being reflected off of a metal object into the courtyard, but the light was actually above the ground in the air. In a few more moments, the light took on the form of a human being. Finally, a man stood before her in a gleaming white robe. He was looking right at her. He smiled and slowly he began to step toward her. Although the angel seemed cheerful and even friendly, Mary found that her heart was pounding and she was somewhat afraid. The man was obviously an angel. Mary retreated backward several steps just as the angel came near to the door.

Then standing in the back doorway of the house he said to her, "Greetings, favored one! The Lord is with you." But she was very perplexed at this statement and kept pondering what kind of salutation this was. The

---

2 Leviticus 23:5-8 NIV.

angel said to her,

"Do not be afraid, Mary; for you have found favor with God. "And behold, you will conceive in your womb and bear a son, and you shall name Him Jesus. He will be great and will be called the Son of the Most High; and the Lord God will give Him the throne of His father David; and He will reign over the house of Jacob forever, and His kingdom will have no end."

Mary said to the angel, "How can this be, since I am a virgin?"

The angel answered and said to her, "The Holy Spirit will come upon you, and the power of the Most High will overshadow you; and for that reason, the holy Child shall be called the Son of God."

"And behold, even your relative Elizabeth has also conceived a son in her old age; and she who was called barren is now in her sixth month. 'For nothing will be impossible with God.' [3]

And Mary said, "Behold, the bondslave of the Lord; may it be done to me according to your word." [4]

After smiling at Mary with a profound tenderness for perhaps a half minute, the angel was again transformed into a shimmering light, and within moments he was gone, vanishing into the air. The doorway now being empty, Mary fell to her knees and began to cry softly. She felt very feeble. At that moment she was not confident that she could continue to prepare the meal and she did not care. She was astounded as she reflected on the words, "The holy Child shall be called the Son of God."

Then she vaguely remembered words of Samuel the prophet as he spoke to King David over a thousand years before:

"When your days are over and you rest with your ancestors, I will raise up your offspring to succeed you, your own flesh and blood, and I will establish his kingdom. He is the one who will build a house for my Name, and I will establish the throne of his kingdom forever. I will be his father, and he will be my son." [5]

---

3 Mary's relative Elisabeth was apparently sterile and had not been able to conceive. She gave birth to John the Baptist about six months before the birth of Jesus. (See the account in Appendix 1, pages 415-418).

4 Luke 1:28-38 NASB.

5 2 Samuel 7:12-14 NASB.

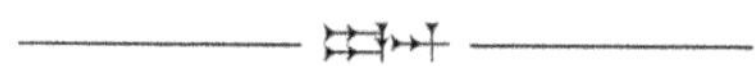

Several days later in the evening, Mary was in front of her house, sitting on the doorstep. She and her mother would soon go to bed. The temperatures had increased during the day, and it was now pleasant to be outside. She and her mother had joined another family briefly for the celebration of Passover [6] since her father and brothers were far off to the south in Jerusalem. Mary and her mother had only stayed a short time because her mother was not feeling well, and she had already laid down to sleep.

Mary was about to enter the house again when looking off to the east; she saw the lip of the full moon rising above the ridge on the eastern horizon. She had already noticed how the sky had brightened before the moon rose. Now the moonlight started to flood the small valley where Nazareth lay. Rising to her feet, Mary waited a moment on the steps of the house. As she lingered, the moon rose higher and finally separated itself from the ridge line.

As Mary contemplated the full moon, other words came back to her mind. She had heard them at the local synagogue only a week before. They were words from the Psalms written by Ethan the Ezrahite. She could not remember all the words, but in essence, God had said,

> *"David's descendants shall endure forever, and his throne shall subsist as the sun before Me. His throne shall be established forever like the moon, and the witness in the sky is faithful."* [7]

Mary felt her knees grow weak, so she held onto the doorpost to steady herself and whispered, "God is going to do this. I will bear a son, and his name will be called Jesus."

A tear came to her eye as she turned to go inside, but she found herself drawn to look at the moon again. The words remained in her mind, "the witness in the sky is faithful."

---

6   According to early Christian traditions, Jesus was conceived during the general time frame of Passover in the spring. He would have been born about nine months later at the end of December or the beginning of January. Jesus' traditional winter birthdate is based on his spring conception.

7   Psalm 89:36-37

Mary then noticed a star just to the left of the full moon. It was barely visible in the lunar glare. She knew very little of the stars or their names. For her, it was interesting that the star was there, but she did not consider it as being important. Mary then decided to enter the house and get herself ready to go to sleep. However, much further to the east, someone else who knew the stars exceedingly well was contemplating the same scene.

Borsippa in Babylonia

Months - Nisan / Ve Addar - Day 14   Evening, March 30, 3 BC

On his way to the observatory, Illis-kutul had noticed that Jewish people in the Borsippa area were preparing to celebrate their festival called Passover. Having arrived at the astronomical viewing platform just before dark, Illis-kutul was firmly expecting to see the full moon rise in the east. As the stars began to shine, Illis-kutul remembered that the moon was in the constellation which the Greeks called Parthenos and that the Romans called Virgo. The Babylonians referred to the constellation as AB.SIN, the Seed Furrow. The "Furrow" was associated with the Babylonian fertility goddess Shala.

Illis-kutul remembered that the principal star of the constellation, known to the Babylonians as the "bright star of the furrow," was very close to the full moon.[8] The star was called Spica, "the head of grain," by both the Romans and Greeks. In much of the Mediterranean world and the Middle East, the star's first appearance in the autumn was associated with the planting of grain.[9]

Illis-kutul raised his finger to blot out the full moon. Having done so, he could just make out the star in the intense light of the full moon. He did not think much about it at that moment, but the "seed of the woman" would soon be manifested.[10]

---

8 (SA4 šá ABSIN in transliterated cuneiform) The star was known as "Stachus" in Greek.

9 Winter barley and wheat were well established in the fields during the winter. The grain was ready for harvest during the following spring. At the end of the first-millennium BC, Spica made its heliacal rising in early October.

10 This phrase refers to Genesis 3:15, which is perhaps the most-ancient promise of a savior for humanity: "And

Shavuot (Pentecost)

Months - Ayyaru / Sivan - Day 5   Monday evening - May 19, 3 BC

A little over seven weeks after Passover in the very late afternoon, Illis-kutul again left his home and went toward the observatory just before sunset. Going up the street, Illis-kutul saw one of his Jewish neighbors outside at the entrance of his house. The two men briefly exchanged a few words, and Illis-kutul realized that this evening at sunset would begin the 49th day of the Jewish "Counting of the Omer."

The 49th day of the count marked the day before the Jewish festival of Shavuot (Pentecost), which took place on the 50th day following the Jewish offering of the first fruits of the annual barley harvest. It was because of this counting of seven weeks that Shavuot was referred to by the Jews as the Feast of Weeks.

When the Jewish neighbor saw that Illis-kutul had recognized the significance of the day, he asked him to wait just a moment.

The neighbor went inside and came out with a small, folded cloth that he handed to Illis-kutul, saying, "I appreciate that you show an interest in our holidays. I just wanted to bless you with this gift. This wrapping contains some delicious cakes that my wife prepared earlier in the day as part of her preparation for the Shavuot celebrations. Enjoy them!"

Illis-kutul took the cakes, thanked the man, and continued toward the observatory. He had lived in the same area for three years, and was well aware of their festivals. A few years earlier, Illis-kutul had been given a greater understanding of the festivals and their significance through conversations with a Rabbi in the neighborhood. Illis-kutul was intrigued by the Jewish calendar system. The aspect of the months and years was very similar both in Judaism and Babylonian thought. The calendars were usually out of harmony with each other for about one year in three. Unlike the Babylonian calendar, the Jewish month of Nisan sometimes began before the spring equinox.

I will put enmity, between you and the woman, and between your seed and her seed; He shall bruise you on the head, and you shall bruise him on the heel."

However, the system of counting weeks was different for the Babylonians and the Jews. Among the Jews, weeks continued sequentially year in and year out. Every seven days was a Sabbath day. In the Babylonian system, the first week of each month began on the evening of the sighting of the crescent moon in the west at sunset. That was the beginning of the first day of the month. On the seventh day of the month, some sacrifices were offered to various gods as on the 14th, 21st, and 28th days of the month. Most people did not stop working, but the priests offered sacrifices. Finally, either one or two additional days were included in the calendar for each month as necessary, making a total of 29 or 30 days. Then with the sighting of the crescent moon in the evening in the west at the beginning of the month, the cycle of weeks began again.

The Babylonians celebrated the 19th day of each month and offered some sacrifices to the gods on that day as well. For them, this represented seven weeks (a week of weeks) from the beginning of the previous month. If the previous month had 30 days, then adding 19 days made 49 days, which is the equivalent of seven weeks. Illis-kutul was not sure why these seven weeks had come to be important in Babylonian thought. However, it was interesting to him that the Jews had a similar idea regarding the seven weeks following their First-fruits offering and their annual festival of Shavuot (Pentecost).

About a half hour after the incident with his neighbor, on the observatory terrace, Illis-kutul began to scan the skies. It was a clear day; the stars would be shining brightly in the evening. The sun was still a bit above the horizon, but Illis-kutul could easily see the moon. It was in the form of a large crescent in the southern and western sky. Illis-kutul was going to watch the moon this evening, because he was well aware that after sunset it would be very near the king star LUGAL [11] in the lion constellation.

Entering the observatory workroom beside the terrace just before dark, Illis-kutul encountered Iqisa. They exchanged a few words. And Iqisa also mentioned to Illis-kutul that the moon was expected to be in close conjunction with the star LUGAL that evening.

Illis-kutul responded, "Yes, I know. I suspect that we should be looking at the old omen texts concerning this event. Our ancestors made much

---

11 Regulus, the principal star in the constellation Leo. It was known as the "king star" for thousands of years in various cultures in the ancient world. The name LUGAL means king.

of such events while they were in direct service to the king. There may be some symbolic significance to this event. However, the general lack of interest on the part of the Parthian rulers for our old omen texts does not motivate one to seek to discover a meaning behind such lunar conjunctions with LUGAL."

Illis-kutul had placed the folded cloth with the cakes on a corner table where there some water jugs and food that the men would sometimes eat when they were hungry. Looking in the direction of the table and the cloth with the honey cakes, Illis-kutul spoke again.

"Oh, I brought some cakes from my Jewish neighbor. He passed them off to me on the way to the observatory, when he realized that I was aware of their holiday and expressed some interest. This evening marks the day before the Jewish festival Shavuot. Tonight marks the beginning of the 49th day or the end of the seventh week of the so-called 'Counting of the Omer,' which dates their festival of Shavuot."

Iqisa responded, "Yes, I am aware of their festival. I am glad you received some of their cakes as a gift. I have enjoyed eating some of their unique festival desserts in the past. Eliab has also brought some similar things to the notary office from time to time."

Neither men thought a whole lot more about the cakes or the Jewish festival during much of the rest of the evening. After the sun had set, LUGAL became visible less than a cubit [12] from the moon. Later in the evening, the moon came closer and closer to the king star until it stood less than two fingers[13] from the lunar disk when both objects sank beneath the horizon.

As the moon and the star neared the horizon, Illis-kutul placed his hand in a pocket in his robe, and he felt the leather sack where he kept his money. As his fingers were touching the leather, he thought of the coins. For an instant, he remembered that the image on the coin was

---

12 A Babylonian cubit was about two degrees. One degree of arc is equal to two average lunar diameters. A lunar diameter is generally equivalent to 30 minutes of arc, although it may vary somewhat. Four full moons side by side would have been the distance. On this day at sunset, the edge of the moon was about 1°35′ from the star. Four hours later they were side by side.

13 In Babylonian terminology, five minutes of arc was a finger. Five minutes of arc is about one-sixth of a typical lunar diameter of 30 minutes of arc (a half of a degree). In this incident, the moon came within nine minutes of arc of Regulus at its setting (one third of a lunar diameter).

similar to the conjunction he saw in the sky. Indeed the two images were related. The Parthians kings had representations of the moon and LU-GAL stamped on their coins.

After the moonset both Iqisa and Illis-kutul went into the workroom beside the terraced observatory. The cakes were still present, and Illis-kutul encouraged Iqisa to eat a few of them before returning home.

Then he continued saying, "I just had a thought on the terrace about how similar some of the Parthian coins are to what we just saw in the sky. LUGAL and the moon together have been associated with royalty for the Parthians, just as they have been for of our kings in the past. I recently also have heard about a beautiful lion monument symbolizing the lion constellation, LUGAL and the moon at the royal tombs of the Commagene kingdom near Samosata.[14] Perhaps I will be able to see that someday. Anyway, do have some of the cakes. I need to get home. I understand that you are staying for a little while longer before you go home. Have a good evening."

---

14 The tomb of King Antiochus I, ruler of Commagene from 70 BC to 36 BC is a central feature of the site. One part of the site has a monument which has come to be called the "Lion Horoscope." Note the presence of the crescent moon with Regulus (LUGAL) below the lion's mouth. Image: Public Domain (Carl Humann 1883).

The men said goodbye, and afterward, Iqisa poured himself some water and sat down at the table beside the folded cloth containing the cakes. Suddenly several thoughts came in succession: "These are Jewish cakes; this is the 49th day of the counting of the Omer; The moon and LUGAL together is a royal symbol for many peoples. The two celestial objects have been on one face of several of the coins of the Parthian Emperors."

Iqisa's mouth watered as he took a few cakes from the cloth wrapping. He wanted to bite into them. Their sweetness was a good reward after a day's work. But Iqisa began thinking of the coins in his own pocket as well. Pushing himself back from the table, Iqisa took out four coins from a small leather pouch which he also carried in a pocket on the side of his robe. He placed the coins on the table in front of him. Two of them had the image of Phraates IV, the Parthian ruler, on them. Both coins were also inscribed with images of the crescent moon and the star Sharru or LUGAL above the image of the king.[15]

The conjunction he had just witnessed was taking place in the lion constellation on the 49th day of the counting of the Omer. He had a fuzzy remembrance that several months earlier, Eliab had mentioned a text from the book of Psalms about David's line of kings.

Iqisa thought, "What was it that Eliab said? David's throne will endure and be established for long ages like the sun and moon?"[16]

His train of thought continued, "Could it be that the God of the Jews might indicate something about the coming of the Messiah through the heavens? After all, today is a significant Jewish date."

But reflecting, Iqisa said to himself, "Well, it is not Pentecost itself. Be-

---

15 Both words meant "king" in Aramaic and ancient Sumerian. The star is now called Regulus, a name which is linked to royalty. Over several generations, the Parthian emperors used similar images on their coins. One can plainly see the moon and Regulus to the left of the kings' heads. These two coins show: Phraates IV, Parthian Emperor from 38 BC to 2 BC and Phraataces, successor of Phraates IV, who reigned with his mother Musa from 2 BC to AD 4.

16 Psalm 89:36-37

sides, the moon is in close conjunction with LUGAL from time to time. Such an event is not so unusual. There is such a small amount of evidence. I do not want to speculate."

With these thoughts, Iqisa then let the idea go. His mind turned to other more pressing occupations.

At home the next morning after breakfast, the image on the coins came back to Illis-kutul's mind, when he noticed two coins containing the image of the Parthian king and a star on a shelf beside his bed. He had placed them there two days before, thinking that he would put the coins back in a pouch to take with him the next day. Over the coming weeks occasionally Illis-kutul thought about the association of the moon and the star. But his regular activities soon swallowed up his thoughts, temporarily submerging the memory of what he had witnessed on the 49th day of the Omer Count. Later in the summer, the lion constellation and the star LUGAL disappeared into the solar glare in the west. They would emerge again in the morning sky from the intense light near the sun about a month and a half later.

Studying Astronomy

Months - Du'ūzu / Av

Weeks after the solstice, the heat of summer became strong.[17] It was at that time that Iqisa met with Eliab and his son at the notary office just after the normal day of work. As foreseen, Eliab and Iqisa's son Bela-num were to come to the observatory to see the annual first visibility[18] of MUL.BABBAR (Jupiter) and each of the various phases of the planet's

---

17 According to the Babylonian calculations, the summer solstice in the first-century BC was sometime after the 24th or 25th of June. July temperatures in modern Baghdad in Iraq vary between 43° C (109.4° F) and 25° C (77° F).

18 The planet's so-called "heliacal rising" is its first visibility in the east, just before sunrise after the planet has spent about one month or more near the sun in the solar glare.

cycle as they occurred. Therefore Iqisa had been asked by Ekur-zakir to give Eliab and Belanum a bit of more instruction about astronomy in general, as well as detailed instruction about the planetary cycle of MUL.BABBAR (Jupiter).

Before they met in one of the rooms of the notary office, Iqisa had diagrammed the phases of MUL.BABBAR on some wax tablets.[19]

Looking at the text and illustrations with Eliab and Belanum, Iqisa explained, "Here is a small diagram showing the phases of MUL.BABBAR. The first phase is the "Nanmurtu," which of course means 'the appearance.'[20] The words used to describe this literally mean 'it appears.'"

"This is when MUL.BABBAR becomes visible in the early morning sky after having been too close to the sun to have been seen. The 'wandering star' (planet) is usually hidden for a little bit more than a month each year. After this, the star moves in an easterly direction among the background stars for almost four months."

"The second phase of the planet follows when about four months later the star becomes stationary in the morning sky among the other stars. For almost four months, it visually moves toward the east (left) at least a little bit each day. Then it comes to a halt in its movements among the background stars. For a couple of weeks, the planet looks like it does not move at all. However, we call the day more or less in the middle of that period literally 'the first station.' One says 'it is stationary.'"[21]

---

19 Several ancient societies used wax covered boards for writing. The boards were reusable.

20 This is referred to in modern terms as a "heliacal rising" and is usually indicated in modern astronomical texts by the Greek letter gamma.

21 In modern terms this is called the planet's first station, which is indicated by the Greek letter phi.

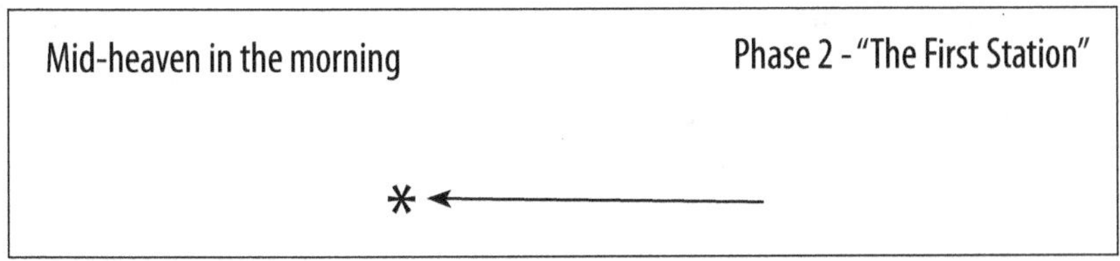

Iqisa continued saying, "Then MUL.BABBAR starts to move again after a few weeks of being stationary, but this time it reverses direction and goes toward the west (right) among the background stars. Two months after the first station, the star rises in the east at sunset. This is called: 'the daylight rising,' or literally 'it rises to daylight.'[22] This happens when the planet rises visibly above the horizon for the last time in the evening."

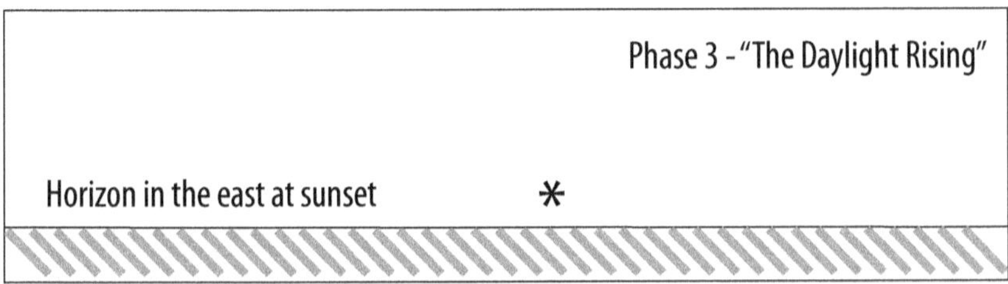

"Then about two months after the rising at sunset the star stops again, but now in the evening sky. This is called the 'second station' The terms mean 'it is stationary'"[23]

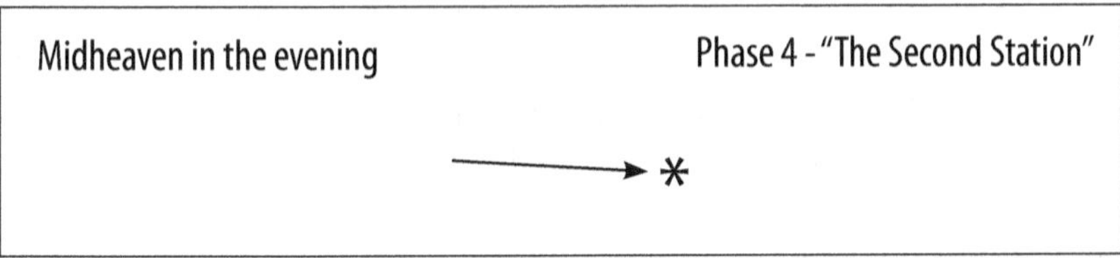

---

22 In modern terms this is the acronychal rising. It is the star's rising in the east at sunset. This is indicated in some modern astronomical texts by the Greek letter theta.

23 This is the planet's second station indicated in modern texts by the Greek letter psi.

After a few questions from Eliab and Belanum, Iqisa continued his explanations, "Following the second station MUL.BABBAR reverses course again and moves east through the background stars. This diagram summarizes all of MULBABBAR's movements among the background stars."

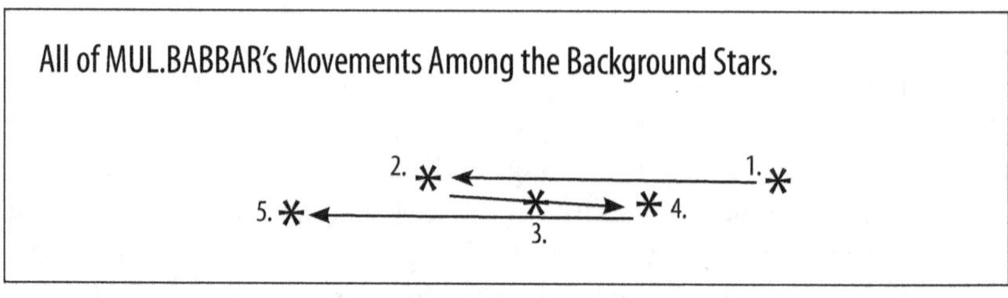

"Finally after four more months, the star disappears with the sun in the solar glare in the west in the evening. This is called 'the setting'" [24] It is about one year after its first-morning appearance.

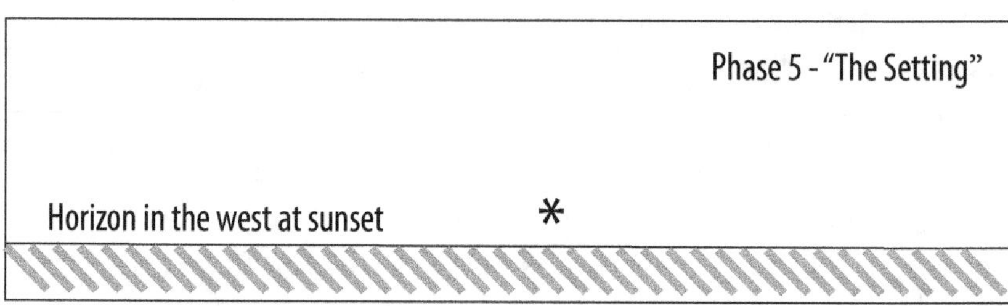

"After its setting, the star is hidden in the solar glare for about 30 days or so, and then it becomes visible again. Then the entire cycle repeats. It is almost like a celestial dance. MUL.BABBAR takes slightly less than 12 years to complete the whole circuit of the heavens and come back to the same constellation where it was at the beginning. It passes through about one constellation in the zodiac every year."

Eliab and Belanum listened attentively and even asked several questions. At one point Eliab said, "I have heard just a little bit about the Babylonian

---

24   This is the planet's heliacal setting. The setting with the sun is indicated in modern astronomical texts by the Greek letter omega.

names for the wandering stars, the planets. Just now you have been speaking to us about MUL.BABBAR. Among us Jews, we refer to the planet as Sedeq, which means "righteousness" in Hebrew. What are some of your other names for the planets and how do they move? Are their cycles similar to the way MUL.BABBAR behaves?"

Iqisa continued, "There is a somewhat similar cycle to MUL.BABBAR's activity for the star we call GENNA and also 'Kajamänu,' meaning 'the slow, steady one.' As you probably know, Eliab, this last name is similar to the Jewish name Shabbatei,[25] which is a name related to your Jewish day of rest, the Sabbath. That name reflects the fact that the planet is slow or 'resting,' as some might want to say. It takes GENNA a bit more than 29 years to make one full circuit through the stars in the path of the sun and moon. The slowly moving star is also referred to as Phainon, meaning the 'shiner' by the Greeks and Saturn by the Romans."

"There is another star called the 'red star' or the 'strange star.' In Greek, this planet was originally called 'Pyroëis,' meaning the 'fiery one' until it became more identified with the Greek god Ares, which is Mars to the Romans. I understand that you Jews call this wandering star Ma'adim, meaning the 'red one.'"

Eliab nodded yes and added, "I do sometimes see Ma'adim in the night sky. It really does have a reddish/orange appearance."

"The star of Ishtar is the brightest evening and morning star. We often call this star Dilbat. The star's cycle is somewhat different because there are morning and evening phases. The star is never visible all night long, but only in the morning or evening. The Jews call this planet Nogah, meaning 'brightness,' and the Romans call it Venus for their goddess of love and fertility. The Greek name is 'Phosphorus,' meaning the 'light bringer.' It probably has this last name because it is very bright."

"There is also a small wandering star which is rarely visible that we call the star of Nabu, that is the god Marduk's son Nabu (Nebo). In Greek, this star is known as 'Stilbon,' meaning the 'gleamer.' The Romans call it Mercury in memory of their messenger god. And the Jews call it Kochav Chammah, meaning the 'sun star.'"

Then Iqisa said something that he did not expect. "You know Eliab,

---

25 GENNA / Kajamänu / Shabbatei is the planet Saturn.

we Babylonians associate our gods directly with the planets, sun, moon, and stars. You Jews make a big difference between your deity and the celestial objects. Your planetary names speak of qualities like 'Nogah' for brightness, 'Sedeq' for righteousness, 'Shabbatei' for rest. Even your name for the star of Nabu does not have anything to do with your idea of deity; it is simply called the 'sun star.' It is interesting that when we do astronomical calculations, really we are not referring to our gods. But we treat the planets, sun, moon, and stars as objects which can be studied, I guess if one thought about it, one could understand many of the celestial movements without ever making any reference to a god at all."

Eliab spoke up saying, "In our understanding, the God of our ancestors spoke the heavenly lights into being. This is written in the first book of our Scriptures. The passage speaks of the creation of all things. God said, 'Let there be lights in the expanse of the heavens to separate the day from the night and let them be for signs and for seasons and for days and years ...'[26] Yes, you are correct. We do not associate the created heavenly objects with our God directly. One can study them like one can learn more about sheep and fruit trees. No one thinks of sheep or fruit trees as being divine. At least I do not think so."

Iqisa was not particularly pleased with this last statement, but he overlooked it as merely part of Eliab's ignorance of the Babylonian gods, him being a Jew. The conversation and Iqisa's instruction soon stopped, but he did not forget what Eliab had said.

Hours later as he was walking through the street on his way home, Iqisa said to himself, "It is true, no one thinks of sheep and fruit trees as being divine. Additionally, our ziggurats are not divine, nor the mountains to the east of Babylonia, nor the sea itself. Water is not worshiped although it is sometimes associated with gods. Why are the Zoroastrians apparently worshiping fire or a god associated with fire? Why worship any of these things?"

Iqisa's thoughts continued, "This Jewish way of thinking is unsettling. In one way, it seems to remove the mystical side of life, but is that not what I am doing already? When I do my astronomical calculations using mathematics one would not need to invoke the presence of a god

---

26 Genesis 1:14.

to explain the movements. I cannot explain why the heavenly bodies exist without thinking of their creation by a god or gods. However, I can explain the regular functions of the heavenly cycles with math and statistics. Eliab's belief in one deity they call Yahweh (YHWH) who made all things bothers me, but at the same time it seems to be realistic."

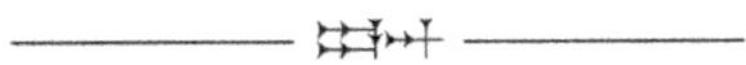

Eliab only had a limited amount of time to devote to studying astronomy. However, he quickly learned enough to be able to understand some of the things which he would see concerning MUL.BABBAR's annual cycle in the coming months.

In the evenings, Iqisa started exploring the 70 tablets of the foundational Babylonian astrological omen catalog, the *Enūma Anu Enlil,* and its associated commentaries in greater depth with his son.

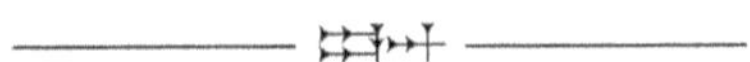

In midsummer about one week before the rising of MUL.BABBAR (Jupiter), Iqisa was in Ekur-zakir's notary office. Seeing Eliab working copying a title deed on his way out of the building, Iqisa stopped and exchanged a few words with him. Iqisa was sometimes still pondering the conversation several weeks before.

At one point, Iqisa found himself saying to Eliab, "I would be interested in reading more about how your deity created all things. Do you have a copy of the first book of your Scriptures in Greek? I know that there is a Greek translation of your Hebrew Scriptures."

Eliab responded, "Yes, I can let you borrow that portion of our scriptures. It is very precious. I was able to make myself a copy several years ago. I will bring it soon here to the office. You can read the passages about the Creation yourself."

MUL.BABBAR Rises in the East

Months IV & V - Dumuzu / Av - Day 16   Early morning, July 29, 3 BC

After having spent three days sick at home, Ekur-zakir was ready to return to work. It was perhaps two hours before sunrise. The 64-year-old man's dimly lit house was filled with shadows despite the presence of the nearly full moon outside. Ekur-zakir knew that he needed to get going soon. He had already woken up his servant so that the young man could accompany him to the nearby astronomical observation platform.

Minutes later in the moonlight, the two men crossed the last courtyard in the temple complex on their way to the bottom of the stairs which ascended the ziggurat. Acknowledging the presence of the armed guard at the base of the stairway with a wave of his hand, Ekur-zakir turned toward the stairway. He thought to himself, "It is amazing to see these men awake; they are usually sleeping at this early morning hour despite my comings and goings."

Ekur-zakir, assisted by his servant, began climbing the stairs toward the fourth level of the pyramid. In the darkness, they had to be careful, the ancient ziggurat of the main temple complex in the city had long fallen into great disrepair.

In the predawn hours, the sky was being dominated by the just past full moon that was approaching the western horizon. However, Ekur-zakir's thoughts were occupied by the constellation of the great lion to the east where MUL.BABBAR (Jupiter) would rise. The constellation was called UR.GU.LA or Aru by the Babylonians, Shir by the Parthians and Persians, Leon by the Greeks and Ari in Hebrew by the Jews. The Jewish name of the constellation came back into Ekur-zakir's thoughts as he stopped briefly on the steps to catch his breath.

While the moon's radiance made their ascent easier, its light blocked out most of the stars in the west. Within a half hour, the stars would begin to disappear in the east as the growing light of the sun caused the darkness to flee. Ekur-zakir wanted to get to the observation platform of the crumbling structure well before sunrise. He desired to see the rising of MUL.BABBAR, the so-called "white star." It had been hidden in the solar glare for about a month. The old astronomer wanted to see its early morning rising one more time before his eyes failed him.

Thinking of the lion constellation's Jewish name, Ekur-zakir also remembered Ariel, Eliab's father whose name meant, the lion of God. Ekur-zakir appreciated the quality of the dates from Ariel's plantation, and he had instructed his servants to buy dates directly from there. Climbing the steps again, Ekur-zakir thought of the local Jewish community, which was very present in Babylonia. They were well established, and a number of families were exceedingly prosperous.

Ekur-zakir had seen how many of the Jews were devoted to YHWH, the God of their fathers. Their beliefs were attractive even to some Babylonians. Secretly Ekur-zakir also was beginning to entertain serious doubts about the high gods Marduk, Sîn, Ishtar, and Nabu. He wondered if the God known as YHWH might not deserve more of his attention. That idea had only been reinforced by the historical research done by Iqisa and Eliab in recent months. Ekur-zakir was not insensible to their discoveries. If their calculations were correct, then there was a strong possibility that the great king, the Jewish Messiah, might arrive in the next several years.

Ekur-zakir had plenty of questions. In addition, something profoundly astronomical intensely irritated the aging priest. The god Marduk's star, MUL.BABBAR, and the other planets moved in regular, invariable patterns that the Babylonians had observed, predicted and recorded for hundreds of years. Were the great gods not able to change their path in the sky? Ekur-zakir did not always like to take the same street to go to the market. Was it impossible for Marduk or Nabu to change their courses? Perhaps the stars were only representative of the gods. But why was there such unending, predictable regularity? Marduk supposedly had created this order of things, but was this the case?

In the Jewish texts concerning the creation of all things, it was mentioned almost in passing that YHWH / Elohim had "made the stars also." It was almost as though the stars of Marduk and Nabu were insignificant to the God of the Jews. That simple statement from the Jewish book of Genesis had bothered and intrigued Ekur-zakir for decades.

Sometimes Ekur-zakir thought privately, "What if the God of the Jews was much more significant than I have ever conceived?"

As he took a final step onto the second level of the ziggurat, these thoughts raced through Ekur-zakir's mind. He then turned toward the next flight of stairs.

It was evident to all, including the priests of Nabu in Borsippa, that the great god Marduk and his son Nabu, did not have the ascendancy at the moment. Marduk's main temple and ziggurat in nearby Babylon had lain mostly in ruins after repeated revolts, centuries of decay, and a futile effort to restore it. Some of the temple complex and much of the mostly deserted old capital city was being used for garden plots. The conquering peoples, the Persians, Greeks, and Parthians, had maintained some, often limited, financial support for the temple of Nabu in Borsippa and its priesthood. Even so, the Borsippa temple and ziggurat were in an extreme state of disrepair. The vast majority of the other ancient Mesopotamian ziggurats had long ago become simple mounds of rubble.

In addition, some astronomers were doing more and more horoscopes to supplement their incomes, even while many of them put little stock in their predictions. After several hundred years of debate, the different schools of astronomers were not in agreement about the usefulness of horoscopes. Some astronomers like Ekur-zakir were positively opposed to the more recent Greek horoscope innovations. However, their primary concern was elsewhere, because the Zoroastrians were continually amassing more religious, political and economic power.

Ekur-zakir continued to ponder these realities as he climbed the steps. The Zoroastrians were not worshipers of Marduk or Nabu. Their god, Ahura Mazda, the supposed creator of the starry skies, was at the center of the Zoroastrian fascination with the heavens. However, Ahura Mazda had left the Zoroastrians with scant technical knowledge concerning the very stars they prized so deeply. Zoroastrianism abounded with devotional practices and meditative texts that inspired the Medes, Persians, and Parthians. Some texts of their religion gave them an interest in the starry heavens.

However, even the origin of the prophet Zoroaster was shrouded in mystery and legend. He was supposedly a great astronomer, but Ekur-zakir thought, with a bit of irritation, that Zoroaster had apparently not succeeded in sharing much of his technical knowledge with his followers. Already for several generations, Zoroastrian priests with royal support had sought the help of the Babylonians because they needed technical astronomy skills. Every year, several young Zoroastrians were trained at the Borsippa temple complex and in other astronomical centers in Mesopotamia. Many of them did not enjoy learning to read and write in cuneiform. However, acquiring skills in ancient languages was necessary to read the vast libraries of astronomical records spanning hundreds of years.

Ekur-zakir reached the third level of the ziggurat and walked the short distance to the next stairway. Finally reaching the fourth level, he was very much out of breath and practically exhausted. He walked around to the southeastern side of the ziggurat until he came to the entrance of a small workroom just inside the pyramid walls. The builders of the ziggurat had placed a few small storage rooms on each level for maintenance and storage purposes.[27] The astronomers had taken over one of these rooms on the fourth level as a workroom.

Entering the dimly lit chamber, the older priest was greeted by one of the two Zoroastrian apprentices on duty that night. Seeing Ekur-zakir's state of fatigue, the young man immediately turned to a side table, poured some water from a pitcher into a small cup. He handed it to Ekur-zakir, who gladly accepted the precious liquid. He smiled at the young man who bowed slightly, revealing the light of a few dim lamps behind him toward the interior of the room. Scrolled documents, wax-covered writing boards and cuneiform tablets were lying on a few tables. Other documents and tablets were stored on shelves around the walls.

After being refreshed, Ekur-zakir went back outside and continued the twenty yards to the southernmost point of the fourth-level terrace where a group of men was gathered. All of them greeted the newcomer in quiet tones. Looking around the group, Ekur-zakir spotted his son, Iqisa, who had also turned toward him. Iqisa was accompanied by his son Belanum, and not far from him was Eliab. The Jewish scribe had been invited to see the first visibility of MUL.BABBAR, which was something that had been agreed upon several months earlier when Iqisa and Eliab had been doing their research.

Ekur-zakir turned away from the group and back toward the east where the sky was very noticeably brightening. Many dimmer stars had already disappeared in the growing light. The astronomical assistant, Anu-Belsunu, who had the best eyes among them, was positioned on a small platform a few meters above the others. He knew more or less where to look because he was well acquainted with MUL.BABBAR's

---

27 To the author's knowledge, it is not known that such rooms actually existed.

yearly cycle. After a few minutes, the astronomical assistant cupped his hands around his face to shut out all peripheral light. The others waited for his announcement. Bright stars like MUL.BABBAR could be seen relatively near the horizon. Other dimmer stars needed to rise much higher to be recognized.

Finally, he spoke. "I see the star; it is very dim in the haze about a lunar diameter and a half from the horizon. Soon another man confirmed the sighting, and then a second and a third as the star rose higher. Several minutes went by, but Ekur-zakir's weaker eyes could not discern the star, except during one brief moment. He was deeply disappointed. Ekur-za-kir had already experienced this in the previous months. After many decades, his eyes were finally failing.

Iqisa spoke to one of the assistants, "Check the water clock, and write down what the gage says."[28]

As their observations continued for a few more minutes, toward the southeast, wisps of mist hugging the ground, were becoming more evident in the growing light. Ariel's date-palm plantation lay somewhere on the horizon six miles away to the southeast. Just beside the city walls to the north and west, a branch of the Euphrates lay hidden in the mist. A few cocks crowed far below in the distance. Ekur-zakir finally suggested that they eat some of the excellent dates and bread waiting in the terrace workroom.

After their light breakfast, Ekur-zakir sat beside his son's work table, while Iqisa spoke to some other men.

Then Ekur-zakir suddenly remembered the sun. He thought to himself, "Exactly where is the sun today? What is its exact position? The star MUL.BABBAR is at the beginning of the lion constellation ...."

---

28 Babylonian documents indicate that the ideal first visual sighting of MUL.BABBAR should have been at about 40 minutes before sunrise. This would have been expressed in degrees (in this case 10°, because the earth turns at the rate of about one degree every four minutes). The planet would have risen a little bit above the horizon before it actually became visible, possibly one degree or less. In the Babylonian astronomical diary from 109 BC we read: *Month V, the 8th, MULBABBAR's first appearance in Leo; rising of MUL.BABBAR to sunrise: 11°. The ideal first appearance should have been on the 7th.* (See The Babylonian Astronomical Diaries Volume III, page 359.) The ideal rising in 109 BC was at 10° before sunrise (probably about 44 minutes after the planet rose above the horizon. The numbers for the incident on July 29, 3 BC are in accordance with the typical Babylonian ideal rising dates.

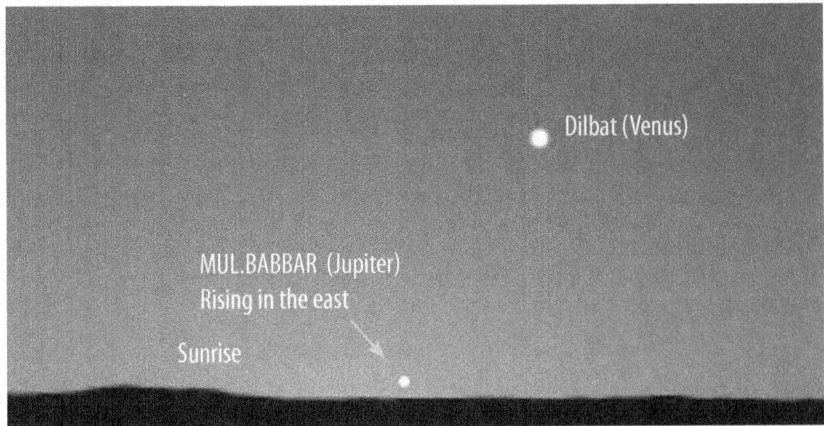

Image: The eastern sky in the early morning July 29, 3 BC.

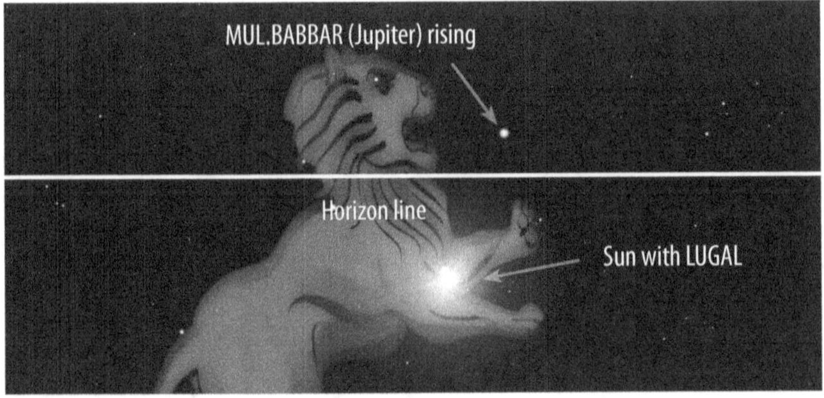

Image: The eastern sky in the early morning July 29, 3 BC without the solar glare.

Ekur-zakir suddenly trembled. He realized ... his mind raced. "The star MUL.BABBAR has risen, the royal planet, ^{MUL}LUGAL, but the sun ... the sun is with ... "

His thoughts multiplied, "MUL.BABBAR must be about four and a half or five astronomical cubits from the sun to be seen, meaning ..."

As he reflected, Ekur-zakir was almost certain where the sun could be found in relation to the stars hidden in the solar glare.

He called one of the young assistants saying, "Please bring me the tablet indicating the sun's daily position for the fifth month of the lunar year."

The young man went across the room, searched briefly in a shelf, took a clay tablet in his hands and brought it to Ekur-zakir. The older man began searching the lines of the cuneiform tablet. His finger went down the lines of text until he arrived at the right day. Because of his sickness during the preceding days, Ekur-zakir had not realized what was happening, until this moment. finally he saw it, the sun is with LUGAL, the royal star.

According to the tablet, the sun was beside the king star LUGAL. The planet MUL.BABBAR had risen in the east while the sun was in conjunction with the king star. Ekur-zakir had never seen this happen previously. MUL.BABBAR rose in the east each year, but only once every 12 years was it in the lion constellation. But just one time in every 83 years could it be more or less in this exact position. The rising of the "planet of kings" at the moment of the solar conjunction with the king star, was an evident sign concerning royalty. Ekur-zakir sat astounded. He had never read anything like this in the omen catalogs either. The event was discreet, but it was also unique and highly symbolic.

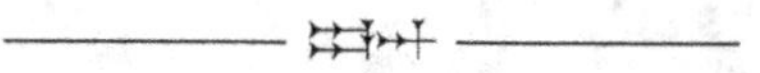

Later in the day, in the archives building at the base of the ziggurat, Ekur-zakir verified the calculations and the historical records, and he finally felt confident about his discovery. The next day, he called together his main colleagues including his son Iqisa, Suen-magir and Illis-kutul. He broke the news to them in this way:

"Yesterday morning, we saw the first-morning visibility of MUL.BAB-BAR.[29] However, something else also was happening that you apparently did not notice. I did not realize it either at the beginning. The sun was in conjunction with LUGAL yesterday morning. Putting the two things together would seem to be a clear sign concerning royalty. According to my memory, there are no omen texts about this type of thing because this has apparently never happened before."

"As you know, over a period of many decades MUL.BABBAR seems to rise later and later. The wandering star MUL.BABBAR follows a sequence

---

29 Heliacal rising.

which repeats itself every 71 and 83 years. Seventy-one years ago the planet was too close to the sun to be seen on the date of the solar conjunction with LUGAL. I found a date for MUL.BABBAR's rising a day after the sun's conjunction with LUGAL 83 years ago. Today the wandering star became visible at the same moment when the sun was in conjunction with LUGAL although the two were hidden in the solar glare."

"From what I can discern through our records, this is the first and only time that this has ever happened in the last 2,500 years of Sumerian and Babylonian astronomical studies. Looking at the records 142, 166, 213, 249, and 332 years ago I see that no one signaled this type of event.

"The sun was not in conjunction with LUGAL at the time of the planet's rising in those years. At that time, MUL.BABBAR was closer to the sun than today. It would have been invisible in the solar glare. That makes yesterday's event special. It is a distinct sign concerning kingship. We can now ask ourselves, 'What does this mean?' I am personally convinced that it must be a royal sign."

Illis-kutul responded saying, "Yes, Ekur-zakir this is an evident royal sign. I too wonder what this could mean. Does it have anything to do with the Parthian royal house? The emperor is quite old, perhaps there will be a change. At the same time, one would not expect that his son Phraataces would be a particularly remarkable successor. It is well known that the emperor's wife Musa is dominating everything which happens in the royal household."

Iqisa agreed with Illis-kutul's statement, while Suen-magir remained silent. Both Iqisa and Suen-magir respected Illis-kutul enormously, and they understood the truth of his statements.

Iqisa also added, "This is such a remarkable royal sign that one could almost imagine that it has to do with the rising of a truly great royal leader. Perhaps it involves someone who is not at all connected to the Parthian royal house or empire."

Illis-kutul sat quietly for a moment. His thoughts raced back to the conjunction of the moon with LUGAL several months before and the possible connections to messianic Judaism. He reasoned, "But that had been on the day before the Jewish festival of Pentecost, not on the Jewish festival day itself. Surely, this incident today and the lunar event a few months previously are unrelated."

But Iqisa continued, "You all know how I did the research with Eliab several months ago concerning the prophesied arrival of the Jewish Messiah. I hesitate to say it, but could there be a connection? Is it possible?"

Illis-kutul held his tongue, but he was surprised to hear Iqisa mention the possibility of a Jewish connection.

Ekur-zakir then spoke again, "I understand you Iqisa, but what interest does Marduk or our other gods have in the Jewish Messiah? Our gods have given us insights into their heavenly writing, but they did not indicate anything about the Jews as such. I am not ready to start speculating about the Jewish messianic hopes. I do not even know their ideas well enough to speculate."

"However, yesterday morning's event was unique. I, like you, think that it could involve the emergence of a truly great world ruler. But at this point, I suggest that we not fix a specific interpretation concerning the event. Perhaps there will be other omens, involving the reading of sacrificial livers or other terrestrial signs.[30] If there are further incidents that point toward kingship, it could be a sign about something which is happening concerning royalty here in Parthian territories or elsewhere. Such signs certainly could indicate the rising of an exceedingly great world leader."

Ekur-zakir continued, "Anyway, I am definitely going to write a report to the astronomers in Babylon and to the Parthian chief magus, the Rab-mag[31] in Ctesiphon. He will want to know about this, even if he is a Zoroastrian. The Rab-mag greatly appreciates our science. Some of the other Babylonian astronomers may have also noticed this event. If not, they will certainly be interested."

Chuckling Ekur-zakir said, "Perhaps you all have noticed that we have two Zoroastrian apprentices here, who are getting instruction about the heavens and our methods. They come from the Rab-mag, and they will return to him. They do not know anything about our present conversation. However, if they do discover what we are discussing right now, you can be sure that they will report it. It is better to be as open and honest as possible with the Parthians. We do still have some financing coming from Ctesiphon, even though it is certainly not enough to live on. There is no need of rattling the authorities."

---

30 Extispicy, the reading of signs through examining the livers of sacrificed animals, was a common.

31 Chief wise man in the Parthian Empire.

The Census Decree

August 3 BC

Chapter Contents:

The Census Decree

Rome - A Census Declaration

The Middle of Dumuzu / Av

During the midmorning, on a warm day of the end of July, Marcus Valerius Messalla Messallinus and his father, Valerius Messala,[2] led a group of ten senators up to the Palatine Hill in Rome. Marcus was 33 years old, and his father was in his 61st year. Augustus, the Roman emperor, was just one year younger than Valerius. As the men advanced up the stairs and narrow streets, the group was accompanied by 12 armed

---

* The image underlying "The Census Decree" title is in Ephesus. It is part of a monument finished in AD 40 in commemoration of Emperor Augustus and his family. Part of the text reads: "From Emperor Caesar Augustus, the son of the god, the greatest of the priests, who was consul twelve and tribune twenty times ..."

1 No one knows the exact date when the census decree was given. It is reasonable to assume that this took place several months before the actual census because a time of preparation and organization would have been necessary to inform and organize the administrators and allied powers across the empire.

Note: The month of July was named in honor of Julius Caesar, who died about 40 years before the events concerning Jesus' birth. In 8 BC, the Roman month of Sextilis was renamed in honor of Caesar's nephew and adopted son Octavian, who had become Emperor Augustus.

2 Valerius Messala did make the speech in the Roman Senate that accompanied Augustus' being awarded the "Pater Patriae" title on February 5, 2 BC. Valerius Messala's son Marcus was consul in 3 BC. The two Messalas may have collaborated with others in setting up the census itself.

lictors[3] because Marcus was one of the two consuls of Rome during that particular year.

All the men were influential members of the Senate. However, Valerius Messalla was also a leading figure among Rome's literary elite and was renowned as an orator. Some people considered him superior to the great orator Cicero, who had died about 40 years earlier. Passing in front of the temple of Apollo, the men walked near several other armed guards standing at the main entrance of the emperor's private residence. The guards came to attention as the Consul, senators, and lictors crossed the threshold of the Emperor Augustus' home on the Palatine hill.

Augustus was inhabited by a kind of humility and discipline which refused to be seduced by outward signs of wealth. He knew that life is short and many coveted his position as well as his fortune. He was careful not to show too many signs of his personal riches. His residence was not overly decorated or richly ornamented although it was beautiful. Such a posture toward wealth made for good politics. If he lifted himself up too high, others would want to bring him down. The Romans were still suspicious of kings. He was not the king of Rome, and he did not live in absolute luxury. Officially Augustus was the Princeps, the first citizen of the empire.

After a short wait, the group was introduced into the emperor's reception hall, which served as an appendage of his office.

Augustus, the adopted son of the assassinated, but now divine Julius Caesar, greeted the men warmly.[4] While evoking some of their past encounters, he made a point of asking some personal questions about the family members of each of his visitors. The entire group was seated, and refreshments were served.

Finally, the time came when the emperor turned to Marcus, the young consul, and asked, "Tell me, what is the reason for your visit here today?"

Marcus indicated that his father, who had been chosen as spokesman, would speak for the group.

---

3 The lictors were security officers attending the consul or possibly other magistrates, bearing the fasces (axes attached to bundles of rods), which were Roman symbols of authority.

4 Augustus official title, Princeps, Imperator Divi Filius Augustus, directly underlined how he was the adopted son of the divine Julius. He was the "son of a god."

Rising, but staying at a respectful distance from the emperor, Valerius Messala raised his voice, "Caesar, we have come today to speak with you concerning the 25th anniversary of your becoming the first citizen of the empire, the Princeps. In about five months, we will begin celebrations of these last 25 years of your administration. The years of your government have been filled with peace and prosperity. Your justice and clemency have filled all of us with confidence for our shared future. We as Roman senators have been more than pleased to serve the greater good of Rome and the empire with you."

"In these last days, we have been informed that the Plebeian Assembly will try to offer you the title Pater Patriae (Father of the Fatherland) in the coming days.[5] You are certainly worthy of this honor. I was also present 25 years ago when the title was already offered to you, but you declined to accept it. In the intervening period, your greatness as a true father to the empire has been demonstrated time and again. Even in these last days, you were acclaimed as Pater Patriae by a large crowd of people when you attended a theater performance."

"The past 25 years have demonstrated to everyone how fortunate we are to have you as our leader. However, we want to encourage you to delay your acceptance of the title Pater Patriae until early in the new year. At that time, we propose to award you this honor during an extraordinary meeting of the Senate according to the finest tradition of our people. This event could mark the official beginning of our celebrations of your 25 years as the Princeps."

Valerius paused briefly and then continued, "But in addition, we encourage you to use the coming time to increase your reputation further and inspire all the peoples of the empire to gratefulness and confident obedience. We want to suggest that this could be done through a census of all the territories and peoples submitted to and allied with Rome. We propose that the census should be carried out in the coming months so that its results may be published during next year's celebrations. Since this census would involve all the states submitted to Roman rule, no new taxes will be involved as is the case in many of our censuses. We do not impose direct taxes on the populations of subject states. No, the main

---

5 This title had only been given to three other people in the history of the Roman people until this time. Others who had received the title were the general Marcus Furius Camillus in 386 BC, Cicero in 63 BC, and Julius Caesar in 45 BC.

purpose of the census will be political, not financial. It will simply be used to establish a detailed enumeration of the number of citizens, the subject peoples as well as the armies and fleets."

"The results of the census could be used to demonstrate to all men the facts concerning the nobility, might, and extensive reach of Roman rule. Indeed, it will take some time to organize and carry out this census across the entire empire. The late fall and early part of winter would be a good moment for this type of endeavor because agricultural activities come to a standstill toward the end of the consular year."[6]

"Furthermore, we suggest that an oath of allegiance to you and Rome be an integral part of the census. The oath could also include the swearing of allegiance to local rulers as well.[7] The pledge of loyalty would only reinforce and secure the unity of the empire. Without a doubt, greater unity under your leadership will also eventually lead us to even further peace and prosperity."

"We suggest that the oath specifically underline your status as a father for us all. A phrase should be included, 'We recognize that the emperor exercises his role among us as a good and righteous father with his children.'[8] Such a pledge could be a preparation for the attribution of the title Pater Patriae early in the new year. We have already discussed the census, as well as its form and goals in a closed-door gathering of the Senate in these last days.[9] You have certainly been well informed of our deliberations."

"Caesar, if these ideas please you, we encourage you to issue a decree with the consent and full approbation of the Senate that this census takes place in all regions and among all peoples of the empire before the end of this year." [10]

---

6 At the end of the first millennium BC, the Roman consular year was from January to December. It is often overlooked that the census could not have been done when agricultural activities were in full swing.

7 The oath included an oath of allegiance to Caesar and to Herod in Judaea. (See Antiquities of the Jews 17.2.4, section 42.)

8 The role of Augustus as First Citizen and Father in the empire was taken as being the major aspect of the census by the historian Paulus Orosius (*Adversus Pagans*, VI.22.7, and VII.2.16).

9 This is entirely the author's own estimation of what may have happened. However, we have no definitive proof that the Senate was involved in setting up the census.

10 December 3 BC (the end of the consular year).

5

The Heavens Speak - II

August through December 3 BC

Chapter Contents:

The Heavens Speak - II

Borsippa - The Rising of the King Star

Dumuzu / Av - Day 30 Morning, August 12, 3 BC

During the two weeks following MUL.BABBAR's heliacal rising, each morning, Illis-kutul, Suen-magir, Iqisa, and Ekur-zakir watched MUL.BABBAR and Dilbat drawing closer together. As the days passed it became obvious through calculations and the nightly visual sightings that the two "stars" would be very close together on the morning of the 30th day of Dumuzu.

Therefore, the entire team was present at the observatory when the planets MUL.BABBAR and Dilbat[1] both rose in the sky about a bit over an hour before dawn. The two "stars" were separated by about two Babylonian fingers of arc,[2] which amounts to about one-third of a lunar diameter.

They were also aware that LUGAL, the king star, in the lion constellation could very possibly be seen again coming out of the solar glare on the morning of the 30th.[3] The team waited together while Anu-Belsunu

---

1 Jupiter and Venus.

2 A finger of arc is about five minutes of arc in modern terms. The separation of the two wandering stars was about nine minutes of arc.

3 The morning of August 12, 3 BC. The star LUGAL (Regulus) should have become visible on either the 12th or 13th

climbed into the small raised platform above the observatory terrace and strained his eyes toward the east. Each one was watching. At about an hour before sunrise, Anu-Belsunu said he believed that he had seen the star flickering above the eastern horizon. Soon Illis-kutul, Suen-magir, and Iqisa said the same. Ekur-zakir's eyes were not able to discern the star. He took consolation knowing that the star would be more easily visible in the coming days.

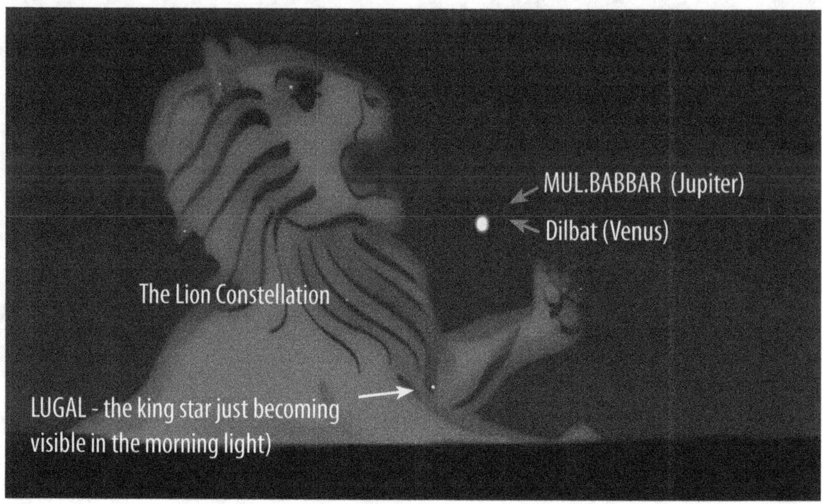

Even while they were all still on the terrace just moments after sighting LUGAL, Ekur-zakir made a comment: "Here we have another amazing incident. I am not sure if anyone has ever seen such a major conjunction of the king planet MUL.BABBAR with Dilbat at the same time as the rising of the king star. I have never seen this before in my lifetime. It is a clear heavenly sign concerning kingship. However, again this is not something that I remember in the omen texts. Conjunctions of Dilbat and MUL.BABBAR are certainly described in the texts. I can cite passages from the *Enuma Anu Enlil* omen catalog from memory. Here are some examples:"

"If Venus reaches Jupiter and passes it, a mighty flood will come.

If Venus and Jupiter come close, then there will be a reign of

---

of August in 3 BC.

Image: Above is a photo of a very similar conjunction to one described in the preceding pages. The photo shows Venus (brightest) and Jupiter in August 2014, as viewed in southwestern France (Author's photo).

destruction concerning the king of Amurru."[4]

"If Venus comes near Jupiter : in the land altogether - brother will become hostile to his brother."

Ekur-zakir continued saying, "However, I am not sure how to interpret this particular event. Yes, we could choose one or more of these lines and declare, 'Here is the interpretation.' However, I am not so sure that is the way to proceed. The omen catalog does not explicitly indicate how to understand the rising of LUGAL at the same moment as such a conjunction. I am going to send a report to the Rab-mag about what we have seen today. The astronomers at the court in Ctesiphon and Uruk and elsewhere may have noticed this as well. However, depending on the weather and their view of the horizon they may not have been able to see the rising star. I am a bit surprised to see two major events which could both be significantly symbolic of kingship within a few weeks."

The others also agreed that a report should be prepared. Certainly, a

---

4 A kingdom which existed in the second millennium BC. It corresponded to the general region of modern Syria and Lebanon.

copy should be sent to Babylon and possibly to Uruk and elsewhere to inform other astronomers who may or who may not have observed today's event depending on the cloud cover and haze.

While Ekur-zakir was talking, Iqisa was only half listening because he was thinking about how he would pay for something which his wife wanted. In addition, for a brief moment, Suen-magir began to wonder about the possibility that a truly great king was making his appearing, but his mind also drifted off concerning what he would be eating for lunch and supper. He was glad that he still had a servant, who could take care of most of his needs, despite his tendency to squander his income through drink and women.

However, the reasoning capability of Illis-kutul was alert and active. Out of the entire group, he was the only one who said to himself, "Could this be related to the Jewish Messiah?"

The idea came, and he entertained it for just a moment. His mind went back briefly to the research that had been done by Iqisa and Eliab. However, like two weeks before, Illis-kutul still hesitated to say anything about the Jewish messianic hope.

He thought to himself, "Well, we will need to have other indications. A royal sign more or less at Pentecost, the visible rising of MUL.BABBAR, and now this event are not enough to establish any certainty about what the gods or a God may be doing. These royal celestial signs may all be significant, but we need greater clarity before we can definitively connect these events to a specific royal figure here on earth."

A week's journey away to the east-southeast of Borsippa in Uruk, the astronomer Selebum was also puzzling over the remarkable rising of LU-GAL at the same time as the conjunction. He also realized that the event was not described in the omen catalogs. The 40-year-old astronomer was saying to himself, "How should one interpret the event? He was not sure. Certainly, it seemed to point to royalty, but was there a specific significance to today's conjunction and the additional heliacal rising?"

Selebum did not inform his staff in his thoughts. He did not want their advice, nor their participation in his plans, and above all he did not want to share any new wealth with them. Over the last months, he had been pondering how to turn various omens and interesting stellar events into possibilities for personal profit. Selebum had thought about writing to the emperor's wife, named Musa. He was well aware through various acquaintances and informants in the capital, Ctesiphon, that the queen desired to ensure her dominance at the court. She also wanted to secure the inheritance of the crown for her son Phraataces. Selebum suspected there might be some stellar events that could be interpreted so that the queen would be pleased. However, Selebum was not sure how to write about today's conjunction so that the queen could get the benefit. He looked at a piece of parchment spread out on a table in front of him. Selebum was ready to write, but he did not sense any inspiration.

He thought to himself, "Perhaps it would be necessary to wait this time, but an opportunity will come."

After a few minutes, Selebum got up, rolled up the parchment and arranged it along with his writing materials in a nearby shelf. Then he picked up his small coin pouch, which also had been laying on the table.

Selebum thought, "This pouch is too light. However, at the right time, I will take action. My astronomical knowledge and cunning will fill this pouch and several others besides. I will enjoy the rest of my life. Finally, I will have everything that I desire; I will not live in want. The rich have the funds that I need. I will devise a plan to get what I desire. My understanding of the skies will open doors of opportunity for me. Whether honestly or dishonestly, I will succeed."

The King Stars Together

Ululu / Tishrei - Day 3   Morning, September 13, 3 BC

One month after the rising of LUGAL and the conjunction of MUL. BABBAR with Dilbat, early in the sixth month of the Babylonian year, MUL.BABBAR came close to LUGAL in the early morning sky. There was a marked royal aspect of the king planet being in conjunction with the king star. However, the two did not touch, and their alignment did not take place on a date which was symbolically important. The astronomical team noted the conjunction, but it was not overly significant for them. MUL.BABBAR and LUGAL had been together like this five other times in the previous 25 years.

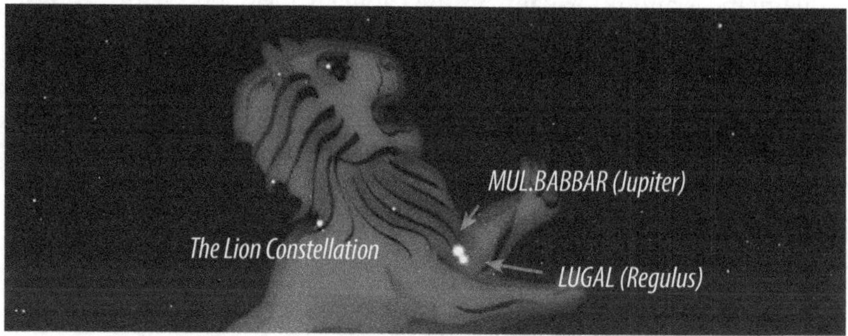

Image: The conjunction of MUL.BABBAR with LUGAL on September 13, 3 BC

The Great Day

Ululu / Tishrei - Day 22   Morning, October 3, 3 BC

In the evening of the 22nd day of the month, Illis-kutul went to bed early. He did not notice that his neighbors in the Jewish quarter were preparing for the celebration of the "Great Day" of the Feast of Tabernacles.[5] Illis-kutul was to be at the observatory for the last of the three watches when he would observe the skies in the hours before dawn.

When Illis-kutul arrived at the observatory, he saw that the moon had risen a short time earlier in the company of MUL.BABBAR (Jupiter) and LUGAL (Regulus) in the lion constellation. Illis-kutul recorded that aspect of the skies as well as a few other details. After dawn, he spent some time in the astronomical archives and then he went home. However, to his surprise, he saw that many of his Jewish acquaintances were well-dressed.

---

5 This was the seventh Jewish month (Tishrei), while it was only the sixth Babylonian month.

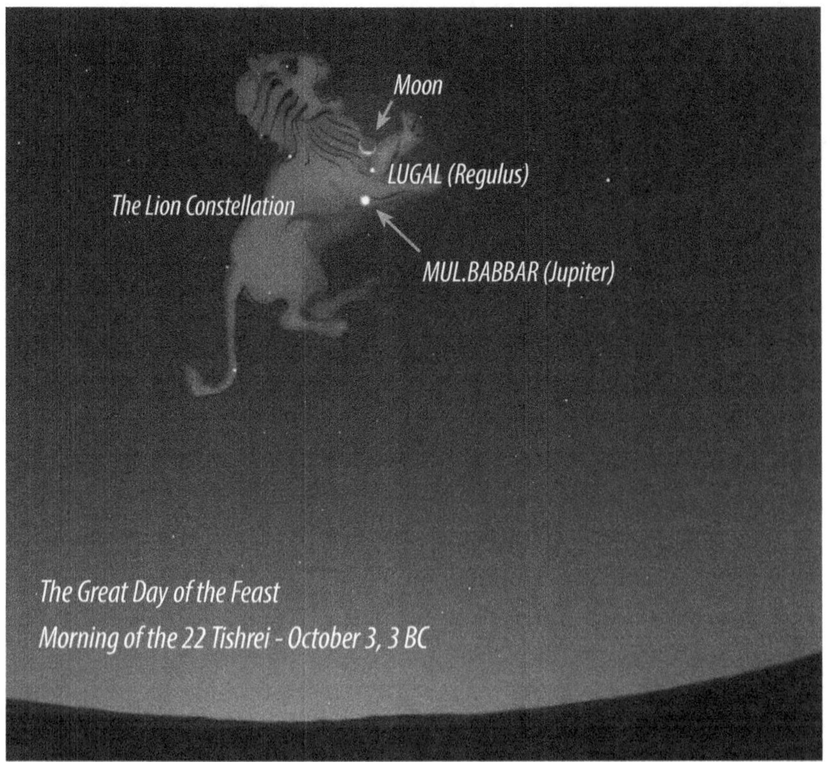

Illis-kutul asked his neighbor Josiah, "What is this event you are celebrating?"To which Josiah responded, "Today is the Great Day of the Feast of Tabernacles. This day marks the end of eight days of remembering how that God had us live in tents in the Sinai Desert many centuries ago when we came out of captivity in Egypt. Since you are relatively new in our neighborhood, you may not have noticed that we do this every year. The neighbor asked Illis-kutul to wait a moment. He went into his house and then brought out a large plate with several Jewish delicacies. Illis-kutul took the plate, thanked his neighbor and proceeded to enter his lodging.[6]

When Illis-kutul shut the door behind him he realized that just hours

---

6 Leviticus 23:39: On exactly the fifteenth day of the seventh month, when you have gathered in the crops of the land, you shall celebrate the feast of the Lord for seven days, with a rest on the first day and a rest on the eighth day.

before, the moon had been present with MUL.BABBAR and LUGAL in the lion constellation. One could think of such a combination of the king planet with the king star and the moon as having royal significance. In fact, a text from the omen catalog called to Illis-kutul's memory that such a combination could mean long life to the king. Certainly as well the lion constellation was also thought of as being royal. However, Illis-kutul found it odd that this combination in the lion constellation happened on the so-called "Great Day" of the Jewish festival.

The other events in the previous months came flooding back as he remembered that four months before there had been a royal sign involving LUGAL and the moon on the day that was the day before the Jewish festival of Pentecost.

Illis-kutul thought to himself, "It is a bit unexpected that two Jewish festivals this year were marked by stellar events involving kingship themes. However, again the kingship sign last spring was the day before Pentecost. It was not on Pentecost itself. Here we are on the date of the Great Day of Tabernacles."

Still thinking about these things Illis-kutul greeted his wife and laid the Jewish delicacies on the table while explaining that they were a gift from their neighbors. In a few minutes, his earlier thoughts got lost as his wife told him about some pressing needs in their household.

It was only several weeks later that kingship symbols in the heavens would again become a subject of considerable discussion among the Borsippian astronomers.

Suen-magir - The Scriptures and Calculations

Tašrītu / Marcheshvan - Day 20   Afternoon, October 30, 3 BC

About a month after the Great Day, Suen-magir came by the notary office looking for Ekur-zakir concerning a mistake that he had noticed in a legal contract. Suen-magir also worked part-time copying documents for Ekur-zakir, but he did the scribal work almost exclusively at his dwelling place or in the astronomical archives building. He hardly ever came to the notary office.

As Suen-magir entered the main room of the office, the whole building seemed to be empty. There was not even a sound. While traversing the central office, Suen-magir noticed a Greek text written on a parchment sheet on a table that Eliab often used for making duplicate copies. Suen-magir realized that this must be a passage from the Jewish Scriptures. His eyes fell on some phrases toward the end of the passage,

"Why are you cast down, O my soul, and why are you in turmoil within me? Hope in God; for I shall again praise him, my salvation and my God."[7]

Suen-magir realized that the person who had written the text understood something about depression, and the words were as sweet as honey to him. Then, even as he called out for Ekur-zakir, again as his eyes scanned more of the passage, but a bit higher up.

"Send out your light and your truth; let them lead me; let them bring me to your holy hill and to your dwelling! Then I will go to the altar of God, to God my exceeding joy, and I will praise you with the lyre, O God, my God."[8]

Suen-magir at times felt so much in darkness. Even the thought of light and truth, which could show him the path forward, was an encouragement to him.

Suen-magir called out again, this time raising his voice substantially, "Ekur-zakir are you here somewhere?"

Eventually, after a few moments, Eliab's voice responded faintly from a room well toward the back of the building, and shortly afterward he arrived with an armload of rolled legal documents.

He greeted Suen-magir warmly saying, "Well, I am glad to see you, it has been a while since I last saw you. I hope all is well. Are you needing to speak to Ekur-zakir?"

Suen-magir responded, "Yes, I just wanted to inform him about a mistake in a certain legal document. Ekur-zakir is not here?"

"No he is not, but he should be back just before sunset. I am expecting him to sign a few documents for clients who will arrive at about that

---

7 Psalm 43:5.

8 Psalm 43:4.

time. However, perhaps I can help you," answered Eliab.

The two men looked at the copy of the legal document that Suen-magir had brought. Afterward, Suen-magir glanced back toward the Greek text on Eliab's work table nearby.

He said, "I happened to notice the Greek text from your sacred Scriptures on the table as I passed by looking for Ekur-zakir. I read a few lines, and I appreciated the text. Can you tell me the origins and the context of the writing?"

Eliab, seeing Suen-magir's interest and apparent sincerity proceeded to give the astronomer some background concerning the passage.

After his explanation, he said, "The reason that this text is here in the office is that sometimes in my spare time even here at the office I copy short passages from the Jewish sacred texts for clients who want their copies in Greek and Hebrew. This particular document is from the Greek Septuagint, which is a Greek translation of the original Hebrew text.

Suen-magir replied saying, "You know, if you have other texts of this kind, I would not mind borrowing some of them to read during the coming weeks."

Eliab said, "I do have an extended copy of a portion of the book of Psalms which I can let you borrow. If you like, being a scribe yourself, perhaps you can make yourself a copy of either a portion or the entire text."

Shifting over toward his work table, Eliab picked up the parchment text and a few others underneath saying, "Here take these short texts for now. Later, if you want to learn more about our Scriptures, you can let me know, and I can pass a longer text from the book of Psalms to you."

Suen-magir thanked Eliab gladly while receiving the parchment documents. It was in this manner that he began to be more personally exposed to the Jewish Scriptures.

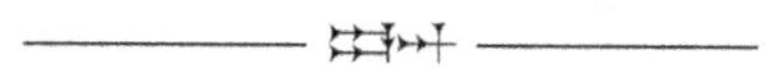

About three weeks later, Suen-magir arrived at the observatory library archives in the afternoon. He had been in the observation team the night before, and after sleeping, he decided to return to the archives building.

Days before he had noticed that the moon was moving closer to the ecliptic, the imaginary line of the path of the sun. Since the king star LUGAL was more or less located on the ecliptic, from time to time, the moon would pass in front of LUGAL (Regulus) during the night. At least half the time such events happened during the daytime and one could not see the star because of the light of day.[9] However, if all went well perhaps the astronomical team could see the moon cross in front of the king star LUGAL, one of the most symbolically significant stars in the sky. It had occurred to Suen-magir that such an event might be important in relation to the other royal celestial events in previous months.

Suen-magir took out the cuneiform tablets of the procedure texts for calculating the lunar latitude and longitude in the zodiac. He spread them out on his work table and took a wax writing board to make notes and calculations. Although Suen-magir knew some of the mathematical formulas very well, he did not want to make a mistake. The rules for calculating the position of the moon had been developed over centuries. It would not be wise to neglect any aspect of the calculation.

After an hour or so of work, Suen-magir was convinced. The moon would indeed pass in front of LUGAL in the middle of the night on the 17th day of the month (one week later). Suen-magir decided to inform the rest of the team. Such events were always exciting, and it was something which no one would want to miss. However, in thinking about the moon and LUGAL, Suen-magir forgot about a detail that he, himself had written in the years' almanac about eight months previously.

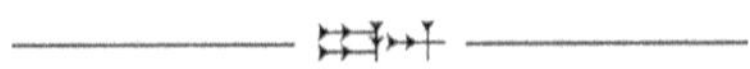

The day after Suen-magir made his calculations, he saw Iqisa in the archives building. Iqisa had just checked the almanac concerning upcoming events because he had planned to invite Eliab and his son Belanum to the observatory on the date the first stationary phase of MUL.BAB-BAR's annual cycle. When Suen-magir arrived, the cuneiform almanac tablet was still on the work table in front of Iqisa.

---

9 An occultation happens when the moon or another object passes in front of a star or planet.

The two men greeted each other, then Suen-magir explained to Iqisa what was going to happen on the night of the 17th of the lunar month.

Iqisa replied, "Well, this is very interesting, I was just looking at the almanac, and the 17th is also the date of MUL.BABBAR's first stationary point. Certainly, we might be off a day or so concerning the stationary point, but it is interesting that the almanac does indicate this day for the first station. Even now, the planet has basically visually come to a halt among the background stars."

Suen-magir was a bit surprised and said, "Yes, this is fairly unique. I do not remember hearing of something like this. You are saying that the lunar occultation of LUGAL happens on the date when the planet is at its first stationary point. Rarely would the principal royal star, LUGAL, be occulted by the moon at the same time that MUL.BABBAR, the king planet, becomes stationary. That makes an event involving the royal star and the royal planet all in the constellation of the lion. Of course, the constellation also has a kingly reputation. I have never heard of such a combination in all my years as an astronomer. This is fascinating. There was the heliacal rising of MUL.BABBAR followed by the nearly equally surprising rising of LUGAL. Now we have another interesting symbolic event with the Moon, LUGAL, and MUL.BABBAR."

MUL.BABBAR's First Station

Samna / Kislev - Day 17   Night, November 26/27, 3 BC

On the evening of the 17th of the month of Samna, the entire astronomical team gathered again and took their meal together just after nightfall in a room beside the archives building. The Zoroastrian apprentices were there along with the Babylonian servants, the four astronomers and Iqisa's son Belunum. They rested for a while and then went up to the observation terrace on the ziggurat. Eliab joined the group just before they went up to the observation area on the ziggurat.

Toward the fourth hour after sunset, the moon rose in the east and minutes later LUGAL (Regulus) also rose above the horizon. After a few hours, the moon moved in front of LUGAL blocking off all of its light.

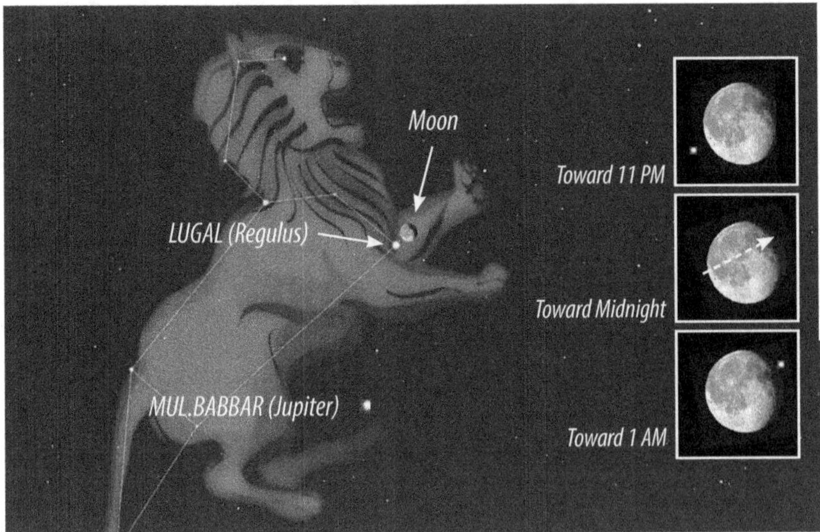

Image: The occultation of LUGAL (Regulus) by the Moon on the night of November 26/27, 3 BC.

The sky was exceptionally clear. Suen-magir was delighted. His calculations were exact. Using the water clock, it was determined that LUGAL had risen to about 26° above the horizon when the occultation began.[10] The timing corresponded with Suen-magir's previous calculations. After about a half a bēru,[11] the star reemerged from the upper dark side of the moon. Many of them had seen this before, but it was a new experience for Belanum and Eliab. Belanum's excited "wows" drew a bit of laughter from the others because his obvious delight was profound. His father and grandfather patted him on the back as signs of affection.

Eliab stood on the terrace as the star emerged from the lunar glare and thought back to Jerusalem and his experiences a little over one year previously. He remembered, "When I was at my cousin's home, I was

---

10 The Babylonians understood that the stars move about one degree higher in the sky every four minutes. They termed this period as an "uš." The occultation began approximately one hour and 44 minutes after LUGAL (Regulus) rose above the horizon. On a clear night, the star probably became visible at about 1.30° above the horizon. One can only see the very brightest stars on the horizon itself.

11 About an hour in Babylonian terms. The bēru corresponded to the time it takes for one zodiacal constellation to rise or set (two hours). Each Babylonian constellation in the zodiac measured 30°. In one hour the earth turns 15°. An uš was the Babylonian equivalent of four minutes = one degree. Thirty uš made two hours = a bēru.

copying the Davidic covenant Psalm and the passage about the sun and the moon being witnesses to the enduring nature of David's throne and the Messiah's reign. Then the next night I had the dream about the inscription at my father's home. But tonight the moon is passing in front of this king star in the lion constellation."

The stream of ideas continued, "It actually makes me think of Jacob's blessing to Judah when he said that the patriarch was like a lion and to him 'would be the obedience of the peoples.' The Messiah will come out of David's line and he was from the tribe of Judah. But the astronomers have told me that from time to time the moon passes in front of LUGAL, I must not read too much into this incident. Really who am I to start seeing signs in the sun, moon, and stars?" With this last thought, Eliab banished all speculation from his mind.

As the night continued, everyone went to sleep since nothing else of any great consequence was expected. However, as Illis-kutul tried to rest, his spirit was somewhat disturbed, he could not sleep. Eventually, he went out on the terrace again while the others slept. He contemplated the stars. He stared into space and waited for morning. It was too dangerous to go home at this late hour, and he was not sure he could rest better there. Illis-kutul had never seen anything like this. There had been several royal celestial signs, but the team did not know how to interpret the events. It was baffling. But Illis-kutul's keen mind had already discerned that the mystery might very well get deeper. What if there were other signs connected to the remaining phases of MUL.BABBAR's cycle?

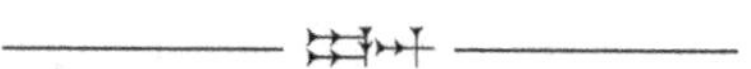

None of the men in Borsippa knew that two royal astronomers in the court in Ctesiphon were intensely pondering the same event. One of them, the Greek astronomer Nikolaus was particularly amazed. He was a man with wide experience, and at the age of 54, he knew that the event was infrequent. Being a careful man, he was not ready to speculate too much on what the occultation and the stationary point combined might mean. In fact, he secretly wondered if any event in the heavens meant anything. He had become skeptical over the years. But he kept his mouth shut, even though a few people knew his opinions. His colleague

Hormizdah, a Zoroastrian, spent some of the next afternoon explaining the event to the Rab-mag, Larvandad, who came from Media.

In Borsippa, the next afternoon the team gathered again at Ekur-za-kir's request in the astronomical archives building. He wanted to talk about the events of the previous night.

Ekur-zakir began by congratulations. "Suen-magir, you did a fine job with your calculations. You are showing your capacities very well. One does not always have all the time necessary for this type of calculation. You are making a good addition to our team. I no longer can keep track of such events."

Even though he had very little sleep, Illis-kutul also commented, "Iqisa and Suen-magir, it is amazing that MUL.BABBAR is also in its stationary phase in the lion constellation at the moment. I would not have expected this. There would seem to be some correlation between the lunar occultation and the stationary point of the king planet. I know of no text from the *Enuma Anu Enlil* omen catalog or other texts which would give us a clear understanding of such an event. Thank you for noticing that MUL.BABBAR was at its station and reminding us of that. Our almanac continues to be useful!"

Both Iqisa and Suen-magir indicated their appreciation to Illis-kutul for his compliments.

Iqisa added, "Unfortunately, essentially we are no closer to having a real understanding of these royal signs than we were four months ago when the rising of MUL.BABBAR took place. This is a very curious circumstance. But it is undeniable. We have no explanation for these remarkable signs which certainly have something to do with royalty. I personally find this to be a bit disturbing. Are we so unintelligent that we cannot understand? Our ancient omen texts do not seem to be of great help. Nothing like this has been recorded previously."

Illis-kutul glanced around the room and almost said something about the Jewish connection, but he held his tongue. There was still nothing obviously Jewish about the series of royal signs. He still wanted some additional evidence. He could not bear to bring up the possibility of the appearance of the Jewish Messiah without more evidence. Inwardly, he sighed because he wanted to talk about that possibility, but he still felt that it was inappropriate.

Ekur-zakir continued, "I agree with you Iqisa. It is a very curious situation. However, we will also need to send a report about this to the Rabmag, the astronomers in Babylon and those in Uruk."

Illis-kutul waited a moment and then said, "I am not sure that it is wise to send our reports to Selebum in Uruk. He will certainly try to take any information we give him and turn it toward his financial advantage. I worked with him for 15 years. You know that one of my reasons for being here in Borsippa is that I could no longer stand his conniving. I am probably a pretty good judge of his character. Even so, Ekur-zakir do as you think appropriate. Hopefully, things will not go too badly. However, I am wary of Selebum."

Ekur-zakir responded smiling, "Yes, I am aware of your reservations concerning Selebum. I also share your concern. We know that profit is his main motivation. Perhaps, I could just forget about sending him a report this time. I am getting older. Such lapses of memory are permitted to older people."

Everyone chuckled heartily including Ekur-zakir himself.

Ekur-zakir continued saying, "We know from previous experience that when LUGAL is occulted by the moon that a second occultation is possible in the months that follow. Usually, this happens during the second month following the first occultation. Therefore, Suen-magir, please make the calculation concerning the moon's position in about two months from now. Hopefully, the moon will pass in front of the star during the night, and we will have clear skies so we can see it. I will be interested in the result of your calculations. The almanac will already give you a good idea about the moon's projected location, but to know if we can see an occultation we will need greater precision. The occultation might happen when the moon and the star are below the horizon. So yes, Suen-magir, please help us concerning these calculations."

After a few moments, Ekur-zakir said, "I just thought of something else. Let's go ahead and check the almanac concerning the date of the evening rising of MUL.BABBAR. That will tell us the phase of the moon as well."

With that Suen-magir rose and went into the next room. In an instant, he returned with the cuneiform tablet in his hand. He sat down again and turned over the tablet to the reverse side since already the first half of the year had finished. Then he said, "The rising of MUL.BABBAR at sunset is on the 14th in Leo.

Ekur-zakir said what they all already knew. "OK, so the last visible evening rising of MUL.BABBAR takes place on the 14th, that is at the time of the full moon. It is very probable that there will be a second occultation of LUGAL during the night of the full moon. The planet and the moon will possibly be within a two, three, or perhaps four cubits from each other.[12] LUGAL will be there as well. Very well, as I said to you, Suen-magir, do the calculation. But also you should find out when the moon is going to pass in front of LUGAL and if that will be visible to us. It seems to me that it is very possible."

Suen-magir replied, "Yes, there is a very high probability that you are right Ekur-zakir. The moon will certainly be at the right latitude to occult the star. I will do the specific calculation later today or tomorrow. If the moon passes in front of LUGAL again during MUL.BABBAR's third phase, like we saw last night, this would truly be remarkable. Such an event would give us a royal sign at three out of the five phases of MUL.BABBAR's cycle."

After a few moments looking at the group, Ekur-zakir saw the expression on Illis-kutul's face.

Ekur-zakir said, "I can see your mind is churning my friend Illis-kutul. I am sure you will continue to do some research about this yourself. I look forward to hearing your results."

Ekur-zakir chuckled and smiled. Illis-kutul smiled back, and everyone laughed. It had been evident to most of them that Illis-kutul's mind was not satisfied, and that he would not wholly rest until the enigma was settled.

---

12 A Babylonian astronomical cubit was usually equivalent to two degrees.

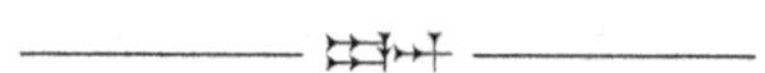

Within a few days, Suen-magir did the calculations and was convinced that the moon would again visibly pass in front of LUGAL (Regulus) at the time MUL.BABBAR's (Jupiter's) evening rising phase. The team received these words with excitement, but also with mixed emotions. What did this mean? For the third time, there would be a visible royal sign associated with the planet MUL.BABBAR's yearly cycle, in addition to the sign at LUGAL's annual rising.

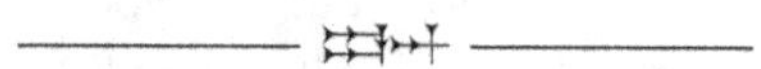

In Uruk, Selebum also was puzzled. He had heard about the occultation during the night from those who were watching the skies at the Uruk observatory. He had been sound asleep. But he was aware that MUL.BABBAR was in its second annual phase. And more than that, the occultation had occurred on the day noted in the year's almanac as the recognized day of the stationary point. This was an interesting coincidence. Selebum was as surprised as anyone by the occultation taking place at the moment of MUL.BABBAR's first stationary point. But even more troubling to Selebum was the fact that he did not yet see any obvious method of how to turn these signs connected to royalty to obtaining a profit.

In general, the moon being near to LUGAL in this manner was a positive omen for the king. Selebum thought, "Perhaps the king would pay to hear that he might live longer than expected." Selebum contemplated writing to him, but as he reflected on the matter, his mind settled on a different approach.

A week after the surprising events, Illis-kutul happened to go by the notary office for a short meeting with Ekur-zakir. On his way out he saw Eliab in a side room, and he decided to speak to him briefly.

After greeting Eliab, he said, "How did you like seeing the occultation of LUGAL the other night? That was fairly amazing wasn't it?"

Eliab answered, "Yes, I was pretty thrilled, it was also amusing to see how Belanum reacted. He was surprised, but I was as well. I had never seen anything like that. It was especially amazing to see the star reappear."

Illis-kutul responded, "You know, I am getting more interested in the things concerning your Messiah. Last spring, I read the text of Iqisa's copy of your report to your cousin. You both did some interesting speculations about the arrival of the Messiah. Suen-magir has told me that you lent him some texts from the Greek translation of the Jewish Scriptures. Do you know of other prophetic passages, which you could show me about the Messiah?"

Eliab said, "Certainly I will bring some of the texts. I can perhaps write out some prophecies and give them to you. It should not take me a long time. There are several texts, but the passages are not long."

"I mentioned some of the prophetic texts when we all had our noon-time meal together during our research last year. Some of my favorites are two passages from the book of Jeremiah. The prophet repeats more or less the same prophecy about a righteous king who will arise from the lineage of David. This 'Righteous One' is the one we are expecting."[13]

Illis-kutul replied, "This is very interesting. I look forward to reading the prophecies in more detail. Perhaps you can give me some greater insight into them. I assume you know the texts well."

Eliab said, "In reality, I was never one who spent a lot of time with these texts, but at least one of the prophecies from the time of Jacob our ancestor has shaped my life. I can perhaps tell you about that at another moment. I mainly got involved in the research because of my cousin in Jerusalem. He encouraged me to get information for him about the history of the Sabbatical periods and the dates of the reigns of the various kings in the Persian, Seleucid, and Parthian Empires."

"You have read the report that I sent to him. It does seem that the Messiah may appear in a short time. Iqisa suggested to me a way of un-

---

13 Jeremiah 23:5-6 and 33:14-16. The second passage is particularly interesting. See 33:1-13 as well. In verses 12 through 13 shepherds are specifically mentioned. It is probable that the revelation that was given to the shepherds concerning the Messiah's birth was meant to be a symbolic fulfillment of the prophecy in Jeremiah 33:12-13.

derstanding the text which may partially explain Daniel's 70 'sevens' prophecy."

Illis-kutul said, "I look forward to possibly hearing more about all the prophecies. We do not have anything like that in our Babylonian religion. I will go now, and let you do some work. Ekur-zakir pays you for your scribal work; I must not distract you too much."

Then as he was just about to leave the building, he looked back, and an idea came to his mind.

He again spoke to Eliab, "You know Eliab, I am not aware of the Jewish names for the wandering stars which the Greeks call planets. The other night we were again looking at MUL.BABBAR during the occultation of LUGAL. What is the Jewish name for MUL.BABBAR?"

Eliab looked up from his desk and said back to Illis-kutul, "We refer to MUL.BABBAR as the star of righteousness, in Hebrew the name is Sedeq, which means righteousness."

Illis-kutul said, "Thanks, I was just curious."

Before the full weight of Eliab's words hit him, Illis-kutul turned again and walked out the door into the courtyard, which led to the street. About midway across the courtyard, he stopped, and he starred at the ground in front of him.

He said to himself in soft tones, "I would have never dreamed, it cannot be ... 'Sedeq,' the star of righteousness! The Messiah is the Righteous One. Does he not see a possible connection?"

After standing in the middle of the courtyard for about a minute with his mind racing, Illis-kutul almost turned back, but then he said to himself. "OK, calm down. Perhaps this is the answer, perhaps not. You will need to do additional research. There is still a lot to discover. Perhaps MUL.BABBAR's Jewish name is a partial key to the enigma."

Going out the gate and into the street where several large wheeled carts pulled by strong water buffalo were passing, Illis-kutul continued to reflect on what he had just heard. He said to himself, "Why does not Eliab see a connection between the star and the Messiah?"

But the answer was obvious. He thought, "Eliab has not been aware of all of our discussions. We always talked about these things as an astronomical team. Eliab was not present. He does not realize that there have been several remarkable signs about royalty involving the Sun, Moon, LUGAL, and MUL.BABBAR (Sedeq). He is not expecting any stellar manifestation concerning his Messiah, and why should he? As I remember the Jewish texts do not give any hint of a special star which would appear when the Messiah would arrive. He would have certainly said so if it had been the case. And also, we were not expecting any stellar manifestation related to Judaism either."[14]

His train of thought continued, "But this does not explain everything. There is not yet enough evidence. Something is certainly happening involving royalty, but what? Kings, princes, governors and high officials are relatively numerous across the entire earth. However, a Jewish connection to these royal heavenly signs seems more and more likely."

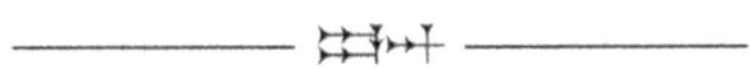

About the same time as Illis-kutul's conversation with Eliab, Suen-magir decided to have another night in one of the local bars gambling and visiting his paid women friends nearby. The result was the same as usual. He felt ashamed and irritated with himself that he had wasted his money again. It took him two days to sober up.

However, this time something unexpected happened. When Suen-magir was at home eating his evening meal, he noticed one of the Greek texts of the book of Proverbs that Eliab had loaned to him. It was on a shelf in the next room. Taking his lamp in hand, Suen-magir walked over, took the parchment scroll and returned to his seat. In the previous days, Suen-magir had read several passages from the scroll. He had found it uplifting.

Unrolling the scroll, he continued to eat for several minutes, and then he read a passage at random, it began:

My son, if your heart is wise, my own heart also will be glad; And

---

14 Christians often cite Numbers 24:17 as an indication that people may have been expecting a stellar manifestation when the Messiah appeared. However, the star in the passage refers to a person, not a visible heavenly object. See Appendix 1 and the section: "The Star and Scepter." David was the prophesied star of Numbers 24:17. Certainly, Jesus is a son of David. However, Balaam's prophecy is very specific concerning a bright shining leader who would crush through the forehead of Moab, etc. See the fulfillment of Balaam's prophecy in 2 Samuel 8:1-15.

my inmost being will rejoice when your lips speak what is right. Do not let your heart envy sinners, But live in the fear of the LORD always. Surely there is a future, and your hope will not be cut off. Listen, my son, and be wise, and direct your heart in the way.[15]

The words were encouraging. It was as though his own father was writing to him. Suen-magir had only known his father until the age of 10 years, but unfortunately, he had died of a sudden sickness. But here in the text, it was as though his own father lived again, encouraging Suen-magir to apply his heart to wisdom, and encouraging him that a new future awaited, if he feared the God of the Jews. Suen-magir pondered the words for several moments.

A new future was something for which Suen-magir so longed. He had hoped that it would happen in making a move from Uruk to Borsippa, but he had been disappointed. His heart was still very heavy from the loss of his wife and child. Suen-magir continued his reading.

"Listen, my son, and be wise, and direct your heart in the way. Do not be with heavy drinkers of wine, with gluttonous eaters of meat; For the heavy drinker and the glutton will come to poverty, and drowsiness will clothe one with rags. Listen to your father who begot you, and do not despise your mother when she is old. Buy truth, and do not sell it. Get wisdom and instruction and understanding."

"The father of the righteous will greatly rejoice, and he who sires a wise son will be glad in him. Let your father and your mother be glad, and let her rejoice who gave birth to you. Give me your heart, my son, and let your eyes delight in my ways."

"For a harlot is a deep pit and an adulterous woman is a narrow well. Surely she lurks as a robber, and increases the faithless among men."

"Who has woe? Who has sorrow? Who has contentions? Who has complaining? Who has wounds without cause? Who has redness of eyes? Those who linger long over wine, and those who go to taste mixed wine. Do not look on the wine when it is red, when it sparkles in the cup, when it goes down smoothly; At the last, it bites like a serpent and stings like a viper."

---

15 Proverbs 23:15-19 NASB.

Suen-magir let the last words roll off his tongue, *"It bites like a serpent and stings like a viper."*

But he was even more impressed by the tenderness of the words from a caring father. The thought of such a loving father pierced his heart, and he began to weep. Suen-magir felt something break in his heart, like the breaking of the link in a chain. There was some freedom. How he regretted these last years. All the waste, all the brokenness of his pain, all the shame.

He went back higher in the text and found the words,

"But live in the fear of the LORD always. Surely there is a future, and your hope will not be cut off. Listen, my son, and be wise."

He repeated the words, saying them softly under his breath. He meditated on each word. For some reason that he did not entirely understand, it was as though his own life seemed to be dependent on these words.

"Surely there is a future, and your hope will not be cut off."

He somehow knew that way forward was through respecting and obeying the God of Israel. It was as though the Jewish God had given him back his father and mother at least for an instant. It was bringing healing to his heart. He began to sense hope for the future.

6

The Birth of the Messiah

December 3 BC and January 2 BC

Chapter Contents

The Birth of the Messiah

Arrival in Bethlehem December 3 BC / January 2 BC[1]

Joseph looked ahead, another one hundred paces and they would be at the summit of a low hill. From that vantage point, Jerusalem would be visible in the distance. Joseph, who was standing beside one of the couple's two donkeys, turned and saw Mary walking several paces behind. Being almost nine months pregnant, walking and even riding was a challenge for her, but looking up, she smiled as Joseph looked back.

Joseph tried to encourage her, "Another one hundred paces and you will be able to see the great temple in Jerusalem. We will sleep in the city tonight."

Mary, almost out of breath, could only manage to say, "I am certainly looking forward to resting."

Joseph thought back over the last week. They had left Galilee eight days earlier. They had decided to travel through Samaria because the distance was shorter than the journey down the Jordan Valley through Jericho.[2] Being pregnant, Mary could not go very far during any one day. Happily, they had friends in a few villages where they had been able to

---

1 These dates represent the end of the month of Jewish months of Tevet and beginning Shevat, 3 BC. This particular year the Babylonian months fell one month after the probable dates of their Jewish equivalents.

2 Jesus and his disciples had traveled through Samaria at one point (John 4:3-42), although Jews often sought to avoid traveling through the region.

spend the night. One day, because it had rained continuously, some of their friends had simply invited them to stay longer. Only one time had it been necessary to stay overnight at an inn. The night before arriving at Jerusalem, they had been able to sleep outside because the area just north of Jerusalem was already much warmer than in Galilee.

Travelers were everywhere on the roads. Augustus' proclamation of an empire-wide census had been announced in Galilee about three months before. Joseph had debated about possibly leaving Mary in Galilee and making the journey to Bethlehem by himself, but she had insisted on coming with him. She wanted to be near her husband. Both of them were terribly conscious of the seriousness of their situation. Mary was carrying the Messiah of Israel in her womb. Part of the time during the previous days, she sat on their second donkey as Joseph led both of the beasts with two cords. The other donkey carried some of their belongings. However, she did not like being bounced around on the back of the donkey. She found it almost as uncomfortable as walking, and she had decided to walk as much as possible.

Once in the last 100 paces, Mary stumbled, giving Joseph cause to worry, but she did not fall. Arriving at the top of the hill, the two of them looked toward the south. The higher portions of the temple and the upper city of Jerusalem were visible less than a mile away. The outer walls of the city were even closer. Joseph pointed out to Mary the three great fortified towers near Herod's palace, where several of the king's soldiers could be seen.

Tears filled Mary's eyes as she said, "I am so glad we have nearly arrived, I try to keep a good attitude, but this is a difficult trip." Joseph took her in his arms to comfort her. Then looking over to his right, Joseph saw a bank of clouds on the western and southwestern horizons.

He said, "We will need to find some shelter in the city. It is probable that by tomorrow morning there will be rain. If there is only a light drizzle, perhaps we can go on to Bethlehem in the morning, but I would prefer to keep us both dry. Leaving Jerusalem, it will only take less than half of a morning or a small part of the afternoon to arrive in Bethlehem."

The two travelers and their donkeys continued down the gently descending southern slope of the hill. Their adventure was well underway. As they advanced, they had no idea that for many months already the heavens far above them had been announcing the arrival of Israel's Messiah.

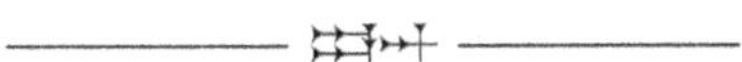

Six weeks previously, Joseph had written to his cousin Uzziel that he would be coming to Bethlehem for the census. At that point, he was not sure that Mary would be joining him. Despite his best efforts, Joseph was not sure that the news of her coming had certainly reached Uzziel. However, they had to keep going, hoping that Uzziel could lodge them.

The couple spent the night in a crowded and noisy quarter of Jerusalem, somewhere behind the temple and below the aristocratic upper city. Joseph did not particularly like being in the city, and he was glad to be back on the road to Bethlehem by mid-morning. Some rain had fallen during the night, but it had stopped, and the sky began to clear toward midmorning. Joseph immediately decided to start the final leg of the trip to Bethlehem. In another two or three hours they would be there. Leaving the city by its western gate near Herod's palace, the couple descended into the upper reaches of the Ben Hinnom Valley and then went up onto the plateau facing Jerusalem from the south. They walked along the well-traveled road under some occasional palm trees scattered among groves of pine and olive trees. The donkeys sometimes slipped on the muddy and somewhat rocky road. Avoiding small and large potholes filled with water along the road also slowed their progress.

After about an hour and a half, they came to a point where the road fell away gently to a lower elevation. From there, they could see Bethlehem on a hill over a mile away with a deep valley to its north and east. As Joseph and Mary advanced with their two donkeys toward the town, a few houses were scattered to the left and right among olive groves. Continuing on along the road, there more and more farmhouses and low walls built out of stones gathered from the surrounding fields. In various places, cactus had been cultivated to form barriers, pens, and corrals for livestock. Some of the houses had an upper story, and the majority of them had flat roofs, which were surrounded by modest walls. However, there were rarer Greek or Roman-style villas, many of which had tile roofs.

Joseph turned to Mary saying, "My cousin Uzziel lives on the southern side of town. We will need to go through the town center and down on the other side to get there. His house is somewhat lower than the main part of town on the hill. They continued to advance, and the day's market activities were drawing to a close as they arrived at the central square. While Mary sat on one side of the open market with the donkeys, Joseph hurriedly bought some necessary food and some bread. He even thought to buy a small jug of wine as a present for his cousin. They had already brought some other gifts with them from Galilee, but he knew that his cousin liked a certain kind of wine produced in the vineyards to the west of Bethlehem. He only needed a few minutes to find the wine after he had made his other purchases.

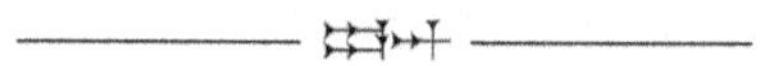

About one-third of an hour after they had entered the market area in central Bethlehem, Joseph and Mary began the short walk on a relatively narrow path enclosed by several homes on either side of the street. Finally, they arrived at Uzziel's home. It was the last one on the southwest side of town. There were even a few palm trees, cedars, and an olive grove just beside it. Some of Uzziel's sheep were feeding under the olive trees. Joseph knocked on the main door of the house, but he heard a noise above him on the roof. An instant later, he heard Uzziel's booming voice.

"Welcome cousin, so good to see you. Oh! I was not aware that Mary was also coming!"

Joseph intervened, "I did try to get news to you in advance, but apparently things did not work out. Sorry that you were not informed as I had desired."

Still looking down from the roof Uzziel boomed out again, "Well, this is no problem at all. You are welcome. I think your name is Mary, is that not right?"

Straining as she looked up Mary nodded, yes. Uzziel continued, "We will be a bit crowded together because of the census. Our cousin Raphu is also here with his wife and two children. They are occupying the upstairs guest room here just beside me on the roof. Anyway, we must stop telling the whole neighborhood about our activities. I will come down by the back stairway and open the door for you."

Moments later after opening the main door of the house, Uzziel embraced and hugged Joseph and Mary as well. He had remarked how round she was. But Joseph had already partly informed him about some of the unique circumstances of his relationship with Mary. Uzziel had decided just not to ask too many questions. Things could get embarrassing for everyone. It was not worth the trouble to try to sort out this pregnancy.

Uzziel was showing them inside just as his wife Rachel came through the back door of the house about ten paces away. Seeing Joseph, she cried aloud, "I am so glad you have finally arrived and, this must be Mary! Welcome to you as well!"

The greetings continued. Just after Rachel had entered the back door, the couple's three little children, two girls and one boy, five, seven, and eight years old poured in through the back door and around their mother into the central living area of the house. They giggled and seemed to be a little bit shy after having made their eruption into the house.

Moments later, Uzziel showed Joseph the space reserved for animals just inside the front entrance of the house. It was lower than the central living area by about three feet. Cousin Raphu eventually made his appearance with his wife and their two boys, of five and six years. Joseph presented his gifts, and his cousin was well pleased with the jug of wine.

Uzziel cried out in his booming voice, "Tonight we will celebrate your coming! The wine is a good means to celebrate in style." But he also reassured Joseph, "Of course, dear cousin, I will not drink too much!"

After a while, Rachel explained the living and sleeping situation. Mary and Joseph would be with Uzziel, Rachel and their children in the main living area of the house while Raphu and his family would be upstairs.[3]

She said, "Tonight after supper we will string up a few curtains between two posts on one side of the main living area to give you both a little bit of privacy. We will let you sleep just above the space for the animals, next to the manger area. That way you will have a bit more heat

---

3 The Greek word καταλυματι "katalymati" used in Luke's text is often translated as "inn." While this is a possible translation of the word, other possibilities do exist. Typically a commercial inn was called a "pandocheion" in Greek. However, during the period, very often houses had a guest room either on the main floor or above in an upper story. The same word was used concerning the "upper room," a guest room, ("katalyma") mentioned in relation to the last supper in Luke 22:10-12. The words "no room for them" in the passage Luke 2:1-7 simply means there was no "place" for them in the guest room. The word "room/place" is τοπος in Greek (as in topographic / topography). The phrase is not referring to a room in a hotel.

during the night. Your two donkeys will keep you company and hopefully give you a bit more warmth."[4]

Supper came and went. The three couples and the children enjoyed themselves during the lively discussions punctuated with jokes. Eventually, after Raphu and his family went back to their room upstairs, Mary and Joseph started to get comfortable in their new lodging. The curtains were put in place. After Joseph laid down, he closed his eyes, and within moments he was asleep.

Meanwhile, Mary was still up arranging a few things. Rachel made ready to extinguish the lamps in the home while her family was getting ready to lay down as well. In the background, Rachel and Uzziel's two boys were teasing each other, striking the other with a piece of rope.

It was at this point that Rachel asked Mary privately in a soft voice, "How much longer before the baby will be born? Have you talked to any midwives recently?"

Mary responded, "The midwives in Nazareth told me that the birth would be in no more than two weeks. However, they were convinced that the trip here might cause the birth to happen sooner. We are prepared to stay for a longer period. I would prefer not to return to Galilee immediately after the birth. The journey here was fairly difficult for me. Joseph wants to look for work here locally, but we will need housing after the census is over. We do not want to be a burden to you. If you know of a place where we might be able to stay for several weeks or even longer,

---

4 Concerning the manger: Joseph would have had relatives and possibly many friends in Bethlehem. Hospitality being a central value in most ancient societies, one can expect that Joseph found lodging in Bethlehem with friends or family. The apocryphal stories of Mary giving birth alone in a cave/stable seem a bit far-fetched from this perspective. At night in typical peasant homes, at least some of the livestock were kept in a physically lower part of the central living area of the house. Mangers were sometimes located between the somewhat higher living quarters where the family actually lived and the lower area reserved for animals.

The "guest room" (katalymati / katalyma) in the house already having been taken, because of the presence of others, apparently Mary and Joseph were received in the main living quarters of the host family just beside a section reserved for livestock. The area was usually open between the main living area and the place reserved for livestock so that heat from the animals would warm the house. When this particular baby had been born, he was placed in a manger situated at one end of the central living area of the host family. Mangers were usually located just beside and above the area where the livestock was housed for the night.

Many of these ideas originated from: Bailey, Kenneth E. *Jesus through Middle Eastern Eyes: Cultural Studies in the Gospels*. Downers Grove, IL: IVP Academic, 2008. Kindle edition, Chapter 1.

we would be very grateful to know about it. We are adaptable to various possibilities.

Rachel responded by saying, "I will speak to Uzziel about this. There is a small house which is vacant not far away. The older lady who lived there died about the time when the census was announced. Her heirs live in Jerusalem, but they do not intend to occupy the house. Perhaps they could be convinced to rent it for some weeks or months. Anyway, I am certain that something can be worked out."

She smiled at Mary, who seemed to be a bit ill at ease. "I am aware that as a new mother you need a home. God will provide. I hope you can stay in Bethlehem for several months at least. It is a long way back to Galilee. Traveling with a newborn can be difficult. It would be perfect for you to be able to present your child at the temple. Of course, if it is a boy that will mean that you will need to stay here or somewhere nearby for at least six weeks because of the purification rules for women who have recently given birth. However, if it is a girl a longer period is necessary. You will need to stay for almost three months."[5]

Mary simply responded, "Yes, I am aware of the requirements of the law. Joseph and I have already discussed the idea of presenting our son at the temple. I am pretty sure this is what we will do."

Stretching out her hand and touching the hand of Rachel, Mary said, "Thank you again so much for your hospitality. We had better go to sleep now."

"Have a good night Mary," Rachel said with tenderness.

After a few more minutes arranging some affairs in the house, Rachel laid down, but knowing Mary's situation, she left a small lamp partially hidden in a corner to give a bit of light if necessary. Finally, the thought occurred to her, "She said 'our son,' That is a really odd thing to say. Why is she so sure that it is a baby boy?"

---

5 See Leviticus 12:1-8 for the precise information concerning a woman's ceremonial purification following child-birth.

The Census Pledge

Mary and Joseph rose early on their third day in Bethlehem to participate in the required census. Their names were recorded, but an exceptionally moving moment for them both was a sermon of allegiance to the emperor and king Herod that everyone was required to say or else pay a fine.

Some local Pharisees had already refused to say the pledge. Mary and Joseph had witnessed one of the incidents, which involved a man who was about 30 feet in front of them in line. That particular Pharisee had even spat on the ground as he refused to say the pledge. There was a bit of tension in the air because of the oath of allegiance, but in general, the census was conducted without too much disorder. The pledge was similar to others that were being said in various parts of the empire. However, the pledge had been adapted to the Jewish situation. It had been posted on a sign near the beginning of the census line. Arriving there, Joseph had read out the words to Mary,

> *"I swear by the Creator of the world, that I will be loyal to Caesar Augustus and King Herod and their descendants all my life in thought, word, and deed. I will regard as friends whomever they so regard, and consider as enemies whomever they so require. In defense of their interests, I will spare neither body, soul, life, nor even my children. Whenever I perceive or hear anything being said or planned or done against them, I will denounce such efforts. I will be an enemy to whoever says or plans or does any such thing. I call God as a witness against me this day that I will faithfully obey the emperor and his servant King Herod all the days of my life. I recognize the good government of Emperor Augustus. He defends us from our enemies and has brought peace to the world. I acknowledge that he conducts the affairs of the empire as a good father takes care of his household."*

Mary and Joseph both agreed that it was possible for them to say the pledge although they were not sure how God himself would react to every aspect of it. In particular, what would God think of one not even sparing one of their children in defense of the interests of the emperor? This aspect of the pledge was particularly worrisome considering the presence of the child in Mary's womb. However, there seemed to be no choice. They did not need to have problems with the authorities. They were not aware that the pledge in Judaea was less severe and less demanding than in other parts of the empire where other words had been added,

> *"But if I do anything contrary to this oath, or not in conformity with what I swore, I myself call down upon myself, my body, my soul, my life, my children, and all my family and property, utter ruin and utter destruction unto all my issue and all my descendants, and may neither earth nor sea receive the bodies of my family or my descendants, or yield fruits to them."* [6]

---

6 The fifth-century AD Christian historian Paulus Orosius mentions the census and pledge, see, *Historiae Adversus Paganos,* VI.22.7, and VII.2.16. The census was political in nature. It was meant to unify the empire behind Augustus and his heirs. The census had nothing to do with taxation. (See also the previous chapter "The Census Decree.")

The actual pledge of allegiance is not recorded for us in any text. However, the pledge written here has been adapted from another one which was sworn by the inhabitants of the newly created province of Paphlagonia in modern-day Turkey in the spring of 3 BC. It is certain that Mary and Joseph could not have said anything like the text which follows. It would have been completely objectionable to them. The text follows.

In the third year from the twelfth consulship of Emperor Caesar Augustus, son of a god,* March 6, in the … at Gangra, the following oath was taken by the inhabitants of Paphlagonia and the Roman businessmen dwelling among them:

"I swear by Jupiter, earth, sun, by all the gods and goddesses, and by Augustus himself, that I will be loyal to Caesar Augustus and to his children and descendants all my life in word, in deed, and in thought, regarding as friends whomever they so regard, and considering as enemies whomever they so adjudge; that in defense of their interests I will spare neither body, soul, life, not children, but will in every way undergo every danger in defense of their interests; that whenever I perceive or hear anything being said or planned or done against them I will lodge information about this and will be an enemy to whoever says or plans or does any such thing; and that whomever they adjudge to be enemies I will by land and sea, with weapons and sword, pursue and punish. But if I do anything contrary to this oath, or not in conformity with what I swore, I myself call down upon myself, my body, my soul, my life, my children, and all my family and property, utter ruin and utter destruction unto all my issue and all my descendants, and may neither earth nor sea receive the bodies of my family or my descendants, or yield fruits to them."

*Augustus was legally the adopted son of Julius Caesar (he was actually his nephew). Julius Caesar had come to be regarded as a god shortly after his death. A temple to Julius Caesar stood on the east side of the Forum in Rome. Augustus was the legal heir and adopted son of the divine Julius, making him a "son of a god."

This text is from: N. Lewis and M. Reinhold, *Roman Civilization, Sourcebook II: The Empire* (New York, New York: Harper & Row, 1966) 34-35.

The Birth

A few days after their census registration toward the middle of the night, Mary tried to awaken Joseph, but he was sleeping very soundly. Nothing she did seemed to arouse him, neither speaking softly, nor gouging his ribs seemed to make any difference.

Finally, after what seemed like hours, but perhaps only after 30 minutes, in desperation, Mary called to Rachel saying, "Rachel, Rachel, do you hear me? I am having regular contractions. Not long ago I lost a lot of water. Can you help me?" Rachel quickly lit an additional lamp and joined Mary. By this time, Joseph was finally awake. He decided to evacuate his sleeping area and let the women handle the situation.

Happily, Rachel had plenty of experience with birthing events. While she was not a midwife, she had participated in at least ten births. She sent Uzziel to get the neighbor lady next door as well. Together they helped Mary through the birthing process. In about three hours the young boy was in Mary's arms as she lay on their makeshift bed of straw covered with a blanket.

The child had cried out loudly within moments of being born. He was apparently very healthy. Joseph had even been coaxed into cutting the umbilical cord. In the next half hour, the child found his way to his mother's breast. Then the children in Uzziel's family were invited to see the newborn. There was much rejoicing. After a few hours the child had fallen asleep, Rachel and Mary together wrapped the baby.

Uzziel placed new straw in a manger, and offered it to Mary as a temporary bed for the baby. The manger was between the main living area of the house and the lower area reserved for the animals. Happily, Uzziel's dozen sheep and Joseph's two donkeys did raise the temperature in the main room of the house. The neighbor lady went back home, and Mary, Rachel, and all the others went back to sleep for a few hours.

Eventually light began to shine through cracks in the shuttered window facing the street. Soon Uzziel got up with Rachel, and they began preparing some food in the back courtyard beside the house. Rachel came into the central living area, she quietly opened the main door of the house and stepped into the street. Her neighbor who had participated in the birth was already talking to another neighbor about 20 feet away. Both women turned toward Rachel with obvious delight in their eyes. They said, "Well, how is the newborn and his mother?"

A lively though muted conversation erupted. Within minutes, the two neighbors had gone their way. One of them went toward the center of town because she operated a stall in the open market. She spoke of the birth to a friend she saw in the street. Within an hour at least 30 women were well informed about the events that had transpired in Rachel and Uzziel's home that night. However, no one in Bethlehem was yet aware of the events which had occurred just about 5,000 paces to the east of the house.

The Angels

During the night of Jesus' birth, it was pitch black except for the visible stars. There was no moon, but some stars were shining although clouds occasionally blocked their light.

To the east of Bethlehem during the last part of the night, Rahim, Azariah, and their partners rested near the big boulders. The two men were shepherds who worked with a team of three others. They and their flock were stationed in fields one or more miles to the east of Bethlehem. The men often changed locations, but that particular night they were on the north side of a field near a small clump of pine and cedar trees. Toward the south about thirty-five yards away, an olive grove covered the flank of the hill which gently fell away into a ravine with a small watercourse.

Beside the cedars, Rahim and his partners had built a small enclosure for their sheep. A few large boulders formed part of the compound. Some low cactus covered about six or seven yards on one side, and a variety of stones and branches had been placed to finish the enclosure. The flock numbered about 70 animals. Azariah became sleepy and awakened Rahim laying a few feet away.

Since there was no chilly wind, Rahim, getting up, placed himself on one of the boulders and made ready for his shift which would last until sunrise. His partner Azariah tried to be comfortable in order to get a few hours sleep before dawn.

Azariah had just closed his eyes, when suddenly he heard Rahim say, "Wow, what is this!"

Opening his eyes, Azariah immediately noticed that the area around the encampment had seemed to brighten very suddenly. The extra lighting was strange because there was no moon or even a fire. Azariah found it really troubling.

As he sat up, the brightness continued to increase, and Azariah spoke softly but audibly to Rahim, "What is going on? This light is very odd."

Azariah even stood to his feet and joined Rahim who was still seated on a boulder about four feet above the ground. The men could now see the olive grove plainly; the light green leaves were clearly visible. The illumination continued to increase. Rahim and Azariah called to their three other partners, and Azariah even shook two of them awake.

He and Rahim were beginning to be in a bit of desperation to understand what was happening. "You guys, wake up, now!!! Something bizarre is happening."

Within moments, all five of the men were well awake and stood beside the boulders. Rahim slid down and stood with them. Then the unexplainable happened. They began to hear a gentle song. It seemed to be coming from the very air itself only yards away. The melody and the loudness of the song seemed to come and go like waves breaking on a beach. It was in a strange, but beautiful language, which none of the men had ever heard before. There seemed to be hundreds of voices. Amazingly the sheep were not aroused or alarmed. They appeared to be in utter peace, not even aware of what was happening.

After about one minute, a single dim flame about the height of a man slowly became visible and began to shimmer about ten yards away in the direction of the olive grove. The singing died away and stopped. In a few instants, a man clothed in a white robe with a beautiful golden headband, as well as a golden sash around his waist was standing in front of Rahim, Azariah and their partners. The man was very powerfully built and had a large sword hanging from his side in a jeweled scabbard. As he stood in front of them, the man seemed to have the appearance of a warrior. His entire being shone, but the light was not so overpowering that the men needed to cover their eyes. The surrounding light only illuminated the clearing and a few dozen yards inside the olive trees.

After a few moments, the man spoke, "Do not be afraid. I bring you good news that will cause great joy for all the people. Today in the town of David a Savior has been born to you; he is the Messiah, the Lord. You have been chosen to be witnesses of His coming. Go into the city after the rising of the sun and search for him. This will be a sign to you: You will find a baby wrapped in cloths and lying in a manger."[7]

A few moments after the man's message had been given, dozens of flames dimly began to appear. Rapidly the intensity of the flames increased, and finally, they were transformed into what appeared to be hundreds of men all clothed in white with golden headbands as well as golden sashes around their waists. The men all had swords similar to their leader, who stood about five paces in front of the first rank of men. About 150 men in four ranks were stretched out all along the edge of the olive grove to the left and right of the first man who had appeared. Several moments later, the song began again, but this time the men could understand it. The massive choir was singing in Judaean Aramaic. The shepherds could hardly believe their ears. They all realized that they were being visited by an entire regiment of angels.

"Glory to God in the highest heaven, and on earth peace to those on whom his favor rests."

Various other lines of the song filled the air but even so the sheep did not move. They did not seem to be aware of what was happening. The entire clearing was filled with light, and the song continued for about two minutes. It was the most beautiful song that the men had ever heard.

As the song reached a crescendo, a change began to take place in the ranks of angels. Their clothing was transformed within a few moments into gold and silver armor. On their heads, they had massive golden helmets. A multitude of shields appeared in their hands. Quickly afterward,

---

7   As Kenneth Bailey points out, for the poor shepherds it would have been "good news" to hear that the child Messiah was wrapped and placed in a manger. The statement would have indicated that the child could be found in a typical peasant home. He would have been in an environment which would not have been either intimidating or hostile to the shepherds. Therefore, Jesus was probably born in the main living quarters of a peasant family just beside and above a "stable" area, which would have housed livestock. One or more mangers could have been in the portion of the house separating the main living area from the livestock. (These paragraphs come from the author's book, The Lion Led the Way, Third Edition, p. 217.)

Many of these ideas originated from: Bailey, Kenneth E. Jesus through Middle Eastern Eyes: Cultural Studies in the Gospels. Downers Grove, IL: IVP Academic, 2008. Kindle edition, Chapter 1.

they drew their swords and raised them high above their heads.

Then they raised their voices in a massive, strong, military style shout three times, "Glory to God in the highest." Then in perfect unison, the angels placed their swords in their scabbards.

The lead angel, who was again looking directly at the shepherds bowed slightly in their direction. Then rising again he smiled several moments at Rahim, Azariah and their partners. Turning to his left, the lead angel then gave some commands and a shout in an unknown language. The entire group of angels pivoted, and the column began to move toward Bethlehem. They seemed to move higher in the air at every moment and then they began to fade from sight. Within a short time, they all had become shimmering flames and then nothing. The light in the clearing dwindled very quickly until there was only darkness again.

Then within moments, all five of the shepherds fell to the ground and wept. They stayed on their knees before God for many minutes confessing their sins, but they also simply marveled at God's greatness. Eventually, each shepherd began to raise his head and look around. Turning slightly to his right, Rahim noticed a faint hint of light on the horizon in the east. Azariah and Rahim spoke first. It was soon decided to go to Bethlehem exactly as the angel had announced to them. Three of them would go at first while the other two stayed with the flock. Then after finding the child, the first ones would come back and relieve the others so that they could in their turn go to Bethlehem and see the child. Azariah and Rahim were chosen to be in the first group.

The Shepherds Find the Child

Reaching Bethlehem about one hour after sunrise, the men went straight to the market in the center of town. They began asking specifically women, who were often still setting up their stands, whether or not they had heard anything about the birth of a child during the night or even in the early hours that morning. Eventually, they stumbled on the stand of a neighbor of Uzziel and Rachel. The woman told them that a young boy had been born during the night in the southwest quarter of Bethlehem. Azariah and Rahim decided to buy some dates and dried figs in the market as a gift for the child and his family.

Arriving at the house, they looked at each other and hesitated for a moment. Eventually, Azariah stepped up and knocked on the door very politely without insisting.

Opening the door, Uzziel greeted the men who were obviously shepherds, but was somewhat taken aback to see the three men facing him. Recovering from his initial surprise, Uzziel assumed that the men had come to do some buying or selling.

He said, "Thank you for coming, but I assume you are here concerning something to do with sheep. Listen, I do not need any more sheep, and I am not ready to sell any of mine."

The men did not seem to react. They stood before him in silence, but with an obvious delight in their eyes.

Then Uzziel said, "You are here about sheep right? Is this why have you come or is their another reason?"

Azariah spoke up, "We have not come concerning sheep. We have come to see the child that was born during the night."

Uzziel, who was exceedingly surprised, responded, "Why in the world would you want to see this newborn? What interest could he possibly hold for you?"

Azariah continued, "You may not believe us, but we were visited by angels before dawn in the fields to the east of Bethlehem. It was completely amazing. They sang the praises of God in our presence. There were hundreds of them."

Tears began to roll down Azariah's cheeks as he spoke. "I assure you that neither I nor the others with me have been drinking. The chief angel instructed us to come to Bethlehem in order to find a special child. Apparently, he has a great future. The chief angel told us that the child would grow up to be Israel's Messiah. He also told us that we would find the child wrapped and lying in a manger."

Uzziel turned and looked over his shoulder. Toward the back wall of the house about fifteen feet away, just above the area reserved for the animals, the manger and its straw were covered with a small blanket. Mary was there, standing over the baby in the makeshift bed. Suddenly becoming physically weak from shock, Uzziel kept standing, but his body fell heavily against the door frame. As he starred across the room, his jaw dropped.

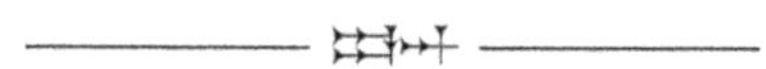

About a week later, Azariah was back in Bethlehem in the market early in the morning. He went back to the same market stand where he had bought the dates and dried figs about seven days previously. The two men struck up a friendly conversation. After a little while, Azariah decided to speak more personally to his friend about his experience a week before concerning the angels and finding the child.

He said, "You may not believe me, but just before my last visit, I had experienced something which was beyond my comprehension. In the hours previous to my coming, I and the other shepherds working with me saw seen a vision of angels during the night. It was the most incredible thing. The angels spoke of the coming of the Righteous One, the Messiah."

Without Azariah being aware, Shelumiel, the chief servant of a businessman in Bethlehem just happened to be standing behind Azariah looking at something on another stand several feet away. Despite his nearly fifty years, Shelumiel's hearing was excellent. He picked up every detail of the discussion. Looking in another direction without giving any indication that he heard anything, Shelumiel lingered for a few more moments. In low tones, Azariah told his story, but even so, Shelumiel got the gist of it. Finally, there was some noisy conversation nearby, and Shelumiel had to move away. Inwardly Shelumiel's heart leaped for joy, and a small smile spread across his face. Shelumiel was a pious man.

Several days after the birth, Elizabeth, Mary's relative came to Uzziel's home for a visit along with her husband Zachariah and their baby son John. The two women were overjoyed to be together again. They had anticipated this moment months previously when Mary had visited Elizabeth and Zachariah in their home in Judaea. However, at that time they did not realize that Mary would give birth to her child in Bethlehem.[8]

---

8 Zachariah and Elizabeth lived in hill country in Judaea where Mary visited them before John's birth (Luke 1:39).

The Presentation - February 2 BC

And when the days for their purification according to the law of Moses were completed, they brought Him up to Jerusalem to present Him to the Lord (as it is written in the Law of the Lord, "Every firstborn male that opens the womb shall be called holy to the Lord"), and to offer a sacrifice according to what was said in the Law of the Lord, "A pair of turtledoves or two young pigeons." [9]

And there was a man in Jerusalem whose name was Simeon; and this man was righteous and devout, looking for the consolation of Israel; and the Holy Spirit was upon him. And it had been revealed to him by the Holy Spirit that he would not see death before he had seen the Lord's Christ. And he came in the Spirit into the temple; and when the parents brought in the child Jesus, to carry out for Him the custom of the Law, then he took Him into his arms, and blessed God, and said,

"Now Lord, You are releasing Your bond-servant to depart in peace, According to Your word; For my eyes have seen Your salvation, which You have prepared in the presence of all peoples, A Light of revelation to the Gentiles, And the glory of Your people Israel."

And His father and mother were amazed at the things which were being said about Him. Simeon blessed them and said to Mary His mother, "Behold, this Child is appointed for the fall and rise of many in Israel,

---

9   According to Leviticus 12:1-5 there were specific rules to be followed following a birth. This shows that the presentation of Jesus at the temple was at least 41 days after the child was born.

Then the LORD spoke to Moses, saying, "Speak to the sons of Israel, saying: 'When a woman gives birth and bears a male child, then she shall be unclean for seven days, as in the days of her menstruation she shall be unclean. 'On the eighth day the flesh of his foreskin shall be circumcised. 'Then she shall remain in the blood of her purification for thirty-three days; she shall not touch any consecrated thing, nor enter the sanctuary until the days of her purification are completed.

The family was apparently relatively poor because the sacrifices that they offered at the temple were the offering of those who could not afford a lamb (Leviticus 12-6-8).

'When the days of her purification are completed, for a son or for a daughter, she shall bring to the priest at the doorway of the tent of meeting a one year old lamb for a burnt offering and a young pigeon or a turtledove for a sin offering. 'Then he shall offer it before the LORD and make atonement for her, and she shall be cleansed from the flow of her blood. This is the law for her who bears a child, whether a male or a female. 'But if she cannot afford a lamb, then she shall take two turtledoves or two young pigeons, the one for a burnt offering and the other for a sin offering; and the priest shall make atonement for her, and she will be clean.'"

Above: A chapel is located at a traditional location of the shepherd's field about a kilometer to the east of Manger Square in Bethlehem. (Author's photo)

Below: The dome of the chapel with the words "Glory to God in the highest ..."
(Author's photo)

Above photo: The area near the Shepherd's Field today. Several large residences dominate the area. Small groves of olive trees can be found nearby. (Author's photo)

Below: Modern Bethlehem, as seen from near Manger Square looking toward the northwest. The Magi would have probably approached Bethlehem on or near the crest of the ridge in the photo. The deep valley in the foreground directly to the north of old Bethlehem would have probably forbidden access to the town from that angle (Author's photo).

and for a sign to be opposed— and a sword will pierce even your own soul—to the end that thoughts from many hearts may be revealed."

And there was a prophetess, Anna the daughter of Phanuel, of the tribe of Asher. She was advanced in years and had lived with her husband seven years after her marriage, and then as a widow to the age of eighty-four. She never left the temple, serving night and day with fastings and prayers. At that very moment she came up and began giving thanks to God, and continued to speak of Him to all those who were looking for the redemption of Jerusalem. (Luke 2:22-38, NASB)

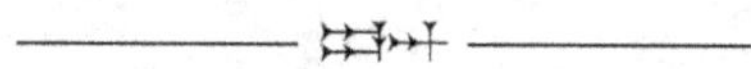

Joseph and Mary decided to remain in Bethlehem. They had seen so much of God's favor in Bethlehem and it would have been difficult to travel back to the north with a small child in winter.[10] Therefore they settled in a house.[11] Joseph found work as a carpenter and was able to provide an income for his family. .[12]

---

10 According to Luke's account, one could have the impression that the 'holy family' went directly back to Nazareth following the presentation.

When they had performed everything according to the Law of the Lord, they returned to Galilee, to their own city of Nazareth. The Child continued to grow and become strong, increasing in wisdom; and the grace of God was upon Him. (Luke 2:39-40)

Matthew tells us that the decision to go to Nazareth was taken following the trip to Egypt. Matthew also indicated that Joseph would have liked to return to Bethlehem following the journey to Egypt, but he was afraid to go there. However, after a dream, Joseph decided to take the family to Nazareth in Galilee (See Matthew 2:19-23). The accounts are not contradictory, but complementary. Luke was probably well aware of Matthew's account. He indicated that several people had written accounts of Jesus' life before he wrote his text (Luke 1:1-4).

11 Matthew 2:11.

12 We know that Herod the Great died about one year or so after the census. See the *Antiquities of the Jews* 17.2.4 through 17.8.4 (17:32-205). The crown prince, Antipater, made a trip to Rome following the census/pledge. He wrote to friends to get an invitation. Then he finally made the journey. A plot to poison the king had been devised with the help of Pheroras, Antipater's uncle. Pheroras was supposed to assassinate the king during Antipater's absence. The entire experience lasted about a year. Herod discovered Antipater's plot about seven months before the crown prince returned from Rome. The king kept this information to himself until his son returned to Judaea. According to one ancient tradition, the young toddler stood by his mother during the visit of the wise men. A child one year old can stand alone or holding onto objects or other people.

Photo: Bethlehem can be seen in far the distance. This photo was taken from the upper part of the massive mound that forms the original emplacement of Herod's Herodium palace southeast of Bethlehem. Some ruins of the lower palace complex can be seen in the foreground (Author's photo).

Historical Note - A Crisis in the King's Family Because of the Census

About 6,000 Pharisees refused to say the pledge of allegiance to the king and the emperor.[13] Usually, such a refusal would have forced the men to pay a substantial fine. However, Herod's sister-in-law, the wife of his brother Pheroras[14] volunteered to pay the penalty for the Pharisees who had refused to say the oath of allegiance. She was aware that many Pharisees were favorable to her husband. They preferred that Pheroras become king in place of his brother.

This willingness of Pheroras' wife to pay the fine caused a great deal of ill feeling between the brothers. Herod was enraged and insisted that Pheroras divorce his wife. Pheroras left the capital to spend time in his tetrarchy which included both Galilee and Perea. At the same time, the crown prince Antipater was actually in league with Pheroras to poison the king and seize the throne.

Seeing the extreme animosity which was brewing between his father and his uncle, Antipater engineered events so that he could be invited to visit Rome. He agreed with Pheroras that an attempt to poison the king would be made in his absence. However, unexpectedly Pheroras died by poisoning sometime after Antipater's departure for Rome. As the king conducted an investigation into his brother's death, it was discovered that Pheroras and Antipater were planning to have the king put to death. Herod kept this information to himself for many months.

However, when Antipater returned from Rome in the fall of 2 BC, he was tried and placed in jail. Varus, the Roman governor of Syria, encouraged Herod to write to Augustus concerning what to do with the crown prince. Herod had written to the emperor, and Antipater was still in prison when the wise men arrived in Judaea in December of 2 BC.

Apparently, the stress of Antipater's betrayal caused the king to become unwell. His sickness was so great that it caused him to reflect on the state of his affairs and to rewrite his will. Even though Herod was seriously ill, he continued to exercise authority over the realm. It was in this context that the wise men arrived in Jerusalem about a year after the birth of Jesus.

---

13 Josephus, Antiquities of the Jews 17.2.4 (17:41-43).

14 Herod's brother, Pheroras, was the Tetrarch of Galilee and Perea (A tetrarch often rules over about a fourth of a kingdom). Pheroras had held these territories at Herod's request and the approval of Augustus since about 20 BC.

Part 3: Interpreting the Star

Oh, the depth of the riches both of the wisdom
and knowledge of God! How unsearchable are
His judgments and unfathomable His ways!

"Who has known the mind of the Lord?
Or who has been His counselor?"

(Romans 11:33-34)

To one there is given through the Spirit the
message of wisdom ... (1 Corinthians 12:8)

7

The Heavens Speak - III

January through March 2 BC

Chapter Contents

The Heavens Speak - III

Borsippa

The Rising at Sunset

Months X & XI - Tebētu / Shevat - Day 14   Evening, January 20, 2 BC

At the time of MUL.BABBAR's last visible evening rising, the astronomical team gathered again, but also several members of the group from nearby Babylon were invited. It was less than a day's journey from the ancient capital of Babylonia to Borsippa. Ekur-zakir wanted the men from Babylon to be present because they considered themselves to be the guardians of the astrological and astronomical traditions. Historically Babylon had the most renowned astronomers, however the city had largely fallen into ruins, and the astronomical team and temple complex there had lost a lot of their former prestige.

The whole group watched "the rising toward the daylight"[1] of MUL. BABBAR (Jupiter) and less than an hour later the beginning of occultation of LUGAL (Regulus). Everything went as expected. Ekur-zakir again congratulated Suen-magir for his excellent calculations. The three astronomers from Babylon maintained that the occultation at the rising of MUL.BABBAR indicated that the king Phraates IV would have a long

---

1 The modern term is an "acronychal rising." It is the last day when a planet or a star visibly rises in the east after sunset. Later the star or planet appears in the eastern sky without rising following sunset.

life. They took the same approach concerning the previous occultation of LUGAL by the moon when MUL.BABBAR had been at its stationary point. They cited a few passages from the omen texts of the *Enuma Anu Enlil* to justify their claim.

Illis-kutul and the others were hardly satisfied with this response. They were well aware that the king was over 65 years of age. While their ruler might live another 20 years, there were persistent and well-known rumors that the Parthian emperor was in poor health. It seemed strange to Ekur-zakir, Illis-kutul, Iqisa, and Suen-magir that all these royal signs concerned the reigning emperor. What was so special about Phraates IV? It did not seem to make sense.

Eliab was also present on the evening of the events. He had been invited to witness all of MUL.BABBAR's phases and he was determined not to miss anything, especially seeing how the entire series of events was so interesting. Although he had been sick for several days previously, Eliab managed to be present at the appointed time. He brought several promised prophetic texts that he had managed to copy for Illis-kutul.

However, since the hour was not late, Eliab left not long after the occultation to go home. Illis-kutul was not able to speak with him more fully, although he earnestly wanted to do so.

But on his way down the ziggurat, Eliab thought, "Here is the practically same event which we saw two months ago. It obviously has to do with kingship. This is a remarkable occurrence. But I am not going to let myself speculate about what the event might mean. After all, such events do happen from time to time. The astronomers have told me so. But the men have themselves said that the moon passing in front of LUGAL was happening at the time of two major phases of MUL.BABBAR's cycle. In their thought MUL.BABBAR is associated with kingship. And for us, MUL.BABBAR/Sedeq is associated with righteousness. The Messiah is the 'Righteous One.' Yes, the sun and moon are witnesses concerning the enduring nature of the Messiah's throne. But I need to stop these speculations. I know very little about astronomy. Why waste my time speculating?"

At that point, Eliab again silenced his thoughts about the Messiah and the heavens. He did not want to get too carried away.

However, none of the men in Borsippa that night knew what had been happening in Ctesiphon, the imperial capital, that same evening.

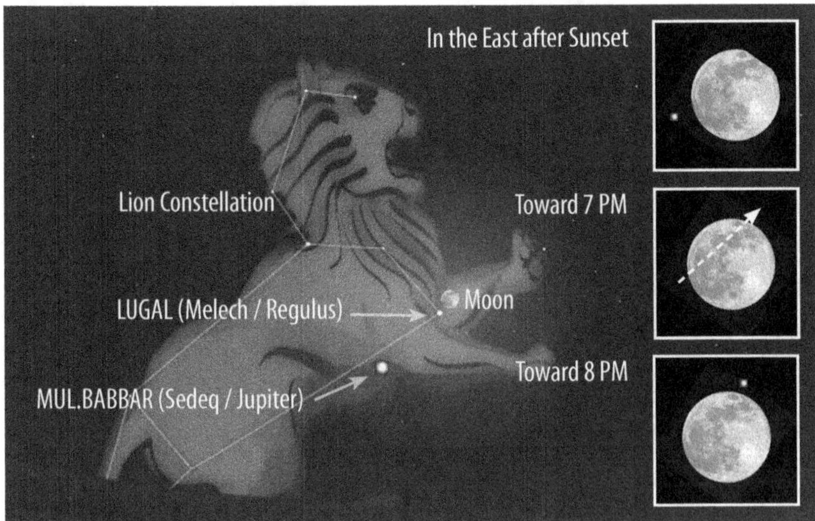

Image: The occultation of LUGAL (Regulus) by the Moon on the night of January 20, 2 BC.

Ctesiphon

Intrigue in the Capital

Months X & XI - Tebētu / Shevat - Day 14

Selebum[2] sat on an ornately carved stone bench beside a side door to the queen's royal apartments in Ctesiphon. The hallway on either side of him was deserted. Beside him, two guards stood on each side of the door. They were clothed with chain-mail on their torsos down to their mid-thigh, and a long white tunic covered them from their shoulders down to just below their knees. Each soldier had a shining silver colored helmet with horsehair coming down in the back, as well as a sword and spear. They would undoubtedly kill without thinking at any sign of danger or at the slightest command of their masters.

The hallway was connected to the palace gardens. As the sun sank in the west, Selebum had entered the palace through the gardens and a back

---

2 Selebum is an old Babylonian name which means "fox."

gate leading to the residence. He had now waited about a half hour on the bench. Not a word had been spoken, and Selebum was not sure that he ever wanted to say anything to the guards beside him.

During the previous four days, Selebum had traveled from Uruk[3] which was to the south and east of both Borsippa and Ctesiphon. His family had lived in Uruk since before the time of Nebuchadnezzar, and had been involved with Uruk's astronomical traditions for most of that time. However, Selebum wanted more out of life. He was looking for a means of enriching himself.

Through some contacts in the palace, Selebum had seen a door of opportunity, and he decided to take his chances. The queen and her son were somewhere on the other side of the massive wooden door beside his bench. Selebum's future was in their hands. Time was of the essence now. Within a short moment, part of the impressive show in the sky outside would be over with, and nothing he could do would prevent that.

Almost two months before, just after the previous occultation of the star LUGAL by the moon, Selebum had thought that he might be able to profit from some of the events in the heavens this year. He did some calculations. He was now sure that the moon would again pass in front of LUGAL during the early part of this night. Selebum had come to Ctesiphon to impress the young crown prince and the queen.

After about another five minutes of waiting, the door opened slightly, and a thin, well-dressed man appeared. Coming over to Selebum he spoke softly in his ear to follow him into the royal apartments. Going through the door, the man led Selebum down a corridor which finally issued into a large well-decorated room. On one side the queen sat at a small table with her son standing beside her. Approaching the queen and her son, Selebum could see a parchment document in front of them on the table. Even from several feet away, he recognized the letter that he had sent to the queen about six weeks previously.

Selebum bowed, and his guide left through another side door. Not a word was spoken until Selebum had ceased bowing.

Queen Musa spoke in Aramaic, "Welcome Selebum, we are glad that you have been able to come. Your communications have been of great

---

3 About 110 miles or 175 kilometers.

interest to us. I am glad to make your acquaintance this evening. I understand that you want to show us something in the heavens."

Queen Musa was a strikingly beautiful woman slight less than 40 years old. Her voice was seductively sweet like honey, but commanding at the same time. Looking at her, Selebum was slightly shaken and certainly drawn to her beauty. Her dark blue dress plunged low toward her breasts in a manner which would not have escaped the notice of any man. The young prince, Phraataces, standing beside the queen must have been about 18 years old. He looked particularly manly, strong and handsome, being dressed in a beautiful yellow robe which had various jewels sown on it in several bands.

Selebum replied, "My queen, I desire to be of service to you. It seemed to me that my observations would indeed be useful. The king has become feeble; it seemed to me that you would be interested in knowing what the skies have declared concerning your common future."

"My queen, as I insisted in my last communication it is of the greatest importance that we discuss these things in detail only after I show you something in the skies. As I wrote to you in my letter, if the weather is good and without clouds, the skies themselves will speak to you this very evening. Is there an upper terrace where we can look to the stars to the east?"

The queen pushed her chair away from the table and stood saying, "Yes, everything has been arranged just as you informed me. We are ready to go upstairs. My son Phraataces will lead us." The queen then wrapped her shoulders in a shawl against the night air.

Up until this time, the prince had not said a word, but now he merely motioned with his hand and said, "Follow me," as he moved toward the side door previously used by the manservant who had disappeared. The queen followed the two men at a small distance.

Going out through the door into a hallway, a stairway shot up to the right and Phraataces immediately began to mount the stairs. Selebum and the queen followed. When they arrived at the top of the stairway about 30 steps higher up, there was a landing with a small corridor and a door facing the stairs. Phraataces opened the door, and within moments all three were on a terrace which provided a magnificent view toward the east. One could see out across the palace grounds as well as some of the surrounding city. There were various larger potted plants in several corners of the terrace. Three chairs and a small table were in place. A servant girl stood over to one side, bowing as the prince and the queen arrived. Phraataces continued toward the balustrade at the edge of the terrace. Once there, Phraataces stopped, looked to the east where the full moon was shining brightly and said, "So Selebum, what is it that you want to show us?"

Illustration: The Moon very near LUGAL (Regulus) while MUL.BABBAR rises.

Queen Musa came and stood beside her son while she too was looking toward the east. A particularly brilliant star was lower toward the horizon. It looked as though it must have just risen not long after the sun's setting.

Selebum lifted his hand and placed a finger in front of the full moon. He then said, "If both of you follow my example you will see. Place your finger in front of the moon." Selebum raised his hand to blot out the moon, and then asked, "What do you see just below the moon?"

Both the queen and the crown prince followed Selebum's example. The queen spoke first, "There is a star, it is just beside the moon. I would not have noticed it without covering the moon with my finger because the moon is so bright. The light of the full moon almost completely hides the star." The crown prince confirmed his mother's statement.

Selebum continued, "My queen, are you aware of how the moon moves in the night sky? Within a very short time, the moon will move in front of the star. Later in an hour or so, the star will again emerge from behind the moon. Some aspects of this event are very rare.

Queen Musa reacted, "Yes, this is fairly amazing. I do not think I have ever seen anything like this before. What are the names of the two stars?"

Selebum responded, "My queen, the star just beside the moon which will soon disappear is the one called LUGAL in our astronomical documents or Sharru in Aramaic.[4] It is in the constellation of the lion. You may even see the outlines of a lion if you look at certain stars." Selebum pointed out the stars making up the head of the vast celestial lion.

He also was quick to point out how the moon would soon cover LUGAL. "Again place your fingers in front of the full moon." Each of them did this. The crown prince said, "Yes, I see what you mean, within a short time it appears that the moon will cover LUGAL completely."

Each of them lowered their hands, and Selebum then continued, "The other bright star further away from the moon is MUL.BABBAR, the so-called "white star," which is associated with Marduk, the king of the gods in the Babylonian traditions. We also refer to it as [MUL]LUGAL, "the king star" as well. This evening, the star MUL.BABBAR rose just after sunset. Tomorrow and in the coming days, the star will already be visible in the sky after the sun sets. Among your servants the Babylonian astronomers, we call this rising in the evening the "elē ūmi," meaning: 'the daylight rising.' This event only happens on one evening each year, and it is one of the key moments of this wandering star's yearly cycle."

He continued, "The stationary star LUGAL is visibly covered by the moon once or twice every nine years. However, I have not been able to determine how often this cyclical event would be accompanied by the last visible evening rising of MUL.BABBAR. Such an occurrence would only happen once in hundreds if not thousands of years. What you see at this instant is exceedingly exceptional. None of us will ever see such an event again. I want to draw your attention to the fact that both of the stars are connected with kingship. Of course, some traditional astrologers might say that such an event could mean a long life for the present king. I am not so sure about this case. It could also mean that the present king will soon be eclipsed, just as the moon is passing in front of LUGAL at this instant. An event like we see this evening could be considered as

---

4 LUGAL is now called Regulus, the king star in the lion constellation.

signaling the beginning of a new great reign. It could signal great things for your futures."

Selebum's words certainly interested his hosts. For another quarter of an hour, he continued to describe the heavens as he pointed out other objects. The queen and her son asked more questions. Finally, after several long descriptions of astronomical techniques and observations, Selebum raised his hand again and placed his finger over the full moon and indicated for the queen and her son to do the same.

The crown prince remarked, "Several moments ago, I could still barely see the star. Now it is apparently too close to the moon to be seen. The star has disappeared. I am very impressed. You knew that this would happen tonight? Amazing, you fellows are quite capable. What a special experience to see this."

Queen Musa, then followed her soon saying, "I am also very impressed. I want to see the star emerge from behind the moon. How long will this take?

Selebum replied, "It will require possibly an hour for the star to be seen again. The light of the full moon is very intense. One cannot see the exact moment when the star will emerge from behind the lunar disk."

The queen said, "Very well, we will stay here. Selebum, you have given us plenty to ponder. I am beginning to like astronomy."

She signaled to the servant girl, who came close by. The air being somewhat chilly, the queen then commanded in soft tones that blankets should be brought for each of them. She also insisted that something warm should be brought for them to drink and eat. Musa then ordered the servant girl to leave so that their discussion could continue without being overheard. Selebum continued to elaborate on how the heavens sometimes could indicate how the future would unfold.

About an hour later, as they all stood again beside the balustrade at the edge of the terrace, eventually they were finally able to distinguish the newly visible star from the moon.

After the star reappeared, the queen said, "I thank you Selebum for your insights. It seems that even the gods are signaling to us that my son and I have a great future before us." Smiling, she looked at her son while speaking to Selebum. "I will reward you handsomely for your efforts to inform us about these heavenly portents."

Then turning her gaze at Selebum, she said, "However, I do ask that you not say anything to anyone about our meeting together this evening. I assure you that if you do, your life may be forfeited. I would prefer not to have to use my authority, but I will if necessary."

These last words visibly shook Selebum. He prostrated himself before the queen, on his knees bowing to the ground. "I swear that no news of our encounter will reach anyone beyond this terrace."

The queen did not stay long, rising she quickly moved toward a door which was to one side. Opening the door, she spoke to a servant waiting just on the other side of the door. The servant left and soon returned with a small pouch, which the queen gave to Selebum.

Queen Musa told him, "I am very interested in any information, which you can give me in the coming months, even five or six months from now. We will remain in contact."

After a few other words, the queen sent Selebum away. Following his departure, she turned to her son saying, "The astronomer is seeking to line his pockets with gold. We will see if he will produce more useful information. I was amazed by the ominous appearance of the moon passing in front of the king star LUGAL. However, we will need to be very diligent if we are ever able to seize the throne. There are huge risks involved in assassination attempts. I will need to see more than one celestial portent to be convinced that we should act."

The two of them moved toward the balustrade again. Turning toward her son, the queen took his hand, then placing it between both of her hands, she looked him in the eyes. The full moon illuminated their faces and the entire terrace.

Musa said in a soft tone, "I very much want you to be emperor, and I want to reign with you. I believe the future will be gracious to us. However, we will need to be careful; fate can sometimes expose one to unforeseen tragedies. Your father has spies everywhere. He must not get wind of any of this."

She then drew him close to her and kissed him on the cheek. Afterward, they turned their gaze toward the moon once more.

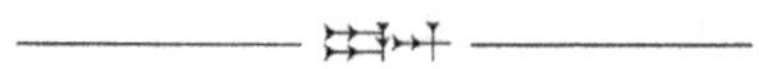

On another elevated terrace about 100 yards away from the queen and the crown prince, the Rab-mag, the Greek astronomer Nikolaus, and Hormizda the Zoroastrian were watching the same scene in the sky, But they knew nothing of Selebum's visit, nor his schemes. However, the Rab-mag and his colleagues were completely aware that they had just witnessed something unique. There was no doubt in their minds that a significant royal sign had taken place.

Borsippa

Months X & XI - Tebetu / Shevat   January / February, 2 BC

Following the evening rising of MUL.BABBAR, Illis-kutul plunged himself into reading the Jewish sacred texts that Eliab had provided. Illis-kutul was able to also obtain other texts from various sources. Some of his neighbors had been more than willing to loan him portions of the Greek Septuagint texts. It was clear that parts of the Jewish Scriptures indicated that there would be a great king who would arise to rule over all the earth. For Illis-kutul, the kingship signs were significant beyond anything that the standard omen catalog ever indicated. It even seemed to him that the Messiah might even be divine. The great king's reign was supposed to be everlasting. Illis-kutul was struck by the text of Daniel which said,

> *"In my vision at night I looked, and there before me was one like a son of man, coming with the clouds of heaven. He approached the Ancient of Days and was led into his presence. He was given authority, glory and sovereign power; all nations and peoples of every language served him. His dominion is an everlasting dominion that will not pass away, and his kingdom is one that will never be destroyed.*[5]

It was as though this individual, "the Son of Man," was to share the

---

5 Daniel 7:13-14.

Jewish God's authority over all things. The "Son of Man," was certainly destined for great things. While the kings in the east were sometimes thought to be divine, none of them could point to prophetic passages in sacred books which would give them such a high destiny. Yes, most of them used the title "king of kings," and they often thought of themselves in exaggerated terms, but here the "Son of Man" did not seem to be presumptuous or boastful. The great king's elevation was the will of the one seated upon the throne.

When Illis-kutul read the prophecy of the "70 sevens" later in the book of Daniel, it seemed as though the Messiah would arrive and eventually he would be "cut off and have nothing." [6] The passage was exceedingly strange and difficult to understand. How could the kingdom and the authority of the Messiah be eternal and yet "he would be cut off and have nothing?" It did not make sense. Besides, both texts were found in the same book of prophecy. It seemed contradictory.

Eliab had promised a copy of a unique messianic Psalm to Illis-kutul, but he had not been able to do it because of sickness. Illis-kutul wondered what could be in the passage. A few more weeks went by.

Melchizedek in the Heavens

Months XI and XII - Šabātu / Adar I - Day 11

In the latter part of the winter, MUL.BABBAR moved closer to LUGAL until on the night of the 11th of Šabātu the two were in conjunction. The astronomers knew that about every 12 years MUL.BABBAR and LUGAL would draw near to one another. However, sometimes the two did not have a visible conjunction because their closest approaches were invisible in the solar glare. In other years, the two were in conjunction possibly two or three times in a single year. But this particular case was unique because on the very night when the two shining stars were closest together, the moon also joined them. Illis-kutul already had seen the moon in the Lion constellation when the planet and the star were closest together

---

6 Daniel 9:26.

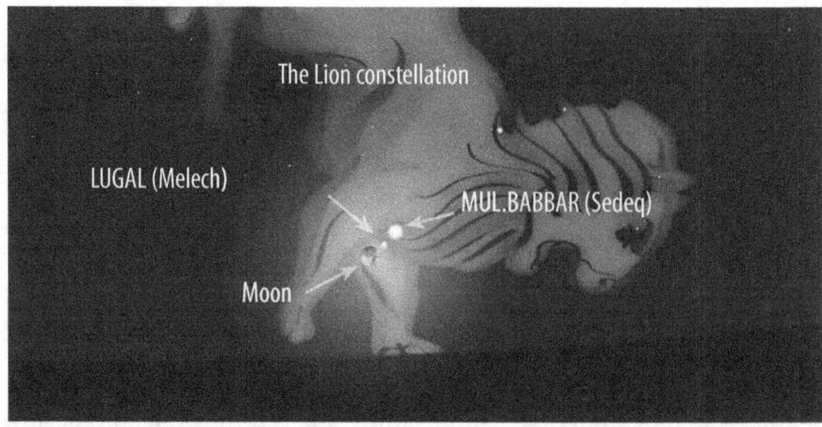

Illustration: The Moon near LUGAL (Melech / Regulus) while MUL.BABBAR (Jupiter/Sedeq) was in conjunction.

but at some distance. In this case, the moon was close to LUGAL, being only about one lunar diameter below the star. MUL.BABBAR was at an almost equal distance above LUGAL. The configuration seemed symbolic to Illis-kutul and his fellow astronomers.

The next afternoon, Illis-kutul was in the notary office. He had come to see Ekur-zakir, but the chief notary was not in the building.

Seeing Eliab in a side room, Illis-kutul spoke to him saying, "Last night MUL.BABBAR and LUGAL came close together as we had foreseen. However, in addition, the moon joined them. The three of them were in a row when they went below the horizon in the west a little over an hour before dawn. It was fascinating. I do not remember having seen this happen before last night."

Eliab responded, "The Hebrew and Aramaic equivalent of LUGAL is the word Melech, which as you know means "king." As I told you previously, the Jewish name for MUL.BABBAR is Sedeq which means 'righteousness.'

"It is interesting that one of the people who is mentioned in our prophecies about the Messiah is an ancient king who was named Melchizedek. Using our Jewish names for the celestial objects gives an intriguing perspective. In all the events which I have witnessed so far there has been an interaction between Melech and Sedeq. The two names make a combination like Melchizedek."

"There is this well-known text from our book of Psalms, but I confess I do not understand all of it. I try to memorize the texts as I write them. As I remember it goes something like this:

"The Lord says to my Lord: 'Sit at my right hand, until I make your enemies your footstool.' The Lord sends forth from Zion your mighty scepter. Rule in the midst of your enemies! ... The Lord has sworn and will not change his mind, 'You are a priest forever after the order of Melchizedek.'"

"The Lord is at your right hand; he will shatter kings on the day of his wrath. He will execute judgment among the nations, filling them with corpses; he will shatter chiefs over the wide earth.[7]"

"As you can understand, the passage is full of royal implications. It is also plainly said that this individual would exercise dominion over the nations and kingdoms. Melchizedek was a king-priest associated with the ancient city of Salem, which is now known as Jerusalem."

"In addition, I also copied an essential messianic Psalm for you as promised. I have it here with me. In this text, there are several references to God's covenant with David that He will place one of the king's descendants on the throne."

Eliab unrolled the small scroll where he had copied the psalm, and he read the passage in Greek while pointing to the words.

"He will cry to Me, 'You are my Father, My God, and the rock of my salvation.' I also shall make him My firstborn, the highest of the kings of the earth. My lovingkindness I will keep for him forever, and My covenant shall be confirmed to him. So I will establish his descendants forever and his throne as the days of heaven."[8]

---

7 See Psalm 110.

8 Psalm 89:26-29

"This text makes it clear that God will establish David's throne forever. But then look at the following passage. Again this text is about David's throne and by implication the Messiah's throne because he will be a descendant of David. I noticed this passage in particular well over a year ago, but I have not brought up this subject with you before today although I have mentioned it to Iqisa. However, thinking about the two incidents when the moon passed in front of LUGAL it does seem important to underline this passage:

"Once I have sworn by My holiness; I will not lie to David. His descendants shall endure forever and his throne as the sun before Me. It shall be established forever like the moon. And the witness in the sky is faithful." [9]

"Is that not interesting concerning the sun and moon? Together they are witnesses that David's royal line will endure."

Illis-kutul stood with his mouth open looking at the text before him in Greek from the Septuagint version of the Jewish Scriptures.

Looking up and facing Eliab, he said, "I am particularly impressed with this text. It could explain the signs we have seen for months. You have seen three of the events yourself. For us, the coincidence of the Moon being with LUGAL twice during the phases of the planet MUL.BABBAR was very odd. It is something which we do not have the habit of seeing."

Illis-kutul shifted a little bit and looked at the Scripture text on the table in front of them both. Then looking at Eliab he spoke again.

"There is something which you did not realize when MUL.BABBAR rose above the horizon in the morning skies about seven months ago. The sun was in conjunction with LUGAL at the same time that the planet MUL.BABBAR rose in the east. We know the daily position of the sun in relation to the background stars. Ekur-zakir was the one who noticed the sun's position last summer when MUL.BABBAR first became visible again. However, MUL.BABBAR's rising when the sun was in conjunction with LUGAL is unknown in our omen texts. Therefore, we were looking for a possible explanation. What you are indicating to me, might be the type of thing that could give a fuller understanding of the signs."

---

9 Psalm 89:35-37

Eliab replied, "Are you saying that there is a possibility that the skies are indicating something about the coming of the Messiah?"

"Yes, that is precisely what I am saying. I have been thinking that as a possible explanation for a few months. I have especially been pondering it after you told me about the Jewish name 'Sedeq.' When one considers this name instead of MUL.BABBAR, things begin to make even more sense. After all, your Messiah is the 'Righteous One.'" said Illis-kutul.

Eliab replied, "When I saw the moon pass in front of LUGAL these two times, I had briefly thought that there might be some messianic connection, but I quickly discounted the possibility. After all, who am I to be reading 'signs' in the heavens?"

Illis-kutul said, "My first thought would not have been directed toward a Jewish Messiah either. But the idea is becoming more and more intriguing. However, I still need to talk in depth with the other astronomers about all of this. There remain some things that I do not understand. For the time being, let us not speak about any of this to other people. I still want to verify certain aspects of these things."

With the last phrase, Illis-kutul excused himself and left the notary office. He was still worried that one aspect of the theory was not making sense.

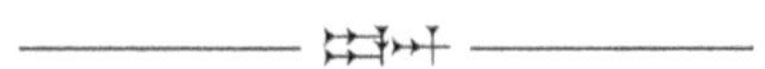

A week after the grouping of the Moon, MUL.BABBAR, and LUGAL Illis-kutul decided to talk to Ekur-zakir about the signs. He was able to speak to him in the astronomical archives area, but he invited Ekur-zakir to go near the base of the ziggurat, away from others, to have more privacy.

After both men had gotten settled, Illis-kutul began, "You know Ekur-zakir, this series of celestial events which is centered on kingship is somewhat disconcerting. We have never seen anything like it. Even if one consults the *Enuma Anu Enlil* and the *Summa Sîn ina tamartisu* one will find nothing that equals this series of royal signs. Our astrological concepts are surpassed by this series of royal signs. We are accustomed to interpreting more or less one event at a time. So far we have had the five significant and unusual events. I will just enumerate them again briefly:

1) The heliacal rising of Jupiter while the sun was in conjunction with LUGAL.

2) The rising of LUGAL while MUL.BABBAR and Dilbat were in conjunction.

3) The first stationary point of MUL.BABBAR taking place at the same moment as a lunar occultation of LUGAL.

4) The visible acronychal rising of MUL.BABBAR at the same moment as the second lunar occultation of LUGAL.

5) The close conjunction of MUL.BABBAR and LUGAL in the presence of the moon that just happened.

And yet, I am not sure what to think yet about the stationary point of MUL.BABBAR this spring in about one month's time. I cannot see a relationship between the Sun, Moon, MUL.BABBAR and LUGAL at that time. The moon will apparently be toward the east when the two stars are in the west. The sun will not be anywhere nearby. At this point, I do not see how that makes any kind of sign. Suen-magir may be able to do some calculations, but simply looking at the almanac does not give me much reason to hope for a royal sign. This is odd. If all the other phases have some type of royal manifestations, then why not that one?"

"I strongly suspect that the heliacal setting of MUL.BABBAR later this coming summer will take place at the same moment as the sun's conjunction with LUGAL. I am familiar with the cycle, and that will probably be the result. Suen-magir will soon finish the almanac, and we will know. Such an event would be the mirror image of what we have already witnessed concerning the heliacal rising of MUL.BABBAR last summer."

"Such a series of manifestations just does not happen in the ordinary course of events. Something extraordinary is happening. I am not sure what else may take place later this year. However, I am dumbfounded. This type of series is unique. It is authentic. We are not dreaming, and it is not just marginally possible in our imaginations. Something is happening concerning kingship. It is like a major announcement about a monarch. It does not fit our usual categories, yet it is obvious. So who is this king? I have a possible idea, but I would like to hear your perspective first."

Ekur-zakir responded. "I am very much aware of what you are saying.

It is an odd circumstance. Our omen catalog was not designed for this type of situation. The catalog was written over 1,000 years ago, possibly 1,500 even years in the past or even earlier. It refers to the governments of Akkad, Elam, Subartu, and Amurru. All of those kingdoms have ceased to exist. We have still been borrowing for the omen catalog to understand the symbolism of a vast number of celestial events. However, the old documents are completely outmoded."

After a brief pause, Ekur-zakir continued, "I am not sure to whom the series of signs corresponds. I have a hard time believing that all of this involves Phraates IV. He is not such a remarkable king. I do not see why the gods would judge it necessary or desirable to prolong his life or give him great honor and success. The repeated events involving the Moon, LUGAL, and MUL.BABBAR seem to be positive signs concerning royalty according to our texts. They could indicate long life and success."

Ekur-zakir seemed to have finished, so Illis-kutul spoke up again, "I spent a little bit of time reading Jewish prophecies concerning their Messiah, and also I have talked with Eliab. Were you aware that their Messiah is referred to as 'The Righteous One' and did you know that their name for MUL.BABBAR is 'Sedeq' meaning 'righteousness'?"

Ekur-zakir replied, "Yes, now that you mention it I was aware of these things, but I have not made any connection in my mind to the signs we have seen and the Jews even though Iqisa mentioned this last summer just after MUL.BABBAR's heliacal rising."

Illis-kutul replied, "Here, you see that I have brought a small scroll, I want to read you a text which Eliab showed me a few days ago. This particular text follows a long passage in their book of Psalms about David the king and their Messiah. The text has the Jewish God speaking prophetically :

"Once I have sworn by My holiness; I will not lie to David. His descendants shall endure forever and his throne as the sun before Me. It shall be established forever like the moon. And the witness in the sky is faithful."

"Have you wondered how to explain the presence of the sun and moon in all these signs? We have not understood the significance of the signs from our omen texts. However, a Jewish perspective may contain the beginning of an explanation. The signs are perhaps royal announcements about the coming of the Jewish Messiah. Such a point of view would make good sense of the sun and moon being present in the signs."

Illis-kutul continued, "Last spring I noticed something on a day that is important to the Jews. You all are aware that the Jews have a festival called Passover and another one called 'the Feast of Weeks,' or as they say Shavuot.[10] This second festival happens after a period of seven weeks which one counts from a specific offering that the Jews make in Jerusalem during their Passover festival."

"Do you remember what happened in the spring last year when the moon made its close conjunction with LUGAL? I thought to myself at that moment: 'This is like the image on our coins.' I do not know how the tradition got started of associating the moon with LUGAL, but we all recognize it as an association linked to royalty. Well, last spring on the 49th day of the seventh week, the moon was positioned precisely by LUGAL in the evening sky. It was the day that signals their festival, but it was not the festival day itself."

Ekur-zakir answered, "I do not know enough about their festivals to understand how the 49th day might be significant. Anyway, keep on pondering these things. I think we may be on the right path in considering that this has something to do with the Jews."

Illis-kutul continued, "As I said, I am still not sure what to think about the second stationary point of MUL.BABBAR. Up until now, there has been an evident royal sign at each of the planet's phases. Perhaps there will be some kind of sign at the next phase of the planet, but it is not obvious to me."

Ekur-zakir replied, "If something does not happen during the stationary phase, it would seem to contradict your theory. We will see. Let's stay in communication about these things. I have been genuinely puzzled. When the astronomers from Babylon came several weeks ago, I said to myself that their explanation sounded rather hollow. It certainly affirmed the traditional interpretation from the omen catalog, but these events do transcend our previous experiences."

Ekur-zakir ended by saying, "Illis-kutul what would we do if we came to understand that these events have something to do with the Jewish

---

10 Pentecost

Messiah? What would we do with such information? It might be interesting, but I am not sure what we would do with such knowledge. And how would we confirm the thing?"

Illis-kutul echoed Ekur-zakir's comments with a knowing nod. Then after a few more words, the two of them went their ways.

Beginning of Months XII and XIII - Addaru / Adar II — Early March, 2 BC

Suen-magir had continued to read the Psalms and Proverbs. He sensed that his faith in the God of Abraham, Isaac, and Jacob was growing. He was staying sober, and his visits to prostitutes had ended. He had indeed changed his way of living. He was concentrating on his work and seeking not to fall into self-pity and all of its accompanying problems. He was also wondering, "If I continue to believe secretly in the Jewish God, what am I going to do if I am called upon to participate in ceremonies for the god Nabu or others? The annual Akitu festival would begin in a matter of weeks. What should be my role? Should I participate?"

Toward the beginning of Addaru, [11] Suen-magir and several astronomers from Babylon were able to finish the astronomical almanac for the next year. They confirmed that the setting of MUL.BABBAR would most likely take place more or less exactly one solar year after the planet's appearing at the beginning of its yearly cycle. When the result was reported to Ekur-zakir, he was very excited. Knowing that Illis-kutul would be extremely interested, Ekur-zakir encouraged Suen-magir to take a copy of the almanac and go directly to tell him about it even though Illis-kutul was resting at home.

When Suen-magir arrived at Illis-kutul's home, he was greeted at the door by a servant. As he entered the interior hallway Kallisto, Illis-ku-

---

11 In this case, the beginning of March, in 2 BC.

tul's 19-year-old daughter was there talking to her mother. Suen-magir greeted them both. At that instant and for the first time, Suen-magir noticed how the young girl Kallisto had now indeed become a woman. He did not see Kallisto very often, but he now understood that she was a real beauty.

He thought to himself, "She is no longer the young adolescent that she had been while we were all living in Uruk." For an instant, it seemed to Suen-magir that Kallisto also looked at him differently. From the smile on her face, it seemed that she was pleased to see him.

The very next moment, Sarpanit, Kallisto's mother, opened another door and introduced Suen-magir into a side room where Illis-kutul was resting seated on a couch with a large cushion behind his head. He had gone to sleep, but he woke when the door opened. Leaving the hallway, Suen-magir did not notice how Kallisto's eyes followed his every step.

She was thinking to herself, "He has changed, I can sense it. He is no longer the man he used to be. I have always liked him ..."

Suen-magir, entering the side room, greeted Illis-kutul and told him just to remain seated. He then opened the leather bag he had been carrying and drew out the new almanac tablet. Then extending his hand toward Illis-kutul, he showed him the lines concerning MUL.BABBAR's setting. Immediately Illis-kutul realized the implications and smiling he looked up at Suen-magir.

He said, "MUL.BABBAR should set in the west when the sun will again be in conjunction with LUGAL. This is remarkable, I would say that this is definitely a royal sign."

The two men continued their discussion. Although Illis-kutul did not say so, for him there remained the question of whether or not there would be a royal sign during the second stationary phase of MUL.BABBAR. He could not think of anything which would be a heavenly sign during the moment of the stationary phase. Illis-kutul knew that Suen-magir and the others had many responsibilities. They would probably not be able to calculate anything else concerning the second stationary phase of MUL. BABBAR. Would there be another sign? They would have to wait and see.

Leaving the house, Suen-magir looked around to see if Kallisto might be somewhere in one of the rooms off the entrance hall, but she was not visible. He had a hard time not thinking about her for several days.

Hours later, when Iqisa alone also saw the new almanac tablet at the observatory library, he looked up MUL.BABBAR's projected setting date. He also knew immediately that the sun would again be in conjunction with LUGAL at about the same period of the year. The date was exactly one solar year after the first visibility of the planet.

Iqisa wondered, "Who is this great king? It really seems strange that there have been royal signs during each phase of the planet's cycle."

Then an idea came to him. "Could this possibly have something to do with the Jewish Messiah as would indicate our research last year? But how is it that the gods have designed something to correspond with the coming of a Jewish king? It does not make sense. Why would Marduk, who made the heavens, be interested in Jewish princes and kings? Marduk is worshiped in Babylonia, not in Israel. I find this confusing. Why would our gods have anything to do with the Jews?"

Iqisa's questioning continued for many days. He did not think too much about MUL.BABBAR's second stationary point.

However, Illis-kutul was preoccupied with this mystery. He asked himself, "Is there a royal connection concerning MUL.BABBAR's second station that was soon going to take place?"

MUL.BABBAR's Second Stationary Phase

Months XII and XIII - Addaru / Adar II - Day 23   March 29/30, 2 BC

On the supposed day of MUL.BABBAR's stationary point, Illis-kutul came to the observatory in the early evening. He could plainly see MUL.BABBAR fairly near LUGAL in mid-heaven. However, they were nowhere near the sun or moon. The light of the sun disappeared, and Illis-kutul was aware that the moon would rise much later in the night. But there was no reason for him to remain at the observatory. There was nothing significant to see.

Illis-kutul was not sure what to make of the situation. There was no evident sign concerning royalty and certainly nothing with the sun or moon as in the previous events. He stayed and talked to the astronomical assistants about various subjects not related to the royal signs. After a few hours, he looked up at MUL.BABBAR and sighed before finally going home, as a very puzzled and frustrated man.

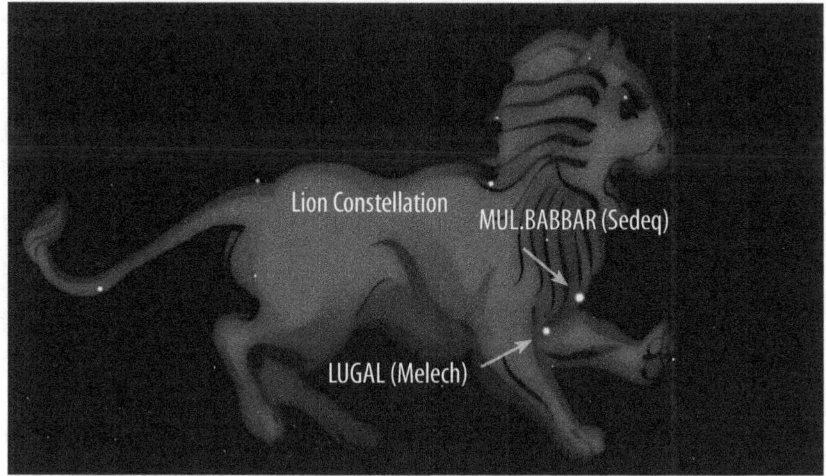

Illustration: MUL.BABBAR (Jupiter) at its second stationary point near LUGAL (Melech / Regulus) at the end of March 2 BC.

Months XII and XIII - Addaru / Adar II - Day 24   March 30/31, 2 BC

The next night, Illis-kutul did not even bother to go to the observatory, thinking that his efforts were useless. However, on the morning of the 24th of Addaru, Illis-kutul arrived at the astronomical archives and spoke to the assistant, Sakkut-tajjar, who had been on duty during the night. Sakkut-tajjar was delighted to see Illis-kutul.

Sakkut-tajjar expressed his excitement by exclaiming, "Something you and I did not expect happened last night. I know that you were looking for some kind of connection between MUL.BABBAR's stationary phase

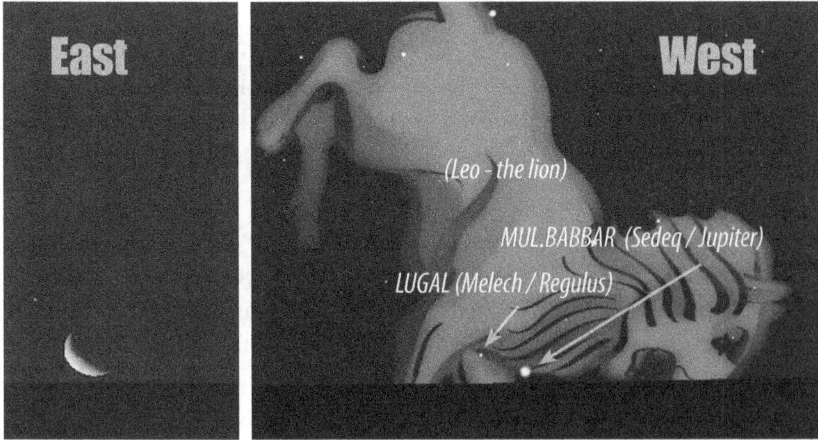

Image: MUL.BABBAR set just as the Moon was rising. LUGAL set almost immediately afterward.

and the sun or moon. Well, last night, just moments after MUL.BABBAR vanished in the western sky, the moon began to rise in the east. Slightly afterward LUGAL also disappeared in the west as the moon rose higher. The two stars and the moon were as we say 'seeing each other.' This is similar to when the moon rises just before sunset so that the two briefly 'see each other.' The same terminology applies here."

Illis-kutul reacted by saying, "Well, I am very surprised. I did not think about this possibility, but you are right, this is very interesting."

Sakkut-tajjar said, "It seems to me that this is perhaps the relationship that you were looking for, but you did not realize the night before last."

He continued, "This event is just one night later than our almanac date for the stationary phase of MUL.BABBAR. However, it is entirely within the acceptable limits for the stationary phase. You know that we often write even in the almanacs 'on about such and such date, the stationary phase of a planet.' That is perfectly acceptable. Your idea that there are royal signs connected to all the phases of MUL.BABBAR during this regular cycle of the planet has been confirmed. Looking at the incident last night, one can make a direct association between the moon and the planet MUL.BABBAR and the star LUGAL."

Sakkut-tajjar then said, "Please know that I have already shared this with the other astronomers. They are all thrilled to hear that the moon was associated with MUL.BABBAR and LUGAL last night."

Surprised and very glad at the same time, Illis-kutul expressed his joy and thanks to Sakkut-tajjar. Moments later, Illis-kutul continued to stand amazed as the assistant left the room. Looking across the rows of shelves in the main astronomical archives, Illis-kutul pondered these events as he gently touched his chin and stroked his beard.

He thought, "Apparently there is a sign at every phase of MUL.BAB-BAR's regular cycle. The almanac calculations have more or less confirmed the only remaining phase (at the planet's setting). It is absolutely unheard for such a coincidence of events to take place. The series of royal signs has completely surpassed the omen texts. The ancient omen texts cannot serve as a guide, at least not for this series of events. We are on our own concerning the true interpretation of these royal signs."

Illis-kutul left the building. The sun was blazing brightly in the mid-morning sky. As the sun's rays fell on his face, he thought back to the Jewish Scriptures again.

"Once I have sworn by My holiness; I will not lie to David. His descendants shall endure forever, and his throne as the sun before Me. It shall be established forever like the moon, and the witness in the sky is faithful."[12]

Babylon - Akitu Festival

End of Months XII and XIII - Addaru / Adar II   March / April, 2 BC

Three weeks after Suen-magir and his co-workers finished the almanac, the annual festivities of the Akitu festival began. The astronomers from Borsippa were expected to participate in the ceremonies and the procession of the gods. The god Nabu had a principal role in the celebrations, as the chief god Marduk's son. The cult statue of Nabu was displaced from Borsippa to Babylon for the festival. The ancient capital of Mesopotamia was only a short day's journey away from Borsippa.[13]

However, Suen-magir asked to be excused. He declined to give his rea-

---

12 Psalm 89:35-37.

13 Borsippa and Babylon were separated by about 11 miles or 18 kilometers.

sons for not participating. But secretly Suen-magir was having a hard time reconciling his growing belief in the God of the Jews with his role as a priest-astronomer. The others went to Babylon to be part of the festivities, but only on the fourth day of the festival that lasted until the first day of Nissanu.

At the same time, Ekur-zakir, Iqisa, and Illis-kutul were beginning to ask themselves profound questions about the truthfulness of their ancestral traditions. The omen catalog was not giving the answers needed to solve the riddle of the repeated royal signs.

On the last day of the festival, which was the first of Nissanu, Iddin-Bel, the chief astronomer in Babylon, spoke privately to Ekur-zakir saying,

"I want you to know that we have been looking at the coming months in our version of the celestial almanac. A couple of our astronomers here in Babylon noticed that MUL.BABBAR and Dilbat will be very close to each other in two and a half months from now, at the time of the full moon. We have the habit of seeing the conjunctions of these two planets. Often such conjunctions are not extremely remarkable. However, this time the two astronomers were inspired to do some calculations. According to them, it seems very likely that the two wondering stars could meet and possibly become visibly joined together.[14] We cannot be sure that the two planets will be above the horizon when they will be closest together, but it is very possible. The conjunction might be very interesting to see. However, we could all be disappointed. Even so, I would like to invite your group of astronomers to witness this event with us. If we get to see something spectacular together, it will be all the better. If the weather is bad or if the closest aspect of the conjunction happens when the planets are below the horizon, well that will just be too bad."

"Looking into our records, I have not found a similar incident in well over a century. The last major event of this type was in the 156th year of the Seleucid era in the month of Dumuzu when MUL.BABBAR and

---

14 It is doubtful that closeness calculations were done for most planetary conjunctions. However, the Babylonian astronomers were well capable of doing such calculations. In the almanac for 162 BC, the Babylonians calculated that Venus would pass about five minutes of arc from the star Spica on the 5th of the lunar month (August 4/5). The almanac text even says "It will be close." In reality, the planet did pass about four minutes of arc away from the star, but it was during a portion of the night that was hidden from the Babylonians when the planet and star were well below the horizon. However, the men did succeed in calculating the close passing of the two objects.

Salbatanu[15] were united as one star.[16] When the phenomenon happens the two wondering stars could be very bright in the western sky just after sunset."

Iddin-Bel continued, "Thank you for inviting our team several weeks ago during the occultation of LUGAL. We would like to return the hospitality by inviting your group to the temple here in Babylon for the conjunction in the month of Simānu. Certainly, we will work out your accommodation."

Ekur-zakir responded by saying, "I suspect most all of the members of my team would be glad to come to the Esagila temple in Babylon to witness this event with you all. I will inform my group. We will probably arrive a day or two before the event."

---

15 Jupiter and Mars.

16 The date of the conjunction was July 13, 156 BC in the western sky, after sunset. Mars was positioned 0°1′29″ from Jupiter at sunset when viewed from the area of Babylon. The human eye cannot discern separation distances of less than one minute and forty seconds in the night sky. The two planets together were like one star in appearance. The Babylonian record reads: "Night of the 19th, the first part of the night, Mars came close to Jupiter, they turned into one star." Jupiter was at magnitude -1.7 and Mars at +1.8 (not extremely bright). There may have been other such incidents, but the author found this in Volume III of the *Astronomical Diaries* produced by Sachs and Hunger on page 71.

The Babylonian Almanac
and Jewish Calendar

2/1 BC

The following is an example of what a Babylonian astronomical almanac would have been like in the years 2/1 BC (Year 310 of the Seleucid Era - Year 246 of the Arsacid Era). This almanac is modeled from copies of the still surviving Babylonian astronomical almanac from 7/6 BC. The Babylonian and Jewish years always started in the spring and continued to the next spring. Many of the Jewish month names have Babylonian origins. The Jewish months had other names in the years preceding the Babylonian exile. Both Babylonian and Jewish days always began in the evening at sunset and ended at sunset the next day. The months began with the first sighting of the lunar crescent in the west at sunset.

In the year 2/1 BC, it is probable that the Jewish month of Nisan and the Babylonian month Nisannu were in synchronization. Once in about every two to three years the two calendars diverged. This almanac example is given simply to familiarize readers with the form and content of the late Babylonian almanacs. (Image above: A portion of the cuneiform Astronomical Almanac from 162/161 BC.)

In the original documents the Babylonians used their own names for the sun, moon, stars, and planets. In the Babylonian Almanac the names of the planets were as follows:
Jupiter = MUL.BABBAR and also the "kakkabu pesu" both meaning "the white star." There were also other names: Sag.me.gar, Sulpae, Neberu (Nibiru), and Ud.al.tar.
Venus = Dilbat (Delebat), It was also called Na-ba-at kak-ka-bu, meaning "the brightest star."
Saturn = GENNA or Kajamänu, meaning "the steady one."
Mars = Salbatanu (unknown meaning).
Mercury = GU4 .UD or Sihtu, meaning "the jumping one" (because of its quick movements).

There may be a number of errors in this almanac. The author has not been able to verify every aspect of the events and dates.

Babylonian Almanac in 2/1 BC

Month I (April 5)   Nīsannu
The first of which will follow the 29th of the previous month.
Jupiter in the beginning of Leo, Saturn in Taurus,
Venus in Taurus, Mercury in Pisces, Mars in Taurus

8th Venus will reach Gemini (April 12/13)
10th Mars will reach Gemini (April 14/15)
11th Mercury will reach Aries (April 15/16)
On the 29th, last lunar visibility before sunrise. (May 3)

Month II (May 5)   Ayyāru
The first of which will follow the 30th of the previous month.
Jupiter in the beginning of Leo, Saturn in Taurus, Venus at the
end of Gemini, Mercury in Aries, Mars in Gemini

1st Mercury will reach Taurus (May 5/6)
4th Venus will reach Cancer (May 8/9)
15th Mercury will reach Gemini (May 19/20)
25th Mercury evening visibility begins (May 29/30)
25th Mars will reach Cancer (May 29/30)
On the 28th, last lunar visibility before sunrise. (June 1)

Month III (June 3) Simannu
The first of which will follow the 29th of the previous month.
Jupiter in Leo, Saturn in Taurus, Venus at the end of Cancer,
Mercury in Gemini, Mars in the beginning of Cancer

1st Mercury will reach Cancer (June 3/4)
5th Venus will reach Leo (June 6/7)
23rd Mercury will reach Leo (June 25/26)
25th Saturn Will reach Gemini (June 27/28)
On the 28th, last lunar visibility before sunrise. (June 30)

Nisan

14 Passover
15 Unleavened Bread
16 First Fruits

Iyar

Sivan

5th end of Omer Count
6th Pentecost

Jewish Dates

Month IV (July 3) Du'ūzu

The first of which will follow the 30th of the previous month.
Jupiter in Leo, Saturn in Gemini, Venus in Leo, Mercury,
Mars in Cancer

6th Mercury evening visibility ends (July 7/8)
11th Venus will reach Virgo (July 12/13)
16th Mars will reach Leo (July 17/18)
21st Mercury will reach Cancer (July 22/23)
27th Last visibility of Jupiter in the West (July 28/29)
On the 29th, last lunar visibility before sunrise. (July 30)

Month V (August 1) Ābu

The first of which will follow the 29th of the previous month.
Jupiter in Leo, Saturn in Gemini, Venus in Leo,
Mercury in Cancer, Mars in Leo

4th Mercury morning visibility begins (August 4/5)
10th Mercury will reach Leo (August 10/11)
17th Venus will reach Leo (August 17/18)
22nd Mercury morning visibility ends (August 22/23)
28th Mercury will reach Virgo (August 28/29)
29th first appearance of Jupiter in the East August 29
On the 28th, last lunar visibility before sunrise. (August 29)

Month VI (August 31) Ulūlū

The first of which will follow the 30th of the previous month.
Jupiter in the end of Leo, Saturn in Gemini, Venus in Leo,
Mercury in Virgo, Mars in the end of Leo

3rd Mars will reach Virgo (September 2/3)
15th Mercury will reach Libra (September 14/15)
18th Jupiter will reach Virgo (September 17/18)
18th Saturn stationary in Gemini (September 17/18)
On the 28th, last lunar visibility before sunrise. (Sept. 27)

Tammuz

Av

Elul

Jewish Dates

Month VII (September 30) Tašrītu

The first of which will follow the 30th of the previous month.
Jupiter in Virgo, Saturn in the end of Gemini, Venus in Leo,
Mercury in Libra, Mars in Virgo

5th Mercury will enter Scorpio (October 4/5)
7th Venus will reach Virgo (October 6/7)
19th Mars will reach Libra (October 18/19)
On the 27th, last lunar visibility before sunrise. (October 26)

Month VIII (October 30) Arahsamna

The first of which will follow the 30th of the previous month.
Jupiter in Virgo, Saturn in Gemini, Venus in Virgo,
Mercury in Scorpio, Mars in Libra

9th Venus will reach Libra (November 7/8)
18th Mercury morning visibility begins (November 16/17)
On the 27th, last lunar visibility before sunrise. (November 25)

Month IX (November 28) Kisilīmu

The first of which will follow the 29th of the previous month.
Jupiter in Virgo, Saturn in Gemini, Venus in Libra,
Mercury in Scorpio, Mars at the end of Libra

4th Mars will reach Scorpio (December 1/2)
7th Venus will reach Scorpio (December 4/5)
13th Mercury will reach Sagittarius (December 10/11)
19th Saturn will reach Taurus (December 16/17)
27th Mercury morning visibility ends (December 24/25)
On the 28th, last lunar visibility before sunrise. (Dec 25)

Tishrei

1 Day of Trumpets
10 Day of Atonement
15-22
Feast of Tabernacles

Marheshvan

Kislev

25 Beginning
of Hanukkah

Jewish Dates

Month X (December 28)   Tebētu
The first of which will follow the 30th of the previous month.
Jupiter in Virgo, Saturn in Taurus, Venus in the end of Scorpio,
Mercury, Mars in Scorpio

1st Jupiter stationary in Virgo (December 28/29)
3rd Venus will reach Sagittarius (December 30/31)
3rd Mercury will reach Capricorn (December 30/31)
13th Lunar eclipse (total) (January 9/10)
18th Mars will reach Sagittarius (January 14/15)
20th Mercury will reach Aquarius (January 16/17)
27th Venus will reach Capricorn (January 23/24)
On the 28th, last lunar visibility before sunrise. (January 24)

Month XI (January 26)   Šabātu
The first of which will follow the 29th of the previous month.
Jupiter in Virgo, Saturn in Taurus, Venus in the beginning of
Capricorn, Mercury in Aquarius, Mars in Sagittarius

3rd Saturn stationary in Taurus (January 28/29)
3rd Mercury evening visibility begins (January 28/29)
8th Mercury will reach Pisces (February 2/3)
23rd Venus will reach Aquarius (February 17/18)
24th Mercury evening visibility ends (February 18/19)
On the 28th, last lunar visibility before sunrise. (February 22)

Month XII (February 25)   Addāru
The first of which will follow the 30th of the previous month.
Jupiter in Virgo, Saturn in Gemini, Venus in Aquarius, Mercury
in Pisces, Mars at the end of Sagittarius

2nd Mars will reach Capricorn (February 26/27)
15th Saturn will reach Gemini (March 10/11)
18th Venus will reach Pisces (March 13/14)
On the 28th, last lunar visibility before sunrise. (March 23)

Tevet (Tebet)

Shevat

Adar

Jewish Dates

The Heavens Speak - IV

April through August 2 BC

8

Chapter Contents:

The Heavens Speak - IV

Borsippa

Month I - End of Nisannu / Nisan

Toward the end of the month of Nissanu,[1] letters addressed to various astronomers arrived in Borsippa, Ctesiphon, Uruk, Nippar, and Sippar. The astronomers in the old city of Babylon wanted to inform their colleagues about a remarkable conjunction. According to their calculations, the star of Marduk, MUL.BABBAR, and the star of Ishtar, Dilbat, could meet in a very close conjunction in the middle of the month of Simannu.[2] The two planets could either become a single star or almost be joined together. The Borsippian astronomers had already been informed of these calculations during the Akitu festival, and they were planning to go to Babylon to witness the conjunction with the astronomers at the Esagila temple. The astronomers elsewhere were at a greater distance from Babylon. Therefore it was understood that they would make their observations from their locations.

However, in Uruk, Selebum took the message to heart, and he remembered texts in the *Enuma Anu Enlil* omen compendium that could be related to such an event. Selebum was confident that he might have finally

---

1 Nissanu is the equivalent of the Jewish month of Nisan (March/April).

2 The conjunction of Jupiter and Venus was on June 17, 2 BC. (The third month of the year: Simmanu / Sivan)

found the means of endearing himself to the queen and her son Phraataces.

After a bit of reflection, Selebum sent a letter to the queen and the crown prince explaining that there was a significant conjunction which would happen in about five weeks. He asked them to summon him to the palace for the day of the event so he could explain to them the meaning. As Selebum was finishing the letter, he reread the words of the omen.

> *If Dilbat enters UD.AL.TAR,[3] then the king of Akkad[4] will die, the dynasty will change ...*

It would not be necessary to inform the queen and her son about the whole passage. The first part would be enough.

Melchizedek in the Heavens II

Month II - Ayyāru / Iyar - Day 5   May 9, 2 BC

During the latter part of the first month of the year, Suen-magir did some calculations concerning the expected third MUL.BABBAR/ LU-GAL conjunction. He discovered that the moon would again be just beside LUGAL on the date of the closest conjunction of the planet and the star. Therefore on the evening of the fifth of Ayyāru,[5] the entire astronomical team was present at the terrace observatory along with Eliab and Belanum, who had been invited by Ekur-zakir. Seeing the conjunction happening at the same moment that the moon was alongside the two stars was amazing. The combination was almost an exact replica of the event that took place about two and a half months previously.

Illis-kutul had still not talked to the entire team about his growing convictions that the royal signs might be signaling the coming of the Jewish Messiah, but he did speak privately to Eliab toward the end of the evening.

---

3 Dilbat = Venus. UD.AL.TAR was used for MUL.BABBAR (Jupiter) in this omen text from the *Enuma Anu Enlil*.

4   Akkad was a kingdom in the second millennium BC in central Mesopotamia. It corresponded more or less with the province of Babylonia in the first-century BC. The Parthian emperor was also the king of Babylonia. In the evening sky, among the Babylonians Venus was regarded as a male war god.

5   Ayyāru is the same as the Jewish month of Iyar (the second month of the year). It was during April and May.

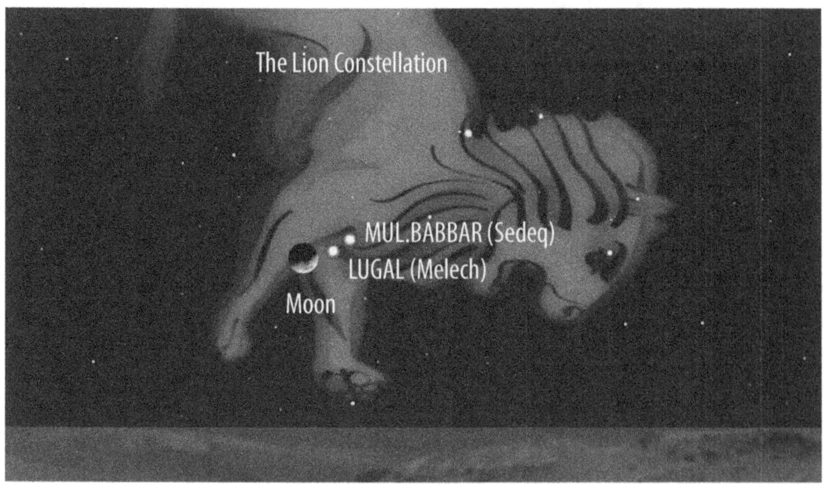

Image: MUL.BABBAR, LUGAL, and the Moon together on May 9, 2 BC.

When Illis-kutul began, the two men stood at the southernmost corner of the terrace, "I remember a text from your Scriptures,

"Once I have sworn by My holiness; I will not lie to David. His descendants shall endure forever and his throne as the sun before Me. It shall be established forever like the moon. And the witness in the sky is faithful."[6]

"It seems to me that this is a good example of exactly what the text seems to be saying. The righteous king's throne will be established forever. The righteous king, Melchizedek will reign."

Eliab responded by saying, "Perhaps you are right. So does this series of stellar events mean that the king has been born? I would like to be certain, but how can we know for certain?"

Illis-kutul replied, "The text of Daniel says that the Messiah will arrive at the end of 62 'sevens.' It would appear that the skies are in accordance with Daniel. Your studies of the Sabbatical cycle and the history of the kings would seem to indicate that the present year is the time of the Messiah's coming. The Sabbatical year starts in the coming month of Tašrītu,

---

6 Psalm 89:35-37

that is your month of Tishrei,[7] is that not right?"

Eliab said, "Yes, my research with Iqisa certainly suggested that the Messiah should be arriving. I think you are right, but I still do not see anything which would directly link the skies to Judaism. Is there any further proof? We Jews are not accustomed to reading the heavens in order to know anything more than the weather forecast. Here you are making a significant claim that the heavens are announcing the coming of the Righteous One. It seems reasonable enough to me, but I would suspect there must be a more significant connection which would make everything very clear. At this stage we are still in a bit of supposition."

Illis-kutul looked at his Jewish friend and said, "You are asking hard questions. Perhaps I will need to go back and examine everything in depth again. I did not expect you to ask such hard questions. You seem to be even more determined to have clarity about these things than I am."

Eliab looked at his friend. "I do want to be certain. Perhaps God will give us a way of knowing which will surprise us all."

Month II - Ayyāru / Iyar - Day 7 Afternoon, May 12, 2 BC

Illis-kutul sat in the astronomical archive library a few days after the MUL.BABBAR/LUGAL conjunction. He was not exactly sure how to prove that the celestial manifestations were associated with the Jewish Messiah, but it seemed to be true. The Jewish God had supposedly created the world and the heavens. If these were his royal signs, then he must have designed things in this manner.

A copy of the almanac for the year was laying on the table. Illis-kutul looked down the cuneiform tablet until he arrived at the date for the setting of MUL.BABBAR. Taking into account the solar year, the date was the day before the planet's rising during the previous year. That was not unusual. However, it was odd that both the beginning and end of the cycle would have been marked by the sun's conjunction with LUGAL, the king star. Such an alinement of circumstances was unknown. Royal signs

---

7 Tishrei was generally astride September and October.

had marked all the phases of MUL.BABBAR's cycle during the past year.

Illis-kutul thought, "Was there anything which connected the heavens with Jewish ideas about the Messiah? Indeed, the text about David's throne and the sun and moon seemed to line up with the events in the heavens. Then there was that curious royal conjunction of the moon with LUGAL on the 49th day of the 'Counting of the Omer' during the previous year. It is a curious thing that 49 days is the total of seven times seven weeks."

Iqisa entered the room at about this time and walked over to the table where Illis-kutul was seated.

The two men exchanged greetings, and Iqisa asked, "What are you doing Illis-kutul? I notice that there is a copy of the almanac in front of you."

Illis-kutul responded, "Yes, the almanac tablet was on the table when I arrived. I did not place it there. It must have been one of the assistants. However, more importantly, I have been pondering the royal signs. It seems to me that there might be a connection between the royal signs and the Jewish Messiah. Have you thought about this yourself?"

Iqisa responded, "In these last days I have begun to think that myself. You know, last year I found our research about the Jewish prophecy given by Daniel to be amazing. However, I am confused. Why would Marduk design the skies to give an announcement about the coming of a Jewish king? I do not understand. Our gods, Marduk, Nabu, Ishtar, and the others have never indicated to us that the Jews are important to them. We have well over a thousand years of astronomical records and documents here in these rooms and also in the archives at Babylon. The *Enuma Anu Enlil* give us interpretations of all kinds of events, but we cannot interpret this odd series of royal celestial signs."

Illis-kutul replied, "I know what you mean. This situation places most of our manner of interpreting celestial signs into question."

During a lull in the conversation, Illis-kutul thought back concerning Daniel's prophecy.

Illis-kutul said, "What if Daniel's prophecy also involved symbolism? Literal years were involved according to your study with Eliab. But what about other periods of seven? Is that possible? Could there also be symbolic periods of time?"

Iqisa simply said, "Well perhaps, I never really thought about that."

Illis-kutul responded, "Iqisa, if these royal signs are connected with the Jews, I think there must be a more direct connection. We can speculate, but I am interested in finding proof. A few days ago I spoke to Eliab about these things. He is glad to think that perhaps there is a connection between the heavens and the arrival of the Jewish Messiah, but he also pressed me very strongly, asking me how we could be sure that the royal celestial signs were connected with the Jewish Messiah. I told him I did not know. However, according to your research concerning the Sabbatical years and Daniel's prophecy, we seem to have arrived at the right moment."

"Last year you remember the conjunction of the moon with LUGAL on the 49th day of the so-called 'Counting of the Omer?' That seemed to have Jewish implications, but it was not on the Jewish festival day. Later in the fall, the Moon, MUL.BABBAR, and LUGAL were all together on the Jewish 'Great Day' of the Feast of Tabernacles. To me, that seemed reasonably royal because it was in the lion constellation. However, I did not say anything at that time. I still do not see how to firmly connect the royal celestial events with Judaism or Jewish messianic thought. Of course, the Jewish names of the stars and planets do seem to be messianically important. And now all of us are in agreement that all the phases of MUL.BABBAR for this year are connected to royal signs."

The conversation continued for several more minutes, but there was no firm conclusion.

Daniel's 70 "Sevens"

Month II - Ayyāru / Iyar - Day 11 Afternoon, May 16, 2 BC

At his home, four days after his conversation with Illis-kutul about the royal celestial events possibly being focused on the Jewish Messiah, Iqisa started thinking about Daniel's prophecy of the 70 'sevens.' He remembered the incident on the 49th day of the "Counting of the Omer," and eating the Jewish cakes that Illis-kutul had brought to the observatory.

Then he had a thought, "What if the stellar events have a symbolic connection with the coming of the Messiah which could be connected to Daniel's prophecy more or less like what Illis-kutul suggested? What if the 49 days, which is 7 x 7 days, are also connected to 62 x 7 days? The separation could simply be Shavuot.[8] What if one counts 434 days from the Jewish festival Shavuot last year? When would that end?"

Armed with these thoughts, Iqisa went to the astronomical archives library.

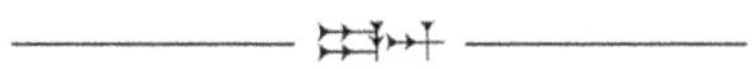

Arriving in the archives, Iqisa went into the main archives and took out the astronomical records from the previous year. He then settled in a small side room away from the astronomical assistants, and none of the other astronomers were present. He found the date when the moon had been in the close conjunction with LUGAL a year before and started writing everything down, also indicating the number of days in each month as well as the Jewish and Babylonian dates.

Conjunction of LUGAL and the Moon, 5th of Ayyāru
(5th Sivan for the Jews).
Pentecost, 6th of Ayyāru (6th Sivan for the Jews).
Begin the count of 434 days on 7th of Ayyāru (7th Sivan for the Jews)
Days until the end of the month of Ayyāru:
(Inclusive of the 7th): 24 days.

Nisannu - 29 days

Ayyāru - 30 days
Simānu - 29 days
Du'ūzu - 30 days
Abu - 30 days
Ulūlu - 30 days
Tašrītu - 30 days

---

8 Pentecost.

Arahsamna - 29 days
Kislīmu - 29 days
Tebētu - 30 days
Šabātu - 29 days
Addaru - 29 days

He then picked up the almanac for the current year and copied out the projected month lengths for the first six months:

Nisannu - 30 days
Ayyāru - 29 days
Simānu - 30 days
Du'ūzu - 29 days
Abu - 30 days
Ulūlu - 30 days

Having written everything out. Iqisa then began to do the addition for the days after Pentecost in the previous year.

24 + 29 + 30 + 30 + 30 + 30 + 29 + 29 + 30 + 29 + 29 = 319

He did the subtraction from 434 (62 x 7) which came to 115 days.

Afterward he subtracted the days in the current year based on the almanac number of projected days in each month.

115 - 30 (Nisannu) = 85
85 - 29 (Ayyāru) = 56
56 - 30 (Simānu) = 26
26 days remaining in Du'ūzu

Iqisa then looked at the almanac to see if any event was projected for the 26th of Du'ūzu. He read the words:

"26th: last visibility of MUL.BABBAR in the west."

This was not what he expected. He really did not know what he had hoped to find by doing the counting, but he had not made the connection with MUL.BABBAR in his mind until that moment.

He said to himself aloud, "This is very interesting.

7 x 7 = 49 and 62 x 7 = 434."

Then another idea flashed through his mind. "Well then, it appears that the end of MUL.BABBAR's cycle is marked by the prophecy, what about the beginning of the cycle? Is it also somehow marked by the prophecy? How many days were there between the Day of Pentecost and the rising of MUL.BABBAR?"

Iqisa decided to count the days from Pentecost the year before until MUL.BABBAR's rising. He began the count as before:

7th of Ayyāru - (7th Sivan for the Jews)
Until the 16th of Du'ūzu (the date of MUL.BABBAR's rising the year before) That made:

The rest of Ayyāru (24 days - including the 7th of the month)
All of Simānu (29 days)
And 16 days of Du'ūzu

24 + 29 + 16 = 69

Iqisa reasoned, "7 + 62 = 69. According to Daniel's prophecy, this is the number of the 'sevens' which must take place before the arrival of the 'Righteous One, the Messiah.' This seems to tie the beginning of the cycle to the two series of 'sevens.'"

Iqisa pushed his chair away from the table, but he kept looking at the numbers. It was indisputable.

He thought, "Amazing. I will need to speak to the other astronomers about this. Who would have dreamed that this could have been possible? Now we can symbolically connect MUL.BABBAR's cycle to Daniel's prophecy. If MUL.BABBAR makes its last appearance before it disappears into the solar glare on the 26th of Du'ūzu as expected; the cycle will truly be complete. The royal celestial signs MUL.BABBAR will be completely integrated into the prophecy. There is no doubt that the Jewish Messiah is connected to the royal celestial signs."[9]

---

9 See Appendix 11, page 455 for a summary of these pages concerning Daniel 9 and the Cycle of MUL.BABBAR (Jupiter/Sedeq) in 3 and 2 BC.

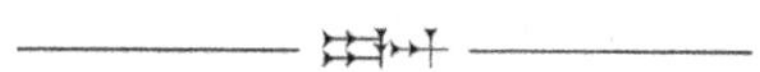

A few hours later, Iqisa explained his calculations to Illis-kutul, Ekur-zakir, and Suen-magir. The three sat dumbfounded for several minutes. Then Illis-kutul said, "We should call for Eliab to come and explain this to him."

Eliab was summoned from the notary office. Then Iqisa spent a good while explaining everything in detail to Eliab as the others also listened. There could be no doubt. The celestial signs involved the Jewish Messiah. The royal signs involving MUL.BABBAR/Sedeq were symbolic messages about the Messiah's coming.

Eliab was amazed and looked around at the whole team of astronomers at the end of the presentation saying, "Well, now we know for a certainty, there can be no doubt. I have also noticed that at least twice there have been events which repeated themselves. There were the two incidents with the moon covering the king star LUGAL and also the gathering of objects with the Moon, LUGAL, and MUL.BABBAR/Sedeq together. In our holy books, there is a passage which tells us that if something happens twice in a dream, then one can be assured that the thing is ordained by God and it will happen quickly." [10]

Ekur-zakir said, "Well, this last bit of information is fascinating. Apparently, the God of the Jews is indicating something about his Messiah. He seems to be underlining it to us."

Illis-kutul responded by saying, "Yes, apparently we are being informed. But what should we do now? A series of signs about the Jewish Messiah is a most unexpected result. However, what should we do with the information? We have learned a real secret. Something which has apparently been arranged by Yahweh, the Creator and Lord of all according to your beliefs."

Then looking at Iqisa, Eliab said, "You remember how we discussed the issue of 'What does it mean that the Messiah would be arriving?' We asked ourselves the question, 'Would this mean that he would become a public figure or that he is born?' I think this is a strong indication the

---

10 Genesis 41:32.

signs are a signal of his birth. It will not be necessary to wait 20 to 30 years to know that he has arrived as a public figure, it would be evident to many. However, one would not necessarily know about his birth unless it was being signaled to us in another manner. God could use prophets to do this. From what we can understand Daniel's prophecy allows us to understand the time of his coming. Now we also see that the Messiah's birth is being heralded by the heavens. The signs are announcing his coming, probably his birth."

Illis-kutul responded, "Yes, if he were now becoming a public figure so that multitudes of people would know about it, then there would be no need for these relatively discreet celestial signs. Only people like us could be aware of these events. Most people do not notice the risings, stations, and settings of MUL.BABBAR. We are privileged to know these things."

The others all agreed, and Ekur-zakir spoke up, "I think you all are right, this is an amazing result. I am not sure what to do exactly. Certainly, I will need to inform the Rab-mag in the capital. But I am not so sure the other astronomers in Babylon, Uruk and elsewhere will be so ready to hear our results. We should not inform Selebum. He would certainly try to turn this information into a means of securing some financial profit."

After looking to see the reactions of the others, Ekur-zakir continued, "The astronomers in Babylon may not be ready to hear us yet. They see themselves as the main guardians of our ancestral traditions concerning the skies and our celestial omen collections. However, we have been prepared for this result. How many other astronomers recently researched their archives concerning Sabbatical years, the reigns of the ancient kings and the coming of the Messiah? I suspect none of them have even thought about such issues. We are almost certainly very far ahead of the others through our understanding the messianic nature of the royal celestial signs."

Iqisa said, "There is a serious side of this entire matter. I think all of us see the implications. Several of us have begun to ask serious questions about our traditional way of thinking about the heavens. These events certainly go well beyond our normal way of understanding celestial signs. There have simply been too many royal signs to interpret them as usual. The events also call into question the validity of our omen texts and our beliefs in our ancestral gods. If the God of the Jews did all of this, then our belief in Marduk, Ishtar, Sin, Samas, and the others is called into question. That is something which is hard for us to accept ourselves. We should not be surprised that others might thoroughly object to any such suggestion."

Illis-kutul responded, "Yes, you are right Iqisa. And we cannot expect others to be very excited or happy about these things. They have not necessarily experienced what we have experienced. It is not every day that one questions his fundamental beliefs."

After some initial hesitation, Suen-magir interrupted, "I need to tell you that during the last months I have been experiencing some unexpected freedom. You all know of my addictions and pain in the wake of my wife's death and that of our child. To my great surprise, I have found help through believing in the God of the Jews, even though I still have many questions. I do not understand everything, but I know that I have had some relief and have been helped concerning my problems. I have been reading texts from the Jewish Scriptures provided by Eliab. I experienced new hope for my life, and the pain of my wife's departure is gone. I am finally able to be free of gambling, drink, and women. I have even been able to save some money."

With this last statement, all the others laughed because their joy was immense. Tears appeared in Illis-kutul's eyes as he heard Suen-magir speak of the changes. He got up, went over to Suen-magir, raised him up from his seated position, and hugged him. Then both men sat down together.

Smiling because of what he had just witnessed, Ekur-zakir continued the conversation, "Well, it seems that we are all undergoing some profound changes for the good. I too have asked myself many questions in the last months. However, as I said, 'What shall we do with these insights?' In about a month from now, we will be in Babylon for the conjunction of MUL.BABBAR and Dilbat. We cannot speak so freely about our new understanding of these celestial events. We will need to find out if the others have been somewhat prepared for this new perspective.

Ekur-zakir added, "How are we to interpret the coming conjunction? You all know the passage from the omen texts. When the star of Ishtar enters and joins MUL.BABBAR, it is supposed to signal the death of the king and the end of the dynasty. You all also know why. In the evening sky, Ishtar is considered to be a male war god.[11] If the planet strikes MUL. BABBAR, it is like violence being done to the king. Without a doubt that is what the astronomers in Babylon will be thinking. However, we do not know for sure that the two stars will become one. They may only come really close."

Illis-kutul said, "One can be certain that Selebum is also aware of the omen text. I would not be surprised that he might try to turn this knowledge for his financial profit. The conjunction could be a bit spectacular. Even if the two stars do not join, they will certainly come very close together."

Ekur-zakir continued, "But the question remains, how do we interpret what may happen in the coming conjunction?"

Eliab sensed that he had an opportunity to be helpful, so he spoke up, "I never have been involved in interpreting the heavens. However, if I may offer a suggestion, I suspect that the Jewish symbols are clear. As you all now know, MUL.BABBAR is known as Sedeq among the Jews. The word means 'righteousness.' Also we Jews call the planet Dilbat by the name Nogah, meaning 'brightness.' I assume because it is the brightest star in the sky. However, combining the two names might make one think of the 'bright righteous one.' It is also probably important that the conjunction is taking place in the lion constellation beside the king planet LUGAL. Among the Jews, the lion constellation is identified with the Jewish tribe of Judah, from which the Messiah will come. As you also now know, the Hebrew equivalent of LUGAL is Melech like the Aramaic word for king. It seems to me that the conjunction is again an announcement of the 'Righteous One.' the messianic king."

In the previous weeks, Suen-magir had also been informed about the messianic psalm concerning the sun and moon. He also spoke up, "I was looking at the almanac a few days ago, and I saw that when MUL. BABBAR and Dilbat come nearest to each other or join, the full moon will rise in the east. Again we will have the lunar witness as we have seen so many times before."

Suen-magir's comment caused Illis-kutul to recite the words,

---

11 In Babylonian thought Ishtar was both female and male. In the morning sky the star was seen as being female, but in the evening sky the star of Ishtar was though of as being a bearded male war god.

"My covenant I will not violate, nor will I alter the utterance of My lips. Once I have sworn by My holiness; I will not lie to David. His descendants shall endure forever and his throne as the sun before Me. It shall be established forever like the moon, and the witness in the sky is faithful."

Ekur-zakir responded, "Illis-kutul you sound like a Jewish scribe. Eli-ab, should you not be the one reciting Jewish texts?"

With this last statement they all laughed, but the entire astronomical team could see that their world was being turned upside down. Everything that they had previously believed about the origins of the world and their usual interpretations of the heavens was being called into question. However, despite their many questions about their ancient traditions, they all now firmly believed in the coming of the Jewish Messiah.

Two days journey to the north,[12] the chief Magus, the Rab-mag, Larvandad, sat on a terrace overlooking Ctesiphon. The Parthian royal capital on the east side of the river from Seleucia on the Tigris was bustling with activity in the early morning hours. Below the terrace, several slaves were struggling with a cart which had a broken axle. Some were offloading the cart while others were loading the same material into another one. All this was happening in the early morning hours because in the afternoon the sun was too hot to continue any activity. At that point, everyone stayed inside sleeping and resting until the late afternoon and the early evening when the temperatures began to go down.

Larvandad enjoyed the early mornings on his terrace. Many of the other dignitaries in the court were still sleeping because of their over-zealous pleasure-seeking activities the night before. However, the Rab-mag was not a man to overindulge his appetites. Larvandad kept part of the morning for his correspondence. Today, there was a particularly interesting letter from the chief astronomer at Borsippa, Ekur-zakir.

The letter began with the typical formal salutations, but soon it plunged

---

12 About 44 miles or 73 kilometers.

into a detail explanation of the royal celestial signs which the Borsippian astronomers were interpreting as being connected to the coming of the Jewish Messiah. As a Zoroastrian, Larvandad read this with great interest. According to Zoroastrian thought a series of leaders who would restore the world to the worship of the supreme god named Ahura Mazda. There were some similarities between Zoroastrian concepts and Jewish ideas, but also profound differences. Larvandad himself had read large portions of the Jewish Scriptures in the Greek Septuagint version. He especially enjoyed the narratives from the book of Genesis about the creation, flood, and the lives of the Jewish patriarchs. While traditional Zoroastrian thought usually applied negative connotations to the movements of the planets, Larvandad saw that the interpretations of the recent celestial events were entirely reasonable.

Ekur-zakir's explanation of the heavenly signs made it very clear that the celestial signs certainly involved the coming of the Jewish messianic king, the "Righteous One." But Ekur-zakir also made an appeal in writing,

> *"Our discovery concerning these signs is a very sensitive subject. It is very probable that there will be resistance toward our interpretation of these signs because the signs themselves call into question our ancestral beliefs. It would appear that the Jewish deity Yahweh was the true creator of the heavens and earth. He has put all these signs in place. This goes beyond our omen texts, it goes beyond our typical Babylonian comprehension of the creation. However, my fellow astronomers and I feel compelled to follow the evidence. The Jewish deity Yahweh seems to be much more powerful than Marduk, Nabu and the other gods of the Babylonians. Please keep in mind that I am writing this as a priest of Nabu.*

> *"You can well understand that we need to be careful about with whom we share this information. The heavenly signs should not be spoken of among the other astronomers without them being prepared. Otherwise, they may resist and even seek to oppose this interpretation of the celestial signs. I would ask that you not discuss these events except with your most trusted advisors. We are not able to share these things in depth with our Babylonian astronomer colleagues at this time. Perhaps a moment will come when this will be appropriate."*

> *"We are convinced that the young Jewish Messiah has been born in*

recent months or he will perhaps still be born soon. This knowledge is marvelous to us. However, we are not sure what to do with these insights. We would be glad to have your perspective and counsel."

Ekur-zakur's letter continued for a few more paragraphs, but Larvandad's thoughts came back to the words, "We would be glad to have your perspective and counsel."

Larvandad pondered the question for possibly an hour or more. He stood up, walked over toward the edge of the terrace and starred off across the city toward the river Tigris and Seleucia on the opposite bank. Suddenly he thought, "I am looking off toward the west, it would be fascinating if someone could go and find out if this Messiah has truly been born. The Borsippian astronomers have an impressive amount of evidence. Perhaps they have been shown these things for a reason."

Larvandad thought of the account of Joseph in Egypt from the Jewish Scriptures. Joseph had understood Pharaon's dreams about the coming years of prosperity and also of famine in Egypt. Following Joseph's interpretation of the dreams, Pharaon had appointed Joseph to be in charge of preparing all of Egypt for the years of prosperity and lack. The Jewish God had given indications of what would happen through dreams.

Larvandad thought, "Perhaps the God of the Jews could also inform men through the heavens as well?"

Then he said to himself, "These men have perhaps had insight into a hugely important birth. The Jewish Messiah is supposedly going to reign over all the nations. Since the men have apparently received this revelation, perhaps they should also be the ones to find out if it is true. Perhaps they should go to Judaea and find this supposed Messiah. If they do succeed, it will be clear that the Jewish deity is the greatest of all the gods. However, if they do not find the Messiah, then we have nothing to fear. Their ideas will have been proven useless. In a way, I would like for them to succeed. I do not like believing in vague religious ideas. I also want to know the truth. There are too many things done in the name of the gods which are simply unjust and unrighteous. What if this Jewish messianic king, the 'Righteous One' exists? I would like to see him change the world for the better."

Larvandad's thoughts continued, "If the men have been shown these things, perhaps they should go to find the young Messiah? For such a journey they will need finances and men. They will need some armed guards and a number of servants. I can supply them with at least some of the resources. If they find the Messiah, it would be appropriate to send gifts as well. A large sum of money would be necessary."

Pondering the possibilities of truly finding the young Messiah, he said to himself, "I would also like to send some of my closest aides. I want to hear from their mouths what they will witness concerning this messianic child. I can trust my men."

The Rab-mag thought, "Maybe I should propose this to Hormizdah, who is Zoroastrian, and Nikolaos, the Babylonian Greek scholar/astronomer who has been a diplomat and royal tutor in Rome. Nikolaos especially would be an excellent choice. He was even skeptical about all types of signs and western astrology. If Nikolaos could be convinced, then one could be confident that the Borsippians were right."

Larvandad reread the last lines of Ekur-zakir's letter. There it was mentioned that the astronomers at Borsippa planned to be in Babylon on the of the next month for a conjunction of MUL.BABBAR and Dilbat. Reflecting on this fact, Larvandad decided to send Hormizdah and Nikolaos to meet the Borsippians. But the men could also be his representatives during the great conjunction of the two planets. Their presence in Babylon would please the Babylonian astronomers as well.

During the next two days, Larvandad briefed Hormizdah and Nikolaos and prepared letters for the astronomers at Babylon and the Borsippians. About one week before the conjunction of MUL.BABBAR and Dilbat Larvandad sent off his two trusted advisors with his blessing and a letter for Ekur-zakir. He watched the men from his terrace 30 feet above the ground as they mounted their horses in a courtyard below and as they rode out of the palace complex. Both men posed briefly and turned to look up as they rode out the gate. Sitting on their horses, they waved to Larvandad before going through the gate. Retaking his seat with a pile of correspondence awaiting him, the Rab-mag did not fully understand that he had just launched one of the most famous adventures of all time.

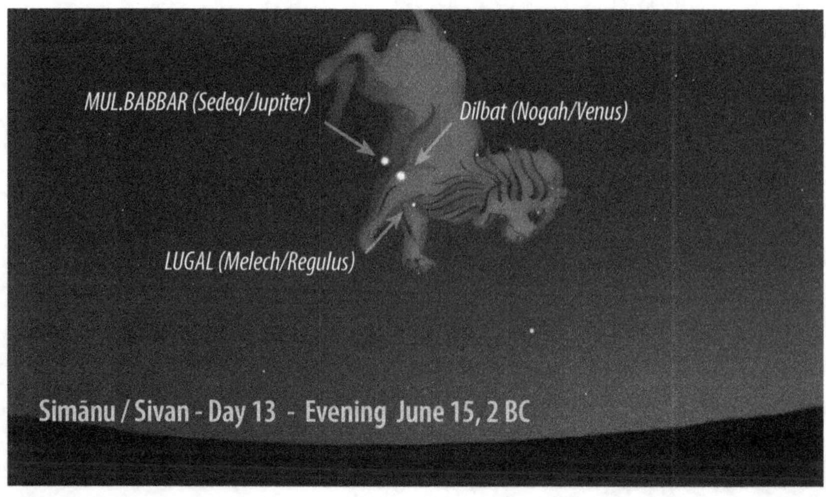

Babylon

Month III - Simānu / Sivan - Days 12 & 13   June 15, 2 BC

Two days later, Hormizdah and Nikolaos arrived in the largely ruined city of Babylon. The city still had a population of perhaps 15,000 people, but it was only a glimmer of its former glory when hundreds of thousands of people had lived there.[13]

The men met the Babylonian astronomers at the Esagila temple complex. The buildings of the temple were still in reasonably good shape although the Parthian administration had neglected much of the financing for needed maintenance. The structures of the temple complex, which spread over several acres, towered over the adjacent streets. At no point were the terraces of the mud brick buildings less than 40 and sometimes 65 feet above the surrounding land and buildings. Most streets near the temple were still inhabited, but the farther one went away from the temple complex, the ruins of the largely abandoned ancient city predom-

---

13 Some scholars estimate that the city's population may have been much higher. The Seleucid kings who followed Alexander the Great's conquest of Babylonia had insisted on moving most of Babylon's people to the new city that they founded, Seleucia on the Tigris. One of the Parthian royal capitals was Ctesiphon on the opposite bank of the Tigris from Seleucia.

inated. Some portions of the old city were given over to garden plots. Goats and sheep grazed on grass were growing on the earthen mounds of ruined buildings.

After supper, the men went to the observation area on the roof of one of the higher buildings. The astronomers from Babylon were observing MUL.BABBAR and Dilbat in the western sky. Already the two planets were very close to each other, certainly giving the impression that they might be joined together a few nights later. The astronomers were excited because their most recent calculations plainly showed that Dilbat would probably touch MUL.BABBAR on the evening of the 15th day of the month as the full moon rose in the east. They were all going to witness what would certainly be a once in a lifetime celestial event.

Later, the newly arrived representatives of the Rab-mag settled in for the night. They were informed that the Borsippian astronomers would come by noontime the next day, a bit over one day before the expected conjunction. As he was getting ready to go to sleep, Hormizdah opened a leather bag containing his personal affairs. He just wanted to make sure that the letter from Larvandad for Ekur-zakir was still there. He smiled, thinking about its contents because he had lent a hand to Larvandad in writing it. He then placed the letter in a pocket in his robe.

Month III - Simānu / Sivan - Day 13   Late Morning, June 16, 2 BC

Toward noon the next day, Ekur-zakir, Illis-kutul, Iqisa, and Suen-magir arrived on horseback from Borsippa. They came with four assistants including Sakkut-tajjar and Anu-Belsunu, as well as a few servants. They were all well received by Iddin-Bel, the chief astronomer in Babylon. At the noon-time meal, Iddin-Bel introduced the two special visitors from Ctesiphon. At that time, the men only entered into friendly conversation. Hormizdah and Nikolaos did not say anything to Ekur-zakir about their having been briefed by the Rab-mag concerning the Jewish messianic implications of the recent royal celestial signs.

To avoid the heat of the afternoon sun, the men went to their lodgings on the side of a major courtyard in the temple complex to rest. At the edge of the courtyard before entering their lodgings, Hormizdah pulled

Ekur-zakir aside a drew out Larvandad's letter from inside his robe. Hormizdah looked Ekur-zakir straight in the face and said in a quiet, but firm way,

"This letter is of great importance. It is from the Rab-mag, Larvandad. You are not to share its contents with the astronomers at Babylon. Please discreetly inform your team of its contents at the appropriate moment."

A bit taken aback, Ekur-zakir took the letter while Hormizdah smiled at him and the men continued walking across the courtyard. Arriving at their separate lodgings, each disappeared into the dimly lit, but much cooler interiors. The summer heat remained outside.

Having closed the door behind him in the relatively dim interior of his room, Ekur-zakir sat down on his bed. He wanted to read the letter immediately, but he decided to rest first. But a question filled his mind even as he was laying down, "What could this possibly be about?"

After about three-quarters of an hour of resting Ekur-zakir rose from his bed and placed himself where a shaft of light was coming in from a small upper window much higher up near the ceiling. Opening the rolled parchment, Ekur-zakir began to read the letter.

There were the usual rather formal greetings, then Larvandad indicated that he well understood the interpretation of the royal signs and found it exceedingly interesting. He was thankful for Ekur-zakir's confidence in informing him of the events. Also, Larvandad agreed concerning telling the other Babylonian astronomers. The other Babylonians did not need to know anything until they had been prepared to receive the message. But the next lines were absolutely amazing.

Larvandad had written:

"If you and your team are willing, I think it would be appropriate for you all to travel to Judaea and seek to find this newborn child Messiah. I am willing to finance a significant portion of your expenses. The journey is long. You will need to be absent for possibly up to six months. Your interpretation of the royal celestial signs is apparently well-founded. However, we will never know if the interpretation is true unless someone finds the child and brings back word about him. You all have received insight into the signs. If the God of the Jews is at work in all of these events, I suspect that he will also help you find the child. Hormizdah and Nikolaos are completely aware of the contents of this

letter. They are ready to discuss these matters with you in depth. I hope that there will be an expedition to the west to find the young Messiah. Hormizdah and Nikolaos are both ready to participate in such a journey. Nikolaos has spent an extended time in the Roman Empire. However, neither of the men are well informed about the situation in Judaea."

The text continued briefly and ended with the words,

"I expect to hear something back from you in the coming days. Hormizdah and Nikolaos can bring word from you back to me personally."

Ekur-zakir sat a bit dumbfounded. He had never dreamed of actually traveling to Judaea to see if the Messiah could be found. He was not sure that he really wanted to do it and he definitely felt a bit out of his league. He was an astronomer. He had been to Susa. He had seen some of the mountains in the direction of Ecbatana. He had been to the sea at the mouths of the Tigris and the Euphrates rivers. He had been to Ctesiphon and Seleucia on the Tigris. However, he had not traveled further to the west than a few days journey into the Arabian Desert near Borsippa. To make a two-month journey to Judaea was well beyond anything he had ever undertaken.

But even so, Ekur-zakir was intrigued. Deep in his soul, he knew that if the child king did indeed exist, he wanted to meet him. How could this happen? Ekur-zakir had no idea, but the possibility of actually meeting the "Righteous One," this Jewish Messiah was very motivating.

Ekur-zakir pondered the possibilities during the next few hours as he waited for the heat of the afternoon to lessen. Just before supper, Ekur-zakir gathered his team and read the letter. Everyone was exceedingly surprised. No one had even dreamed of going to find the young Messiah. Iqisa suggested that Eliab might make an excellent addition to the group. Eliab had already traveled to Judaea. But in addition, he was well aware of important aspects of Jewish thought and practice.

In the evening, the men all gathered on the roof of the Esagila Temple complex. They were on the highest building towering 65 feet above the surrounding ground. Dilbat appeared in the evening sky just before sunset. The planet was exceedingly bright. Shortly after sunset MUL. BABBAR also appeared, and the men marveled at the closeness of the two stars. For several days they had been drawing closer together, and now they were about one and a half lunar diameters apart. Considering their positions and their trajectory it certainly appeared that the two stars would meet and join the next evening.

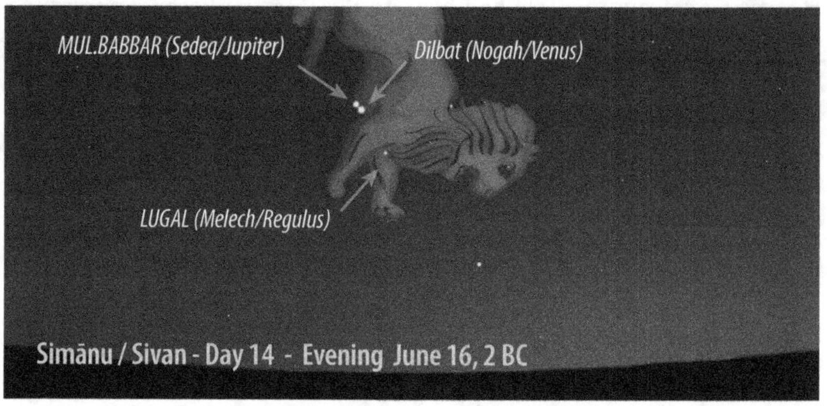

As the men were leaving the observation platform later in the evening, Ekur-zakir touched Hormizdah's shoulder and spoke to him briefly.

"I have read the letter, and I have shared it with my group of astronomers. We do need to talk in depth. I am willing to do this tomorrow morning. We will continue to think about the Rab-mag's proposal during the night. Perhaps we can give you a word about our perspective on the proposal in a few days. We are astonished. Give us a bit of time to digest this proposal. We are certainly intrigued."

Month III - Simānu / Sivan - Day 14 — Early Morning - June 17, 2 BC

The next morning, all the men met for breakfast, and they started to get to know each other a little more. After their early morning meal, Ekur-zakir asked Illis-kutul, Iqisa, and Suen-magir as well as Nikolaos and Hormizdah to come apart to talk about the Rab-mag's proposal. Discreetly Ekur-zakir requested a private room from one of the servants without informing their Babylonian hosts. The men would have perhaps a half hour or so before they were missed, so the discussion had to be limited.

Iqisa and Illis-kutul made a brief presentation of the facts concerning the celestial signs for Nikolaos and Hormizdah. Ekur-zakir explained why the astronomers thought that the signs signaled the birth of the Messiah rather than a public manifestation of an adult leader.

Nikolaos and Hormizdah had a few questions, and then Hormizdah asked, "We will need to return to the Rab-mag with a response. We know very well that all of this is very new. It would be understandable that you may not be able to give us a certain answer about the Rab-mag's proposition. But please tell us soon, 'Will it be a possibility for you to travel to Judaea seeking the child Messiah?'"

Ekur-zakir replied, "Well, nothing is definite yet, but for my part, I may be interested in going. Such a trip is not something which I have done before. If I did participate, I would need to make plenty of arrangements. It would be similar for the other astronomers. We cannot simply leave our responsibilities in the notary office, the observatory, and the temple complex. We will need to find some people who can at least partially replace us during our absence."

Ekur-zakir continued, "We can stay in touch in the coming months. If the trip does indeed take place, we will only leave for Judaea after the heat of summer is well past. The eastern Mediterranean region does not have a harsh winter climate like some countries to the north. It will be less difficult for us to travel there in the fall and winter than in the summer heat. Sometimes there will be rain, and we might even briefly see some snow, but this will be much more agreeable for the journey than the summer heat."

"If everything comes together and we can make the journey, you both are welcome to join the group. I appreciate the Rab-mag's financial proposal as well. The journey is long. It will be expensive, and we will need to have some armed guards and servants. I suspect our group would need to be a minimum of about 20 people."

Ekur-zakir concluded by saying, "I think that you can tell the Rab-mag that we are seriously considering his proposal. We will need to see if we can make all the arrangements. I suspect that we can give Larvandad a definitive answer in about one month. The Rab-mag has explained many things to you about this situation. I think both of you certainly can understand how we need to be fairly discreet concerning our opinions and interpretations concerning the celestial signs."

"We would be glad to talk to you some more about these things. However, the local astronomers are going to want to see us all. Personally, I would be glad to talk to you all later this afternoon before we eat and go to the observation platform to see the conjunction. However, to avoid having the others ask too many questions we should end our time together for the moment and join the other local astronomers. We have some things which we need to discuss with them. I would also like to propose to you both to come to Borsippa for several days. That way we can discuss these things in depth."

After a short discussion, Nikolaos and Hormizdah agreed that it would be best to continue the conversation in Borsippa. Before noon, Ekur-zakir sent a servant to Borsippa to arrange things for the arrival of Nikolaos and Hormizdah. It was foreseen that they would all leave for Borsippa the next morning. Afterward, the entire group of astronomers from Borsippa and Babylon spent several hours together talking about different kinds of projects. The noontime meal came and went, and in the early afternoon, the men rested.

A Single Star

Month III - Simānu / Sivan - Day 15   Evening - June 17, 2 BC

In the late afternoon, some of the assistant astronomers from the team in Babylon reported seeing Dilbat[14] even before sunset. This was not unusual. The planet was in an extremely bright phase, making it visible even in daylight.

Later in the evening before sunset, all the astronomers arrived at the observation platform atop of one of the temple complex buildings. There, 40 cubits [15] above the surrounding temple courts, the conjunction of MUL.BABBAR and Dilbat could be seen with great clarity. One could not tell the two stars apart, positioned as they were about one-third of the distance between the western horizon and the zenith. It looked as though they had become one single object. In addition, just after the sun went down, the moon rose in the east. It was a grand spectacle. However, if one had not followed the movements of Dilbat in relation to MUL.BABBAR during the previous days, one might not have been as impressed.

While the two stars together were noticeably brighter than when they were separately, their brightness was not completely abnormal. An untrained eye might not have fully appreciated the difference in intensity.[16]

---

14 Venus.

15 About 65 feet or 20 meters.

16 Some amateur astronomers and Bethlehem Star theorists have speculated that the combined light of the two planets together was much brighter than the two separately. However, according to two scientists that the author contacted, the apparent magnitude of the combined "star" would have only been about one tenth of a magnitude brighter than Venus. See Hutchison, *The Lion Led the Way*, Third Edition, pages 238-239.

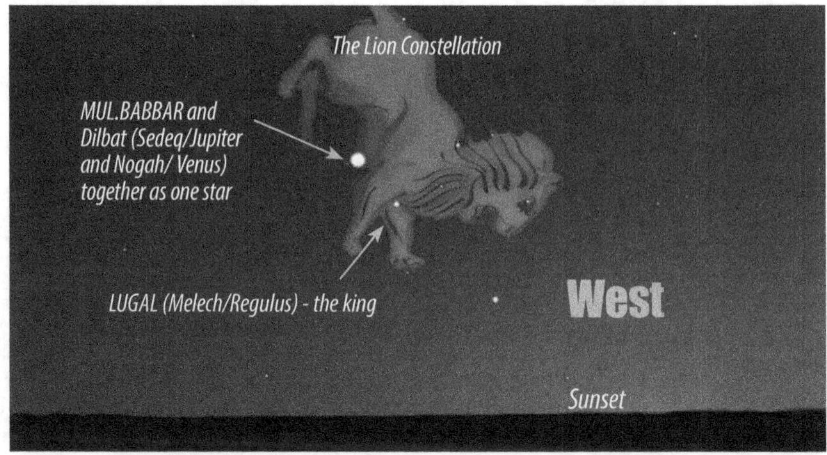

Above: The western sky on the evening of June 17, 2 BC.

Image: The moon rising in the east on June 17, 2 BC.

As the evening went on, the combined "star" descended further and further toward the horizon, while the moon rose higher. Before the single star set in the west, Illis-kutul found himself with the other astronomers from Borsippa. He quietly recited one of his favorite passages from the Jewish Scriptures just so the other Borsippians could hear him:

"Once I have sworn by My holiness; I will not lie to David. His descendants shall endure forever, and his throne as the sun before Me. It shall be established forever like the moon, and the witness in the sky is faithful."

The others smiled and nodded their heads.

Later as the "star" passed below the horizon, Iddin-Bel, the head of the astronomers in Babylon, gathered everyone near an olive oil lamp beside a small shelter on the observation platform. He had a cuneiform tablet in his hand. He signaled for everyone to be silent for a moment and he read out some words from the Babylonian omen text, the *Enuma Anu Enlil:*

> *If Dilbat (Venus) enters UD.AL.TAR (Jupiter),* [17] *then the king of Ak-kad* [18] *will die, the dynasty will change, either a soldier will go out, or the enemy will send a message to the land (asking for peace).*

Iddin-Bel said, "According to the omen text, the king of Akkad, that is the one we now know as Babylon, will die and the dynasty will end. As you all know, the star of Ishtar is a masculine war god in the evening sky. This event is like a war god hitting the king planet."

"I will inform the Rab-mag concerning the omen. However, I do not want to write this to the Parthian Emperor himself."

Looking around the group in the light of the full moon, and with the light of the small lamp, Iddin-Bel's eyes fell on Hormizdah and Nikolaos, then he said, "Can you take this message to the Rab-mag for me?"

Both men nodded their heads, but they each knew that the Rab-mag would not be impressed.

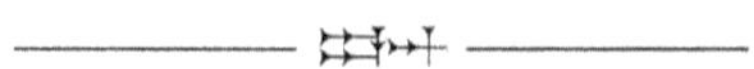

At about the same moment as the astronomers were observing the conjunction in Babylon, in the capital Ctesiphon, Selebum was with Queen Musa and the Crown Prince Phraataces on a terrace of the palace which faced toward the west. Selebum had arranged to be with them even though the Rab-mag had desired to spend the evening watching the conjunction with the principal members of the royal family. Finally, only the king spent the evening with the Rab-mag.

Selebum, Queen Musa, and Phraataces directed their eyes toward the

---

17 UD.AL.TAR means the "heroic one." It was another name for MUL.BABBAR, the king planet [MUL]LUGAL (Jupiter).

18 Akkad was a kingdom in the second millenium BC in central Mesopotamia.

single star sinking in the west. Selebum had told the queen and the crown prince that he would reveal an especially interesting omen to them at the end of the evening. He only read the following words,

"If Dilbat (Venus) enters UD.AL.TAR, then the king of Akkad will die."

Selebum then spoke, "My queen, the ancient kingdom of Akkad was a dominate power when our omen texts were written. Akkad was basically the equivalent of your present province of Babylonia. The Emperor Phraates IV, your husband, is now the ruler over the present equivalent of Akkad."

The queen was noticeably moved, then she said, "My son it appears that your time has come. You and I will soon reign over the Empire."

Looking at Selebum, the queen thanked him for his services. Within less than an hour, Selebum left the palace with a small bag of coins. The queen and the crown prince had warned him if he breathed a single word concerning the evening's discussion to others, that he would forfeit his life within days. The queen and her son were determined to act for their advantage.

Discussions in Borsippa

Month III - Simānu / Sivan - Day 19   Evening - June 21, 2 BC

The Borsippian astronomers and their guests returned home the day after the conjunction. Nikolaos and Hormizda were delighted to spend part of several nights at the observatory on the Borsippa ziggurat. It was not often that they had such a high place to look at the heavens.

The guests were lodged at Ekur-zakir's home. On their fourth day in Borsippa, Ekur-zakir invited the whole astronomical team for a meal in the evening. He hoped that this special meal might provide an occasion for the astronomers to get to know Nikolaos and Hormizdah in greater depth. Ekur-zakir's wife Ispubarza ate earlier and retired to another part of the house for the evening. Servants brought the food, and they were constantly in and out of the room trying their best to meet every need, whether with bread, wine, or more of the principal dishes.

During the last part meal, Hormizdah opened up a bit more about himself. He was not a particularly talkative person. However, he had gotten to know the Borsippians better, and the relaxed atmosphere of the meal seemed to give him more inclination to talk. He spoke for a while about his former life as a scholar in the imperial city of Ecbatana in Media. In recent years, he had been called into the Rab-mag's service in the capital, Ctesiphon, but he preferred his native Media. He was a Zoroastrian, but he liked to study different kinds of religious beliefs. He was intrigued by the possibility of traveling to Judaea. However, he was a bit disturbed because, like the men from Borsippa, he had questions.

At one point he said to the others, "If we do go on this adventure, as a Zoroastrian, what will this mean to be seeking a Jewish Messiah? Am I now slowly but surely changing my beliefs? Even the Rag-mag himself must understand how big a challenge this is to our way of thinking. If this righteous world ruler is Jewish, what about our Zoroastrian ideas of a world savior from Zoroaster's line? I am no longer sure what to think."

Finally after about a half hour listening to Hormizda, Illis-kutul and Iqisa indicated that they would be interested in hearing more about Nikolaos' life and activities. Everyone agreed, and the focus of the evening shifted to the Greek astronomer/scholar and diplomat.

Nikolaos began by saying, "I grew up in Seleucia on the Tigris and was a student of some noted scholars in that city. Because my father was quite well-off, he desired for me to have an extensive education, including nine months with Babylonian astronomers in Sippar when I was 19 years old. It was a magnificent experience. I was able to learn your Babylonian astronomical science first hand. I had already studied cuneiform in the years previously."

"When I was in my early twenties, I also studied Greek astronomy and some philosophy in Alexandria. I know the writings of Hipparchus in detail. The astronomer Aristarchus has been one of my favorites. As you know the Greek astronomer Seleucus of Seleucia, who lived over 125 years ago, was a champion of Aristarchus' theory that the sun is the center of the universe. I inherited those ideas, and have rejected some of Hipparchus' thought. I do not think that the earth is the center of the known universe."

At this point, Illis-kutul spoke up grinning and chuckling, "Everyday it looks to me like the sun comes up and later it goes down. I have stayed in the same spot for several years. I do not want to claim to be at the center of the universe, but the sun and moon seem to move around my location. I know this does not sound very profound but is about all I can speculate after such a fine meal."

Looking at their host, he continued saying, "Ekur-zakir the wine was great, but it makes my mind a bit dull."

Ekur-zakir responded jokingly, "I have really made a mistake by inviting you all here tonight. All of us know that Illis-kutul has the sharpest mind here. If I have made his mind dull with my wine, we will all have more work to do to pick up the slack."

Everyone roared with laughter including Nikolaos. However, Suen-magir did not laugh as much as the others, knowing how he had been terribly drunk many times in the last many years. He preferred not to even think about it. He remembered how Illis-kutul had to cover up for his intemperance.

After the laughing died down, Nikolaos started again, "I am well aware that you Babylonian astronomers do not delve into questions about the structure of the universe very much," he said smiling.

"However, being from a Greek background, of course, I am interested in the geometry of the universe. The Greek astronomers have had many debates on this subject. At this time Hipparchus' concepts have the ascendancy, but I hope that will eventually change and that Aristarchus' ideas will prevail."

"I am now a little bit over fifty years old. I am married, and I have three children who are all living in Seleucia or Ctesiphon. I have been in the royal court in Ctesiphon and outside the Parthian Empire for much of the last 25 years. I was privileged to do some extensive traveling during the previous ten years. My trips have included a major journey to Rome via Athens. I was sent to Rome as a tutor to the sons of Phraates IV. The young men are still living as hostages in the Roman capital to guarantee the peace. I will say this here in confidence; I speculate that the boys had been sent away on Queen Musa's initiative to secure the throne for her son, Phraataces."

For a few moments, Nikolaos hesitated and then apologized saying, "I may shock you all a little bit by the things I would like to share now. My thinking has been changing in recent years. I am no longer the same scholar that Phraates sent to Athens and Rome. My views have changed."

"During my travels, I was thinking about the perspectives on astrology which have been proposed here in Babylonia and Assyria during the last few thousand years. It has been commonplace in Mesopotamian astronomy to speculate about 'celestial writing.' You and I have thought that there have been messages in the sky written there by the gods. I am certainly not as impressed by any celestial events listed in the *Enuma Anu Enlil* texts or others as I was in my youth. As a result of my trip to Greece and Rome, I can now say, 'I no longer want to believe just anything that either eastern or western scholars or astronomers may say about the heavens and man.'"

"While I spent time in Rome and in Athens on the way, I began to explore ideas about divination proposed by some Greek thinkers and the Roman statesman Cicero. I was particularly intrigued by Cicero's statements about the recent wave of Hellenistic astrology."

"Cicero developed several arguments against astrology in his books *De Divinatione (Concerning Divination)* and *De Fato (Concerning Fate)*. As you already know Hellenistic astrology is gaining a more significant hearing here in Babylonia thanks to the many Greeks who live in the region."

"The older Mesopotamian ideas about astrology are being called into question. The Hellenistic astrologers often think that one's 'fate' or destiny is directly or at least indirectly caused by the heavens. However, I myself have come to question this entire approach."

"I also call into question the approach presented in the ancient Babylonian omen catalog, the *Enuma Anu Enlil*. I am not sure that any of these methods are accurate for understanding messages in the heavens, even if such messages exist. For example, here is a text that I took by chance the other day and wrote down. Nikolaos shifted in his seat and took a leather bag on the floor at his feet. Pulling out a small parchment text, he unrolled it and read the passage for everyone. It went as follows:

> *When in the month Ayyāru,*[19] *during the evening watch, the moon eclipses, the king will die. The sons of the king will vie for the throne of*

---

19 The second month of the Babylonian year in the spring. It was the equivalent of the Jewish month "Iyar" after the month of Nisan, when the wheat was ripening.

their father, but will not sit on it.[20]

Then Nikolaos commented, "It seems odd to me that a lunar eclipse could foretell or even cause specific events. I know there are famous examples like the lunar eclipse which happened just before Alexander won his great victory over Darius at the Battle of Gaugamela, thus gaining control of the Persian Empire. But did the eclipse really foretell Alexander's victory? One could consider that it predicted his possible defeat as well depending on one's perspective. It is only because he won the battle that men believe that the eclipse signaled his triumph. Ultimately, it could have indicated Darius' victory."

"I am happy that Alexander won the battle. My ancestors came to live in this region because of it," he said with a smile and a bit of a chuckle.

Illis-kutul also responded with a comment as he smiled, "Yes, I guess you are happy about that."

Nikolaos continued, "In your Babylonian tradition, the eclipses signaled something which could happen concerning the king. You then offered certain sacrifices and sometimes even installed a temporary substitute king to ward off evil. You Babylonians have thought that the future can be changed and that the signs are not deterministic."

"However, among the Hellenists from the West, the emphasis is shifting to deterministic 'Fate.' I am not sure that one needs to believe in 'Fate.' Perhaps the choices of men are more important than we think. I know how easy it is to get into an argument with my wife by merely saying certain words. Is it my destiny that I would choose to say those words? It seems to me that every time I decide to avoid saying certain things life goes better in our home."

Ekur-zakir said, "I can relate to your last example. My wife and I have experienced this on many occasions! As for the rest, as you know, there is starting to be a lot of debate about these questions among the different schools of astronomers here in Babylonia.[21] I am not sure where I stand

---

20 *Enûma Anu Enlil* 17.2

21 In Strabo's book, *Geography* 16.1.6-7 we read: "In Babylon a residence was set apart for the native philosophers called Chaldæans, who are chiefly devoted to the study of astronomy. Some, who are not approved of by the rest, profess to understand genethlialogy, or the casting of nativities. There is also a tribe of Chaldæans, who inhabit a district of Babylonia, in the neighborhood of the Arabians, and of the sea called the Persian Sea. There are several

on all these issues in every detail. It is evident that our Babylonian gods no longer have sway over events. The Zoroastrians may soon be dictating everything to us. Hormizdah may know their plans," he said with a snicker, and everyone including Hormizdah laughed.

Then Ekur-zakir continued, "It seems like the world is changing. Perhaps we do not understand everything as well as we once thought. I have been astounded by the apparent connection between the heavens and the Jewish Messiah. If all this is shown to be true, perhaps all of our thinking about the gods should be called into question. I am open to having all the relevant evidence. You all understand that this is something which I am declaring to you all in private. It would be better not to broadcast it too loudly."

All the other men at the table smiled, and some nodded their heads. Iqisa even said, "Yes, father we hear you very well, some things cannot be spoken outside this room."

The others also nodded their agreement and Illis-kutul said, "I never thought I would say such things myself, but I also agree."

Around the table, eyes then shifted back to Nikolaos, who continued by saying, "I do want to talk to you about the Jewish connection, but I would like to describe some important points from Cicero's books to you. These things should be considered. I made a short list. I know I have already said a lot, but I want to express my doubts about horoscope astrology in a very concrete and somewhat detailed way."

Ekur-zakir, spoke up, "We have the rest of the night. Only Iqisa needs to be at the observatory for the last watch of the night. We are all ears."

Nikolaos shifted in his seat slightly while he took out a small parchment roll from his robe. Then after unrolling it he began to elaborate on several points: [22]

(1) "The stars are apparently so far away, in what manner could they

---

classes of the Chaldean astronomers. Some have the name of Orcheni, some Borsippeni, and many others, as if divided into sects, who disseminate different tenets on the same subjects. The mathematicians make mention of some individuals among them, as Cidenas, Naburianus, and Sudinus. Seleucus also of Seleuceia is a Chaldæan, and many other remarkable men."

22 The seven points in the following paragraphs can be found in many places online. Below are two references: www.astrology-and-science.com/A-divi2.htm (Note 1) and also: www.astrology-and-science.com/H-cice2.htm

influence life on earth? Yes, it is evident that the sun and moon exercise some influence, but what power can a small point of light like Mercury exercise? Most people do not even see the planet when it is visible."

(2) "The Weather does influence humanity greatly. If it does not rain, there are famines. However, the weather is entirely ignored by astrology."

(3) "Cicero also points out that parents have a very significant influence on their children, do not only the physical traits but also their traits of character, attitudes, values and general comportment. Their influence must be stronger on anyone's life than the position of a few planets and one's birth sign."

(4) "It is clear that twins are born almost instantaneously. The heavens are the same concerning them both. However, twins are often very different in their character, abilities, and careers. Indeed it is similar for two children born of different parents but at the same instant. While the position of the heavenly bodies at each child's birth would be the same, the lives, character, abilities, and aspirations of the two children may be profoundly different. Cicero says, 'this makes it very clear that the time of birth has nothing to do in determining man's course in life.'"

(5) "When one considers the different peoples over the face of the world such as the Indians and Persians, it is evident that one's birth and life is more affected more by the local environment and the everyday experience than by the condition or position of the moon and the stars."

(6) "Cicero also brings up one of the great Roman military disasters at Cannae when their enemy Carthage under the command of Hannibal destroyed an army of 70,000 Romans.[23] All the Romans suffered and grieved terribly. Cicero asked, 'Did all the Romans who fell at Cannae have the same horoscope? No, they did not. Most of the men would not have been born on the same day. However, their fate was the same.'"

(7) "As well we can consider the greatest minds among us. Were all the knowledgeable and wise men, like yourselves, all conceived and born under the same star? Certainly not. Was there ever a day when countless numbers of people were not born? However, very few of them become well-known great men or scholars."

---

23 The battle of Cannae took place in 216 BC.

Nikolaos continued, "Considering such things, I have very little confidence that Hellenistic astrology or the ancient Babylonian omen texts mean very much at all. I doubt their predictive power. Cicero himself wrote, 'The stars may have power over some things if you like, but they certainly do not have power over all things.'"[24]

"Even so, I am very interested in the heavenly signs which you are associating with the Jewish Messiah. As I already told you in our previous discussions, Larvandad has let me read your reports about the signs which include a possible Jewish perspective. I have also been watching this series of events with great interest even from the rising of MUL.BABBAR last year. In the history of the world, I am not sure that there has ever been a series of royal signs like what we have witnessed during the past year."

"This is certainly different than horoscope astrology. Your proposed interpretation scheme does not try to establish the destiny of the person because of the positioning of particular heavenly bodies at his birth date. Also, you are not proposing that this might be a favorable time for his birth because of the position of the sun, moon, and certain stars. You think that the series of royal celestial events is a single message. The signs simply announce the arrival of the expected messianic Jewish king."

"I like this idea. An announcement is different than saying that the stars, planets, sun, and moon caused something. The heavens are only announcing that this birth has happened or that it will soon happen."

"The signs themselves do not tell us very much about the man's qualities or if this is an auspicious moment for his coming. Essentially without the perspective given by the Jewish Scriptures and the particular Jewish dating system one could not even discern what or whom the signs are indicating. Indeed, these connections with Judaism are different from what most of us have considered when we have thought of astrological prediction. In fact, it is not an astrological prediction. It is the discernment of a specific royal announcement concerning something which is happening in the present."

Nikolaos waited a moment to see if anyone wanted to react. Then he continued.

"I am intrigued. Perhaps all these signs amount to a real announce-

____

24 *De Fato,* 8.

ment of a birth. If so, the Messiah is certainly a great king, the greatest of kings. It seems to me that this is indeed a birth which is being signaled. If the king who is announced by the signs were already of significant age, surely we would have heard something about him by now."

"I want to be part of any group that eventually goes to Judaea. If it is possible to find the child, then I want to see this wonder with my own eyes. The Rab-mag encourages me to do so."

Each of the men said something similar. However, emotionally Ekur-zakir was moved as he thought to himself, "I would really like to go, but I still hesitate, and I know why. I perceive that this journey risks to cost me dearly."

A week after the conjunction, toward mid-morning, Nikolaos and Hormizdah made their preparations to return to Ctesiphon to see the Rab-mag. The men were in the courtyard of Ekur-zakir's home getting their baggage ready while some servants were saddling their horses. Ekur-zakir was there as well. Just before the men mounted their horses to leave, Shukura, a good friend of Ekur-zakir came through the gate. He was out of breath, he had been walking hurriedly, which is something he would normally not do.

Seeing Ekur-zakir from ten yards away, Shukura spoke, "I have just heard some unexpected news in the marketplace. Phraates IV, who has reigned over the Parthian Empire for 36 years, is dead. Musa and her son Phraataces are the new rulers in Ctesiphon."

Hearing the news, Ekur-zakir, Nikolaos, and Hormizdah looked at each other with a bit of disbelief. For most of their adult lives, Phraates had been on the throne. It was hard to believe that he was no longer alive, exerting his authority as usual. Things could be very different with Phraataces and Musa in power.

Nikolaos said to Ekur-zakir, "I suspect there will be some substantial changes in the court. Hopefully, our project will be maintained. The Rab-mag's position is probably safe. He has cultivated good relations with the queen and the crown prince. Anyway, we will keep you informed about events in the court. Musa and Phraataces will probably leave Ctesiphon as soon as possible to go to Ecbatana and Rhagae for the summer. It is much cooler up there on the high plateau."

In a few more moments, Nikolaos and Hormizdah were on their mounts. Nikolaos looked down at Ekur-zakir saying, "I really want to go on this adventure to Judaea. We will stay in touch. I will make every effort to be ready for a date near the beginning of the month of Tašrītu."[25]

Hormizdah indicated the same and the two men turned their horses toward the gate.

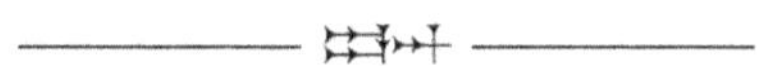

Phraates' death came swiftly, as soon as the queen and her son felt confident to act. The queen introduced one of her guards into the king's bedroom with orders to kill the aging monarch. The deed was done, and as the guard exited the palace with his pay, and three men jumped on him in the darkness about 200 yards from the palace. They put the guard to death and pocketed his salary.

No one ever really knew who had killed the king. But there were suspicions that the two remaining royals had acted for their own advantage.[26]

Within days, a joint coronation ceremony was performed for the queen and her son.[27] Many of the Parthian nobles were already in Ctesiphon to consult with the king about some military matters. Therefore it was not necessary to wait very long for the coronation. About a week after the ceremony, Musa and her son left for the high plateau of Media. Niko-

---

25 The month of Tašrītu/Tishrei (September/October) began toward the beginning of October in 2 BC.

26   No one knows the actual circumstances of the death of Phraates IV, however it seems certain that he was assassinated (Josephus, *Antiquities of the Jews*, 18.39-52). Coins indicate that Phraataces and Musa were certainly reigning from July 2 BC onward. A couple of coins exist which suggest that Phraataces was perhaps even emperor as early as December 3 BC. However, the month names are not clearly marked on the coins. The author has decided to leave the assassination of Phraates IV at this date in order to illustrate how the June 17, 2 BC conjunction would have been interpreted by Babylonian astronomers under normal circumstances.

27 Queen Musa and her son Phraataces reigned together. It seems that they also formed an incestuous couple (Josephus, see the note above). The Parthian nobles were not pleased with their reign, and the couple was overthrown and apparently put to death in AD 4. The details concerning their end are not known.

laos and Hormizdah arrived days before the court's departure. The Rab-mag was delighted to hear that the Borsippian astronomers were ready to embark on the adventure. He left with the royal entourage along with Hormizdah and Nikolaos. They would spend three months in Ecbatana and Rhagae.

Month III - Simānu / Sivan - Day 24   Friday evening June 26, 2 BC

Inspired by his experience in Babylon during the conjunction and their discussions with Nikolaos and Hormizdah in Borsippa, Ekur-zakir was interested in the possibility of a great adventure. However, before reaching a firm decision, Ekur-zakir had wanted to speak to his wife, Ispubarza,[28] but he had hesitated. She was only one year younger than he. They had now been married for forty years. While she was still very attractive in her old age she had lost much of her very remarkable youthful beauty. Her dark black hair was now mostly gray. Her eyes and eyelashes, which had melted Ekur-zakir's heart in years past were no longer very evident, except if one looked closely. Even so, life was still deep within her eyes. She had a keen perception and deep understanding in her relations with others.

After supper a few days following the departure of Nikolaos and Hormizdah, Ekur-zakir broached the subject with his wife of him possibly going to Judaea to find the messianic king.

"Ispubarza, my lovely wife, I want to tell you about my thoughts in the days following my short trip to Babylon. You have already heard me describe the star from time to time. We witnessed seeing the union of MUL.BABBAR and Dilbat several nights ago. You saw it as well because I informed you in advance.

Ispubarza said, "Yes, I am glad you told me. As I already said, I watched a few nights before and after the conjunction. It was very interesting to see the two planets come together as one single star."

---

28 Ispubarza was the name of a Parthian Queen in the Seleucid Era year 234 (78/77 BC). This name was chosen for the wife of Ekur-zakir because it is an original name from the period (The queen's name is mentioned in the *Astronomical Diaries*). The author is not sure about the name's origins or etymology.

The Ekur-zakir continued, "However, I did not mention to you a project which has been proposed by the Rab-mag. As I have also mentioned to you, we have come to the conclusion that the star is related to the Jewish Messiah, whom the Jews believe is destined to reign over the world."

Sensing already that something consequential for her and their couple was going to be discussed, Ispubarza responded, "What do you want to tell me Ekur-zakir? I am open to anything which you want to say to me."

Ekur-zakir summoned his courage and said, "You know that this series of heavenly signs concern a royal figure. We astronomers here in Borsippa are more or less convinced that the signs indicate the birth of a Jewish royal leader. We informed the Rab-mag in Ctesiphon about all this, even though we did not speak to other Babylonian astronomers. We think that they would not want to believe us anyway."

"Nikolaos and Hormizdah brought a message from the Rab-mag. It really surprised me. The Rab-mag would like for some of us to attempt to find the young king in Judaea. We think that this Messiah has been born in the land of Israel. In recent days we have been in the process of determining whether or not some of us should go. It seems that Illis-ku-tul, Iqisa, and Suen-magir will certainly be involved as well as Eliab the Jewish scribe. He has been invited to go for three reasons: 1) because he knows the Jewish religion better than any of us. 2) He has been involved in giving us understanding concerning the Messiah and various Jewish prophecies. And 3) He has already made the trip to Judaea. He knows more about what to expect than all of us who are from Borsippa. In addition, Nikolaos will probably also make the trip along with Hormizdah."

Ispubarza interrupted Ekur-zakir, "So what are you going to tell me, my husband? Do you want to make this journey as well?"

Ekur-zakir simply nodded to indicate that he wanted to make the journey to Judaea.

After a few moments, Ispubarza continued, "I think I understand your heart. These celestial events involving the star are surprising and well beyond anything which you have experienced before. Therefore you want to see with your own eyes if this amazing Jewish king exists? Am I right my husband?"

Ekur-zakir responded, "Yes, my lovely wife, you have understood."

But Ispubarza continued, "However, there are some other things which you have still not told me. The trip is dangerous, and you are not so young. Do you need to tell me that you may not come back? My love, I think you also want to tell me this, am I right?"

Ekur-zakir hesitated a moment and then replied, "Yes, my dear. If I go, it is possible that I will not return, because of the dangers and my age. You may spend many years without me. The thought of this grieves me very much. Even the idea that by going to Judaea I may not see you again is difficult for me to conceive. And yet, I am having more and more the desire to go to Judaea with the group to find the messianic king. I cannot deny that I am strongly drawn to the prospect of seeing this prophesied king."

Ispubarza smiled, "I do not want you to be concerned Ekur-zakir. You are my husband. I have loved you for a long time. You have respected me, you have given me five wonderful children and many grandchildren. I understand your heart. Looking at you now, I can see the light of adventure in your eyes. Indeed, I can think of no greater quest than to find this young king. I have been inspired as you have told me about this series of signs during the last many months."

She looked at him tenderly, reached out her hand, while taking his saying, "I cannot refuse you the possibility of going to Judaea. It is a once in a lifetime opportunity."

Ekur-zakir replied, "So you are willing for me to make the journey, even knowing that physically I may not be able to accomplish the entire trip?"

"Yes, my husband. It seems to me that you will always regret not going or at least wonder what might have been if I retain you here. Please know that I love you dearly. That is why I want to release you to go. Perhaps this is your destiny, to be part of the group which meets the messianic king. Your curiosity has been aroused. My greatest desire is that you would end your days as a man who experienced life to the maximum. I believe such a trip would be good for you, even if you are not able to return."

Ekur-zakir responded, "Ispubarza, I know that our children will be more than gracious with you, if I never return. My heart is certainly torn. I do want to make this journey. This series of signs is like nothing I have seen before. I am coming to think that our gods really are no gods at all in comparison with the wisdom and power of the Jewish God. I know that Iqisa thinks the same as I. My other colleagues have similar thoughts. I doubt if such a prolonged series of royal celestial events has never been seen by any other astronomers in the entire history of the world."

"I do sense that I very well may not return, and this grieves me, but I am greatly drawn to the adventure, I want to be there when the child is found. I do not yet know how we may find the child, but I do desire to see him," said Ekur-zakir.

Ispubarza then came even closer to her seated husband. Standing in front of him, her hands touched both sides of his face as he looked upward at her.

She said, "Do not worry my darling. I want you to go. I also want to hear of your success. Even if you do not return, I believe that Iqisa certainly will. Our lives may end even before the morning light. There is very little which we can control. I cannot retain you forever, either here or in a foreign land. I release you. Make plans and go. Otherwise, I will regret trying to retain you. However, I will cherish your last kiss."

At that point, Ispubarza, kissed Ekur-zakir on the cheek. After an instant, he held her in his arms.

MUL.BABBAR Sets in the West

Month IV - Du'ūzu / Tammuz - Day 27   July 28, 2 BC

In the days following the joining of MUL.ABBAR with Dilbat, the two planets separated and MUL.BABBAR continued to move lower and lower in the evening sky. Forty-one days after the great conjunction, MUL.BABBAR disappeared into the solar glare. Several days later Dilbat (Venus/Nogah) also disappeared in the western solar glare.

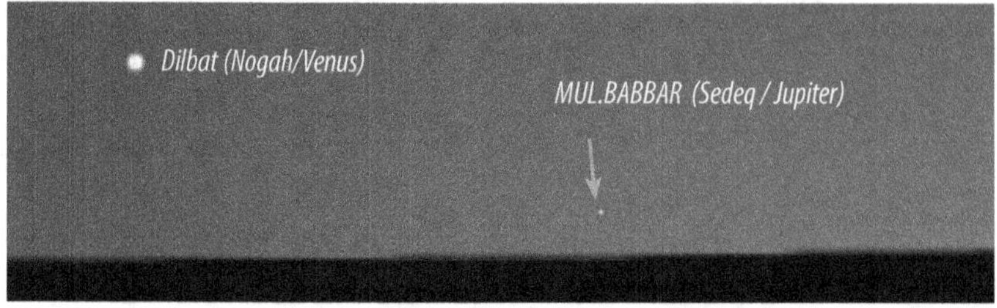

Illustration: This image shows what the Magi could have seen in the early evening on July 28, 2 BC.

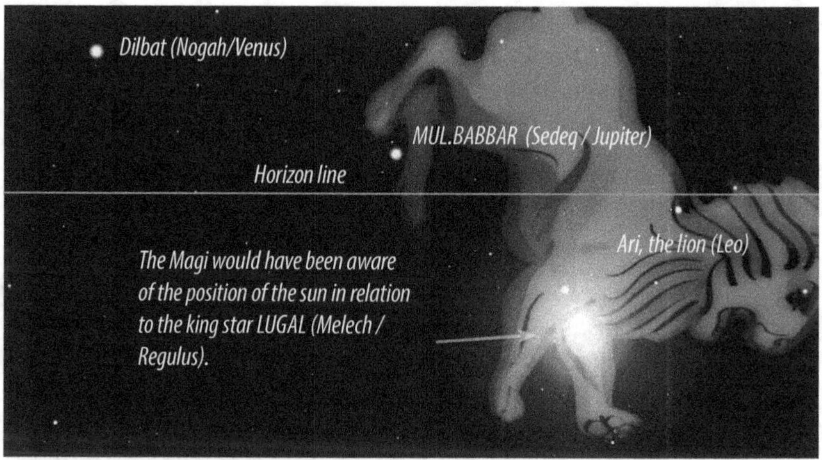

Illustration: Below the horizon out of sight in the early evening on July 28, 2 BC.

MUL.BABBAR disappeared into the solar glare at the same time when the Sun was in conjunction with the king star LUGAL (Regulus /Melech). The planet's setting was noted in the records of the Borsippa astronomical team. It had not escaped notice among the astronomers in Borsippa, Babylon, Uruk or Ctesiphon that several events centered on kingship had happened at the precise moments of MUL.BABBAR's planetary phases. But only the astronomers in Borsippa saw the symbolic event concerning MUL.BABBAR's second stationary phase. In addition, only the Borsippians understood the messianic Jewish nature of the signs.

MUL.BABBAR Rises in the East

Month V - Abu / Av - Day 28   August 29, 2 BC

Thirty-one days after its setting, MUL.BABBAR again became visible in the morning sky. Several days before, Dilbat had again become visible. On the day of MUL.BABBAR's appearing Ekur-zakir, Iqisa, Illis-kutul, and Suen-magir were all together at the ziggurat observatory. Each of them saw that Dilbat and MUL.BABBAR become visible on the eastern horizon within moments of each other. It was remarkable to see the two "stars" appear almost at the same time.

From a Jewish perspective, one could again think of a "bright and righteousness" event involving the king planet based on the meaning of the Jewish names of the two planets. The men also noticed that the other visible planets excepting GENNA (Saturn / Shabbatai) were near MUL.BABBAR in the solar glare. The invisible sun and moon were both there as well. The men estimated that such a close gathering of so many of the celestial objects had not happened for many years. At least no one could remember such a generalized gathering of this type. Then during the days that followed MUL.BABBAR rose higher and higher in the eastern sky.

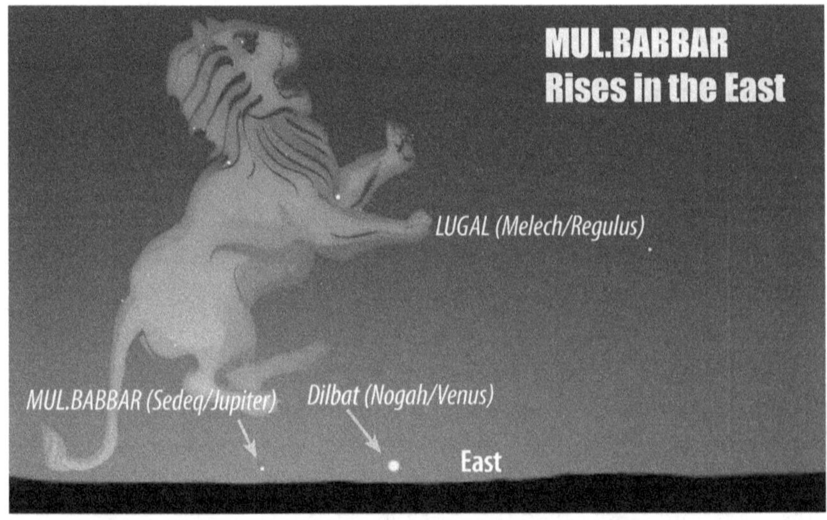

Illustration: The rising of MUL.BABBAR on August 29, 2 BC.

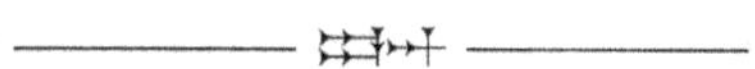

In the weeks preceding MUL.BABBAR's morning rising, and afterward, Sarpanit spoke to her husband, Illis-kutul, repeatedly about inviting Suen-magir for a meal. She said that she wanted to give encouragement to Suen-magir because he had changed or was in the process of changing his lifestyle, and she wanted to be supportive of his efforts. So Suen-magir was invited to eat with the family three times during the summer.

It was only toward the end of their third meal together that Illis-kutul finally more fully understood Sarpanit's profound interest in Suen-magir's well-being. While they were eating a delicacy that Kallisto had prepared, Illis-kutul saw that his daughter's lively eyes were attempting to look at Suen-magir at every opportunity. At various moments, during the evening's good conversation and abundant laughter, Kallisto's eyes seemed to be deeply centered on Suen-magir's face. Then, as Illis-kutul also looked at Suen-magir, he realized that the young man was making every effort to say kind words to Kallisto.

Illis-kutul thought privately almost with a chuckle, "It seems that the women of the household may have been preparing more than food while they spend time together in the kitchen."

The discussion became more serious when Sarpanit mentioned the projected trip to Judaea. The decision had been taken just days before that the trip would certainly take place. Both Suen-magir and Illis-kutul tried to reassure the women that everything would be done concerning their personal safety. They also encouraged the women to think of the great adventure, more than the possible perils.

As the conversation about the projected journey died down, Kallisto said, "We will miss you Suen-magir when you all leave to go to Judaea." But for Illis-kutul, there was something in the tone of her voice which actually said, "I will miss you."

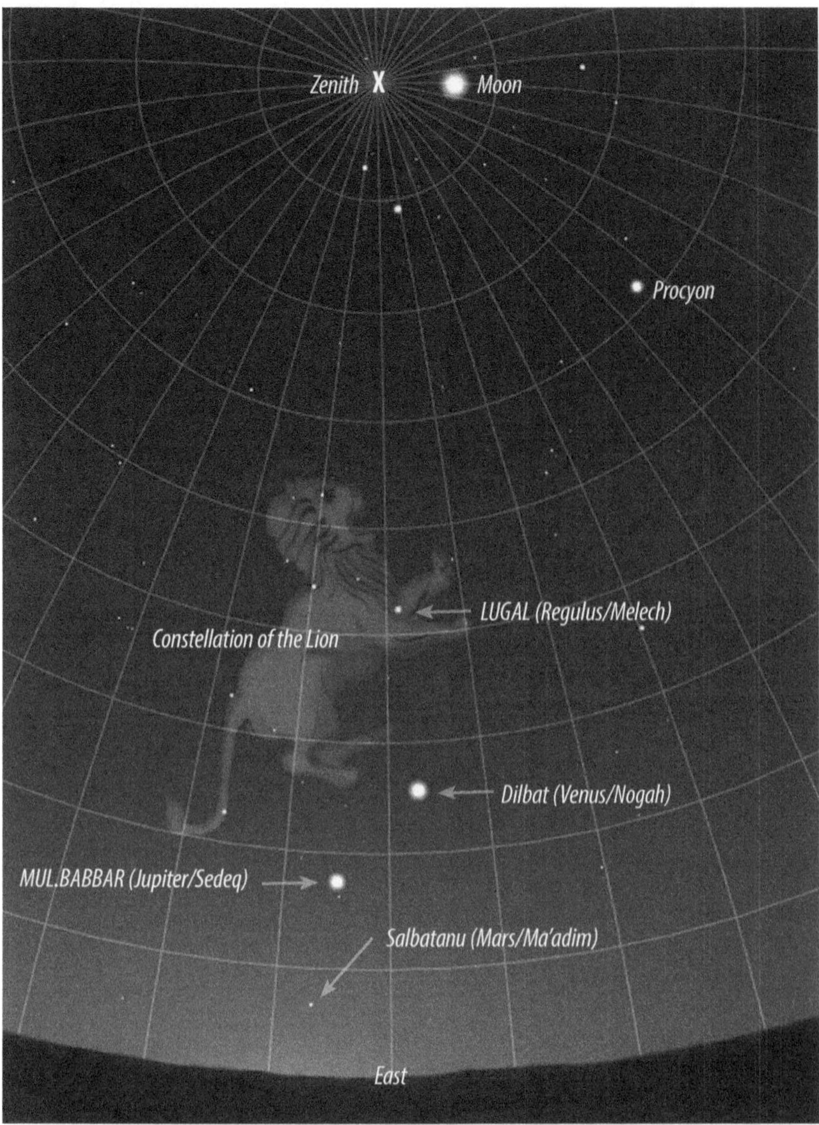

Illustration: The early morning sky in the east and toward the zenith on September 20, 2 BC. After its rising MUL.BABBAR (Jupiter/Sedeq) had changed positions. Three weeks after the heliacal rising of the planet, it was much higher in the morning sky as the sun began to rise. Dilbat (Venus/Nogah) had moved even higher, and Salbatanu (Mars/Ma'adim) had also appeared.

Part 4: The Star in the West

But as for you, Bethlehem Ephrathah, too little to be among the clans of Judah, from you One will go forth for Me to be ruler in Israel.

His goings forth are from long ago, from the days of eternity."

Therefore He will give them up until the time when she who is in labor has borne a child.

Then the remainder of His brethren will return to the sons of Israel.

And He will arise and shepherd His flock. In the strength of the LORD, in the majesty of the name of the LORD His God.

And they will remain, because at that time He will be great to the ends of the earth. This One will be our peace.

(Micah 5:2-5a)

9

The Journey to Judaea

Fall 2 BC

Chapter Contents:

The Journey to Judaea

Borsippa - Preparations

Year 310 of the Seleucid Era - Year 246 of the Arsacid Era

After the decision was taken to make the journey, it took several days to establish specifically who would make the trip and who would stay in Babylonia. Finally, it was decided that all the principal astronomers in Borsippa would make the journey. The travel preparations took some time. Servants and competent armed guards were chosen. Alexis, a man who had served Ekur-zakir for many years, was selected to oversee the servants and handle the logistical side of the journey. He, in turn, chose six capable servants to take care of the daily needs of the group.

The Greek astronomer Nikolaos had heard of a man with a Greek background who had been a soldier with a good reputation. This man, named Callisthenes, lived in Seleucia on the Tigris. On Nikolaos' recommendation, Ekur-zakir invited Callisthenes to come for a visit, and they thoroughly discussed the journey to Judaea. Ekur-zakir was satisfied with Callisthenes' abilities and asked the former soldier to be in charge of their security. He was to select eight other guards to form a team. All the men were expected to be expert archers who could also wield a sword.

Altogether the group was to be 23 men, including six magi, Eliab, nine guards, and seven servants. Of the servants, three had significant fighting abilities as well. Therefore just over half of the group was armed. Everyone would be on horseback, including the servants, while ten camels [1] were to carry baggage and several tents. It was planned that the group would travel up to about 25 miles per day, with at least one day of rest every six to seven days. Since most of the group did not have the habit of traveling very far, it was decided that sometimes they might need to halt for two or three days before continuing to their next major destination.

In preparation for the trip, Ekur-zakir and the astronomical team officially appointed their assistants Sakkut-tajjar and Anu-Belsunu as associate astronomers, a rank a bit higher than their astronomical assistant status. The two men were to be in charge of the observatory and the archives during the absence of the others. Ekur-zakir relinquished his role as priest of Nabu to Anu-Belsunu. Already for several months, Anu-Belsunu had been replacing Ekur-zakir and others for various aspects of the regular sacrificial offerings. Since the funding for the cultic activities was minimal, significant sacrifices were only offered once a month. Ekur-zakir also hired some additional help in the notary office to tide things over until he and the others could return. With these preparations having been made, the men could leave Borsippa knowing that their principal source of livelihood would be sustained in their absence.

Over a period of days, the men all said good-bye to their families. However, they did not make a great public show of their departure. In general, they did not inform their extended families or too many friends about their projected absence that could last up to six months. They all agreed that the reasons for their journey would not make much sense to most of their entourage. It was simply pointless to try to explain everything concerning the celestial signs and the proposed quest.

Alexis and some servants established a type of base camp three miles northwest of Borsippa at a large plantation belonging to one of Ekur-zakir's clients. There, the men and material could be assembled in preparation for their departure. The group wanted to do everything without attracting too much attention.

Finally, Hormizdah and Nikolaos arrived at Borsippa two days before the beginning of the journey. They brought a small fortune of gold and silver donated by the Rab-mag which was to finance the group's travels.

---

1 Dromedaries.

In addition, Larvandad supplied them with gifts befitting a king, including a small highly decorated carved wooden box filled with gold coins. Through their priestly connections, the astronomers as a group were able to obtain some myrrh and frankincense at a reasonable price. These gifts were put in two other small boxes.

After sunset on the evening of the 20th of Tašrītu, the astronomers and Eliab bid farewell to their families, knowing that they would rise well before dawn to leave for the journey. Although their excitement was palpable, most of the men had a good night's sleep. Ispubarza rose with Ekur-zakir well before dawn and ate breakfast with him. A servant who would be traveling with Ekur-zakir had prepared their two horses and was waiting in a side courtyard when Ekur-zakir emerged from the house along with his wife. Above them, the last stars were disappearing in the growing light.

Ispubarza, looked deeply into Ekur-zakir's eyes and kissed him. They were both deeply moved. Ispubarza herself now felt that this would probably be the last time Ekur-zakir would be with her. She embraced him with all her might while the couple lingered on the doorstep for several minutes. Finally, after those tender moments, they separated, and Ekur-zakir turned toward the servant and the waiting horses.

Looking up, Ekur-zakir noticed that the moon was shining relatively near to LUGAL in mid-heaven.[2] He could not help but remember the all the incidents involving the moon and the king star during the previous months. It almost seemed symbolic that the two celestial objects were together when the great journey was beginning. MUL.BABBAR and Dilbat[3] were also visible in the east in the constellation AB.SIN.[4] Dilbat was

---

2 LUGAL = Regulus.

3 Jupiter and Venus (Sedeq and Nogah in Hebrew).

4 The name means the "furrow / the barley stalk." The constellation and its chief star Spica (the "bright star of ABSIN" in Babylonian terms) were associated with the planting of winter wheat and barley in the fall months. At the end of the first millennium BC, Spica made its heliacal rising in early October. At present, the constellation is known as the constellation Virgo, but the Babylonian constellation was very different from the western Greek one.

slowly moving toward the horizon each day, while MUL.BABBAR rose higher and higher in the night sky. MUL.BABBAR had given its message, no one was expecting any other symbolic announcements from the star.

Moving away from his wife with great gentleness, Ekur-zakir mounted his horse and approached the gate with his servant. Then, looking around back toward Ispubarza, he waved. She waved back with tears rolling down her face. She felt weak with emotion, but inwardly she was glad. Her husband was embarking on an adventure of a lifetime.

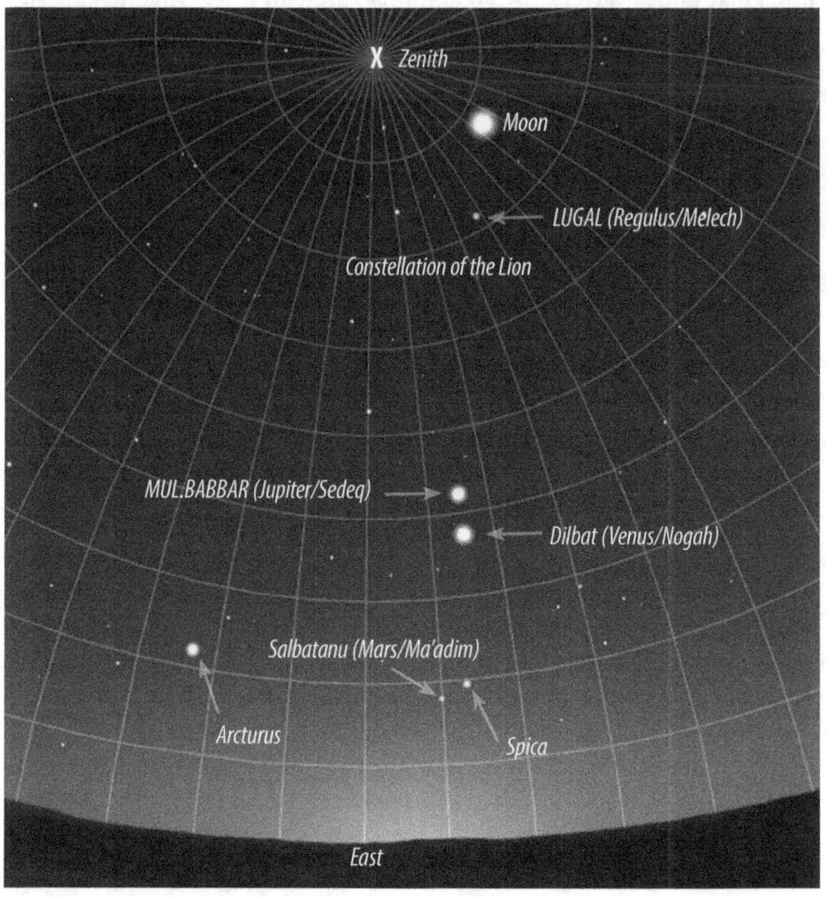

Illustration: The sky toward the east and above. (Tašrītu / Tishrei - Day 20) Morning - Oct. 20, 2 BC

Borsippa - The Journey Begins

Month VII - Tašrītu / Tishrei - Day 20 — Morning - Oct. 20, 2 BC

In the early morning hours, either in small groups or individually, each man made his way to the rendezvous point. The plantation owner and some servants welcomed them all. The very last arrangements were made, and the astronomers, servants, and guards again mounted their horses for their departure. Ekur-zakir's plantation owner friend and a group of at least 20 servants bid them a pleasant journey. Enthusiasm and excitement filled the entire group. While Nikolaos and Hormizdah were well-traveled, Several of the men had never been more than 250 miles away from their homes.

It was already about two hours after sunrise when the expedition finally began. The wind was blowing from the north, but a glorious blue sky stood overhead. Just after noon, they arrived within sight at the largely ruined city of Babylon which was located to their right toward the east. The Borsippian astronomers had decided months before not to stop in Babylon during the journey. Their fellow astronomers would not understand their quest, and they would not be in agreement with their reasoning. It was useless to even think of trying. Perhaps after the journey to Judaea things would be different.

Instead of stopping at the city, several weeks before Alexis had been dispatched to arrange housing for the astronomers at a large estate about five miles north of Babylon, on the east side of the Euphrates. The last hours of daylight on their first day were dominated by a somewhat tricky ferry ride across the great river. Three large boats had to make three crossings each to get the entire group onto the east bank. As the first stars began to appear in the evening sky, they all arrived at the villa where the astronomers would spend the first night.

Ekur-zakir knew the owner of the estate well, and he was happy to host the team for a night. The soldiers and servants spent their first night in tents, but the astronomers were housed in the owner's vast villa. The next morning, the caravan was able to leave relatively early although over breakfast their host insisted that his scholar guests tell him more about their projected journey. On the first day of travel, the expedition only managed to move 17 miles.

On the second day, the company managed to advance 22 miles and the following day the group did 26 miles. They proceeded through the fields and date plantations relatively close to the Euphrates while avoiding wide meanders in the river. In most places, the wise men including Eliab stayed in local inns or some type of arranged housing. The soldiers and servants often slept in tents, while continuously surveying the animals and most of the baggage. The weather was still warm, but occasionally there were some rain showers as the group advanced up the Euphrates valley. Happily, the expedition only had to stop one day because of rain.

During the first weeks of the journey, almost everywhere farmers were tilling their ground in preparation for the planting of winter barley and wheat. In the second week, as the men advanced, the farms along the Euphrates became more sparse. The desert to the east and north sometimes seemed to draw very close to the river on both banks. However, there was still a band of green stretching away from the river about a mile or so in most places.

After two weeks, the group finally arrived facing the city of Dura Europus [5] situated on the west side of the Euphrates River. The city had been founded by Greeks who had arrived in Mesopotamia following Alexander the Great's conquest of the Persian Empire. The expedition could have crossed the Euphrates a few days before and struck out directly across the desert, but the Magi preferred to profit from the good accommodations at Dura Europos before they began their journey through the Syrian desert. They were not used to the stresses and difficulties of traveling over long distances. Their next destination, the city of Tadmur, was at least six to seven days of travel beyond them across the Syrian desert.

---

5 The ruins of this city became a major archaeological site in the 20th century AD, until it was destroyed by Islamic State pillaging and bulldozing from 2014 to 2017.

Dura Europos

Month VIII - Arahsamna / Marcheshvan - Day 9 — Nov. 9, 2 BC

The group stayed three days in Dura Europos before exiting the city and entering into the vast sandy and rocky Syrian desert early in the morning of the 9th of the month of Arahsamna. Two guides joined the expedition for the trip to Tadmur.

Most of the men had spent a bit of time in the desert on the western side of the Euphrates near Borsippa. However, few of them had ever gone very far from the relatively well-watered areas along the two great rivers and canals of Mesopotamia. About a mile and a half out of Dura Europos, when the city was almost out of sight, Ekur-zakir turned his horse and looked back. He realized at that point how deeply they were now engaged in the adventure. During the next week, before they reached Tadmur, there would be little comfort. Ekur-zakir and most of the others did not relish the thought of sleeping in tents for almost a week or possibly longer depending on the weather. However, Ekur-zakir was determined to go to Judaea. After one last look he pulled the reins of his horse in order to turn back toward the west.

He thought to himself, "One hardly does anything without hardship. Be courageous, Ekur-zakir. Six days in the desert will not completely sap all of your strength."

But then he thought, "After Tadmur there are at least six to eight days of hard travel to Damascus. This may be a more difficult trip than I have imagined."

On the third day out from Dura Europos, the group encountered an intense sandstorm. In the morning, not long after the column had begun to move, a light wind rose up from the south. After a few hours, the wind had become strong and sand was starting to cloud the air. Within three hours, they were not able to make any further progress, and one could not see more than 30 or 40 paces.

The guides encouraged everyone to dismount. The horses were all roped together so they would not wander off. The men then unloaded the camels and everyone tried to take some shelter beside the pile of baggage and a few parts of two tents which the men held firmly with ropes and their bare hands. Yet it was impossible to set up any tents because of the forceful sand-laden southern wind.

Toward the middle of the night, the storm ceased, and by dawn, the stars were shining brightly again. Happily, the men were all able to sleep for four or five hours when the wind stopped blowing. In the early morning sky, Dilbat (Venus) was visible near Spica and MUL.BABBAR (Jupiter) was almost in conjunction with a small star that was later called Zaniah [6] by the Arabs. At dawn, after having dusted off much of the baggage and themselves, the journey to Tadmur continued. Happily, the guides knew the area well, and they had no problem leading the men to several wells along the route where both the men and beasts could be refreshed.

After three more nights, before dawn on their seventh day in the desert, MUL.BABBAR passed within about a fourth of a lunar diameter from the star Zaniah in the eastern sky. MUL.BABBAR and Zaniah were still generally toward the east and south at dawn. However, MUL.BABBAR was rising very high in the night sky. As the sky brightened toward dawn, it was positioned well above the horizon, over halfway to the zenith.

Tadmur

Month VIII - Arahsamna / Marcheshvan - Day 15   Nov. 13, 2 BC

While advancing toward Tadmur, at about noon, the group of astronomers met dozens of Jews who were returning from the celebration of the Feast of Tabernacles in Jerusalem. They were traveling to Seleucia on the Tigris, Babylon, Borsippa and other towns and cities in Mesopotamia. Eliab asked the pilgrims about the festival, but most of them seemed to be in a hurry to cross the desert. They were not willing to be delayed. Throughout the afternoon, hundreds of pilgrims passed the group. During that day perhaps 1,500 men, women, and children of all ages moved on toward the east.

After many more miles under the sun's intense rays, toward sunset, one could finally see the independent city of Tadmur. The town was signaled by a broad band of green date palms far in the west. People in the

---

6 Eta Virginis, we do not know the ancient Babylonian, Aramaic, Roman or Jewish names for this star.

Mediterranean world had begun to call the city Palmyra based on the Greek name "palame" referring to the palm trees. The caravan entered the town just as darkness fell. Shortly afterward, the just past full moon rose in the east and flooded the city streets with light.

The horses seemed delighted to find water, abundant hay, and even some grain. Near the caravansary,[7] the whole group noticed the small temple dedicated to the god named Yarhibol, who was called the "lord of the spring."[8] One of the primary local water sources, the Efqa spring, was reputed to have Yarhibol's divine presence accompanying it.[9] The water was not salty, but it did have a sulfurous odor as it came out of the earth. After a short time, the smell disappeared, and the water was good to drink. There were also temples to Bel (Jupiter/Marduk) and other gods in the town.[10]

Tadmur was renowned for its hospitality, however, the hotels were small and filled with Jewish pilgrims, who had now arrived by the hundreds. Many of them were also camping on the edges of town. Several tent cities had sprung up in the previous two or three days as the pilgrims arrived from Judaea via Damascus. The people of Tadmur had made their preparations. The Magi marveled at the abundance of supplies which almost seemed to spring forth from every building in town.

The daily arrivals and departures of Jewish pilgrims in route for the Parthian domains were to continue for about two weeks. The people of Tadmur took special care of the flocks of pilgrims. Some of the travelers were shorn like sheep by their greedy hosts during their stay in the oasis. However, in general, the local population treated their guests well.

In addition, the city also specialized in certain vices. Suen-magir was tempted to visit the local brothels and find some strong drink after the harshness of the desert. It almost seemed like some of the local prosti-

---

7 Caravansary: An inn with a central courtyard for travelers in the desert regions.

8 Yarhibol is an Aramean god who was worshiped mainly in ancient Palmyra in central Syria. Yarhibol was depicted with a solar nimbus and styled "lord of the spring". He normally appears alongside Bel, who was a co-supreme god of Palmyra, and Aglibol, one of the other top Palmyrene gods.

9 Smith, Andrew M. Roman Palmyra: Identity, Community, and State Formation. (New York, NY: Oxford UP, 2013). p. 63.

10 It was only later that the famous temple of Bel was built. It was completed in AD 32 and destroyed by the Islamic State in 2015.

tutes had an insight into his soul. He could barely look in their direction without being tempted, and the girls could see his weakness easily. They tried their best to entice him, but Suen-magir stood his ground. His interior will was becoming stronger. He was not as ready to slide into the mental traps of self-pity and dissipation.

Suen-magir had seen marvels in the heavens during the last year. He was now convinced that his life could still have meaning. Without making his thoughts known to the others, he had even begun to ponder the possibilities of getting married again. He wondered if the God of Abraham, the one who had written such a clear message in the heavens, might not also have a new future in store for him personally.

The group of Magi was split in two because there was not enough room for all of the men in any one location. For a price, the local hotels were happy to provide whatever services they could.

Fortunately, there was enough water available so that all the men could get clean again. A full week of warm desert sunshine, a sandstorm, and the cold nights under the stars had made them all rather unpleasant to look at and terribly smelly. None of the men had changed clothes during the journey from Dura Europos. There really had not been any good reason to do so because within hours any fresh change of clothing would have been as sweaty and probably as dirty as the previous clothes.

The group rested for four days in Tadmur, being refreshed and allowing the horses and dromedaries to eat adequately. Alexis occupied himself with all the logistical details. He and the servants were busy for three days trying to clean clothing and equipment. But Ekur-zakir also tried to make sure that the servants and Alexis had enough rest. Callisthenes did his best to ensure the security of the men and their belongings.

Ekur-zakir and Eliab profited from the presence of the returning Jewish pilgrim to send messages back to Borsippa and also to the Rab-mag in Ctesiphon concerning the progress of the expedition.

Damascus

Month VIII - Arahsamna / Marcheshvan - Day 20   Nov. 18, 2 BC

The group began what would normally have been a six-day journey on to Damascus on the 20th day of Arahsamna. Already one month had passed since their departure from Borsippa. They traveled to the southwest beside the rocky Hayyal mountain chain. Toward the middle of the second day out of Tadmur, they passed three or four thousand Jewish pilgrims who were coming from Damascus and going in the opposite direction.

On the third day, the expedition entered the region of Syria under Roman control. The band passed the border with no problem. There were no soldiers or even any visible presence of Roman authority apart from a border monument in the form of a round stone column about five feet tall indicating the jurisdiction of the Roman authorities. On the face of the column toward the east, it was written in Greek and Aramaic, "Beyond this point the region is under the authority of the Emperor Augustus and the Senate and people of Rome." The symbolic letters SPQR (Senatus Populusque Romanus) were carved at the top of the column.

A few days journey from Damascus, the men were able to find some lodging in a small village, but the servants and soldiers slept in tents. During the night rain began to fall, lightly at first and then fairly heavily. This continued for two days. The local people were delighted with the rain, but the expedition could not proceed until the downpour ceased. With the rain, the temperatures fell significantly and several servants and some soldiers in the group fell ill.

On the morning of the third day, the skies cleared and by noon the group began to move toward Damascus again, but a number of the men remained sick. They passed through an increasing number of cultivated fields, and the land continually became greener with vegetation. After spending a night at a small spring where there were a few houses, the expedition finally arrived in Damascus.[11] It was decided that they would remain in the city for at least three days of rest since several had fallen

---

11 November 26, 2 BC

sick due to the colder weather. Ekur-zakir even sent two servants to see local doctors so that their health could improve before the next step of the journey.

Eliab and Iqisa encountered some people from the local Jewish community in the market, but they did not reveal anything about the reasons for their journey. Most people would have never dreamed why the men were traveling to Judaea. Not far from the market the men noticed that foundations were being prepared for a new temple. Asking some of the local residents, they were told that an extensive temple complex was being planned in honor of the god Jupiter. This would enlarge and replace the ancient Aramean temple of Hadad. Depending on funding, the temple complex would take several years to complete.[12]

Month IX - Kislimu / Kislev - Day 2   Sunday - Nov. 30, 2 BC

Although it had rained during the night, the sky was clear at daybreak of their fourth day in Damascus. Leaving the city and traveling toward the southwest, by evening the group had reached a low ridge where they intended to set up a camp for the night. To their right, they could see the majestic Mount Hermon freshly covered in snow. When they stopped, the sun was starting to set among some high clouds in the west. However, its beams sometimes brilliantly illuminated the snow on the summit. Everyone admired the view for several minutes before they descended a few dozen yards into a somewhat secluded hollow on the other side of the ridge.

Knowing that robbers sometimes followed travelers leaving large cities, Callisthenes discouraged the group from lighting any fires to avoid attracting too much attention. He posted two guards on the top of the ridge and one nearer the camp. He and the other six guards would take turns during the night relieving the sentries. During the second hour after dark, while the moon was still shining in the west, the sentries on the ridge perceived six men who appeared to be drawing near to the camp. However, the sentries on the ridge were able to alert Callisthenes in time.

---

12 The temple of Jupiter in Damascus was completed in about AD 14-15 or so.

Photo: Mount Hermon as seen from the Golan Heights.

Gathering his men, Callisthenes and the eight guards positioned themselves near the top of the hill with their bows and swords ready.

Finally, the robbers arrived near the top of the ridge. In the darkness only illuminated by the stars and the young moon in the west, Callisthenes suddenly spoke firmly, but calmly, "Halt, drop your weapons or die."

At the same moment, one of the archers released an arrow that arrived within a foot of the man in front. The intruders were taken aback by such unexpected and deadly hospitality. They were quickly disarmed, bound and gagged. Callisthenes made sure that the robbers were firmly tied to each other and also to a small, deeply rooted tree not far away. The robbers were placed not exceedingly far from the road, but they were still out of sight. Someone would probably find them in a day or two and release them. The robber's weapons were buried under a large rock in the hollow, and some leaves were scattered to hide the location.

The journey the next day was somewhat similar to the first. Mount Hermon dominated more and more the sky to the northwest. It was covered with snow even well toward its base. A cold wind from the direction of the mountain to the north motivated the men to keep moving. While they felt the penetrating cold, the lower parts of their bodies were warmed by the horses' flanks.

Toward the middle of the second day, another group of pilgrims resting beside the road informed everyone that they had reached the dominions of Herod, king of Judaea. The expedition had entered a region of lower Syria, which was called Gaulanitis.[13] The Emperor Augustus had put the area under Herod's authority about 20 years before. On the third day, the group reached and passed the line of old extinct volcanic hills which dominated the south of Mount Hermon and the region northeast of the Sea of Galilee.[14] After continuing several miles, they camped just beside a deep ravine, in a place which gave them a commanding view of the sea in the distance. The night was cold, and Ekur-zakir especially had trouble staying warm despite being well covered in a tent. The cold prevented several of the men from sleeping well.

Bethsaïda / Hippos

Month IX - Kislimu / Kislev - Day 6   Thursday - Dec. 3, 2 BC

On the morning of the fourth day out from Damascus, with the Sea of Galilee occasionally visible in the distance, the group descended from the plateau[15] down toward the Jordan river. By noon they were near the gates of the town of Bethsaida[16] beside the sea. Callisthenes, Alexis, and a few servants were dispatched to acquire some roasted fish and other provisions from the market in the port town. No one had any idea that this small port would soon be the birthplace of some Galilean fishermen who would become well-known across the entire world.[17] Without realizing it, the men from the expedition may have crossed paths with the parents of several future apostles in the market.

---

13   The name Gaulanitis has its origins from the town named Golan (Γαυλών; גּוֹלָן), which was apparently located about seventeen miles east of the Sea of Galilee near Sheikh Sa'd.

14   Including Mount Bental and Mount Avital

15   Golan Heights

16   The city would be renamed as Julias about thirty years after the Magi passed through the area by Philip the Tetrarch. Philip did this following the death of Livia (Julia), the Emperor Augustus' wife and adopted daughter. Livia received the name Julias and was legally adopted as Augustus' daughter through the emperor's will following his death in AD 14. Livia (Julia) became a goddess by decree in AD 42. It is possible that the New Testament only refers to the town as Bethsaïda because of the idolatry which came to be associated with the new name for the town, Julias. See Frederick M. Strickert, *Philip's City: From Bethsaida to Julias,* (Collegeville, MN: Liturgical, 2011), Chapter 12.

17   Philip, Andrew, Peter (See John 1:44 and 12:21). Bethsaïda was perhaps also home to James and John.

Just after passing Bethsaida, Ekur-zakir did not look well, and expressed some general weariness. He said that he needed a rest. The journey was taking its toll on him. Iqisa started to be a bit alarmed. His father was obviously ill. Taking his father aside, they discussed the situation. Finally, after also talking to Alexis, Callisthenes and their guide, Iqisa spoke to the whole group including the servants and guards.

"There is a town named Hippos not far away on a ridge to the south. It is near the lake, but quite high above it. The town is large enough to have proper quarters for us all. Going on to the large town, Scythopolis, will cause us to spend at least another night or possibly two outside. I would prefer to stop here for at least two or maybe even three days. Ekur-zakir needs a good period of quiet rest. If we stop at Hippos, there are fewer people. It may be more restful than Scythopolis. Perhaps we will only spend one night in Scythopolis. Do you have any objections to staying a few days in Hippos?"

Everyone agreed to stop in Hippos. They did not want to press Ekur-zakir too hard. He was the oldest man in the group, and his health was being affected by the constant movements and sleeping outside in tents. So the Magi's caravan left the lake shore and proceeded to climb the steep hill where Hippos was located. The road wound around to the back side of the town to the city gate which faced east.

At Hippos the magi were settled into some excellent quarters in the only caravansary in town. Their animals and equipment were well housed in facilities provided by the hotel owner. After a good night of sleep. Ekur-zakir began to recover his strength.

The next morning after breakfast,[18] Eliab went to the western edge of the city. A large square formed a sort of terrace. There the city itself was at practically the same height as the city wall since the hill fell away

---

18 December 4th.

sharply just below the ramparts. The view from the wall just beside the terrace was magnificent. The lake and the land facing it were just catching the first rays of sunlight through some holes in the clouds to the east. The waves on the waters far below sometimes seemed to sparkle reflecting the sun's light. Standing looking through a gap in the stones of the ramparts, Eliab realized that facing him across the lake was the region of the tribes of Zebulun and Naphtali.

Suddenly Eliab remembered words from a text he had memorized long ago. The words of the prophet Isaiah seemed to have new meaning there on the terrace facing the so-called "Galilee of the Gentiles" in the distance.

> *But there will be no more gloom for her who was in anguish; in earlier times He treated the land of Zebulun and the land of Naphtali with contempt, but later on He shall make it glorious, by the way of the sea, on the other side of Jordan, Galilee of the Gentiles. The people who walk in darkness will see a great light; Those who live in a dark land, the light will shine on them.[19]*

Eliab thought, "It is odd that these tribes are described as people who walk in darkness and that at some point they will see a great light. Why these people in particular?" Eliab began to remember more of the text.

> *You shall multiply the nation, You shall increase their gladness; They will be glad in Your presence as with the gladness of harvest, As men rejoice when they divide the spoil.[20] You shall break the yoke of their burden and the staff on their shoulders,*

These were promises for the nation. He seemed to forget some lines but as he searched his memory more of the text flooded back into his mind. Only then did Eliab finally remember the following verses. He stood fixed on the scene, and he began to say the phrases aloud. He found that he was greatly moved as the words flowed from his lips.

---

19 Isaiah 9:1-2.

20 Isaiah 9:3-4.

For a child will be born to us, a son will be given to us;
And the government will rest on His shoulders;
And His name will be called Wonderful Counselor, Mighty God,
Eternal Father, Prince of Peace.
There will be no end to the increase of His government or of peace,
On the throne of David and over his kingdom,
To establish it and to uphold it with justice and righteousness
From then on and forevermore.
The zeal of the LORD of hosts will accomplish this.[21]

There it was, a messianic prophecy. It seemed to Eliab that the great light mentioned in the earlier part of the text might very well be linked with the child. The realization almost moved him to tears.

He thought, "A great light, yes that is what he shall be. There will be none greater. He will establish his government of justice and righteousness."

The phrase, *"The zeal of the LORD of hosts will accomplish this..."* stayed in Eliab's thoughts for a few more moments. Apparently, God Himself was determined to bring this about. David had been a 'star' in his generation as Balaam had indicated in an ancient prophecy.[22] The Messiah would be a descendant of David, and a light for the peoples. Eliab rejoiced in thinking of a world transformed. It would become a world where everything good, right, and correct before God would be respected.

Month IX - Kislimu / Kislev - Days 7-8   Sat./ Sun. - Dec. 5-6, 2 BC

The following night, MUL.BABBAR (Sedeq/Jupiter) rose in the east just before the middle of the night and in the early morning Dilbat and Salbatanu[23] were drawing near to each other in the eastern sky. Later during the day, the blue sky disappeared behind thick clouds, and a downpour began. The rain continued the next day and part of the third.

---

21 Isaiah 9:6-7.

22 Numbers 24:17.

23 Venus and Mars.

This was an unexpected benefit of stopping in Hippos. Ekur-zakir could not have stood two nights under the rain with no warmth. However, he was responding well to the comfortable lodgings in Hippos. When the time came, he was ready to travel again. It was decided to leave Hippos, weather permitting, in the early morning on the day after the Sabbath. Eliab was pleased that the men had agreed to honor the Sabbath day, and the rain stopped during the night.

Month IX - Kislimu / Kislev - Day 9　　　　Monday - Dec. 7, 2 BC

The caravan was ready before dawn and left Hippos as the first light of day was becoming apparent in the east. They intended to reach Scythopolis by evening.[24] There were no plans to stop for more than brief moments before reaching the city. Having descended the steep road from Hippos with relative ease, by sunrise the group had already reached the road by the lakeshore and gone on beyond. By late morning, as they advanced with the sea to their right, they arrived at the Jordan River at the southern part of the lake. King Herod had built a usable bridge a half-mile, or so south of the lake, otherwise it might have been difficult to cross the river. It was swollen because of the rain in the preceding weeks. After crossing the river a guard and Alexis were dispatched to ride quickly to reserve some kind of accommodation for the night in Scythopolis. Finally, after a couple of brief halts, the caravan appeared at the northeastern gates of the town as darkness was beginning to fall.

---

24 About 40 kilometers / 25 miles

Scythopolis

Month IX - Kislimu / Kislev - Day 10   Tuesday morning - Dec. 8, 2 BC

The next morning, Ekur-zakir was doing well, so it was decided that one more night in the caravansary was not necessary. Iqisa was encouraged. His father was in better health. Even so, they were delayed in departing because Alexis needed to make some purchases in the city's extensive market. The weather was good although relatively cold. The caravan left Scythopolis by midmorning moving south toward Jericho, which they hoped to reach on the evening of the third day. Their plan meant that they would only spend two nights in a camp before reaching Jericho. As it turned out, they did find some lodging in a small hamlet on the way during the first night, which allowed them all to have a good night's sleep.

Photo: The present-day ruins of Scythopolis, modern Beït Shéan (Author's photo).

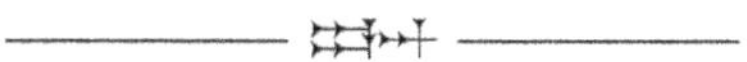

The next day toward noon, the group encountered a large caravan loaded with dates, which was moving north up the valley toward Scythopolis. Eliab struck up a lively conversation with some of the men in the caravan concerning his father's date plantation in Babylonia. A chief servant in the caravan named Ezikias took an interest in Eliab.

Ezikias said, "I am an overseer on a large date plantation about 10 miles to the south. My master, Phineas, would no doubt be hospitable toward you. The dates of Babylonia have a good reputation even here in the Jordan Valley. Even though we esteem that our dates are just as good, I know my master would enjoy making your acquaintance. Please make an effort to see him. You should reach his plantation about an hour before sunset. I will send one of my own servants back to inform my master of your arrival."

Later in the afternoon as the group passed through large date plantations, they arrived at Phineas' villa. Eliab presented himself to the plantation owner, who had some guests from Jerusalem and Egypt in his home. Phineas' father had moved to the Jordan Valley during the reign of Cleopatra. Her husband, Mark Antony, had required Herod the Great to cede some of the magnificent date plantations to the Egyptian queen almost 35 years previously. The owner's father had been sent to work as an administrator at one of the plantations. In time, he had been able to acquire a plantation for himself and had married a Jewish woman.

Phineas was delighted to be able to host such a group of magi. At first, he hoped that the men would possibly tell his horoscope based on his birthdate. He had already had this done in one of the temples of Sarapis near Memphis years ago.[25] However, Eliab explained that among the Babylonian astronomers there were differing opinions concerning horoscopes.[26] This group was not so oriented toward horoscopes. But more importantly, this group was going up to Jerusalem on a sort of pilgrimage and had other activities in mind.

---

25 James Evans, *The Astrologer's Apparatus: A Picture of Professional Practice in Greco-Roman Egypt*, Vol. 35, Part 1, No. 118, p. 1 - 44 (2004).

26 Strabo, Geography, 16, 5-6

When Phineas discovered that Ekur-zakir was suffering physically from the journey, he offered to host the older man in the main house, while the rest of the Magi had housing in a small annex. Meanwhile, the servants and guards in the group were permitted to establish a camp in an open area and to sleep in an adjoining farm building. The night was clear and calm, being dominated by the moon. It was a bit warmer in the area of Jericho than it had been in the region near Damascus, Hippos or Scythopolis.

Jericho

Month IX - Kislimu / Kislev - Day 14 — Thursday - Dec. 11, 2 BC

The next morning, the caravan left Phineas' plantation before noon to reach Jericho by the middle of the afternoon. As usual, one of the guards was dispatched with Alexis to ride ahead and to reserve accommodation in Jericho well before the arrival of the others. In the evening, everyone was installed in a comfortable inn in the center of Jericho. The date palm plantations spread out from the city in all directions. However, above the palms, increasingly the sky was becoming charged with clouds. Rain began to fall as the men entered the city. By the time they arrived at the caravansary, they were all starting to get a bit wet, but they soon found shelter.

Month IX - Kislimu / Kislev - Days 14-15 — Friday / Sat. - Dec. 12/13, 2 BC

Since the rain continued to fall, there was no choice but just to stay in Jericho for another entire day. In the evening the Sabbath began. The next day Eliab went to the main synagogue in Jericho. The service included Bible readings and a little singing. Eliab did not particularly find it uplifting, but the word of God was proclaimed.

Eliab was leaving the building under a covered gallery with arches when he overheard two men speaking near the entrance of the synagogue. They were talking about King Herod. Eliab had already heard several weeks before that the crown prince was in prison because of an attempted assassination plot.

But the men continued to speak, saying, "Yes, one of my friends in the palace told me that the king is in bad health. He has been greatly disturbed by being betrayed by his son. It has made him physically sick."

Eliab tried to linger for another moment to hear more, but several other people came out of the synagogue and interrupted the conversation. Afterward, walking back to the caravansary in the softly falling rain, Eliab thought about their situation.

He said to himself, "We are arriving in Jerusalem seeking a newly born king at the moment when the king has been betrayed by his son and heir. In what kind of position does that put us? There is political turmoil. The king may feel greatly threatened. We are bringing news about a newborn king, which may not be welcome." These thoughts continued as he arrived at the caravansary.

The next day it rained heavily, so traveling further was forbidden, but during the late afternoon, the rain ceased. In the evening, the skies cleared and the stars began to shine.

Month IX - Kislimu / Kislev - Day 17   Monday - Dec. 15, 2 BC

The decision to go on to Jerusalem had been made the night before, so the caravan left Jericho early in the morning. Much of the road was very muddy, and the servants and the baggage animals sometimes had some difficulties as they went up the road beside the large creek in what would later be called the Wadi Qelt. The caravan went along the creek for a considerable distance. Finally, the men arrived at a small hamlet and found lodging for the night in an inn for travelers.[27] At the end of the first day, they were only half a morning's journey east of Jerusalem. They had already ascended a couple of thousand feet above the plain of Jericho.

---

27 This was in the general area of modern Ma'ale Adumim. Jericho is about 250 meters below sea level and Jerusalem is at about 750 meters above sea level. There is 1,000 meters of difference (over 3,000 feet).

Arrival in Jerusalem

Month IX - Kislimu / Kislev - Day 18　　　　Tuesday - Dec, 16, 2 BC

Everyone was up early the next day, well before dawn. The sky was clear, Sihtu, Salbatanu, and Dilbat [28] were shining in the morning sky. MUL.BABBAR (Jupiter) was overhead not far from the waning moon. The men were particularly excited because within another four to five hours they would be entering Jerusalem.

After breakfast, the caravan continued as before with three guards in front including Callisthenes. They were followed by the wise men, Eliab, and the servants. Five other guards closed the column as they advanced, climbing slowly on the road toward Jerusalem. Alexis and one of the other guards had gone on ahead to the city very early to secure lodging for the coming night for the entire group. Three hours later, the column of men, horses, and dromedaries came to its goal.

When the group reached the lower portion of Bethphage, Eliab had shouted out to everyone that they would soon see Jerusalem. Rounding the southern flank of the Mount of Olives their excitement grew. First, they could see the lower city of Jerusalem to the south toward the Hinnon Valley. Above that was the upper city which dominated all the rest. It contained Herod's palace which was visible behind some massive fortifications. Then as they rounded a bit more of the hill, the temple became visible in the foreground. It was dazzling in the sunshine. The front of the building was partly covered with gold metal plates and gold leaf causing the entire front of the structure to reflect the sun's rays.

After advancing about 150 feet further up the road, Callisthenes stopped the column so that everyone could behold the sight. On the right, north of the temple, the massive Antonia fortress offered a backdrop. Toward the horizon, behind the temple, Herod's great fortified towers named Phasael, Hippicus, and Marianne near the king's palace watched over the access to the city from the west. Each tower was from about 110 to 145 feet tall. To the left and below the lower city with its multitudes of poor was spread out before them.

---

28 Mercury, Mars, and Venus.

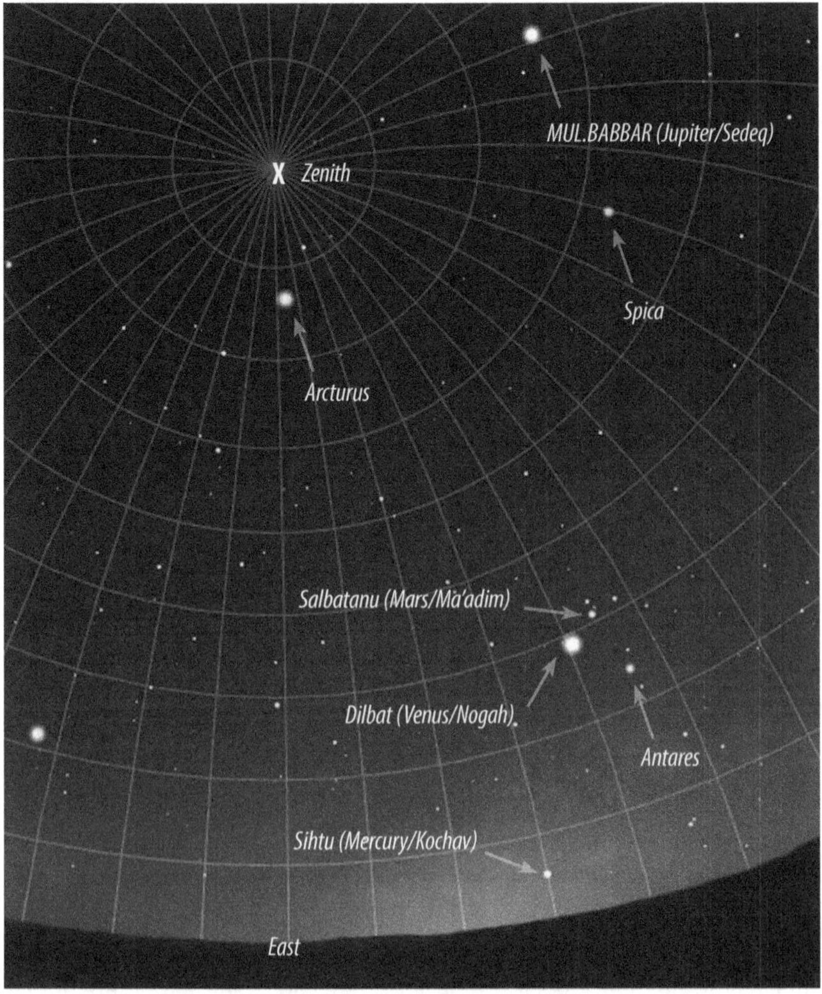

Illustration: The sky toward the east and above. Dec.16, 2 BC.
MUL.BABBAR was much higher in the sky at dawn than most of the fall.

Ekur-zakir spoke up saying, "This is truly a great city and what a glorious temple. I am impressed. We have some great temples in the ruins of Babylon, Seleucia on the Tigris and elsewhere in Babylonia, but none of them are partially covered with gold plates or gold leaf. This is amazing, it is dazzling how the gold reflects the sunlight. You will notice as well that it is all in cut stone, there are no baked mud bricks here!"

Suen-magir chimed in, "Seeing how the reflection of sunlight from the temple is so impressive, I wonder how the front of the temple reflects the light of the moon. That might be really interesting to see as well."

Eliab said, "King Herod rebuilt, enlarged and embellished the temple building a bit less than 20 years ago. My father, Ariel, has only seen the temple from the time before Herod's rebuilding project. But now I have seen the new temple twice in three years."

Homizdah kept his thoughts to himself, he did not want to express his emotions too freely. He was still struggling with his attachments to the Zoroastrian religion and culture. But he marveled at the majesty of the temple building and found himself to be very moved emotionally.

After at least a quarter of an hour, and with Ekur-zakir's consent, Callisthenes gave an order to continue. Within another third of an hour, they were all at a gate toward the northeastern corner of the city. As foreseen, Alexis was there with the other guard. They had been able to arrange housing in the upper city between the temple and Herod's palace.

Entering the city, it was evident that some of the inhabitants were well aware that the men were foreigners. Some people did let their gaze linger on the Babylonian astronomers as they passed, but in general, the Magi were not dressed so much differently from the inhabitants of the great Jewish capital. The differences in clothing did not seem to bother or interest the inhabitants of the city too much. They were accustomed to seeing thousands of foreigners each year, especially during the great annual pilgrimage festivals: Passover (Pesach), Pentecost (Shavuot) and Tabernacles (Sukkot).

The group arrived at the caravansary shortly after noon. They were able to confide their horses and beasts of burden to the stable staff, while the innkeeper hurried to make sure a good meal was prepared for his new guests. The hotel was well built and very comfortable. However, it did have one fault which was bothersome for astronomers. The roof was below some of the surrounding buildings. One could only see the portion of the sky which was more or less directly above the hotel. Also even if the surrounding buildings had been lower, parts of the temple complex blocked portions of the eastern sky. The physical circumstances of the inn would undoubtedly limit the possibility of the Magi doing any significant astronomical observations for several days.

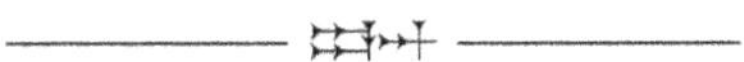

The men rested for part of the afternoon and then went exploring for a few hours just before sundown. The Magi all wanted to go near the temple but time was lacking so they decided to visit the area near Herod's palace instead because it was closer. The three great towers named Phasael, Hippicus, and Mariamne, which stood at the northern part of the palace, had caught their attention when they first saw the city. The Phasael tower was named after the king's deceased brother, and it stood 145 feet tall. The other two were named for the king's friend Hippicus (132 feet) and his second wife, Mariamne (110 feet). Mariamne had been executed on the king's command following some false accusations about 25 years earlier. Later, Herod greatly regretted his mistake of executing his wife. All the towers were heavily fortified, but they also housed luxurious apartments and baths. The most beautiful was the tower dedicated to the former queen. After observing the buildings and a great gate of the palace, the astronomers and Eliab made their way back to the caravansary as the sun was setting.

10

The Magi In Jerusalem

December 2 BC

Chapter Contents:

The Magi in Jerusalem

First Days in Jerusalem

Month IX - Kislimu / Kislev - Day 18

During breakfast on the morning of the first full day in Jerusalem, the astronomers and Eliab met together in a side room at the caravansary. Ekur-zakir, as usual, tried to find a consensus among the wise men concerning how to approach the next phase of their quest.

He said, "Happily, we have been able to arrive in Jerusalem, but now how are we going to find this young Messiah? It seems to me that the most logical approach is to contact the major religious leaders connected with the temple. They may perhaps be aware of local events concerning the Messiah, which escape our knowledge. Just meeting people on the street and asking questions does not seem to be an appropriate approach. Without a doubt, all kinds of wild rumors concerning messianic figures are found among the general populace."

"As several of you know, the Essene community near Jericho and elsewhere in Judaea has very highly developed ideas concerning a Messiah or Messiahs. Generally, they believe that there will be a kingly Messiah and some also believe there will be an additional priestly Messiah. The Essenes do have plenty of ideas about the future reign of righteousness that seems to be indicated by the Jewish prophets. Perhaps we should also make contact with the Essene community as well."

Iqisa spoke, "Yes, father perhaps it would have been a good idea to stop in Qumran, not far from Jericho. However, as you remember we wanted to honor the priestly authorities in Jerusalem. As in all religions, the God of the Jews is a God of order. The high priests and others are the main religious authorities here in Jerusalem. They should be informed about our discoveries first."

Ekur-zakir continued, "I remember our discussions about these things back in Babylonia. You also cited the text of one of the Psalms. Remind me of the passage."

Iqisa looked across the room to Eliab and then said, "Eliab you would do better reciting the passage."

Eliab cited the text from memory,

> *"The Lord swore an oath to David, a sure oath he will not revoke: One of your own descendants I will place on your throne. ... For the Lord has chosen Zion, he has desired it for his dwelling, saying, This is my resting place for ever and ever; here I will sit enthroned, for I have desired it."* Eliab continued, "Later in the same text it is written, *"Here I will make a horn grow for David and set up a lamp for my anointed one."* [1]

Ekur-zakir replied, "As I remember in earlier discussions this passage seemed to indicate that the descendant of David, the Messiah, would prosper in Zion, that is in Jerusalem. Therefore we decided to come to the Jewish capital. However, in coming to the capital, I doubt that we should try to see the present reigning king. I find it difficult to imagine that Herod will be enthusiastic concerning the birth of any kingly figure who is not from his royal line. The present king is not from the house of David and as you all know this affair is specifically centered on David's family and his royal line. I know we have already discussed these issues several times, but now we must make a decision. Whom are we going to contact about these matters? How are we going to proceed?"

Suen-magir said, "Yes, you are right Ekur-zakir. It seems to me that approaching the members of the present royal family and the king is excluded. Kings are always interested in their own royal line. If at all pos-

---

1 Psalm 132:11-17

sible we should avoid contacting anyone at the palace. However, exactly how are we going to make contacts among the priests and important temple authorities?"

Nikolaos finally spoke, "I could not agree more, you are right Suen-magir. Contacts with the palace should be avoided if at all possible.

Hormizdah added, "It is my opinion that some of us who are less renowned should go to the temple to make the first direct contacts with the Jewish religious authorities. It would not be very honorable for you, Ekur-zakir to wait for hours at one of the gates of the temple complex. I suspect that the Jews will not converse with us in their holy precincts. While I am the direct representative of the Rab-mag, I do not have the scholarly reputation of Nikolaos or Illis-kutul. I propose that Eliab, myself and Iqisa could be the representatives of our group. We could make the first contacts. If the main leaders invite us, then we can all go to meet them at their appointed place and time. At that point, Illis-kutul could make a full explanation of the symbolism involved with the star. He is undoubtedly the best speaker among us, and he has a high reputation."

Looking around Ekur-zakir saw that Hormizdah's proposition met the general approval of the entire group. He then said, "Very well, Eliab, Hormizdah, and Iqisa will make the first approach. Perhaps you should try to see someone later this morning. We might as well attempt to make contact with the authorities as soon as possible. We came here specifically to find the Messiah. We need not waste our time."

As noontime approached and the day grew much warmer, Eliab, Hormizdah, and Iqisa left the caravansary and traveled down various streets in the upper city of Jerusalem. They finally arrived at an elevated causeway bridge west of the temple area. It was packed with men, women, and children going to and from the temple. The back of the building was visible about 175 yards away. Even from the back, the building was very imposing. It stood well above the other buildings in the area being about 90 cubits[2] above the surrounding esplanade. That was about 54 cubits above the east end of the causeway bridge that they were traversing. Only the high fortified towers on the hill behind them on the west side of the upper city stood higher. As they crossed the bridge above the inhabited area in the valley to the west of the temple, they looked off toward the south. They could easily see the arched staircase leading to the southwestern gate of the temple. The underside of the archway was about 36 cubits from the street that ran below parallel to the western wall of the temple. At its extremity, the southwestern wall of the temple stood about 64 cubits[3] above the street at the base of the wall. The royal portico was visible above the wall.

They entered the temple complex through the large gate on the western wall at the end of the causeway. They had entered the court of the Gentiles. Before them, a few dozen yards away, stood the inner gate of the Court of Israel. Armed levitical priests were posted there beside the low wall to guard the entrance so that no foreigners should be able to enter the Court of Israel. Eliab alone penetrated into the Court of Israel and made his way toward the council house beside the southwest corner of the main temple building. There at the entrance, he explained briefly to one of the guards that he and a small group of scholars had come from Babylonia with a message for the chief priest and his entourage. Eliab explained that the scholars were not Jews. Therefore they had remained near the western gate in the Court of the Gentiles.

One of the guards disappeared into the interior of the building. Eliab stayed at the door of the council house. About 20 minutes later, the guard reappeared with a senior priest.

The guard introduced the priest saying, "This is Elkanah, who often has the role of being the spokesperson for the chief priest. He is willing to listen to you for a few minutes."

Eliab explained that he had come with some astronomers who were waiting in the Court of the Gentiles. Sizing Eliab up based on his appearance and demeanor, Elkanah decided to go with Eliab to meet the men. Arriving at the gate, they found Hormizdah and Iqisa seated on a

---

2 About 46 meters, 151 feet.

3 36 cubits is about 18 meters and 64 cubits about 32 meters.

small stone bench south of the entrance. The noontime sun had started to make its strength known. Elkanah greeted each man respectfully, but he was very well aware that Hormizdah and Iqisa had different religious origins than Eliab.

Elkanah, noticing that the sun was beaming down rather brightly said, "Let us go across to the shaded area of the portico of the western wall of the temple complex. We can discuss things briefly there with more privacy. That will give me an opportunity to understand why you have made your great journey."

The men arrived among the pillars that upheld the portico of the western wall facing the back of the temple. Few people were there because the crowds usually remained on the south side of the temple toward the causeway and at the Royal Portico. Finding some stone benches over to one side which were free, all the men sat. Elkanah introduced himself as did all the others.

Elkanah then proceeded to ask some questions, "So tell me some more. Exactly why have you all come to Jerusalem?"

Hormizdah and Iqisa looked to Eliab to respond. For a moment Eliab gathered his courage and then said, "We represent a group of astronomers from Babylonia. Hormizdah is the direct representative of the chief of the wise men in the Parthian Empire. Iqisa is the son of the leading astronomer in our group. The group has become convinced that the God of Abraham has signaled the arrival of his Messiah, the son of David, through various signs in the heavens. Indeed they believe the young Messiah has been born in these last few years. There has been a series of royal signs in the heavens which began at least one and a half years ago. The men believe that these signs signal the coming of the 'Righteous One,' the Messiah."

Elkanah, who was a bit taken aback by these revelations, interrupted Eliab at this point. "This is indeed unexpected news. It appears that you believe that the men are correct in their understanding. How is it that you, Eliab, a Jew, came to be involved in this affair?"

Eliab then briefly proceeded to describe his involvement in Ekur-zakir's notarial office for more than 20 years. He also explained how that a few years previously during a visit to Jerusalem, his cousin had caused him to have a renewed interest in the coming of the Messiah.

Elkanah then continued, "Well, I will speak to the high priest about this matter. I suspect that he may want to meet with you. I will first speak to a committee of the chief priest's advisors and some of the Pharisaic leaders. The committee may want to see you as well before we speak to the high priest. However, please be aware that the high priest is a Sadducee. He is not particularly favorable to messianic movements. He may be less interested in these types of events than the Pharisaic members of our main governing religious body the Sanhedrin. They believe in the coming of the Messiah as well as the resurrection of the dead and a coming just world under the government of the Righteous One. Tell me, how long are you staying in Jerusalem and where may we find you in the city?"

Iqisa responded, "Basically we have decided to stay in Judaea for at least a month or more if necessary in order to find the young Messiah. We are staying at a caravansary located behind the temple area. Eliab can give you the exact location. I am still a bit disoriented. We only arrived yesterday morning."

"Very well then," said Elkanah. "We will contact you again either tomorrow or the day following. I wish you well, may you have a good visit of the city. Perhaps I will even be able to offer some hospitality to your group in the coming days."

With that, the men said goodbye and walked away from the spot where they had been meeting. Elkanah returned to the inner temple complex, and the others decided to move south and east to get a better view of the front part of the temple before finding their way back to the caravansary.

Having crossed a portion of the vast esplanade of the Court of the Gentiles south of the temple, Eliab, Hormizdah, and Iqisa passed several gates on the low wall which gave entrance into the Court of Israel. The men could see a little bit through the gates as they passed. The main temple building towered over everything. However, three other structures lined the south face of the temple. The house of the council on the southwestern side of the temple was the high priest's headquarters. Elkanah had come from there and gone back there. The middle building was used for stocking wood for the sacrifices. Eliab informed the men that the third building at the southeastern corner of the temple building itself was the meeting place of the Sanhedrin.[4] Further along, the men could see a significant gate which opened onto what was called the Court of the Women. The female sex could only penetrate into the Court of Israel and the Court of the Women. They could not go further toward the main temple building.

Finally, arriving toward the southeast corner of the complex at the edge of the so-called Royal Portico, the men admired the front face of the temple to the north and west. Eliab also pointed out the front gate facing east, which they could all see in the distance. At the temple itself, they were surprised to see a great golden eagle over the main gate. The men had not seen the eagle upon their arrival in Jerusalem because of all the other sites which had held their attention.

Reacting to the presence of the statue, Iqisa said, "Eliab, I thought Judaism was against idolatry and any representations of animals or men, which could be seen as idolatrous. What is this object doing here at the very heart of your religious worship?" Hormizdah also echoed Iqisa's words.

Eliab responded, "Herod the king somehow thought that the main entrance of the temple should be adorned with this particular statue. He certainly did not ask the opinion of the priests or the people who are most faithful to God. I have heard some stories about how many people were outraged that the king has done this. His rebuilding of the temple a bit less than 20 years ago caused many people to worry, and many were upset. However, he did ask for much advice. The priests were employed doing most of the work, and the sacrifices and temple services proceeded unhindered. The result has been a wonder for our people. The king was praised for his good works.

However, a few years later the king wanted to add this eagle to the structure. This addition was designed to please Augustus' friend and ally, the Roman politician and general Agrippa, who came on a state visit about 13 years ago. I am told that Agrippa's name is inscribed on the front gate as well. The fabrication of the eagle cost Herod a great deal

---

4 By the time of Jesus' trial before the high priest three decades later, the Sanhedrin had moved its meeting place to the far eastern end of the Royal Portico on the southeastern extremity of the temple complex.

of money. The craftsmanship is excellent, and of course, the gold used in making the object represents a sizable treasure. The king said that he made the eagle to honor our God. However, his placing of the eagle above the main door of the temple has been universally opposed. Even so, the king insisted, and the eagle was crafted and installed. I understand that about 100 of Herod's mercenary guards were posted continually over a period of several days, while the eagle was being put in place. Their presence was also very much detested by the priests. At this time only the Levitical temple guards are posted at the temple. Frankly, I am surprised that no one has ever made an effort to remove the statue."

After looking through other aspects the temple complex including the magnificent Royal Portico to the south, the men returned to the caravansary and made their report to the rest of the group.

None of the men who had been gathered together during the encounter with Elkanah had noticed that a young 15-year-old boy had been seated behind one of the columns of the western portico. He was memorizing a short text from the Jewish Scriptures as part of his schooling. The young man had heard the entire conversation even though the men had spoken in low tones so that their voices would not carry. The boy knew that he had been privy to something significant. Looking around the column and seeing the men going their respective ways, he felt confident that he had not even been noticed.

Gathering his things, in a few minutes he crossed over to the Hulda Gate tunnels, and he disappeared down the steps. After a short moment, he came out of the southern gate of the temple below the Royal Portico. Within 15 minutes he was deep in the old city. Finding one of his school friends, he told his companion the entire story. Within four hours about 15 people had heard portions of the story. Later that evening at least 100 people had heard something about the arrival of this group of eastern astronomers, who claimed that the skies were announcing the coming of God's appointed king.

Two days later at nightfall, about 2,500 people already had heard that signs involving a star in the heavens had signaled the birth of a Messiah, who would bring in an age of righteousness and justice.

On the morning of the third day, a few people even arrived at the caravansary wanting to meet the astronomers from the East. The innkeeper had plenty of difficulties sending them away, so his guests could be at peace. However, one of the men would not be put off. He waited much of the morning outside the inn for the men to appear. The man, who was extremely zealous for the liberty of the Jewish people, always carried a dagger in the folds of his robe. He wanted to know more about the signs in the heavens. He waited for several hours before finally giving up later in the morning. He was only one of many who believed that the coming of the Messiah could mean a war of liberation. Herod's collaboration with the pagan Romans would one day cease. The waiting man especially hated the image that Herod had set up over the main gate of the temple. Later the man made his way to see Matthias and Judas, two popular Pharisaic teachers.

Month IX - Kislimu / Kislev - Days 21-22   Friday - Saturday - Dec 19-20, 3 BC

During the following days, the wise men continued to get more and more familiar with different sections of the city near their lodging. The temple continued to be a major attraction for the men. The entire group marveled at its construction, and they decided to revisit it as a whole group the day after their initial meeting with Elkanah. While the men were visiting the temple district, Eliab explained more about the Jewish sacrificial system and festivals.

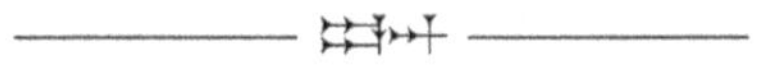

Several hours before the beginning of the weekly Sabbath, Elkanah, the priest, came for a visit on the afternoon of the 21st. He brought word that he had been able to arrange a meeting with several prominent members of the Jewish religious council, the Sanhedrin, on the day after the Sabbath. He also asked for a bit of clarification about the stellar signs, since he did not have the habit of thinking about the heavens.

On the same afternoon, Eliab's cousin Joram came by and thanked the group of astronomers for their help in establishing the possible dates associated with the Messiah's appearing. He said that he would alert some of the Essene teachers that the Magi had arrived in Jerusalem. He thought that several Essene teachers might want to visit the wise men during the next week. Within a day or so, he sent word to the Essene community at Qumran and a few other places about the arrival of the wise men from the East and the heavenly signs.

In the evening, the Sabbath began. The Magi remained in the caravansary most of the next day. However, Eliab attended a synagogue service in the upper city not far from the king's palace.

While it was still unknown to the Magi, several thousand people in the city had already become aware of their coming. On the fourth day after the men's arrival, in the lower city, a few shopkeepers who were secret informers for the king made their report to an official at the palace. They said that many rumors were circulating in the lower city about a group of astronomers from the East who had arrived in Jerusalem several days before. Supposedly the men were saying that the Messiah had been born based on specific signs which they had seen in the heavens. However, the shopkeepers did not have any other details. They were not even aware of where the men could be found.

Meeting Members of the Sanhedrin

Month IX - Kislimu / Kislev - Day 23   Afternoon, Sunday - Dec. 21, 2 BC

After the astronomers had been in the city for four days, a small committee from the Sanhedrin met with the eastern visitors. The group of religious dignitaries was composed almost exclusively of Pharisees who believed in Israel's messianic hope. Matthias, the Sadducean high priest, let it be known that he was not immediately interested in meeting the men, but he did send a few representatives, who would report to him directly about the content of the meeting. The rendezvous happened in a large room, which was often used for wedding receptions. The meeting room was about 75 yards from the astronomers' hotel. The Magi and the Pharisaic party together amounted to about 25 men. Elkanah and Eliab handled the introductions.

The group of Pharisees asked the wise men to briefly explain the celestial events. Ekur-zakir did some of the speaking, but it was Illis-kutul and Suen-magir who gave most of the information. Eliab was invited to say a few words as well because his insights into the 89th Psalm had proven to be a critical aspect of understanding the signs.

The men from Borsippa explained that they had all previously had responsibilities as priests of various Babylonian divinities, however because of their discoveries concerning the coming of the Jewish Messiah they all had more or less discreetly renounced their priestly roles. They continued to be associated with the observatory at Borsippa. Ekur-zakir, in particular, insisted that they did want to find the young Messiah, who in his opinion must not be over two years old. He indicated that the royal signs had begun about a year and a half previously. Ekur-zakir also invited Hormizdah and Nikolaos to say a few words.

Nikolaos indicated that he was still a bit skeptical that they could find the Messiah. However, he was more or less convinced that the celestial signs did indicate the coming of the prophesied Jewish king. Hormizdah explained that his own Zoroastrian beliefs predisposed him to think of the need for a world savior. However, he had not expected this savior figure to be Jewish. He also explained that he had come to Judaea as the official representative of the Rab-mag at Ctesiphon.

The Jewish Pharisees expressed their appreciation concerning the men's presentation. Elkanah added that some people had heard the year before concerning a young child who had been dedicated at the temple.

He continued saying, "Apparently prophecies had been given by two aged believers. A man named Simeon had given the first prophecy upon seeing the child and his parents in the temple complex. A woman prophetess named Anna had also confirmed the prophetic word. However, unfortunately, both of the aged individuals have since died. It is no longer possible to question them."

Elkanah finished by saying, "To my knowledge, no one among us is certain where the couple and the child can be found at this time. An ancient text seems to indicate that the Messiah would be born in Bethlehem, which is a small town no far south of Jerusalem. However, I do not see any compelling reason to think that the child would still be there. What is certain is that the child will come from King David's line and he was certainly from Bethlehem. That may be the main meaning of the text."

Finally, after some more deliberation, it was decided that the men would disperse until a later date and then possibly meet again.

Impressed with the men's seriousness, Elkanah continued questioning the astronomers and Eliab. After more conversation, he decided to extend full hospitality to the Magi and asked the men to stay at his home. It was agreed that the men would leave their accommodations at the caravansary the next morning and come to Elkanah's house. Most of the servants and guards would continue to be lodged at the caravansary.

Matthias and Judas, two well favored Pharisaic teachers, were present at the meeting with the wise men. They had already heard of the men's arrival in Jerusalem from various sources even before the official meeting was scheduled. The men were very impressed by the visitors from the East, and they were sensing that their greatest hour was perhaps at hand. The young Messiah might even be able to play a role. They had heard that the king was ill. They wanted to see him replaced, but even before his replacement, they wished to remove Herod's idolatrous eagle from above the main door of the temple. The evil bird was plainly an offense to God. It could no longer be tolerated.

If the men were able to eliminate the eagle quickly, perhaps the king would not have time to replace it before his death. They began to make plans to gather a group of men who could do the job. It was necessary to destroy the eagle during the daytime because the temple precinct was firmly locked and guarded at night. However, if the effort happened with enough rapidity, then perhaps no one would intervene, and the conspirators could all escape before the king's guards, or the temple police could stop them. Matthias and Judas hoped that the temple police might be complicit and allow the destruction of the great eagle without hindrance.

As they were discussing how things could be done, Judas turned to Matthias and said, "Do you realize that in just a few days it will be the Festival of Lights, Hanukkah? We as a people will be celebrating the cleansing of the temple about 165 years ago. The Seleucid ruler Antiochus IV Epiphanes had desecrated the temple's holy places and the Maccabean leaders cleansed it. If we were able to destroy the eagle during the festival, we would even be giving a new and deeper meaning to the yearly festivities."

Matthias replied, "Do you think we might be able to organize a group to destroy the idolatrous bird in such a short time? I am not sure it can be done. We also need to be careful so that the news of our plans is not proclaimed too widely."

Judas said, "We can certainly try to make the effort to destroy the eagle. I know several young men who may be willing to risk their lives to glorify God in this way."

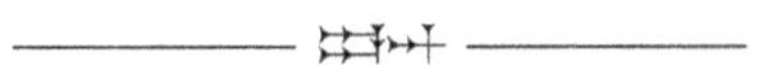

On the same day that the wise men meet with the Jewish religious leaders in Jerusalem, Uzziel, Joseph's cousin, was in the lower city of Jerusalem. While speaking with a friend in the market, Uzziel overheard a conversation about the wise men from Babylonia who had come to Jerusalem looking for a recently born Messiah. Uzziel was very curious, and he sensed that one of the men might be willing to say more.

So he questioned him saying, "I just happened to overhear your conversation. It is fascinating what you were saying about a recently born Messiah. How did the men from the East know anything about this?"

The man in the market responded, "They saw royal signs in the heavens which have announced the coming of God's Righteous One, the descendant of David, the king prophesied by Jeremiah. Unfortunately, that is all I know at the moment. The men arrived here five days ago. More and more people in the city are speaking about this."

Returning to Bethlehem and arriving there in the late afternoon, Uzziel went directly to see Joseph. He found Joseph outside his home sawing through a large piece of wood. He was shaping the wood designated as a crossbeam for a house. A conversation sprang up concerning various things, but finally, Uzziel sensed he should tell his cousin about what he had overheard.

Uzziel said, "Joseph, earlier today, when I was in the market in the lower city of Jerusalem, I overheard a conversation. You might find this very interesting and even perhaps a bit alarming. I questioned one of the men further, and this is what he told me: A group of wise men, who are astronomers, have arrived in Jerusalem from the Parthian Empire. They have come seeking Israel's Messiah. They think that the Messiah was born recently."

Joseph replied, "Yes, this is surprising."

"But you will find this hard to believe." Uzziel added, "It is said in Jerusalem that the men discovered that the Messiah was recently born through signs in the heavens. It appears that there have been a series of celestial signs during the last year or so that indicated that the Messiah had been born."

Joseph was a bit taken aback, "Well this is a revelation to me and of course to you also. It would indeed be interesting to talk to these men. I wonder if we could trust them with our insights into these things? I have never met any such men. Who knows what they are like? How would they have understood these things unless God himself had shown them the truth? I do not believe in astrology. God does say that He made the sun, moon, and the stars to give light, and also, it is written that they are 'for signs, seasons, days and years.'"[5]

"You know Uzziel, we are not completely uninformed about the coming of the 'Righteous One,' isn't that right?" Joseph said with a grin."However, I am not going to go looking for these men. If they find God's Messiah, they will have to be guided by the Lord himself. I am not volunteering any information. They will need to find the young child themselves."

About that time, Mary opened the door. She stood in the doorway and greeted Uzziel while she announced to Joseph that she had finished preparing the evening meal. Bending down a bit, she placed her right hand on the head of her infant son who had just appeared. The young Messiah was standing, although precariously, holding onto her leg. He had also grabbed a large portion of cloth from Mary's dress in his small hand. He looked at Uzziel and smiled.

---

5 Genesis 1:14

A Letter to the King

Month IX - Kislimu / Kislev - Day 24   Sunday night - Dec. 21, 2 BC

After hearing the report given by Elkanah hours after the meeting with the Magi, the High Priest Matthias requested that the wise men also meet with him in private. It was decided that the meeting would take place after dark on the same evening at Elkanah's home. The high priest preferred this arrangement in order not bring too much attention concerning his presence with the men.

During the meeting, Matthias was very impressed by the evidence given by the astronomers about the star and its meaning. He thanked the men and preceded back home in the darkness escorted by a few guards. Arriving at his home, he decided to write up a short report for Herod, the king.

Matthias, High Priest of Israel to Herod, king of Judaea, Greetings.

It has no doubt come to your attention my lord that a group of astronomers has come from Babylonia and Persia concerning a star which supposedly indicates that the Messiah of Israel has been born. The news of their arrival has spread across the entire city of Jerusalem.

A body of men from the Sanhedrin met with these men earlier. I suspect that you also heard about their meeting. Following a report from the Pharisaic leader Elkanah, I also decided to meet the men myself. I finished that meeting this evening. The encounter happened in a discreet manner because I do not want to attract any more attention to these men and their message than is necessary.

I assure the king that the men are very persuasive in their presentation. It may be that you will want to learn more about this yourself. I am willing to brief you personally about what I have learned, but it may be right that you would receive counsel from several of the prominent scribes. Several of the men were present at the meeting on the 24th. They could also give their opinion about the situation.

The coming of these wise men from the East has caused the inhabitants of the city to ask many questions. For my part, I do not want the situation to deteriorate into a robust messianic fever which could cause difficulties both for the king and the kingdom.

Your servant Matthias, High Priest.[6]

Matthias prepared this short message to be delivered to the king. He instructed one of his servants to take the communication to the palace at the break of day. He was well aware that Herod was probably already aware or soon would be of his meeting with the Magi. Hardly anything of importance escaped the attention of the king. Matthias, needed to have the king's confidence, so he had decided to inform the king immediately about his encounter with the wise men.

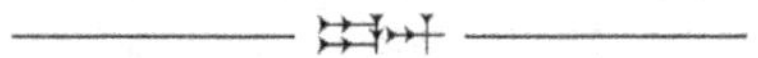

Herod received Matthias' message in the later part of the next morning. The king was not feeling well. Lamenting his diminished physical abilities, he was sitting on a comfortable chair in his bedroom waiting for the servants to bring him one of his favorite foods for breakfast. He had not wanted to eat earlier because his bowels were disturbed and he had little or no appetite.

However, when Herod opened the message from the high priest, the aged king sat upright in his chair and began to take command of his thoughts and feelings in a conscious manner.

He sat a bit dumbfounded for a moment and finally quietly said to himself, "I never thought that something like this would happen. It is just another frustration for me. My son is in prison because he wanted to assassinate me through poisoning in order to seize the throne. Now others arrive proclaiming the birth of a savior king."

---

6 For clarity, this is not the same Matthias who was plotting to destroy the golden eagle.

A Model of the City of Jerusalem and the Temple

Above: A general overview of a model of Jerusalem, the temple and the Antonia Fortress.

Above and Below: The Jerusalem temple and the fortress of Antonia in the background (below only).

Above: Part of the upper city of Jerusalem including the great towers near Herod's palace.

Below: A model of Herod's palace. (Author's photos and public domain.)

Hanukkah Begins

Month IX - Kislimu / Kislev - Day 25

In the early evening of the 25th of Kislev, lamps were lit all over Jerusalem in celebration of the cleansing and rededication of the temple over 160 years previously. In the windows of each home, lamps were shining. The Magi were fascinated, and Eliab led them for a walk in the upper city of Jerusalem where hundreds upon hundreds of lamps were lit. It was truly a communal experience without equal in Babylonia although many Jews did celebrate Hanukkah even in Borsippa.

In the Court of the Women in the temple, the priests illuminated four great lamps about 30 cubits[7] above the ground as possibly 20,000 people gathered in the temple courts. There was a short time of prayer, and a choir of priests sang several Psalms. The ceremonies would become more elaborate and well-attended toward the end of the festival.

Meeting Essenes

Month IX - Kislimu / Kislev - Day 26

In the afternoon of the 26th day of the month, Eliab's cousin Joram did manage to assemble three prominent members from the Essene movement. They came from the Essene community in Qumran and two other Essene groups. Altogether the Essenes numbered about 4,000 in Herod's kingdom. The men who came together with the Magi were fascinated when they heard the account of the manifestation of the star.

They spoke about how they believed that the appearance of the Messiah was imminent through their theory of history centered on Sabbatical Jubilees. They also evoked the possibility that there would be two Messiahs, one who was a kingly Messiah and another who would be a priest.

---

7 About 45 feet.

One of the Essene leaders pointed out how that the sons of darkness and sons of light would fight in the coming time. There would be an immense conflict, but finally, the sons of light would prevail over all the forces of darkness. They seemed to want to underline to the Magi that idolatry would not be permitted.

In the discussion, the Essenes mentioned some books which they prized very highly. These were the so-called "War Scroll" which was about the "sons of darkness and sons of light" and the *Book of Enoch* which also spoke of the arrival of a king of righteousness.

After the departure of the Essene representatives, a discussion arose among the astronomers about the Essene ideas concerning the role of the Messiah or Messiahs.

Illis-kutul said, "I am well conscious that the Essenes believe in the teachings of a man that they call the "Teacher of Righteousness." This person who lived well over 100 years ago supposedly gave them insight into the Jewish prophetic Scriptures. However, he put a lot of emphasis on a time of battle between the so-called sons of darkness and the sons of light. Essentially this concerns those who are the 'chosen ones' who do the will of Yahweh and the pagan idolaters, as we were ourselves only very recently."

"There is even a text which some have called the war scroll, which speaks of the order of battle of the righteous over the wicked. However, I am not so sure that their approach to the Jewish prophetic Scriptures is accurate. I am wondering if their emphasis on armed combat is the way of the God of Israel concerning the Messiah. There is a text in the early part of the Isaiah scroll that reads something like the following. I am citing it more or less from memory, but I have not memorized it. The passage concerns Judah and Jerusalem: [8]

> *"In the last days the mountain of the Lord's temple will be established as the highest of the mountains; it will be exalted above the hills, and all nations will stream to it. Many peoples will come and say, 'Come, let us go up to the mountain of the Lord, to the temple of the God of Jacob. He will teach us his ways, so that we may walk in his paths.'*

---

8 Isaiah 2:1-5.

The law will go out from Zion, the word of the Lord from Jerusalem. He will judge between the nations and will settle disputes for many peoples. They will beat their swords into plowshares and their spears into pruning hooks. A nation will not take up sword against another nation, nor will they train for war anymore. Come, descendants of Jacob, let us walk in the light of the Lord."

"It is interesting that we have come ourselves to the Lord's temple. We, the former sons of darkness in Essene terms, have come to believe in Israel's Messiah as well as God's project for a world of righteousness. Is it not possible that many people from other nations will learn to appreciate the God of Israel?"

"None of us here are particularly interested in fighting any battles. 'Beating swords into plowshares' is something upon which we can agree. Righteousness on the earth would be attractive to us, but not unrighteous warlords. Also in thinking about our recent experience with the star, God's ways do seem to be more discreet than some people might assume. Our experience with the royal signs we saw in the East tells us something about God's ways."

"I am just a little suspicious of this idea concerning a great war. Perhaps it could happen, but the God of the Jews seems to have followed another course with us, and happily so."

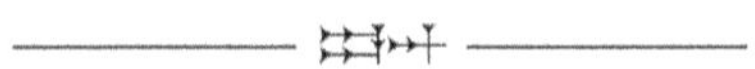

On their eighth day in Jerusalem, Hormizdah, Nikolaos, and Illis-kutul were in the market in the Cardo district of Jerusalem not far from Herod's palace. While they were looking through the various shops about a half hour after their arrival in the market, a man with a black beard spoke to them. "Excuse me, but are you not from Babylonia. I can see the style of clothing which you have on."

Illis-kutul nodded his head indicating that the men did come from the East.

The bearded man continued, "I am wondering, are you the men who have come from Babylonia with news about the Messiah's birth? Everywhere in the city people are speaking of your coming. It is said that you learned this from some signs in the heavens concerning a star. Could you explain this briefly to me?"

Hormizdah, Nikolaos, and Illis-kutul were all astounded.

Nikolaos responded, "Yes, we are here seeking to find the Messiah, and we believe that a star has indicated that he has been born. However, I do not understand, how is it that much of the city is aware of our presence? We have only been speaking to some of the leading religious leaders in the city about our reasons for being here."

The man continued, "I am not sure how the news of your coming has gotten out across the entire city, but it has happened. Almost everyone is aware that men from the East have arrived speaking of the birth of the Messiah."

As the conversation continued, two or three others stood beside the questioner and then more and more men joined them. Within minutes about 30 men were listening to the discussion.

Hormizdah, Nikolaos, and Illis-kutul made a little effort to explain the signs concerning the righteous king. However, the crowd continued to grow. Soon there were 50 men.

Hormizdah, in particular, began to be a bit alarmed and said to the other Magi in hushed tones, "I see that we have become exceedingly popular. I am not sure that the authorities will view this gathering in a positive manner. Perhaps we should regain our lodging."

Then, Illis-kutul thanked the men in the crowd for their interest said, "We will be returning to our lodging."

However, the assembled group of men did not disperse, and several people followed the Magi and even continued to ask questions. About a half hour later when the men had finally arrived at Elkanah's house, there were still about 25 men accompanying them, and some did not leave but remained near the house hoping to see the Magi again.

Because of this marketplace incident, the men finally realized that their project was well-known in the city. As the inhabitants became more and more aware, the Magi found it to be impossible to move about without being noticed.

Herod Calls the Religious Authorities

Because of information that he had received from the high priest and his own network of spies, the king was deeply troubled. He did not like foreigners to be in his capital city looking for a newly born heir to the throne. This young child could be a real threat.

Herod decided to call together some of the principal scribes and religious leaders to the palace. He wanted this done as discreetly as possible, so he gave specific instructions to the high priest and the others about arriving at the palace without much show. The invited people were not to tell others that the king had requested to see them.

The king wanted to know when and where the child would have been born. But even more, he wanted to understand just how genuinely the religious leaders believed in this sort of prophecy and what he could expect from the general population now that the word of the Magi's coming was so widespread.

The High Priest Matthias and others made their way to the palace just after sunset. The evening air was cold, so it made it appropriate to wear hooded cloaks, which also had the advantage of being relatively discreet. Almost anyone seeing the high priest going toward the palace would not have recognized him. Herod had given orders that the group was to be granted entrance through a small rear gate of the palace.

Once inside,, the group of 15 men was presented before the king in his private library. There were hundreds of scrolls neatly placed on extensive and finely crafted shelving. The room itself was about 30 by 45 feet in surface area, and decorative rugs covered much of the white marble floor.

The king was already there when the men arrived. Seeing the king, all of the men bowed low to the ground. Herod invited the High Priest Matthias and three other prominent men to take seats facing the king. There were no other chairs, so the other men stood more or less behind and beside the four who were seated.

Herod could be charming if necessary. He had deemed it appropriate in this context, and he summoned his strength and determined not to allow anyone to see the full extent of his illness. At first, Herod questioned the men about themselves and their families. But in addition, the king genuinely appreciated their qualities as scholars and even pointed out several expensive scrolls of biblical texts in his collection. After an extended time of informal socializing, the king finally addressed the group concerning the messianic rumors.

Herod said, "I called you here this evening to get your opinions concerning the astronomers who came from Babylonia and the messianic aspirations of our people. Tell me what you think of these men and their ideas about the coming of the Messiah. Do you think the Messiah's coming has been announced in the stars?"

Matthias, the high priest, asked three scribal scholars to respond. Each of the men affirmed that the Babylonians should be taken very seriously although the Sadducean scholar said he was not convinced that a Messiah would undoubtedly make his appearance anytime soon.

Afterward, Herod also asked, "If this Messiah was born recently, do the Scriptures indicate where that he may have been born?"

At this point Matthias, the high priest, decided to respond to the king directly in person, "My lord the king, the holy texts indicate that the child will be born in Bethlehem of Judea; for this is what has been written by the prophet Micah many centuries ago. Micah spoke of the hometown of King David and his ancestors:

> 'And you, O Bethlehem, in the land of Judah, are by no means least among the rulers of Judah; for from you shall come a ruler who will shepherd my people Israel.'" [9]

Matthias continued, "The text would seem to indicate that the child would probably be born in Bethlehem. Does the text certainly mean that the child would be born in Bethlehem itself? It is hard to be sure, but that is the way it is often interpreted. It is certain that he will be from the royal line of David, the king. However, as we all know, there are descendants of David living all across the country."

Concurring with Matthias' opinion, some of the scribal scholars indicated that the high priest's understanding was correct.

After a bit more discussion Herod dismissed the assembled persons

---

9 Matthew 2:3-6 ESV.

while thanking them for their aid. In the hours that followed in his private chambers, Herod was torn between fits of anger and a type of resignation.

He asked himself, "If God himself is raising up this child how can I resist him? However, I have tried so hard to pass on my kingdom to my sons so that their rule could be firmly established. How can I let a pretended Messiah come and take their place? I cannot, and I will not see my years of work destroyed. Did I not rebuild and embellish the temple for the God of Israel?" How is it that He will now take the kingdom from my sons? How could God do such an injustice to me?"

The King Summons the Magi

Month IX - Kislimu / Kislev - Day 27

On the evening of the 27th day of Kislev, the rain began falling in abundance and this continued through the night. There was so much rain that hardly any lamps were lit in the windows across the city in celebration of Hanukkah. People stayed inside keeping their shutters closed firmly to keep out the ever-increasing downpour. Several very loud claps of thunder in quick succession were heard before dawn, waking everyone in the city. The deluge continued through the morning and into the early afternoon.

In the late afternoon just before dark, a messenger arrived at Elkanah's house from the palace asking to speak with Elkanah privately. The servants called their master. Reaching in the entryway, Elkanah recognized the young messenger because occasionally he had come to the Council House at the temple with messages from the palace. The young man had a sealed parchment roll in his hand, which he offered to Elkanah as soon as the priest appeared in the entrance hall of the house.

Elkanah took the parchment roll, broke the seal and began to read its contents. It was a message from the king's secretary, indicating that the king was summoning the Magi to the palace for an interview in the evening at the end of the Sabbath on the 30th of the month (two days later). The meeting would take place after dark. The king's secretary insisted that Elkanah not even mention this to any of his contacts, even the high priest. The king wanted to see the men personally and in private. The king would send some men to accompany the astronomers to the palace during the early evening.

The message ended with the words, "Make sure that this rendezvous is not known to others in your entourage, even to your servants."

Elkanah sent the messenger back to the palace with a short written communication that he had well received the king's message and he would do his best to make sure the men from the East would be ready for their interview with the king.

Later that evening after supper when all of the servants were no longer within earshot, Elkanah shared the news with the astronomers and Eliab. The men were a bit surprised, but they did not react negatively. It was an honor to be invited to the palace. But Elkanah insisted that the king was inviting them in secret. They were not to let anyone else know about the invitation.

Even so, Nikolaos thought to himself without saying anything openly to the others, "This is not good. We do not want to be dealing with the king about a young messianic leader. Kings do not appreciate any other heirs to the throne apart from their offspring or their own chosen successors. We will need to be careful. One can lose his life dealing with kings and their line of succession."

Month IX - Kislimu / Kislev - Day 28   Thurs./Friday - Dec. 25/26, 2 BC

The news about the Magi continued to spread throughout the region. Having heard of the astronomer's presence in Jerusalem, some Pharisees arrived from various surrounding towns and villages. The men wanted to meet the Magi because they too were interested in the Messiah. With Elkanah's advice and direction Ekur-zakir and the others received the visitors, but the Magi were a bit frustrated because it seemed that their group was not making any visible progress in achieving its goal of actually meeting the young Messiah.

Otherwise, the Magi spent a little time touring a portion of the upper city near the high towers which fortified the northern part of Herod's palace. Elkanah introduced the men to a seller of parchment manuscripts in the same area. Nikolaos was especially interested in the documents written in Hebrew and Greek, as well as some in Latin.

However, when Nikolaos came out of the shop with a newly acquired parchment roll, he looked toward the great fortified towers at the north side of Herod's palace. He could just make out a few guards who were peering down at the city below. For Nikolaos, it was almost as though they were looking directly at him. He felt a deep sense of foreboding looking toward the palace. It was almost as though the danger of the king's summons was something which he could almost physically touch.

Meeting with the King

Month IX - Kislīmu / Kislev - Day 29

In the evening, the Jewish Sabbath began. Elkanah and his entire household rested. That evening and the next day, meals were served cold, but the Jews had specially prepared dishes which were specifically reserved for the Sabbath day. The men spent time resting, discussing and reading in their rooms. However, during a two hour period in the afternoon, the whole team met with Elkanah. The group had a lively discussion about the Jewish Scriptures, and Elkanah also gave them some counsel about the upcoming interview with the king.

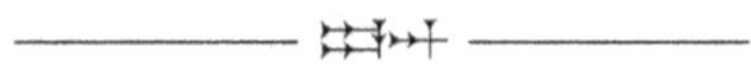

About one hour after sunset, while most of Jerusalem was at home behind closed doors and many were preparing to go to sleep, a discreet, relatively silent escort of ten soldiers arrived outside of Elkanah's house. The soldiers were dressed in winter apparel, including long cloaks which disseminated their weapons. They had also been ordered to change their usual heavy metal studded military sandals for lighter ones which did not make so much noise. However, for an attentive eye, it would have been evident that they were soldiers. A man named Leandros, who was a trusted servant of the king, accompanied the soldiers. He was dressed in the clothes of a businessman. Leandros knocked on the door and spoke to Elkanah's servant, asking to see the master of the household.

Elkanah then summoned the Magi. When the group of wise men arrived at the entrance, Leandros spoke briefly in hushed tones to Elkanah and Eliab, who then turned to the others, indicating that they should follow this man to the expected rendezvous. Soon Elkanah and the men from the East were in the street. The soldiers, who had dissimulated themselves here and there in the street, quickly drew close together. Then the whole group led by Leandros and the commander began the relatively short journey to the palace.

The men took an irregular pathway toward the king's palace, zig-zagging a bit in the maze of narrow streets. They had received instructions not to attract any more attention than necessary, and to not take a direct route to the palace. After about a quarter of an hour and a few more turns than necessary, the entire group arrived on a small square facing a side entrance to the palace. The two guards at the gate acknowledged the detachment commander as he drew near and opened a small, easy access door placed inside one of the more massive main doors. As the men entered the interior of the palace walls, the soldiers soon peeled away from the group and let the wise men advance, with their guide, to another relatively unimposing door toward the back of the palace.

Leandros led the men through some small rooms, and soon they found themselves in a great hall. Looking to one side as they traversed the room, they could see Herod's throne. After a few more paces down an adjoining hallway, the men arrived in a beautiful wood-paneled room with various cushions and several Roman style chairs in a circle positioned to the right side. Leandros told the men to find a seat, and he disappeared through a side door.

Curiously, besides the armed guard at the small entrance door which they had used, the men had not seen a single servant during their entire journey into the palace interior.

Within about ten minutes, Leandros reappeared accompanied by Herod. The king was visibly not in good health, but he advanced steadily as a man of authority. The Magi all rose and bowed in the direction of the king who continued to walk toward them.

The king looked the men over from head to foot. He thought, "Yes, they came from the East. Their clothing and demeanor show it very well."

Deep in his being, Herod just wanted to threaten the men and send them running for home, but he realized that it would probably not be a good strategy. As much as possible he wanted to maintain good relations with the Jews in Babylonia, and he also wanted to find this young Messiah himself.

Arriving at his seat the king prepared to sit down. Then Herod spoke, "Please let me see your faces."

As the group rose from its bowed position, Herod greeted the men by placing his hand on the shoulder of Ekur-zakir who was closest to him and evidently the oldest man in the group.

The king continued, "Welcome to the palace. I have heard many things about you during these last days, and I decided that I wanted to meet you myself. I understand that you have come from Babylonia. I would like to know more about your journey and the reasons for your presence here in Jerusalem."

Within moments, two servants arrived from a side door with trays of refreshments. The king and everyone sat down, and the discussion began. Leandros introduced Elkanah, Eliab, and Ekur-zakir in particular, but the other men were also presented individually to the king.

Herod then asked for a detailed explanation concerning the star. He wanted to know when it had first appeared and how the men had discerned that the star had something to do with the Jewish messianic hope. Illis-kutul was elected to explain the incidents involving the star, but Eliab helped him because there were moments when the king did not fully understand the Babylonian's Aramaic.

While Herod put on an agreeable facade, he inwardly desired to take a sword and put the men to death. They seemed to have no idea how disturbing their appearance in Jerusalem had been for him. He only sensed a threat to his throne. They were fascinated by a star, but he was attempting to preserve his kingdom. Star or no star, he would accomplish all his desire. He would find this so-called Messiah.

After about a half an hour, the king continued his questioning by saying, "Could you show me the star? Is it visible at this moment?"

Illis-kutul responded, "Yes, my lord if the sky is clear to the east in less than an hour we can show it to you. Is there an upper terrace here in the palace which has a view toward the east?"

The king responded by saying yes and encouraged Leandros to make the necessary arrangements so that the group could get to a place where the star would be visible. Herod then continued to question the men about their lives in Babylonia.

However, toward the end of their time together Herod finally spoke up saying, "My advisors among the Jewish religious leaders have told me that the Messiah is to be born in Bethlehem, a village which is well known because of its connection with David, the king. David was born there over one thousand years ago. There is a passage in the book of the prophet Micah to the effect that a ruler for Israel will come out of the town of Bethlehem in the future. I encourage you to go to Bethlehem and make a thorough inquiry. The town is nearby. It is just south of Jerusalem. It seems to me that you will certainly find the child. You have already been well informed about this recently born future ruler through the message which you have ascertained in the stars. It would appear that fate has decided to allow you to find him."

Herod then adjusted himself in his seat and continued, "When you have found him, please come back here to tell me, and we will go together so I can also pay homage to this messianic king. Even if my health has not been particularly good in these last days, I will certainly be able to make a journey to Bethlehem or have the child brought here instead."

The king hesitated a moment and then began again, "Although some people may think otherwise, I am a pious man. No doubt you have seen how I rebuilt the Jewish temple. God is worthy of our best efforts."

Ekur-zakir spoke, "Please know my lord the king, we have certainly noticed how you have rebuilt and adorned the Jewish temple. It is truly a marvel."

Herod continued, "Thank you, I am glad you appreciate it. I do have a request to make of you. I ask you in all seriousness, please, do not tell others about your interview with me. There has been so much excitement in Jerusalem because of your coming; I would prefer that the city be less stirred up."

Herod paused briefly and then said, "Later, when you have found the child, and I am able to see him, then the people will be encouraged to see their king alongside this heaven-sent savior. At that point, they can rejoice to know that I too am a pious man who is seeking the best for the nation. Therefore please keep the knowledge of our rendezvous to yourselves until the appropriate moment. Then all can rejoice."

"In addition, I will send a servant early tomorrow morning to speak with one of the businessmen in Bethlehem. He will probably be able to host you in his home. However, we will try to work this out in a discreet manner so that you will not be disturbed more than is necessary by curious people. My servant will probably be back with word from this businessman by midmorning. You can envisage a trip on to Bethlehem either in the afternoon or perhaps even the next day depending on your commitments here in Jerusalem. I understand that you have gotten to know a number of the religious authorities. It is possible that they would like to question you some more about the star. Therefore I understand if you are not able to leave immediately."

Herod said this although inwardly he hoped that the men would make their departure almost immediately the next day.

About a half hour later, everyone present was guided up to the terrace on the roof of the palace. The sky to the east was clear, and there was no moon. Various lamps had been lit to illuminate the surface of the terrace. The king came up after the others. He had himself carried up on a portable chair by four servants.

There on the palace terrace, Illis-kutul explained to the king what was about to happen. Suen-magir estimated that the first main star in the constellation of the fertility goddess Shala, named GÌR ár šá A (Zavijava) was about five cubits (10°) above the horizon. MUL.BABBAR (Jupiter) would soon become visible. While the king an the others waited, the famous star soon appeared over the eastern horizon. The king did remark how the star was the brightest object in the sky at that moment.

No one among the Magi thought very much about where MUL.BABBAR would be later in the night. They all believed that the star had already given its message. After about ten minutes of looking at the star, Herod thanked the men and again instructed them to proceed to Bethlehem to look for the child. Then the king gave orders to be carried downstairs in his chair. The wise men followed and were accompanied by Leandros toward the small entrance where they had entered the palace.

Herod, arriving in his bedroom and having sent his servants away, took a cushion from his bed, placed it over his face and screamed with all his might. "I will kill this child. He shall not live." He repeated the phrase several times.

Then he continued with determination but less effort, "My sons will inherit the kingdom. I have worked so hard! They will inherit the kingdom, and I will not be outdone by this Messiah."

In a back room, a chief servant threatened the men who had seen the wise men in the palace that night saying, "Be warned, if you say anything to any other slaves or anyone in the city concerning what you have seen this night, you will be put to death. I have received this command from the king himself. No one is to know that the wise men were here this night. Do you understand? No one is to know what took place here this evening. Be warned; your lives are at stake. I will see to your execution myself. Do not breath a word of this to anyone."

After having spent a few hours at the palace, the men went back to their lodging. Exiting the palace by a small side door, again the group of cloaked soldiers led the wise men through the streets. Although from time to time the planet was visible on their journey, no one in the group particularly thought about MUL.BABBAR while the men were walking back to Elkanah's house. Arriving back at their lodging, they discussed what had happened while they were at the palace.

Elkanah reacted by saying, "Who knows, perhaps Herod himself will become a true follower of God. He rebuilt our temple for us and embellished it magnificently as you have seen. However, at the same time, the king has given money to rebuild pagan temples for other nations. Here in our land, he has built three temples dedicated to Rome and the emperor. These temples are in Sebaste in Samaria, Caesarea on the coast and the other is in the far north of the country in Panais, just at the western edge of Mount Hermon. There is a large spring there that is the source of the Jordan River."

After pausing, he continued, "Herod is a complex person. He cannot be entirely trusted, but he has also astonished us. Perhaps he will indeed want to meet the young Messiah."

Ekur-zakir spoke up saying, "It would be marvelous if the king himself were convinced and he would be able to meet the young king."

Iqisa, Eliab, and Suen-magir nodded in agreement, but Nikolaos and Illis-kutul did not say a word.

The Warning

Toward midnight, the men dispersed into their bedrooms. Illis-kutul shared a room with Eliab and Suen-magir. They finally all settled in for a much needed night of rest. Each one drifted off to sleep fairly quickly. They were at ease. They had specific direction concerning where to seek the Messiah. Their quest seemed to be nearing its goal.

However, during the night Illis-kutul had a dream, in which he and the other Magi were riding down a road. Illis-kutul somehow knew that they were going to the place where they were supposed to meet the young Messiah. It was during the daytime. Olive groves lined each side of the dusty road. As the group was advancing, unexpectedly and strangely about twenty-five paces in front of them several flames of fire began to appear. Quickly the group of Magi, servants, and guards came to a stop.

Slowly at first and then more fervently, the glimmers of flame grew from stationary points in the air in front of them. Soon the flames stretched down to the ground and became as tall as human beings. Finally, the glimmering flames were transformed into five angels dressed in white tunics and gold armor. After their transformation, a glow of light rested in the air around each of the angels. The angels completely blocked the road ahead. Each one was dressed for battle in armor with their swords drawn. In the dream, the angels were only 20 paces away from the Magi, and it was clear that they would not be allowed to advance any further.

Finally, after a pause, the angel in the middle of the line advanced five paces and looked at Illis-kutul directly. Even while the angel directed his gaze toward him, Illis-kutul was not fearful, although the sight was awe-inspiring. He was genuinely filled with wonder by the presence of this shining warrior angel. He knew that the vision was of utmost seriousness.

The angel spoke, "You have been chosen to meet the young Messiah, the true king of all the earth. We are protecting the young child and his family. You are forbidden to return and see the king and to tell him the location of the child. We have been sent to warn you. Do not fear to disobey the king. Fear God. As it says in the book of Proverbs 'The fear of the Lord is the beginning of wisdom.' Therefore be wise. You are to return to your homeland by another route. After your visit to Bethlehem you will not return to Jerusalem, nor are you to travel back to Damascus. You will soon discover the route that you are to follow on your way home. Some of our company will help you return to your land. I repeat, do not trust or fear the king. Do not return to the palace to inform the king concerning the child's location."

The angel then bowed slightly. He turned and walked back to his companions. Then the band of angels turned and began walking down the road in front of the Magi. In a few moments, they seemed to vanish as they had appeared. Slowly they were transformed into glowing flames which gradually became dimmer until they were gone entirely. Again the road between the olive trees was clear. In the dream Illis-kutul looked at his companions, they all seemed utterly mystified. The message was clear. They were not to return to see the king.[10]

Almost immediately after the dream, Illis-kutul came out of his slumber. His senses were wholly awakened, and his mind was clear. He could hear Suen-magir, and Eliab breathing and both seemed to be still sleeping soundly. Realizing that his friends were still quite asleep, Illis-kutul said nothing. The other men were in another room. Illis-kutul decided that in the morning he would tell the others. Manifestly the angel's words were to be taken with the utmost seriousness. Illis-kutul closed his eyes, rolled to one side and allowed himself to go back to sleep. He felt completely at peace.

---

10 The men were warned in a dream not to return to Herod (Matthew 2:12). Matthew does not tell us when this took place. The dream is mentioned after the Magi's visit to Jesus' family. However, it is not certain when the dream took place chronologically. The dream could have happened either before or after the Magi's encounter with the child Messiah.

Month IX - Kislimu / Kislev - Day 30   Sunday morning - Dec. 28, 2 BC

The next morning at breakfast, Elkanah greeted all the men warmly. However, as they began to eat, he asked the servants to leave and to close the doors.

He then spoke with hushed tones saying, "Yesterday evening before I went to sleep I had the distinct impression that I should encourage you to be especially careful concerning the king. The king is ill. He was very civil and even charming with you last night. But, although he still has all his wits, he is known to be seized with fits of anger."

"I do think I need to warn you. The king has suffered great disappointments in these last years. Even at this moment the crown prince, Antipater, is in prison on charges of conspiracy. While the king desires for you to return to see him and tell him where he can find the child, I am not sure that the king can be trusted. He put two of his sons to death less than three years ago with hardly any proof on the simple suspicion of treason. Your own lives may even be in danger at this moment."

Illis-kutul had not forgotten his dream. However, in the busy atmosphere of getting washed and dressed, he had not yet sensed that he had a good opportunity to share anything with the others. Now Elkanah had given him the perfect context to relate the dream.

Illis-kutul raised his hand and said, "I have something to tell you all. Last night, I had an amazing dream."

He then recounted his experience in detail. Hearing Illis-kutul's account of his dream astounded everyone.

There was a moment or two of silence, then Eliab intervened. While still speaking with confidence he spoke in hushed tones like Elkanah and Illis-kutul before him, "God has spoken very clearly. He will also show us exactly what to do. We will need to explain some of this to Callisthenes since we will not be able to return to Babylonia by the normal route."

Nikolaos then spoke up, "As you all know I have been somewhat skeptical from the beginning about this entire endeavor, however now I am convinced. The gods or the God of the Jews seem to be involved in this affair. I cannot deny it. I have never before seen so many symbolic astronomical events involving kingship. Now, in addition, there are angelic manifestations in dreams. This is amazing."

Nikolaos then continued, "I have also spent several decades of my life observing and counseling high officials and even the Parthian emperor. We have some serious security issues facing us. I should tell you now my inner thoughts. We do not know if we can trust Herod's appointed host for us in Bethlehem. It is obvious that we should go to the town, but how are we going to find the child without some local help? As the dream indicates, there is a danger both for us and the young child."

"There is another aspect of things which we need to consider. Without a doubt the king also has spies. Will the spies be in the household of our host? Will our host be one of the king's right-hand men? Will spies and informants be watching our every move? The king probably will make an effort to be informed of our activities through every means at his disposition."

Everyone knew that Nikolaos was right. Moreover, inwardly they all asked themselves, "How will we find the child without the king being aware of it?"

11

A Sign Over Bethlehem

December 2 BC and January 1 BC

Chapter Contents:

A Sign over Bethlehem

The Preparations for Departure

Month IX - Kislimu / Kislev - Day 30

After breakfast, the Magi, servants, and guards began to make their preparations for the departure to Bethlehem. The servants had additional responsibilities packing and going to the large markets in Jerusalem to make some necessary purchases. The Magi, Alexis, and Callisthenes all agreed to wait until a messenger came from the king before their departure. They wanted to be sure that at least enough housing for the astronomers had been secured. It was no small affair to lodge the entire team even if some of them would be in tents.

Meanwhile, Herod sent his messenger early in the morning to Bethlehem, well before the wise men ate breakfast. The messenger traveled on foot, although ordinarily royal messengers were sent on horseback so they could arrive quickly and hasten a response. However, this day a somewhat common messenger who had often been employed for less important messages was being sent on foot from the palace to Bethlehem. The king was determined not to draw too any attention to his involvement in sending the wise men to Bethlehem. The messenger had not seen the king, but he had received the message from a minor scribe in the king's service. The messenger did not know that he was carrying a personal message from the king although there was a rather unceremonious royal seal on the document.

Arriving in Bethlehem, the messenger found his way to the business-man Malachi Ben Nahshon's home. After a short wait, the messenger was received by the chief servant Shelumiel who tried to keep his master from being bothered except by the most pressing and essential communications. Shelumiel received the young man kindly and was not surprised to see a royal seal on the message.

After looking briefly at the discreet royal seal on the parchment roll, Shelumiel took the document into Malachi's office and presented it to his master. It was not unusual for Malachi to receive messages from the palace in Jerusalem, so Shelumiel did not pay a lot of attention to the note. Yes, there was a royal seal, but it was one used by an undersecretary, not the principal authorities at the palace.

Malachi had been involved in business affairs concerning the king's palace and fortress at the Herodium for years. He had worked on several building projects on both sites. Various palace officials in Jerusalem often sent messages to Malachi concerning the projects at the Herodium. Malachi's servant had thought to himself, this communication was probably no different, but the messenger wanted an immediate response.

Malachi was seated in his office just off the Roman style garden which dominated the central section of the house. Taking the message from his servant, who immediately stepped outside, Malachi opened the note and discovered that it was a rather surprising text, which had come directly from the king himself.

My Dear Friend Malachi,

I want to thank you again for your loyal service these last many years. Your services rendered to me at the Herodium have made my stays at that palace a real pleasure. At this time my health has declined, and I am not so easily able to travel to my palace near Bethlehem. Hopefully, my health will soon improve.

I have a favor to ask of you. Some men from Babylonia have arrived. They are astronomers who are interested in the Jewish Messiah. They claim that a series of celestial signs centered on a particular star has announced the birth of the Messiah. I have had indications from the priests and scribes in Jerusalem that the Messiah is probably to be born in Bethlehem. Therefore I am sending the men from the East to your town to contin-

ue their research. If at all possible, I desire that you would host these men and do anything necessary to facilitate their searching.

It is not my desire that others would know that I sent them to you. You can even pretend that they came to you from another contact. As a favor to me, I would appreciate it if you host these men for a week or more while they seek to find the supposedly recently born young Messiah in the area of Bethlehem. I understand that the whole group is more than 20 men of whom two-thirds are servants and guards. I only ask you to take personal care of the scholars from the East. The others can camp nearby and be ready to serve their masters when needed.

Herod, King of Judaea

Malachi almost dropped the letter. His mouth and throat became a bit dry. He did not like being asked to be involved in what could be a sensitive matter. He did not mind building structures at the Herodium palace or even providing food and entertainment for the king. However, hosting and aiding a group of foreigners to find the Jewish Messiah was not to his liking.

Just a day or so earlier, one of Malachi's servants had informed him that all of Jerusalem was talking about a group of scholars from the East who had come looking for the Messiah. Now the king had become involved as well, and finally, Malachi himself was also being implicated in the affair as the host for these foreigners. It was the will of the king.

Several minutes went by until Shelumiel re-entered Malachi's office saying, "Master, the man who brought you the letter is waiting for a response from you." Malachi, raised his hand just indicating that he would like a few minutes to respond. He then took a small piece of parchment and wrote the following words:

Malachi Ben Nahshon to Herod the King, Greetings.

Thank you for your communication, which I have received early this morning. I am sorry to hear that the king is not in good health. According to your request, I am willing to host the men who have come from Babylonia. I will do my best to facilitate their research. My household will certainly be ready to receive the men later today. Most of their servants and guards can camp in an olive grove to the east of my home. I will try to make their time in Bethlehem agreeable.

Your servant,

Malachi Ben Nahshon

Having rolled the small piece of parchment, Malachi partly melted a small piece of wax with a lamp which was placed on one corner of the desk. He then fixed the parchment with his seal. Malachi called Shelumiel and indicated that the messenger should be introduced into the office. The messenger, having arrived in the room, stood before Malachi, who was still seated beside his desk.

Malachi raised the note toward the messenger saying, "Return to your master. Here is my response, and please hurry." The young man left the office and walked hastily toward the center of Bethlehem and then toward the capital.

Malachi turned toward Shelumiel and said, "We have some visitors, who are being sent here by the king. Perhaps you have already heard of a group of foreigners who have come from Babylonia searching for our Messiah? A group of over 20 men, of whom two-thirds are servants and guards, will be here before nightfall. If you can believe it, the guests are astronomers! I would suspect that some of the servants will arrive earlier. You have about half the day to prepare."

Shelumiel's mouth opened, he wanted to say several things about how difficult it would be to get everything ready, but he stopped himself. He merely replied, "Yes, master. We will make everything ready."

With that, he turned and left the room and Malachi tried to return to his routine work. However, he found his mind dominated by the thought of scholars from the East arriving at his house.

He thought, "A group of eastern astronomers is looking for the Messiah! How can this be happening? Much of the next week will probably be filled with entertaining this group. How will I ever get any work done?"

But Malachi was also a pious man. The idea came to him, "What if this is all true? What if the Messiah is close by?" Malachi stood pondering this for a short moment. Then looking at his desk, he saw several apples in a dish on one corner of his desktop. Picking one up and biting into the fruit, he thought, "I hope we have more apples in the reserves, but they will probably soon be gone. I am glad I can enjoy this one."

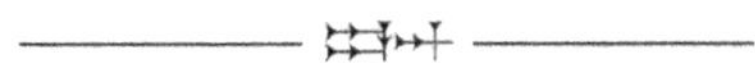

A few hours later, the messenger arrived at a small office toward the back of Herod's palace. He delivered the message and went about other affairs. The undersecretary discreetly took the note and gave it to a servant who often carried messages to the king. Even the undersecretary was not aware of the reason that the correspondence was being sent, but he had been informed that this particular man carried an important message. Within fifteen minutes, the king had read the message and had a scribe write another short text to Elkanah and the Magi who were staying at Elkanah's home. The king, through his intermediaries, also had two guides hired to take the scholars to the right location. These men were not even aware that they were in the king's service because the entire matter was handled with considerable discretion.

Elkanah received the information about the arrangements. The Magi continued their preparations to go to Bethlehem in the late afternoon. The king indicated that Malachi would be ready to receive them just before nightfall. Two trusted men would guide them to their host. However, the king also suggested the Magi arrive just before dark, allowing them to enter the town without making an enormous impression on the local population. At that hour, most everyone would be home eating and preparing themselves for the night. Most of the servants and guards would be guided to a place where they could camp.

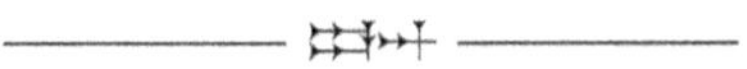

In the early afternoon, Theron, a short man of 27 years, with a curly brown beard left Herod's palace. He was making his way to Bethlehem on foot on a mission for the king. As much as possible, he was to watch the eastern scholars' activities from afar, and he would consult with some of Herod's informers in Bethlehem. The king had instructed Theron to inform him immediately if there were any suspect activities involving the foreigners. Theron had been given a thorough briefing about the men and the messianic quest, which had brought the men to Judaea. The young man was not particularly religious. However, the king's silver and gold were immensely attractive to him.

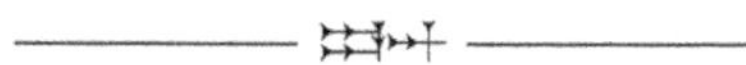

In the late afternoon, when Shelumiel was coming into Malachi's office to arrange some papers, he saw an apple core sitting on the corner of his master's desk. Malachi had eaten it sometime during the day.

Shelumiel thought, "This needs to be removed and thrown away." Immediately, he reached out his hand to grab it, and his thoughts continued, "This was an apple from the reserves in the house which was being stored for the winter. In the next few weeks, most of those apples will be gone. One will still probably be able to buy dried fruit in the market, but happily, we also have some dried apples stored in the house."

Then Shelumiel had a flash, "Oh, Yes, of course, the market! What about the men that I heard last year in the market?"

He suddenly remembered the conversation that he had overheard concerning the shepherds, the angels, and the Messiah. In the daily rush of life's activities, Shelumiel had almost forgotten the discussion which he had overheard about one year earlier. But now the scene came back to him with full force.

Going to Bethlehem

Kislimu / Kislev - Day 30 — Sunday Afternoon - December 28, 2 BC

By early afternoon, Alexis and Callisthenes had made their preparations for the journey to Bethlehem. Some necessary items had been purchased, and the baggage had been prepared for the short journey. Four of the guards would go with the servants. Four other guards, along with Callisthenes, stayed with the astronomers and Eliab. After some final preparations, an initial group with tents and the baggage went first toward Bethlehem with one of the guides in the early afternoon.

Hospitality in Bethlehem

Tebētum / Tevet - Day 1 — Evening - December 28, 2 BC

When the Magi arrived at the door of Malachi's home, the guide alerted the household servants. Soon, Malachi, himself appeared in the entrance of the house and Shelumiel stood behind him. Malachi smiled and seemed to be very welcoming, but he was a bit reserved. Although he did not wholly betray his emotions to the group, in his own heart he was still wondering about these men and their mission. In his mind, he was being assailed by a cohort of questions: "What will all this bring? Will these men succeed? How can I help them? Will my home and manner of living be offensive? What will I say to the king if somehow we fail to find this young Messiah?"

Shelumiel's mind was still filled with details about the lodging and food situation, but he too looked over the small crowd of Magi and their guards. He immediately noticed a man who looked a bit different and somehow realized that he was Jewish. He said to himself, "Who is this man? What is he doing with these foreigners? Is he from Babylonia as well?"

In front of Malachi's home, the Magi's other servants arrived with a few guards. They were camping in the olive groves further to the east of the house. The servants who had come earlier had already unloaded the necessary clothing and personal effects for the wise men at the house. They gave their report, and then they led Callisthenes, and the other guards and servants to the camping area. Only Alexis and one servant were destined to be lodged in Malachi's home. Callisthenes was convinced that the wise men would certainly be safe in the big villa.

As the men entered the house, Nikolaos pretended to look at the ground around him and over his shoulder for a moment, but then as he continued the pretense, he trained his eyes down an adjoining street. In the growing evening shadows, he saw a man about 50 yards away at the edge of a building. He was looking down the street toward the wise men.

Nikolaos thought to himself, "Yes, there he is, that must be one of the king's spies, just as I suspected." The fifty-year-old, Greek astronomer and skeptic did not even pretend to have noticed the man. He merely scratched his forehead as he continued to appear to glance quickly at the ground and the outside of the villa. He then turned entirely toward the front door of Malachi's house and entered.

Fifty yards away, Theron had not noticed that Nikolaos had seen him. Herod's spy thought he had done a good job avoiding being seen. However, he did not know that he had adversaries in the developing game of hide and seek.

Several rooms were available in Malachi's home. He lived alone except for his servants. His children lived in the area, but none of them were still at home because they had all founded their own families. Unfortunately, Malachi's wife had died suddenly after a few days of illness only two years previously. Seeking to please his guests and offer them the maximum of safety and privacy, Malachi felt inspired to place the wise men in two rooms above the main floor of the house on the upper terrace. He knew how much he enjoyed going up to the roof terrace and looking at the stars. Without a doubt, this would be an excellent spot for his guests.

The men entered the inner courtyard and had something to drink to refresh themselves in the dining area. Malachi informed them that they would eat after the men were able to see their rooms and the upper terrace. Then, Malachi had a servant lead the men up the stairway on one side of the inner court garden to the upper floor. The servants in the household were busy taking the men's belongings to their lodgings. The sun was well set, and the stars were starting to appear when the men arrived on the terrace. Immediately they reacted with pleasant jokes about having been deprived of the stars for almost two weeks, even though they had been on the king's palace terrace the night before.

The two rooms designated for the wise men were toward the western part of the villa. No windows in the rooms looked out over the street facing the main entrance of the house. The buildings facing the house to the west also had two stories which partially blocked the view in that direction. A small pergola was in front of the terrace rooms to the east, but the terrace was open toward the north, south, and the east. The eastern portion of the terrace was completely free of obstructions, giving a marvelous view out toward the olive grove where the guards and most of the servants were encamped. At the end of the terrace, the camp could be seen about 100 yards away, a little lower down the ridge. A fire had been started at the campsite, and the guards and the other servants had already managed to set up a few tents. Soon others would quickly be put in place.

Standing on the southern part of the terrace under the pergola, Suen-magir immediately remarked the crescent moon in the west. He said, "Look, everyone, the new moon, the month of Tebētum has begun."

The moon was already very low in the southwestern sky, being almost hidden by other buildings. While the others were getting their first look at their rooms, Suen-magir placed himself at the edge of the terrace to watch the moon as it disappeared. To the west and southwest, the center and southern parts of town were slightly higher than Malachi's home. Therefore the buildings hid the moon from his view fairly quickly.

When the moon had disappeared, Suen-magir found Alexis and asked him if the astronomical materials had been unloaded at the house. Alexis replied that they were in the camp and Suen-magir asked him to send the other servant to bring back the astronomical documents, the cuneiform almanac for the current year, a few instruments and some writing materials, which could be useful in the coming nights. Alexis then sent the servant to look for the material in the camp.

Having gotten installed in their rooms, the men were only able to wash up briefly before going down below for supper. Downstairs Malachi was happy to hear that the men were pleased with their lodgings. They praised his choice of the terrace location. Certainly, they would take advantage of the situation for doing some astronomical observations. All during the meal the wise men were being sized up by Malachi, and similarly, Malachi was being keenly observed by his guests. The conversation was fairly subdued. Malachi asked about the Magi's journey from Babylonia. They provided him with a few details of some of the highlights.

As the men arrived back in their rooms, they discussed doing some astronomical observations during the night. The previous eight weeks had been hectic. The journey from Borsippa to Dura-Europos had allowed the men to observe the sky from time to time, but afterward going to Tadmur, Damascus, and on to Jerusalem they were often exhausted from their daily travels. Happily, the sky was readily visible from the eastern part of the terrace. In the discussion about the night's astronomical watch, it was decided that everyone would first sleep for several hours.

Suen-magir then said, "I would like to do observations during the last part of the night until dawn." The others were in agreement. Malachi's servants had placed beds for each man and everyone found a place to sleep.

When the wise men went to bed on their first evening in Bethlehem, they had no idea that their night would be interrupted. Malachi and the servants also went to sleep.

Shelumiel had a bit of difficulty going to sleep because he kept thinking of the conversation he had overheard in the market almost a year previously. He thought, "The man said that he had seen angels announcing that the Messiah had been born, now these men also arrive. What will happen? Should I say anything to Malachi about the incident a year ago? Yes, I probably should."

A Revelation During The Night

Tebētum / Tevet - Day 1   Late Night - December 29, 2 BC

When Suen-magir eventually woke up, he could see about the room because the servants had placed a small lamp toward the door. It was there in case the men needed to get up during the night. The lamp was partially hidden behind a small wooden box so that it did not give too much light. There was no moon, nor were there any lights in the town to provide any indications of how to move about in the house or on the terrace. It was a luxury to have a lamp all night, but it was helpful.

Having gotten up and gotten dressed, Suen-magir went outside and observed the sky all around. MUL.BABBAR had arisen several hours before, so it was already most of the way to mid-heaven about three-quarters of the way to the zenith when Suen-magir got onto the terrace. After another hour, Dilbat (Nogah/Venus) rose.[3] About an hour previously Salbatanu (Mars) and Antares had risen in the east. Betelgeuse in Orion and GENNA (Saturn) were setting just as Dilbat rose. Some of the stars in Sagittarius were shining brightly in the south, and Sirius was just at the point of setting toward the west-southwest.

A little while after Dilbat (Venus) had risen, Suen-magir was looking up toward MUL.BABBAR (Jupiter) again. The star was nearing the zenith. Looking at Venus rising higher in the sky, Suen-magir thought back to the heliacal rising of Jupiter four months before. Venus had risen at almost the same moment as MUL.BABBAR. He remembered seeing it so clearly. It was somewhat rare for two planets to rise on the eastern horizon at almost the same moment. That had taken place almost exactly four months previously.

Then the thought came back to his mind again and again, "Four months, four months, yes, four months! Of course, it was four months after the heliacal rising." A light was coming on in his mind. He then thought, "I need to verify things."

Entering into his room Suen-magir lit another small lamp off of the light of the primary lamp and again opened the door to the terrace. He placed the little lamp on a table on the terrace and went back into the room. He searched in a bag for the almanac of the current astronomical year. He found the cuneiform document on a baked mud tablet. It had been protected and it had traveled well all the way from Mesopotamia. Taking the tablet, Suen-magir went back outside on the terrace. Turning the tablet over on the reverse side, Suen-magir looked down through the list of months until he arrived at the tenth month of the year and the first day.

There it was written, "On the first, MUL.BABBAR will become stationary in AB.SIN (Virgo)."[4]

---

3 Toward 3:00 AM local mean time (LMT).

4 The actual stationary point was on the late evening of the 27th of December (almost on the 28th). However, the Babylonians may have been off by a day or two. The often referred to the stationary as taking place on "around a certain day."

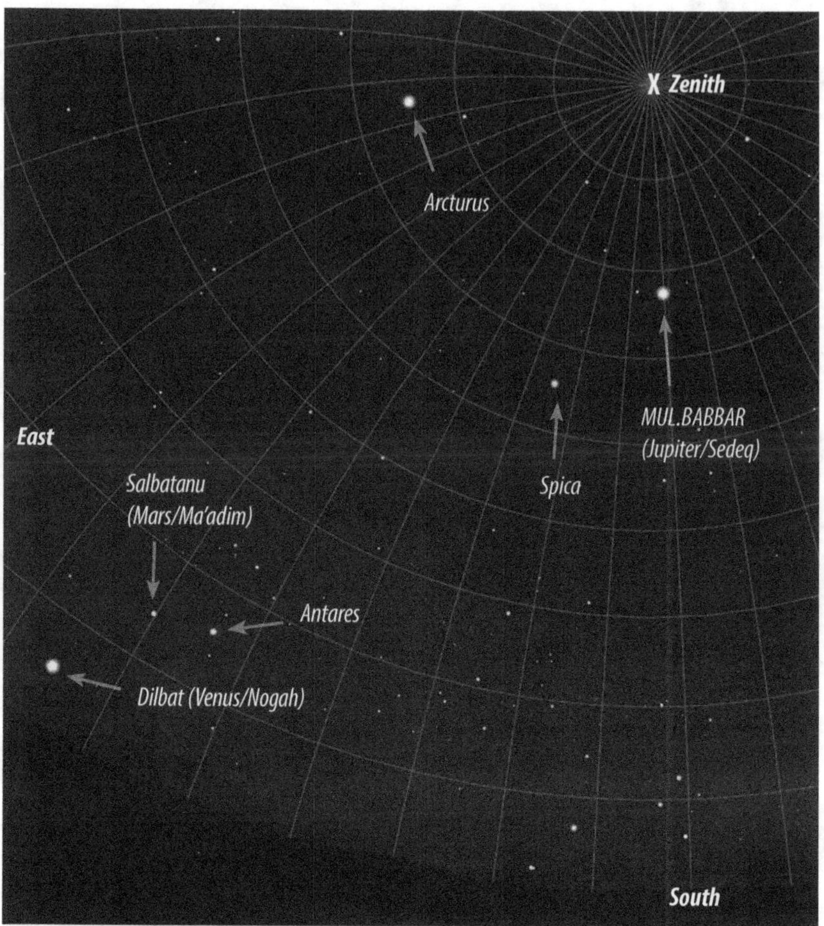

Illustration: The sky toward the east and above. Dec. 29, 2 BC.
MUL.BABBAR was approaching the zenith toward 3:00 AM local time in Bethlehem. The star was close to being directly overhead above Bethlehem. It was well above the heads of the Magi.

Suen-magir thought, "Considering everything else we have experienced during the last year and a half, it is evident that this is a heavenly sign. MUL.BABBAR is at its first annual stationary point, standing over Bethlehem, the place where the young child was undoubtedly located. The star being at its stationary point follows the same sort of sequence which we have experienced in the east. The star has preceded us to Bethlehem. Essentially it has been waiting for us to arrive."

The stream of ideas continued, "The star is giving us one last message. It is confirming that the Messiah is indeed present in the Bethlehem area. Previously, the stationary point was a sign in the series. No one besides an all-powerful and wise God could have planned this sequence of events. Only a day and a half previously we had been making preparations to visit the king at the palace. Now we are in Bethlehem exactly at the time of the planet's stationary phase."

Suen-magir began to laugh to himself quietly. He was elated with emotion. He rose and went to his room and woke up the other members of the team asking them to come out onto the terrace, saying, "There is something which you all must see and hear."

Then he went to the second room and did the same thing. Some said, "What can be so important, we are sleeping?" But Suen-magir could not be put off. After several minutes everyone was gathered on the terrace.

Suen-magir said, "I want you all to look up, the object is very high. It is about three-quarters of the way to the zenith. We can all strain our necks looking up for a short moment. What do you see?"

Several of the men replied in soft tones, "It is MUL.BABBAR."

Standing in front of them all, Suen-magir took the tablet and raised the small lamp. He continued saying, "Here is a phrase from the almanac for this year on the first day of the tenth month. That is right at this moment. 'On the first, MUL.BABBAR will become stationary in AB.SIN.'[5] Does this little phrase mean anything to you? What day is today? Where was the moon located last evening? What does this mean?" After just a moment he added, "We did not dream that we would be in Bethlehem tonight or any night."

Everyone stood astounded for a moment and then Illis-kutul responded in the dim light with a very evident smile on his face, "It is evident that this is a sign for us. The celestial sign is affirming that the Messiah is indeed here. This stationary point is a continuation of the series of signs connected to MUL.BABBAR's normal cycle."

---

5 AB.SIN was the Babylonian astronomical name for the constellation of the Virgin (Virgo). However, the name means "The Furrow" as in a furrow for seed planting. The constellation was not conceived of by the Babylonians in the same way as the Hellenistic Greek-speaking peoples to the west.

Illis-kutul's statement caused Iqisa to begin to chuckle, followed by Suen-magir, Ekur-zakir, Eliab, and the others. Soon they were all laughing quietly, but very hard. They were trying their best not to wake the entire household in the rooms below.

While still laughing, Hormizdah sat down on a bench against the wall and struck his hand against his thigh because of his emotion. He bent over holding his stomach and simply could not stop laughing. Everyone was filled with an incredible joy. None of them had ever experienced such a clear divine heavenly "wink" at a specified moment. Their adventure was undoubtedly going to succeed, and God was making it very clear, first by the dream, but now by this evident stellar sign. The king planet, MUL.BABBAR, was announcing the Messiah's presence. The young child was indeed within a short distance. They were going to find him. At this point, there was no denying it. God had arranged everything.

After about ten minutes the laughing died off, and Eliab dropped to his knees, lifted his hands and began to pray. Some of the others sat down or kneeled, but a few men just stood and raised their hands in praise. Eliab prayed, "You, oh Lord are certainly the great God of all the earth and the heavens. We have come here because of your heavenly signs. You continue to speak in a most amazing manner. Obviously, you have granted us your favor, and we shall certainly find the Righteous One."

When their prayers ended, looking over to one side in the darkness, they saw a man standing at the top of the terrace stairs, which led down to the garden below. Suen-magir lifted the lamp, and in the dim light, one could see Malachi with tears streaming down his cheeks. Shelumiel was standing right behind him. His eyes were not dry, and he knew that he needed to speak to Malachi at the first opportunity.

Planning the Search

Tebētum / Tevet - Day 1   Monday Morning - December 29, 2 BC

Several hours later over breakfast, the Magi and Eliab learned that not only Malachi and Shelumiel, but several members of the household staff had been awakened by the heavy, but mostly restrained, laughing on the terrace. Malachi had gotten his response. He could trust the men. They were serious about the Messiah. It took him about a half-hour to understand the depths of the significance of the evident sign which the men had witnessed during the night. He had no previous knowledge of Babylonian astronomy.

However, now they all needed to sit down and discuss how to find the young Messiah. After breakfast, Malachi summoned everyone into his office. He arranged for there to be enough Roman style chairs, and even though space was a bit restrained all the wise men as well as Eliab, Alexis and Callisthenes joined them. Also in attendance was Shelumiel, Malachi's chief servant. Shelumiel still had not had a moment to speak to Malachi in private.

Malachi opened the discussion by saying, "When we discovered you on the terrace last night, I understood the depths of your commitment to the young Messiah and your uprightness before God. I believe that I can trust you. I am delighted that things have worked out for you to be in my home. However, you should be aware that our king is a dangerous man. We will need to be careful."

"I am not very excited to be involved with you in an affair which concerns the governance of the realm. This business about the Messiah is not simply a matter of religious belief to the king. It is a matter of utmost seriousness, which concerns the future of his kingdom. I will not say much more about this at this moment, but we are going to need to reflect on how we are going to deal with the king even if you find the young Messiah. We can discuss this in the coming days."

Malachi continued, "Now there is a more urgent affair. How are you going to find the young Messiah? Or perhaps I should say, How are we going to find the child Messiah? Yes, the king has instructed me to help you with this matter as much as possible."

Malachi continued, "I would suggest the following procedure. All the Jewish Rabbis in the area know more or less when children have been born, especially young male children because the Rabbis are very often involved in the rites of circumcision which normally take place on the eighth day following the birth. Therefore, please know that it would be a good idea for us to make contact with the local rabbis and work through them to discover the identity of the families who have very young male children. From what you have already told me, the child is less than two years old. But there is a fundamental problem. How are you going to be able to discern which child is the correct one?"

Ekur-zakir signaled to Eliab to explain the perspective of the Magi concerning the child.

Eliab began, "We do not know any way of discerning whether or not any young child might be God's appointed Messiah. However, it may be that the parents of the child know something about his destiny."

Shifting slightly in his chair and clearing his throat, Eliab said, "Let me explain. Already while we were in Babylonia, we thought about the problem of identifying the child. We concluded that in one manner or another we had to have confidence that God himself would probably guide us to the child. The God of Abraham has apparently revealed a message about the coming of the Messiah. It seemed probable to us that God had not revealed this message without also desiring for us to inform others in Judaea about the discovery."

Eliab continued his explanation, "After we finally arrived in Jerusalem we heard that two older people who were something like prophets had an encounter last year with a couple who had brought a young child to the temple. Anna the prophetess and Simeon a righteous and devout man who was looking for the coming of the kingdom of God spoke to the couple and prophesied over their son."

"Unfortunately, both Anna and Simeon have since died. Simeon died only weeks before our arrival in Judaea. And although we asked several people in Jerusalem who knew Anna and Simeon, no one was able to indicate to us where we might find the couple or the child. One person even told us that according to his memory the couple was from Galilee, but he had no other details."

Malachi interrupted, "This is already an excellent start. Since the parents know about the future of their son, then the child can be identified. However, if they have gone to Galilee, we will not be able to find them."

Illis-kutul then said, "It would seem to us that the child is still certainly close by from the sign we were given through the star this past night."

Malachi replied, "Yes, I suppose that you are right. It would seem that the child is still here, even if his parents are possibly from Galilee. Alright, as I proposed earlier, we can contact the local rabbis and inform them about your desire to meet the parents of children of less than two years of age. The rabbis can set up some meetings with various parents. I can insist that you be able to see all the children less than two years of age. It will take several days before a series of interviews with the parents can begin. Things go slowly here as they probably do in your small towns in Babylonia."

Malachi continued, "I will also reflect on this situation some more. God willing, perhaps there are other means of reaching the family. I would suggest that you get some rest. I will contact the rabbis myself this afternoon. I suspect that we could have some small children here with their parents in the coming day or so. However, people do not like to be disturbed. So it may take some coaxing."

After the astronomers and Eliab went to their lodgings, Shelumiel tried to speak with Malachi, but there were other pressing issues concerning buying food in the market and some household affairs that needed to be settled. It seemed impossible for Shelumiel to speak privately with Malachi at that moment.

Hearing Malachi and thinking about the situation, Shelumiel said to himself, "The king is handling all this with a lot of discretion. The messenger was not one who would normally have been recognized as coming from the palace. He also came on foot, not on horseback. The king does not want anyone to know that he sent these astronomers to Malachi."

Shelumiel could understand that the situation was potentially very serious. But he held his tongue although he desperately wanted to reveal his secret concerning the shepherds. He would need to speak with Malachi privately before mentioning the secret to the others.

An Unexpected Connection

Tebētum / Tevet - Day 1   Afternoon - December 29, 2 BC

After the noon meal, Malachi hurriedly went off to meet the local rabbis. They had already heard about the arrival of the Magi in Jerusalem, but all of them did not yet know that Malachi was hosting the men in Bethlehem. While news travels quickly in small towns, it does not always reach everyone so rapidly. The two local rabbis were more than happy to help out and soon after Malachi visited them they drew up a preliminary list of families who had small children the right age. They said they would send Malachi a complete list by the next day.

Malachi then returned to his house and office for a few hours. When Shelumiel had been informed that his master had returned, he hastily went to Malachi's office. There, he entered the office and closed the door gently behind him. Then Malachi's eyes left a document on his desk and looked directly at Shelumiel.

The chief servant said, "Master I have something of great importance to tell you. I have not found an appropriate moment until now."

Smiling at Shelumiel, Malachi responded, "Well, if there is a problem with your accounts or other matters in the household I have absolute confidence in you. As long as it is not too serious do not worry about it. Mistakes are often made. You do not need to bother me with details."

But Shelumiel replied, "Actually, this concerns the Magi and finding the young child Messiah. As you know, I do not have the habit of telling everything that I know. So I have kept a secret since about this time last year. Somewhat after the festival of Hanukkah last year, one morning I was in the market here in Bethlehem. I happened to overhear a conversation that was extremely interesting. A man who was unmistakably a shepherd was speaking with another man who was selling vegetables. They seemed to be friends. I must have been positioned at exactly the right spot because I overheard several phrases of their conversation."

"Anyway, the shepherd explained to his friend that about a week earlier he and other shepherds had been guarding their flock in an area outside of Bethlehem, when suddenly in the darkness, a large number of angels had appeared to them. One of the angels told the men that the Righteous One, the Messiah, had been born here in Bethlehem that very night and that they would be able to find him in the town."

"Unfortunately at that point there was some noisy conversation nearby I was not able to continue to listen. Also if I lingered any longer, my presence could have attracted their attention, so I walked away. I did not see the men's faces well. I am not sure that I could identify them again. However, it seems that one year ago the Messiah's presence in Bethlehem had been announced by angels to a group of shepherds."

Malachi starred at Shelumiel with a bit of disbelief and said, "You are not joking. This story is amazing. I am surprised. I had not heard anything about this story. Do many people in the area know about this? It would be interesting to see how widespread this story has become."

Shelumiel replied, "I have since heard a few rumors about the shepherds, angels, and the young Messiah from a few people whom I trust, but I did not hear any other solid details. It seems that some of the people in Bethlehem are aware of these stories. However, I do not know how widespread the knowledge of all this has become."

Malachi added, "If what you are saying is true, then the child must have been born at about the time of the census. He would be about one year old."

Malachi then thought it right to tell Shelumiel more. "Well, you heard me yesterday and when I was speaking with the Magi this morning. The king is involved in this affair."

Shelumiel interrupted, "Yes, Master. It seems that the king is trying to be very discreet about the entire matter. The messenger, who came yesterday from the palace, came on foot. He was not riding a horse. One could have thought that his message was from anyone but the king."

Malachi looked keenly at Shelumiel and said, "I see you have well understood that these Magi and even ourselves could get into difficulties concerning this young child."

Shelumiel replied, "Yes, Master one can even lose one's life in dealing with kings."

Malachi said, "Until now my relationship with the king has been good. However, up until now, I never was involved in anything concerning the royal line and the destiny of the nation. It was easy for me to do construction projects for this king. However, this affair is much more delicate."

Then as Malachi's thoughts raced forward, he said, "You know Shelumiel, as you have indicated, some people in town know where to find this young Messiah. It should be possible to do some research discreetly. A few well-placed questions to the right people might help us find the child even before we can interview 20 or 30 couples concerning their children."

Malachi sat upright in his chair and said, "I want you to go out among the shepherds in the area and try to find out if any of them know something about a visit from angels last year. Try not to attract too much attention. You can pretend to be buying sheep, but in reality, you are to be seeking information about the angelic visitation and the messianic child. You can begin tomorrow. Perhaps you will have more success than the rabbis."

Malachi beckoned Shelumiel to come closer to where he was seated, took hold of Shelumiel's hands, looked him firmly in the eyes and said, "This is of great importance, be discreet, be careful. As the presence of the Magi becomes more known in the town, all the eyes will be on this house in the coming days."

Tebētum / Tevet - Day 2   Monday Evening - December 29, 2 BC

On the second evening in Bethlehem, about two and a half hours after sunset, the Magi observed the crescent moon as it set in the west. Illis-kutul was chosen for the late night watch. The whole team then tried to get some sleep, and they were not awakened during the night. Since clouds had accumulated in the skies in the hours before sunrise, Illis-kutul's shift was shortened. But before he went to bed, Illis-kutul thought of his wife and Kallisto back in Babylonia. They would certainly be thinking of him and the others ...

Illis-kutul said to himself, "My daughter is interested in Suen-magir. Well, it would appear that the young man also meets the approval of the

God of Israel. He was the one who first got the revelation about the star over Bethlehem!"

He almost laughed aloud thinking of their experience the night before.

Then his thoughts continued, "Suen-magir seems to have sorted out his pain and personal grief. He is no longer a drunkard. He is no longer visiting young women who would lead him astray. Perhaps I can trust him with my daughter."

Illis-kutul smiled as he thought of the possibilities. "Yes, it will work. I remember Suen-magir before his wife died. He was a good husband. He will be wonderful for Kallisto. My daughter will be blessed. I will speak with Suen-magir about this at the appropriate moment."

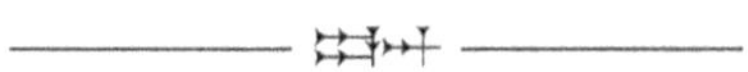

During the long hours of the following day, the men tried to occupy themselves with various activities. Some of the men went to the public square where the daily market was taking place in the morning. Many of the local people were curious about the visitors. Unknown to the Magi, Joseph, also saw Suen-magir, Hormizdah, and Nikolaos in the market, but he stayed over to one side and did not draw near to the men.

Late in the afternoon, some Rabbis came with two families who had recently had children. The meeting was a bit awkward. The Rabbis did not entirely trust the Magi, and it was evident that the two couples did not often visit the inside of a large house belonging to a wealthy family. In the discussions which followed, it was evident that the people who had come did not know anything about a child Messiah. The day ended without any measurable progress, however, at least they had eliminated two families and their children from the Rabbi's list of possible candidates. The Rabbis had assembled a list of over 35 families who might need to be interviewed. Therefore much still was to be done.

The Shepherds Prove Themselves Valuable

Tebētum / Tevet - Day 3   Early Morning - December 31, 2 BC

During the following days, Shelumiel did as Malachi had desired. He started talking to shepherds about possibly buying some sheep. At the same time, he asked a few well-placed questions. Upon meeting the fifth set of shepherds, he found the men whom he was seeking. They were about four miles from Bethlehem on a small ridge not far from Herod's palace fortress called the Herodium.

Shelumiel began by asking questions about the quality of the men's sheep in preparation for a possible acquisition, but at a certain moment, he asked them his main subject of interest.

"I also have a question for you. About one year ago there was a rumor in Bethlehem that some shepherds had seen angels who bore a message about the Messiah. Do you men know anything about this? I would be very interested in hearing the story of how this happened. I have met some people who have heard the story, but they did not have any details. I believe in angels, but like most of us, I have never seen one. For me, it would be fascinating to hear the story."

Shelumiel looked around the group, and he noticed that each one of them was eyeing the other as though they were trying to make a decision. Finally, two of the five men seemed to nod to each other, and the younger one spoke first.

"My name is Rahim, and this is Azariah, he said motioning to another man who was just slightly older. We were about a mile and a half from Bethlehem during the night about one year ago when a large number of angels appeared to us. In fact, all of us saw the sight, but Azariah and I were the first ones. The field around us seemed to light up. There was not any single source of light, but within a few minutes, one could see clearly in the general darkness as though there was a fire in the field where we were. However, all around us, there was no source of light. We woke our companions, and we all started to hear a song which seemed to be coming from the very air itself, only several feet away. It was in a strange, but beautiful language, which none of us had ever heard before. There seemed to be dozens if not hundreds of voices. Amazingly, the sheep were not aroused or alarmed. They did not even seem to notice what was taking place."

Rahim continued, "Within a few moments, a man clothed in white with a beautiful golden headband, as well as a golden sash around his waist was standing in front of us. The man was very powerfully built and had a massive long sword hanging from his side. He seemed to have the appearance of a determined warrior. His entire being shone with light. The man spoke to us saying that the Messiah had been born during that very day in Bethlehem and that we were invited to find the child in the town. He told us that we would find the child wrapped in swaddling clothes and lying in a manger. That seemed odd to us, but who are we to argue with angels?"

"Then in the next moments in front of our eyes dozens of shimmering flames appeared, and after that, there were even hundreds of these glittering flames about the size of grown men. Eventually, the flames took the form of men who were clothed in white robes. They seemed to have been in a type of military formation stretching from one end of the clearing to another. The song we had heard previously began again. I could tell you more, but eventually, the entire group disappeared. Three of us went to Bethlehem as soon as the morning light allowed it. Arriving in the market in the early hours of the morning, we asked several questions about the possible birth of children during the previous hours. Reasonably soon, some women told us that a couple on the south side of Bethlehem had had a child during the night. We went to the location and knocked on the door. A man opened, and when we said that we had come to see the child ..."

You should have seen his eyes," interjected Azariah. "It was amazing to see how surprised he had become."

Rahim continued, "Yes, it was almost amusing, but at that moment the man stepped away from the center of the doorframe. In fact, he more or less fell on the right side of the doorframe from the shock of our words. Then, as we looked into the house through the door, we could see a woman standing over a manger which obviously had a baby in it. The people then allowed us to come into the house and we saw the child. The man at the door was the cousin of the couple with the child. We discovered afterward that the couple had come from Nazareth in Galilee and that they had arrived last year for the census. Both of the man and the woman were from the line of David, so their families are originally from Bethlehem although they were living in Nazareth before the census. The child must be about one year old at this time. The couple had the names, Joseph and Mary."

"When we met the couple and saw the child, we explained to them that angels had appeared to us, telling us that the Messiah had been born. They also explained to us that an angel had appeared to them both about the time when Joseph's wife became pregnant. Apparently, the child was conceived by some sort of miracle, but the couple did not tell us everything."

Shelumiel then asked, "Is the family still in Bethlehem? I would also be interested in seeing the child. This is an amazing story."

Azariah continued, "A few months ago, we were in Bethlehem, and we saw the man named Joseph in the market one morning. We talked with him for a short while. He told us that the young boy was growing normally. The couple had decided to settle in the southern part of Bethlehem for a while. I assume that they are still in town. Joseph is a carpenter."

Shelumiel found that his mouth had come open with stupefaction following the revelations. He was a bit at a loss for words, and then he said, "Yes, I find this entire story is very remarkable."

Shelumiel continued, "I know some other people who would like to meet this couple and hear your story. Would at least the two of you, Azariah and Rahim, be willing to come to Bethlehem in the coming hours? There are some special visitors there who have come looking for the Messiah. They are men from a foreign country."

After a short discussion with the other three shepherds who were present, it was decided that Azariah and Rahim would be allowed to go into the town and meet the men.

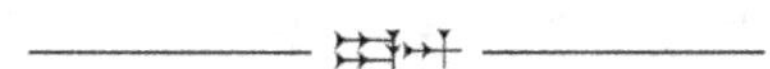

Six hours later in the middle of the afternoon, Hormizdah, Iqisa, and Eliab gathered in the encampment in the olive grove clearing. Alexis was also invited. Shelumiel wanted to avoid having the other servants know about the meeting with the shepherds. The household servants would almost certainly start asking too many questions if the shepherds arrived at the house. Also for the same reason, there was no need to including all the astronomers in the meeting with the shepherds.

The shepherds described their experience to the small group. It was decided that Alexis and Eliab would go with one of the shepherds to find out where the family was living and at least try to meet the man Joseph. Azariah volunteered to take the men to meet the family if they were still in Bethlehem. Within an hour Eliab, Alexis, and Azariah had found their way to Uzziel's house. Rachel answered the door because Uzziel was away. She recognized Azariah, and the shepherd explained why they had come. For a few moments Rachel hesitated, but finally, she told Azariah and the others where they could find Joseph, Mary, and the young child.

Minutes afterward, the men were approaching Joseph's house. Joseph himself was in a shed on one side of the house working with some wooden beams. He was a bit distracted as the men arrived because he had a splinter in his hand. He was focused on getting it out of his hand when as he turned his gaze upwards, he saw the three men looking at him. He knew intuitively that this must be connected to the wise men that he had been hearing about in recent days.

Azariah spoke first, "Joseph, I am sorry to see that you have a splinter. That can be real trouble. Sometimes with my sheep, I have to get into thorn bushes. It can be very painful. I can sympathize."

Joseph acknowledged Azariah's statement with a nod of his head, while he was sizing up the other two visitors. Inwardly, he was wondering, "Can these men be trusted?"

Eliab then spoke-up. "I have come a long way to meet you. We understand from speaking with Azariah that you have an exceptional son. I and Alexis, who is a trusted servant of my employer have come to meet you. There are others who would like to meet you as well."

Still mentally appraising the two unknown men, Joseph signaled for them all to enter his work shed. He encouraged them to be seated on a pile of lumber while he placed himself on another heap of wood a few yards away.

Eliab continued, "I am from a Jewish family in Babylonia. I made a journey to Judaea for the Festival of Tabernacles a few years ago. I was thrilled to be able to attend the festival, which as you know has a special place in the history of our people. I am a devout Jew.

I work as a scribe for a Babylonian notary, who is also a professional astronomer. He and some of his astronomer colleagues believe that the heavens have announced the coming of the 'Righteous One,' the Messiah."

Smiling broadly, Eliab continued, "Apparently you know something important about the young Messiah."

Joseph sat more or less stone-faced, but he encouraged Eliab to continue saying, "Tell me more."

Eliab described the situation, "My employer and several of his colleagues have come all the way from Babylonia to meet the young Messiah in person."

Joseph sat a bit amazed, thinking, "Now this beats everything. People are traveling for months at a time to meet Jesus. This is truly incredible."

He then asked, "That is interesting, can you explain to me just a little bit about how the heavens have been announcing the coming of the Messiah?"

Eliab then mentioned the "star" for the first time, saying, "There has been a series of relatively discreet but highly symbolic heavenly events during the last year and a half. The signs have a profoundly royal aspect to them. My master and his colleagues were surprised by this series of royal events, and they became very inquisitive. Eventually, through their contacts with me and others, they came to the conclusion that the signs must have been related to the coming of Israel's Messiah. Several of the men are in the process of converting to a belief in our God. Already the men have seen God at work. In recent days, while we were in Jerusalem, one of the men even had an angelic visitation in a dream during his sleep.

Joseph's eyebrows rose when he heard about the angelic visitation, and all three of his visitors saw it.

Eliab continued, "As you know Azariah also had an angelic visitation concerning the Messiah. He has told us that the child is now about one year old. According to the stars, the astronomers think that the child is less than two years old."

Joseph said, "How is it that you fellows met Azariah?"

Eliab explained, "After arriving in Jerusalem we asked several religious authorities where we could find the Messiah. Eventually, we were able to establish that the young Messiah must be here in Bethlehem. We had a contact who put us in touch with a businessman named Malachi who lives on the east side of town. Last year about this time, one of Malachi's servants had heard about some shepherds who had been visited by angels, who announced the coming of the Messiah. Through various contacts, the servant was able to find the shepherds."

Alexis understood what Eliab was trying to do and remained silent even though Eliab had neglected to share many important details.

Eliab deliberately did not mention the king because he was concerned that Joseph would be particularly wary of letting the men see the young child if it was immediately known that the king had sent the astronomers to Bethlehem. Also, there was no need of informing either Azariah or Joseph that the men had been with King Herod only days before.

Joseph thought about everything. He said to himself, "The story was indeed believable, but I never expected to hear that the heavens had announced the coming of the Messiah."

Seeing that Joseph was thinking pretty hard, Eliab continued after a few moments of silence, "The astronomers want to see the child. Do you think it might be possible?"

Joseph looked Eliab squarely in the face and said, "I have heard about the coming of the astronomers. The rumor is everywhere. My cousin was in Jerusalem several days ago, and someone mentioned it in his hearing. Then I learned a few days ago that your astronomer friends had come to Bethlehem. I even saw some of them in the market."

After pausing a brief moment, Joseph continued, "I determined in my mind that if the men succeeded in finding the child that I would be glad to meet them myself. Apparently, God has allowed you all to find our little family. The men are welcome to come here, but it cannot be during the daytime. I do not want anyone else to know that the Messiah is living under my roof. There are already possibly too many people who are aware of the unique nature of our son. My wife Mary gave birth to a son in special circumstances last year. The child is indeed the Messiah. I will not tell you more about how we know this thing at this time."

He paused and looked out of his shed toward a house and an orchard not far away.

Finally, after a few moments, Joseph said, "Perhaps we could allow the men to come tomorrow night, but well after dark. As much as possible, I do not want them to be seen approaching our home. When you come to the door, knock twice, pause and then knock three times. By this, I will know that you have arrived."

It was agreed that the astronomers could visit the family the next evening. As Eliab and the two others stood up, Joseph rose as well and thanked the men for their visit.

As the men left the shed, Eliab turned to Joseph saying, "Thank you for your confidence. The astronomers realize the importance of the child. They will be so glad to meet him even for a short time."

After those last words, Eliab, Azariah, and Alexis turned and walked down the road back toward the center of Bethlehem. Joseph sat down again. The beginnings of a few tears filled his eyes. After a moment, he remembered his splinter, and he thought, "I will need to tell Mary about these men and the upcoming visit tomorrow."

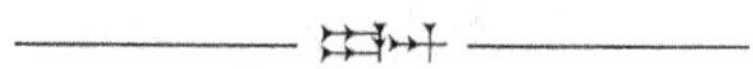

An hour later, the entire group of wise men and Eliab were gathered in their quarters. Shelumiel was also invited because he had heard the shepherds first hand. However, Malachi was not in the house. Shelumiel explained his meeting with the shepherds in more detail. Then Eliab explained what had happened during the interview with Joseph. Everyone was excited about the planned meeting the next evening.

After hearing everything, Ekur-zakir said, "Well, this is amazing. We will soon be seeing the young Messiah. It seems that the entire journey has been worth it."

After hesitating a moment, Ekur-zakir continued, "I guess we need to talk briefly about another detail. When we have seen the child, what is the next step? I suspect we need to begin to imagine our departure and the return journey. We know that we cannot return to Jerusalem. That means we need to get serious about finding another way home."

Ekur-zakir paused again briefly and looked around the group before continuing. "I need to speak about this with Callisthenes. Certainly, Malachi will need to be completely informed. as well."

Then turning to Alexis, Ekur-zakir said, "I know that we have only just arrived, but have you been thinking about our departure?"

Alexis responded, "Yes, master. Be assured, I have been thinking about it already. The Sabbath will begin on the evening of the day after the planned encounter, so everything will have to be prepared reasonably quickly. I will look into some of the details. I will make an effort so that our departure can take place as soon as the Sabbath has ended.

Nikolaos added, "Ekur-zakir, you are so right to think about our leaving. We should not be lax. As soon as our business is done, we had better make our departure. The king will not be expecting us to leave quickly and unannounced. If we do this properly, we can possibly fool the king's spies for many hours, and even possibly gain one or two days of advance on any search parties which may be sent to find us."

Jerusalem Filled With Rumors: The King is Dying

Three days after the Magi had gone to Bethlehem, Herod had fallen into a sad state. His health had declined severely. Already before the Magi's visit, he had been very stressed emotionally and physically. The series of treasonous disappointments caused by his son Antipater had been hard to digest. For months, even before Antipater returned to Judaea from Rome, the king had been grieved and was increasingly bitter. Finally, Antipater had returned. He had been placed in prison. Now the visit of the wise men had stirred the whole city of Jerusalem concerning the Jewish Messiah. These events seemed to doom his desire to pass on his kingdom to worthy heirs. Even that task seemed to be impossible.

As Herod considered these things, he realized more and more how much he detested passing his kingdom on to Archelaus and his other sons Antipas and Philip. It was as though everything that he had so long fought for was dissolving before his eyes. The young men were not ready to take their roles. They were still very inexperienced. Herod had placed such confidence in Antipater. However, his trust had been betrayed.

Herod now thought to himself, "Whom can I trust? Who is worthy of receiving this kingdom as an inheritance?"

But also another question haunted his thoughts, "What if my ill health and the sad state of my affairs is the judgment of God? I murdered God's high priest; I put to death my wife Mariamne, I had my sons Alexander and Aristobulus put to death on suspicions raised by Antipater. What have I done?"

On the morning of the second day after the departure of the wise men, Herod refused to rise from his bed. He seemed to pass from self-pity to fits of anger within minutes. He threw objects at the servants and spoke to them with hatefulness.

The servants, knowing how severely that Antipater's betrayal had affected the king, began to speak openly among themselves about the coming end of the king's reign. The final days of the reign seemed to be confirmed by the visits of several doctors. A rumor started to spread in the palace that the king was dying. Within a day the rumor had spread well outside the palace as well. Already it had been well-known that Herod had been sick for weeks following Antipater's trial. The king was grieved and bitter.

Jerusalem - The Golden Eagle is Destroyed

Month X - Tebētum / Tevet - Day 5   Thursday January 1, 1 BC

The religious teachers Matthias ben Margoloth and Judas ben Sariphraeus were aware of how the king's health had been affected by Antipater's betrayals. In the previous two weeks, they had seen how the coming of the Magi had stirred the city. Having heard the rumor that the king's days were numbered, Matthias and Judas were determined not to allow the great eagle to remain over the main gate of the temple for much longer. Already for many days, secretly the men had been planning how to destroy the golden eagle.

Judas and Matthias, two of the most eloquent men among the Jews, and the most celebrated interpreters of the Jewish laws were men well beloved by the people, because of their efforts to educate the youth.[6] These two religious scholars, when they heard rumors early in the day that the king's sickness might be incurable, stirred up many young men to pull down the golden eagle which the king had erected contrary to the law of their fathers. The law forbids those who wish to live according to it, to erect images or representations of any living creature.

Toward mid-morning, Judas and Matthias persuaded other young men to pull down the golden eagle, encouraging them to destroy the graven image even if they might be punished. They were all convinced that such an act would be meritorious before God and a good example to all men who sought to follow God's decrees.

About noontime, in addition to the persuasive words of Judas and Matthias, a report came to the men that the king had died. Without taking the time to verify the information, in the very middle of the day, a group of over 40 men entered the temple courts and worked their way up to the emplacement of the statue above the great gate, and they pulled down the eagle, and cut it into pieces with axes. Hundreds of people, who were present in the temple courts, witnessed their actions.

One of the king's military leaders, hearing what was happening and assuming that the incident might even be more significant than it was, came upon the group with a large number of soldiers. He caught about 40 men and the leaders in the very act of destroying the eagle, however, some others were able to escape. A huge crowd gathered as the men were marched through the streets to Herod's palace. The king was not dead. He also had been informed of the destruction of the eagle almost immediately. Herod ordered that the commander and the entire group of prisoners should be brought to the palace directly, before nightfall.

The king summoned his strength, ordering that he be transported in a curtained litter to the courtyard facing the main gate of the palace. An

---

6 This section is an adaptation of Flavius Josephus' account in *The Antiquities of the Jews,* 17.6.1 through 17.6.4, Sections 146-167. Several significant incidents led up to the death of Herod the Great. It is probable that the Magi were secretly invited to Herod's palace just before these events. Herod became seriously ill partly because of the betrayal of his son Antipater. It may be that worries connected to the visit of the wise men also caused the king's health to decline. Apparently, in late December of 2 BC or early January of 1 BC, the wise men may have been in Bethlehem at about the same moment when the following events took place.

ornamental chair was positioned at the top of the broad steps in front of the palace. From that vantage point, Herod was several feet above the soldiers and the prisoners on the main pavement of the courtyard. With a large crowd peering through the open gate and at least 300 soldiers present in the courtyard, the king summoned Judas and Matthias to come forward and give an account of their deeds.

Both men confessed their guilt and even added, "We will undergo death, and all sorts of punishments which you can inflict upon us, with pleasure, since we are aware that we shall die, not for any unrighteous actions, but for our ancestral beliefs."

Their courage was remarkable in the face of death. The king ordered them to be bound, and he sent them to Jericho, where he called together the principal men from among the Jews. The king himself was planning to leave for Jericho because his doctors wanted him to continue to Calirrhoe on the north-eastern shore of the Dead Sea. The king's doctors thought that the hot springs might be helpful in restoring the king's health.

Meeting the King of Kings

Month X - Tebētum / Tevet - Day 5   Thursday afternoon, Jan. 1, 1 BC

The Magi maintained an air of not knowing where the Child could be found even though they had a scheduled rendezvous for the evening. During the same afternoon as the troubles in Jerusalem, the Magi interviewed six families, who were sent from the local Rabbis. All of the families were received respectfully in Malachi's office in the villa. Of course, the families were amazed and generally had no idea what to say when they heard more about the wise men and the star. Since all the Magi knew that they would see the young Messiah in the evening, the atmosphere was relaxed.

The astronomers were in good spirits, and many of the families felt blessed by being with them. The men even spoke to the children with much care as Eliab sometimes translated. Most of the men, being fathers themselves, tried to put the families at ease.

After all the families had left the villa, the time came for the evening meal. Malachi was present. He had ordered the servants to prepare a proper light meal. Malachi knew that the Magi were probably not ready to eat a lot just before their encounter with the young Messiah. He had heard all about the success of Shelumiel and the interview with Joseph the day before. He also was in great excitement.

When the servants had gone, Malachi also spoke in quiet tones with the wise men about his plans and how he desired to handle the situation.

"I am aware of your preparations for tonight and these coming days. Ekur-zakir and Shelumiel are keeping me informed. It is good that Alexis is making plans for your departure as well. I think Ekur-zakir has been speaking with Callisthenes also. We will make sure you have at least one guide when it becomes necessary to leave."

"Neither Shelumiel or I will be going with you tonight because we need to remain ignorant of the location of the child. I do not want the child's security to be in danger. As Nikolaos has reminded us from your first days here in my household, we are all being watched by the king's men. There is at least one spy, and without a doubt, there are a few other informants in Bethlehem. The king has insured his success and security for these last decades through a network of spies."

"Eliab and Alexis are aware of how to get to the place where the child is living. As planned, you will need to leave during the night at the end of the Sabbath day. I will make every effort to help you, but all this must be done carefully. I am fearful of how the king will react to your departure. He is very unpredictable. It has been reported that the king may be dying. His health has been greatly affected by the betrayal of his son, Antipater, the Crown Prince."

Malachi then continued, "Because of this situation I will be going to Jerusalem tomorrow in the late afternoon, and I will be there on the Sabbath day. In this manner, I hope to avoid being implicated in your plans to leave without seeing the king. Shelumiel will be present here, but I am insisting that he not be too involved with your preparations for departure. There is a small possibility that both of us could be questioned and even tortured to obtain information about your departure and travel plans. Although we know that you will be accompanied by a couple of shepherd guides, we are trying not to be too familiar with your plans."

Everyone was very uncomfortable with these last statements. The seriousness of the situation sank into their hearts, but no one wanted to speak of the circumstances openly.

Finally, after some hesitation, Ekur-zakir responded, "May the God of your fathers deliver you from all evil that could fall upon your household because of our visit. Of course, none of us could have foreseen this course of events. We understand your efforts to ensure the child's security."

Several of the men made verbal affirmations that this was so.

Afterward, Malachi also informed the Magi about the next day's activities saying, "The local rabbis have arranged for three more families with their young children to pay you a visit tomorrow afternoon. Let us continue the pretense that you are still looking for the child, even if you will meet him tonight. It will be wise to continue to fool the king's spies. Shelumiel has described to me how kindly you have treated the children and their parents. Please continue this tomorrow even after encountering the young Messiah. I am sure the families will appreciate your kindness. All of them will certainly remember your visit for years to come, and they will tell the stories to their children."

Of course, Malachi had no idea that many of the children would die within a short time.

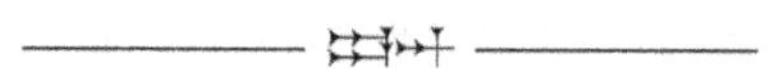

About two hours after sunset, the wise men were prepared to leave for the encounter with the family. The men dressed in their best clothing, not to impress anyone, but in honor of the young king. They all had overgarments to protect them from the cold and hide their fine clothing. Three of the men carried small wooden boxes which contained gifts for the young Messiah. Shelumiel made sure that the rest of the servants were distracted and not aware that the men were leaving through a side door.

Leaving the house, Eliab led the way while Ekur-zakir, Iqisa, Hormizdah, Nikolaos, Suen-magir, and Illis-kutul followed. Alexis went a bit ahead of the group and checked to see if the way was clear. None of the men wanted to encounter anyone on the way to Joseph's home. The moon, which was in its fifth day, was still two days before the first quarter. The moonlight well illuminated the evening sky. There remained about three hours before its setting. The lunar rays made it possible for the men to find their way without difficulty.

The streets were indeed deserted. Once, Alexis signaled to the group to wait a few moments while one man came out of his house and emptied a bucket. Eventually, the group arrived at the limit of the southern section of Bethlehem. Alexis led them to the door of the inconspicuous home, where Joseph's work shed dominated the northern face. The entrance was on the southeastern corner of the house. Alexis knocked twice, and after pausing, he knocked three times again, as had been agreed concerning the predefined signal that the group of foreign astronomers had arrived.

The door opened, revealing Joseph's robust presence in the doorframe. From outside, the interior only appeared to be very dimly lit. Joseph stood back from the doorway and motioned for the group of eight men to enter the house. In the relative darkness, the men perceived Joseph's face for the first time.

The home was typical of Bethlehem. Near the entrance, there was a lower section which housed some farm animals. Above that was a somewhat higher section where the family lived. A mature ewe sheep and two lambs were in the lower area, along with two donkeys farther back away from the door. The lambs seemed to be asleep, but their mother was a bit surprised by the large group and moved further away from the door upon the men's arrival. There was an intense odor of sheep near the entrance.

Going up four steps to the higher part of the house, the men saw one small lamp burning on a wall shelf at the back of the house. At the far side of the main room, a young woman with a beautifully proportioned face, a timid smile, and long somewhat curly black hair, sat calmly. She rose to her feet as the men came up the steps. Each of the men acknowledged her by bowing slightly.

After closing the door quietly behind him, Joseph followed the group of men up the steps to the upper living area. While the others were standing around the sides of the room, Joseph went to the lamp on the shelf and used it to light two other larger olive oil lamps on additional wall shelves in the small house. Soon one could see much more plainly. A curtain stretched across part of the back of the room behind Mary. The child was nowhere to be seen.

Joseph encouraged everyone to find a place to sit, and he made it evident that speaking quietly without making much noise was to be preferred. There were a few benches and a couple of stools on the various sides of the room. Within moments the men had found their places, and Joseph and Mary also sat down. Mary sat on a stool with her back to the wall, and Joseph found a portion of a sturdy low shelf situated next to the wall beside Mary. The wooden shelving easily supported his weight. The couple was dressed in their usual manner. The men were still in their cloaks which they had worn in the streets.

Eliab spoke first, "We are very thankful that you have allowed us to come to see the child. Our lives have all been changed by the things which we have experienced concerning the star and our journey to Judaea."

Joseph followed by saying, "We are glad to receive you. This is my wife, Mary. The child is sleeping behind the curtain. That is part of the reason I am asking you to speak softly."

Eliab continued, "It would be appropriate for us all to be presented. Joseph, you met me yesterday, I am Eliab, a Jew who lives in Borsippa in Babylonia. Most of our group comes from Borsippa. I work in a notarial office in the city, which is run by Ekur-zakir, the formal leader of our group. He is also the chief astronomer in Borsippa. As Eliab pointed out Ekur-zakir, the older man bowed his head again before Joseph and Mary.

Then Eliab introduced Ekur-zakir's son Iqisa and the other astronomers one by one.

Afterward, Joseph continued, "We would like to hear briefly about your experience with the star."

Eliab allowed Illis-kutul and Iqisa to explain their reason for being in Bethlehem, but he intervened when it was apparent that their Babylonian Aramaic posed a problem for Mary and Joseph. Illis-kutul explained that the star had been associated with royal signs while they had been in the East. He also explained that upon their arrival in Bethlehem, the men had again understood that the star's presence over the town was a new royal sign. The star had in a sense "preceded them" to the skies above Judaea. It was essentially waiting for the men when they arrived in Bethlehem.

At the end of a summary explanation about the star, Ekur-zakir asked a question, "We heard from the shepherds something which was indeed marvelous to our ears. It seems that a miracle was involved in the child's conception. Could you explain what happened?

Joseph spoke, but Mary interrupted a few times with further details and clarifications. They explained that the angel had announced the conception, but they had not had any sexual relations as a couple before the conception of the child. They were simply engaged to be married. Amazingly, the conception took place by a miracle from God.

The group of Magi, Eliab and Alexis sat a bit amazed and even speechless at the end of the story of the conception and the subsequent birth. They were especially impressed by the child's name, Jesus. When Mary shared concerning the child's name, the idea that this child would "save his people from their sins" had never before occurred to the Magi.[7]

Having come to the end of their respective stories, Joseph said, "Well, you have come to see the child. The time has come."

With those words, Mary arose and went behind the curtain. In a few moments, she reappeared carrying the young boy who was one year old. He was wrapped in a multicolored striped blanket. Mary retook her seat and made an effort to turn the boy toward the men so he could be seen.

Joseph spoke up again, "As we explained in the story, his name is Jesus, which indicates that he is a savior for his people."

Ekur-zakir reacted, "Yes, he is a savior for your people and indeed the whole world."

Iqisa spoke as well, "It is amazing to think that this child is destined to reign over the entire world."

It was at this moment that the child moved and began to open his eyes. Mary shifted the child on her lap so that he would be looking at her. Jesus reacted to the light by hiding and rubbing his eyes for a moment, but then he allowed them to stay open. He saw his mother and was clearly delighted. Mary smiled at him and even touched him under his chin.

---

7 Matthew 1:21: She will give birth to a son, and you shall give Him the name Jesus, because He will save His people from their sins." Note: The name Jesus has the same signification as the names Jehoshua (Numbers 13:16), Joshua, or Jeshua (Numbers 14:6; Nehemiah 8:17), meaning "Jehovah is salvation."

The child reacted with a small laugh of delight. At the same time, everyone grinded with pleasure.

Then Mary pointed the child toward Joseph, who smiled abundantly. In another moment or two, Mary turned Jesus so that he could see the group of men scattered around the other parts of the room. The child looked around and seemed a bit surprised. He looked back at his mother as if to say, "Who are these men?" He drew a bit closer to his mother for a moment as he also looked at the men.

For an instant, it almost seemed as if he was going to hide his face between his mother's breasts or shoulders. However, finally, he sat up determinedly and looked at the men, letting his gaze settle on each man individually for several moments. The men smiled back. Jesus also smiled and then it appeared that he wanted to get down from his mother's lap.

He was, of course, one year old and he could stand. Fairly soon with his mother's help, he was standing beside his seated mother holding onto the folds of her robe and her leg. The boy continued to look at the men and sometimes would laugh as the men smiled back and made signs with their hands.

Finally, Ekur-zakir spoke, "Mary and Joseph, we have brought some gifts which we want to present to the child." Mary and Joseph nodded back, and Ekur-zakir rose. At that point, he finally removed his cloak, and the finery of his clothing was revealed. Both Mary and Joseph were a bit surprised, and even Jesus seemed to notice the difference in clothing. Then Illus-kutul, Iqisa, Hormizdah, Suen-magir, and Nikolaos rose each in there turn followed by Eliab and Alexis. All the cloaks had come off; the men stood before the holy family in their finest apparel.

Illis-kutul, Hormizdah, and Ekur-zakir had the small wooden boxes. With Ekur-zakir leading, the men bowed before Jesus. Then Ekur-zakir allowed himself to fall on one knee and then down on the other. He started to be noticeably moved emotionally and began to fight back some tears. All of the men got on their knees.

At this point, Mary could not retain herself any longer, and tears began to roll down her cheeks. Joseph was also moved and his eyes pooled with tears as well. Jesus seemed to be fascinated and smiled although he appeared to be thinking, "What does this mean?"

Finally, Ekur-zakir moved forward on his knees holding one of the boxes in his hands. It took him a couple of minutes to very slowly move toward Jesus as Illis-kutul and Hormizdah followed. Ekur-zakir placed the wooden box on the ground well in front of him, and he bowed all the way to the ground. Illis-kutul and Hormizdah then imitated his actions. The other men all bowed low to the ground.

Jesus looked at his mother and then at Joseph. He allowed himself to fall to the ground and began to crawl on his hands and knees toward the men and the boxes. He touched one of the boxes and then moved toward Ekur-zakir. Arriving near his head, Jesus placed his hand on the astronomer's hair. One could hear Ekur-zakir crying softly. Most all the men were moved to tears as were Mary and Joseph. Mary held her head in her hands as the tears flowed. Eventually, Ekur-zakir raised his head, and the child touched his face and beard.

In about a quarter of an hour, it was all over. Jesus regained his mother's lap, and the men quietly sat on the floor nearby. Eventually, it was clear that the boy was again getting sleepy, he yawned even as he looked at the men and sometimes smiled. Then after a few instants, he closed his eyes and fell asleep. The men did not want the encounter to end, but rising, Mary took the boy behind the curtain and laid him down to sleep. Afterward, she rejoined her husband. Then the Magi encouraged the couple to open the gifts.

Mary and Joseph were again moved to tears when they opened the boxes and realized the immense value of the gifts. After more conversation, the men placed their cloaks on their shoulders and set out one by one into the darkness. Mary touched Ekur-zakir's shoulder as he neared the steps to go down to the door. He was the last one to leave. The old man looked at her, and she reached out and took hold of both of his hands saying, "Thank you for coming. Our son will hear about this event in the years to come. Your coming has blessed us immensely."

Ekur-zakir looked at her and smiled. The two stood together for a long moment. More tears came from his eyes. Then Ekur-zakir released Mary's hand and turned toward the steps and the door. Iqisa and Joseph were at the door looking on. Iqisa smiled at his father as the old man walked out of the house, and then he shook Joseph's hand. He turned, and Joseph closed the door.

About a quarter of an hour later, the group of astronomers was back in their lodgings in Malachi's house. The moon was setting as they discreetly entered the house through the unlatched side door. No-one could imagine going to sleep. They discussed the evening's events quietly with each other. Even so, within a bit more than an hour, they were all asleep. Several hours later, some beams of light began reaching into their rooms through cracks in the shutters. Everyone slept soundly for more than an hour after sunrise.

12

Flight and Aftermath

January 1 BC and Afterwards

Chapter Contents:

After Meeting the King of Kings

Month X - Tebētu / Tevet - Day 6

The next day after meeting the young Messiah, the men were busy with three more interviews with Jewish families. They continued to pretend that they were still looking for the Messiah. More interviews were scheduled after the Sabbath day as well. Malachi and Shelumiel made a definite effort to maintain the servants out of earshot of the discussions. They did not want any of the servants to be too familiar with their guest's activities. The wise men described to their hosts their encounter the previous night over breakfast and later during lunch.

Toward mid-afternoon, Malachi came into his office at the end of one of the Magi's prearranged interviews to say his goodbyes. He was leaving for Jerusalem to visit one of his cousins and spend the Sabbath in the capital. In this way, he would not be present as the men departed. It seemed to be the only way to protect himself and his household from being directly incriminated in aiding the Magi to flee. He could not easily be accused of helping the Magi to escape if he had not been present when they left Bethlehem.

Moved to tears thinking about their time together Malachi said, "I am very fortunate that I was able to be part of your adventure. God has certainly surprised me. I am confident that things will go well. May the angels of God help you."

A little while later, Malachi slipped out of the house and discreetly mounted his horse with Shelumiel's help. Seated on his horse, he instructed Shelumiel to take care of the last things that still needed to be arranged for the Magi's departure, and he left Bethlehem for the capital. Shelumiel was feeling the full weight of his responsibility.

Month X - Tebētu / Tevet - Day 6 — Evening and Daytime - Jan. 2/3, 1 BC

In the evening, the Sabbath began. Alexis had already moved the essential belongings to the camp during the day before the beginning of the Sabbath. Later, the men settled in for a good night of sleep.

The next morning, the men ate well and rested. Some of them read various texts and copies of Scriptures which were in Malachi's library. Iqisa found a scroll containing the later portion of the book of Isaiah. Beside it, there was a copy of the same text in Greek.

Eliab helped Iqisa with some passages which seemed to be harder to read. They both pondered the words:

... You should be My Servant to raise up the tribes of Jacob and to restore the preserved ones of Israel; I will also make You a light of the nations so that My salvation (yeshua) may reach to the end of the earth." [1]

The word "yeshua" (Jesus) had taken on a new meaning for Iqisa.

"I bring near My righteousness, it is not far off; And My salvation will not delay. I will grant salvation in Zion, and My glory for Israel. [2]

They both marveled at the words righteousness "tsadaqah" (Sedeq/ Tzedek) and salvation "yeshua."

In a later passage when Eliab had gone away to rest, Iqisa read further as best as he could. His Aramaic was, of course, impeccable, but the Hebrew language did have many differences although Hebrew and Aramaic are related. But when he had difficulties, he consulted the Greek text as well. Iqisa read the words,

---

1 (Isaiah 49:6)

2 (Isaiah 46:13)

Who has believed our message? And to whom has the arm of the LORD been revealed? For He grew up before Him like a tender shoot, And like a root out of parched ground; He has no stately form or majesty That we should look upon Him, Nor appearance that we should be attracted to Him.

He was despised and forsaken of men, A man of sorrows and acquainted with grief; And like one from whom men hide their face He was despised, and we did not esteem Him. Surely our griefs He Himself bore, And our sorrows He carried; Yet we ourselves esteemed Him stricken, Smitten of God, and afflicted.

But He was pierced through for our transgressions, He was crushed for our iniquities; The chastening for our well-being fell upon Him, And by His scourging we are healed. All of us like sheep have gone astray, Each of us has turned to his own way; But the LORD has caused the iniquity of us all To fall on Him. He was oppressed and He was afflicted, Yet He did not open His mouth; Like a lamb that is led to slaughter, And like a sheep that is silent before its shearers, So He did not open His mouth.

By oppression and judgment He was taken away; And as for His generation, who considered That He was cut off out of the land of the living For the transgression of my people, to whom the stroke was due? His grave was assigned with wicked men, Yet He was with a rich man in His death, Because He had done no violence, Nor was there any deceit in His mouth. But the LORD was pleased To crush Him, putting Him to grief; If He would render Himself as a guilt offering, He will see His offspring, He will prolong His days, And the good pleasure of the LORD will prosper in His hand.

As a result of the anguish of His soul, He will see it and be satisfied; By His knowledge the Righteous One, My Servant, will justify the many, As He will bear their iniquities. Therefore, I will allot Him a portion with the great, and He will divide the booty with the strong; Because He poured out Himself to death, and was numbered with the transgressors; Yet He Himself bore the sin of many, and interceded for the transgressors.[3]

---

3 Isaiah 53:1-12

Iqisa thought to himself, "The writer is undoubtedly speaking of the Messiah when he writes about the Righteous One, the Servant of the Lord. But how could this be, how is it that the young boy whom we saw less than a day ago will experience these things?"

Iqisa puzzled over the text for a while. Eliab did not return. Eventually, the time came for Iqisa to stop reading, but the last paragraph lingered in his mind:

As a result of the anguish of His soul, He will see it and be satisfied; By His knowledge the Righteous One, My Servant, will justify the many, As He will bear their iniquities. Therefore, I will allot Him a portion with the great, And He will divide the booty with the strong; Because He poured out Himself to death, And was numbered with the transgressors; Yet He Himself bore the sin of many, And interceded for the transgressors.

As the sun set, the men gathered for a meal. Each of them knew that it was probably the last time they would see the interior of the house and the servants. They all remembered Malachi's kind hospitality. But as the day ended, each of them also found his thoughts racing back to the evening two days before, when they had been preparing to see the young Messiah.

Ekur-zakir, Iqisa, and the others all wondered, "What are they doing now? Will we ever see this young child again? What will become of this child? How will he enter into his reign?"

Their questions overflowed, but now they had to turn their minds to their return journey. They somehow had to slip out of Herod's kingdom without attracting too much attention. Each man asked himself the same question, "Our plans have been established, but will they work?"

In the meantime, with Shelumiel's help, Alexis had done an excellent job with the preparations, even with the limited time. Everything was ready as foreseen. Shortly after the last light of day had faded, the servants loaded the camels and saddled the horses. The animals were located several dozen yards away from the tents in the grove of olive trees. They were out of view for anyone watching the camp from afar. Only the tents and some unnecessary equipment would be left. Five shepherds appeared out of the gathering darkness as the last lingering glow of sunlight slid away in the southwest. Alexis had hired them to stay with the tents and keep a small fire going through the night, to deceive anyone who might be keeping watch on the camp from afar.

The shepherds approached Alexis looking for their pay, but they also had questions. An older gray-bearded man with a dirty blue turban pushed down on his head said, "Is it true that your masters have come looking for the Messiah? We have heard rumors from some people in town that this is so."

Alexis hesitated a moment and replied, "Yes, it is so. My masters have come seeking to find the expected Jewish king."

The shepherd continued, "Some other shepherds nearby were visited by angels about one year ago, they were told that the Messiah had been born in Bethlehem. Apparently, some of the men saw the Messiah."

A lively discussion continued for several minutes, but eventually, Alexis had to break it off to continue the preparations for their departure.

Leaving Bethlehem

Month X - Tebētu / Tevet - Day 7   Saturday Evening - January 3, 1 BC

When the time had come, Shelumiel arranged that the other servants would be distracted in their quarters. Previously, he had told them that the astronomers were going to spend part of the night observing the heavens in their encampment. Shelumiel then mounted the stairway and found several of the Magi already outside on the terrace in the darkness.

Shelumiel addressed them in hushed tones saying, "The time for your departure has come."

Alexis was also there on the terrace with four of the Magi's servants. Each of the servants silently grabbed several bags laying on one side of the terrace while Eliab quietly called the others from inside the rooms. Within a few minutes, the entire group was on its way down the steps and out of the villa through a side door. As they left the building, Shelumiel stood just outside the door and said goodbye to each man. When the last one left the house, Shelumiel followed their steps with his eyes until the men were only dark patches in an alley between the olive trees. He then climbed the two steps back into the house and closed the door behind him. He stood there, just inside the door in the villa courtyard all alone. Tears rolled down his cheeks for several minutes.

Alexis led the men to the encampment. Callisthenes was there waiting for them. He greeted Ekur-zakir smiling and said, "Well, the adventure of our return journey is beginning."

Ekur-zakir smiled in return at the robust soldier and signaled with his hand for Callisthenes to lead the way. The other servants and the guards were already with the horses.

Arriving in the small clearing, everyone waited for a moment while the servants loaded the last bags on the dromedaries. Then at Callisthenes' signal, the men, leading their horses, began walking down a path which led toward the east. Within two hundred yards they arrived at a narrow, dirty path which eventually fell into a somewhat chaotic, stony road. But the men remained on foot; it was not safe to ride in the limited moonlight on the uneven and rough road.

Two shepherds, hired for the occasion, led the way followed by Callisthenes and two guards, then the wise men, the servants, and other guards. The moon was two-thirds full. Its light would be available during the coming seven hours, but as it would draw closer to the western horizon, there would be even less light. The group could make a lot of progress before dawn. After that, the men would need to stop because no light would be available.

Staying well concealed as they advanced among the olive groves near Bethlehem, the group moved at a slow pace and as much as possible without making any noise. No one spoke. Toward the south, in breaks between the surrounding hills, the men occasionally caught glimpses of the Herodium fortress in the distance.

After less than an hour, the group was walking through terrain that was much more arid. There were hardly any trees; however, because of the winter rains, some grass was on both sides of the rocky roadway. The infrequently used road became even more difficult so that riding was utterly out of the question.

After three hours, the group stopped for about a half hour at the entrance of a cave. Ekur-zakir, in particular, had lost the habit of traveling during their stays in Jerusalem and Bethlehem. He was happy to have a brief break. A mile or so further along, the fleeing wise men, as well as their group of guards and servants intercepted a watercourse, which was the extension of the Kidron Valley coming down south and east from Jerusalem. This mostly dry valley continued through the Judaea Desert, towards the Dead Sea, descending about 4,000 feet along its 20-mile course.

The group continued on another three miles in the valley. As the men moved forward the valley walls of the watercourse became cliffs which began to shut out the moonlight. Finally, the group came to a halt in a very steep walled side valley which was a bit out of view from the watercourse. It was not easy to find a good place to hide the large group. Most of the land was fairly naked terrain. However, there was a curve in the side valley which would conceal them from anyone passing on the Kidron watercourse.

After a bit more than five hours of travel, the moon was now too low in the west to be of much help, and it was impossible to continue. Callisthenes posted two guards, and the men settled in for a bit of sleep in the fresh night air.[4]

East of Bethlehem / Lower Kidron Valley

Month X - Tebētu / Tevet - Day 7   Sunday Morning - January 4, 1 BC

Several hours later, as the sky began to brighten in the east, Callisthenes woke everyone. It was not easy for any of the men to get up; almost everyone wanted to sleep longer. However, their security depended upon them being able to move quickly down the wadi and on toward the

---

4 This was near the present Mar Saba Monastery.

Dead Sea. They all had some bread and a few dates before beginning to move about a half hour before dawn. The group was now very low in the valley. Much of the time, as they were winding through the cliffs, the sun did not appear on the crest of the hills even well after sunrise.

As they continued along the path, some sections were safe for riding. Ekur-zakir was having much trouble maintaining the pace, so he was glad for every opportunity to remount his horse. There were occasionally ponds of rainwater along the watercourse, where the horses and the dromedaries were allowed to drink their fill.

By mid-morning, the group had gone south down the Kidron watercourse and eventually turned east. In the middle of the afternoon, the party crossed a large more or less flat area between more rugged terrain allowing them to cover several miles relatively quickly.

Five hours after noonday, the men came out of a stretch of the winding valley surrounded by rugged relief and cliffs. They were entering the Dead Sea valley. Slightly further along, occasionally the group caught glimpses of the vast watery expense of the sea as they continued down the wadi. Finally, Callisthenes said that it was time to come to a halt. About 22 hours after leaving the olive grove campsite the men were getting close to the western shore of the Dead Sea. They had arrived only about a quarter of a mile west of the main north-south road from Jericho to Masada. Without a doubt, there was some traffic on the road, so Callisthenes preferred to stop away from the main road for the night.

Ekur-zakir was completely exhausted. He and the others had something to eat and then immediately went to lay down. Iqisa began to be worried about his father. Hormizdah and Nikolaos both exchanged concerned looks with each other as they watched Ekur-zakir. He did not look well, and the journey was rather trying for them all. Callisthenes and his guards kept watch in groups of two all during the night. So far they had not met anyone, except a few Bedouin in part of the Kidron Valley leading to the Dead Sea. The next day, they were almost certain to encounter one or more caravans and possibly some of Herod's troops traveling near the Dead Sea.

The Flight of the Magi Discovered

Month X - Tebētu / Tevet - Day 7   Sunday mid-morning - Jan. 4, 1 BC

Herod's spy, Theron, came near to Malachi's villa as usual early in the morning on the day after the Sabbath. He even walked by the villa at one point. By mid-morning, he had not seen any of the servants who were in attendance on the Magi. Eventually, Theron saw one of Malachi's servants come out of the main door. The man then walked toward the center of town. Theron followed.

A hundred yards from the house, Theron caught up to the man and asked him, "I am interested in seeing the wise men from the East. Are they going to be at your master's home later today? I suspect they must be very busy. I do not want to bother them too much."

The servant replied, "Last night the men spent some time in their camp to the east of my master's house in the olive grove. They were planning to do some astronomical observations at that spot if the weather was good. We were expecting them back this morning for breakfast, but no one arrived. Therefore some of us went to the camp. No one was there. Two large tents are still standing there. A fire had been kept burning during most of the night beside the tents, but the men had vanished."

The servant hesitated a moment and then added, "Perhaps they will be coming back, but I am not certain. My master went to Jerusalem on the afternoon before the Sabbath. He should be returning to the villa by noontime today. We do not know what we will say to him. It is a very curious situation."

Having given his explanation, the servant bid Theron good day and went on toward the center of town on his appointed task.

Theron stood speechless for a few minutes. He realized that the men had vanished. He had not been expecting this type of event. He then decided to go and consult with the three men who were Herod's usual informants in Bethlehem. He had seen them from time to time in the previous days. Now he went back and found each man and explained the situation. No one was aware of anything particularly suspicious that would have signaled such a hasty and unexpected departure. For an hour or so the men did a bit of a searching while Theron went to the camp where the guards had been lodged in Malachi's olive grove.

Arriving in the clearing of the olive grove, Theron saw the two large tents still standing. It seemed to Theron that the men had probably been gone for many hours. Curiously there was a pile of used water and wineskins over on one side. It was evident that some of them were quite used. Also, some articles of clothing and a few other objects had been left. Theron discerned that it was likely that they had fled under cover of darkness. No doubt the men had departed in the moonlight the previous evening. They could be over 20 miles away by now.

Theron returned to the town center and met with the informants. No one had learned anything except that the Magi's chief servant, the Greek Alexis, had made a series of purchases during the days leading up to the Sabbath. He was apparently buying provisions for a trip including grain for the group's horses. He had replaced all their wine and waterskins. They had also purchased some small tents. The informants finished a careful search around town, but they did not see any trace of the wise men or their servants and guards. The men had all disappeared without a trace.

By early afternoon, Theron decided to return to Jerusalem. Not having a horse, he was obliged to walk back to the capital. Arriving in the city at the palace, he discovered that the king was in Jericho. He also heard more about the incidents concerning the destruction of the golden eagle and the king's illness. By late afternoon, Theron was able to obtain a horse from the king's stable and began riding to Jericho. As night fell, he continued in the moonlight as long as it was possible. Arriving at a small inn a few hours after sunset Theron stopped for the night. He was perhaps seven miles from Jericho.

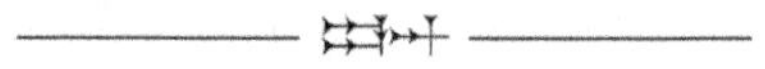

The next morning before dawn, he again mounted his horse, and within a few hours, he arrived in Jericho. He went through the streets until he was able to get to the king's properties and villa south of the center of town. Arriving at Herod's Jericho palace, Theron asked to see the king on a matter of great importance. Even so, it was late afternoon before the king was able to receive him.

When Theron saw the king, it was evident to him that he was in a horrible state of health. Only ten days previously Theron had left Herod to go to Bethlehem. But the king's health had significantly declined in the interim.

The king was much incensed that the astronomers had left without returning to see him. He erupted in anger in Theron's presence. Seizing a golden cup on the table beside him, Herod threw it across the room while he cursed the men.

He yelled out, "So they did not trust the king, and they had decided to flee. I will dispatch men to find them. They will certainly fear me when this thing is over."

Then taking a deep breath, he asked Theron, "Do you think the men succeeded in their quest?"

Theron was noncommittal, "Sire, I am not sure. I never saw them give the appearance that they had succeeded. And yet it is hard to imagine that the men would have left Bethlehem without having accomplished their goal. There was no outward sign that they succeeded. They met with several families. However, I even asked your local informers, and they never had the impression that the men had met the right family."

Herod erupted again, "Damn them; I will send men everywhere immediately to intercept them. I want them back here before me on their knees. They will not escape me, and I will make them pay for their treachery."

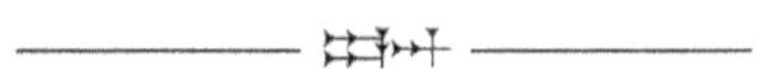

Concerning the child, Herod was not sure what to do about the report from Theron. The Magi had tricked him. They would not be returning to see him. However, the men must have achieved their goal of meeting the young Messiah. Otherwise, they would probably have stayed longer. But Herod was sick and preoccupied in his mind concerning the incident involving the golden eagle. For a few days, Herod mostly forgot about the Babylonian wise men. The king summoned the principal men of the kingdom to assemble at Jericho within a week. He wanted them to witness the punishment of the conspirators who had destroyed the golden eagle. The king's doctors encouraged him to go to the springs of Calirrhoe on the same afternoon as Theron's report. They believed the mineral water baths at that location might help improve the king's health.[5]

Beside the Dead Sea

Month X - Tebētu / Tevet - Day 8 — Monday morning - Jan. 5, 1 BC

When Theron arose to go to Jericho, Callisthenes also made sure to wake everyone in the expedition before sunrise. Two shepherd guides, who had accompanied the men from Bethlehem, said goodbye and returned up the wadi after explaining a few more details to Callisthenes. A third guide stayed with the group. As they were getting ready to leave, the chief guard got everyone's attention.

Clearing his throat, Callisthenes said, "I would suspect that Herod's informants and spies are now well aware of our departure. Without a doubt they have informed or will soon inform the king. I want all of you to know that fairly quickly there will almost certainly be messengers sent in all directions with orders for Herod's troops to intercept us."

Callisthenes looked around the group to see how people were reacting. He thought, "So far so good; they are not scared to death, yet."

Then he continued, "An alert will certainly be sent even to the Masada fortress, so we need to get beyond it quickly. According to our shepherd guides, we will not need to pass less than a mile and a half from the fortress. In the daytime, we would certainly be seen by the sentinels stationed high above the road. They tell me that the fortress is several hundred yards above the surrounding plain. However, if we travel at night, we can bypass the fortress without being seen. Hopefully, we can pass before word gets to the garrison to be on the watch for us."

---

5 Calirrhoe was on the eastern side of the Dead Sea about 25 miles or 40 kilometers from Jericho by road, but less by boat.

Callisthenes continued, "We should try to go about 20 miles and then camp somewhere well off the road for several hours. This will allow us to rest and hopefully avoid some contacts with either caravans or Herod's troops. Then during the early part of the night, we should continue in the moonlight. There would probably be no problem with robbers during the night near the fortress, so it should be safe to travel. However, this means an extended period of travel during the day and the early part of the night."

Looking around at the group again, Callisthenes could see that Ekur-zakir was not so comfortable with the proposed course of action, simply because of the stress involved.

Callisthenes addressed him directly, "Ekur-zakir I know that the last day and night have been trying for you, but we need to get as much distance between Herod's men and us as possible. It is probable that Herod will be informed of our disappearance today if he was not informed yesterday."

The older man simply said, "Yes, I am aware of our situation, so let us do as you suggest. It cannot be avoided. We must hurry."

Within minutes, everyone was on horseback and Callisthenes gave the signal to advance. They made rapid progress. Coming out of the Kidron Valley the group found the road running from Jericho and Qumran to Masada. The road went beside the Dead Sea. Sometimes it was relatively close to the inland sea, but at other points, it was a mile or two from the great salty lake. At certain spots, there were strong odors of sulfur and other chemicals which filled the air reminding one of death.

The group advanced five miles before encountering anyone. The first encounter was with a caravan of over 100 heavily laden dromedaries and twenty men coming from Egypt on its way to Damascus. Usually, such a caravan would have traveled on the King's Highway across the Jordan, but because of the relative abundance of water because of the winter rains, they were moving along the western side of the Dead Sea. A few good-natured jokes were exchanged, and the others excused themselves for taking up most of the road. It was more or less necessary for the group of astronomers, guards, and servants to stop as the caravan passed.

A little while later, a small patrol of five soldiers appeared which seemed to be headed toward Jericho. They merely acknowledged the presence of the Babylonians without asking any questions; then they disappeared in a low cloud of dust as they continued further north. They were riding at a good pace. Apparently, they had their orders and were on a mission.

By late afternoon, the column reached the watercourse coming from the springs at Ein Gedi. The wadi was not empty; there was plenty of water flowing down toward the sea because heavy rains had swelled the stream. The animals and the men drank their fill. Several skins were filled with water in provision for the coming travel.

After a few more miles, the column found a place, which was off the main road and out of sight, to set up a temporary camp. The men ate some of their dried fruit and bread and laid down to rest. Callisthenes even encouraged everyone to try to sleep a bit. As the sun set, the moon began to shine in midheaven toward the southeast. Soon GENNA (Saturn) and the star "Jaw of the Bull" (Aldebaran) appeared just below the moon accompanied by MUL SIPA.ZI.AN.NA "the Shepherd of Heaven" (Orion). The bright "Arrow Star" MUL KAK.SI.DI (Sirius) was toward the horizon in the east south-east across the Dead Sea.

Callisthenes waited about an hour after sunset before summoning everyone to remount their horses. They would continue in the moonlight. The moon was now toward the south-east and south, but it was very high in the sky over the heads of the travelers. The terrain was relatively easy to distinguish, and the road was in good condition. Within an hour, they had covered two and a half miles. They more or less continued at this rate for the next three hours. At some higher points on the road, one could see the reflection of the moon on the vast expanse of the sea.

At the end of the fourth hour, Callisthenes called for a short halt as he was talking to the remaining guide, who indicated a great stone cliff off in the distance.

Soon he turned to the others and said. "Up ahead about five miles away you can see the outlines of the rock of Masada. Herod's great palace fortress is up there on the heights."

Not long afterward in the east MUL.BABBAR made its appearance, shining brightly above the eastern range of mountains high above the lake. There was a profound silence which was only broken from time to time by the cry of an occasional far-off night bird.

The column started to advance. But after a bit more than a quarter of an hour, Iqisa realized by chance that his father riding beside him was wobbling. Then Iqisa was just able to catch Ekur-zakir as he started to fall from his horse. Calling for help, Iqisa held on to his father, while the column stopped. Ekur-zakir was then lowered off of his horse. The older man apologized profusely about almost falling, and he indicated that he desired to be put back on his horse. He was given some water, but he was exhausted. He made a small effort to stand but was unable to rise from the ground. With everyone gathered around, Callisthenes asked the older man, "Can you remount? Can you go on? We must decide."

With difficulty, Ekur-zakir sighed and responded weakly, "I am sorry, I cannot."

Callisthenes looked around at the group; it was evident that everyone was looking to him for leadership. He had to decide what to do. Callisthenes remembered that there was a rocky wadi just about fifty yards further back which they had just passed.

He mentioned this to the group, "You remember we just passed a wadi not far behind us. I want to explore the watercourse to see if there might be a place where we could hide for the rest of the night and perhaps the day tomorrow. If Ekur-zakir recovers his strength, we can try to go on tomorrow night."

Callisthenes took one of the guards, and they went back up the road. After dismounting, they entered the watercourse on foot. It was mostly dry and very stony. Some of the flat stones making up the bottom of the wadi covered several square yards or more on the ground.

Callisthenes thought to himself, "If we enter here no one will probably notice because of the gravel and the flat stones, the footprints of the men and animals will not appear on the surface of the ground. We are lucky; things could have been more difficult."

Going about 150 yards up the curving wadi, Callisthenes found an acceptable spot to camp which was isolated from view. Over the next hour, the servants made a makeshift stretcher out of some blankets and several tent poles. Then the servants, Iqisa, Eliab and some guards took turns carrying Ekur-zakir to the hiding place chosen by Callisthenes. They would have to wait through the rest of the night and the next day. It was too dangerous to travel past the Masada fortress before the next nightfall. It was hoped by all that Ekur-zakir would be in good enough health to continue the journey after resting. The servants did their best to help by giving Ekur-zakir some of the more nutritious food. They also made him more comfortable. Then everyone except two of the guards went to sleep. Later in the night under the almost clear sky, the temperature fell to just above freezing.

Month X - Tebētu / Tevet - Day 9 — Tuesday - Jan. 6, 1 BC

The next day, the men were shivering from the cold as they ate breakfast. A bend in the dry watercourse hid their camping location from anyone passing on the road and the fortress to the south. By going up on the south side of the wadi, one could plainly see the great rock of the Masada fortress separated from the cliffs to the west about four miles away. Even at that distance, it was possible to see some of the towers, walls and palace buildings on the upper portions of the massive rock.

Callisthenes, accompanied by a guard, went down to the road avoiding any spot where their feet might leave a footprint. Looking around, they found a few places where there were a few hoof marks and footprints. Before returning to the camp, both men did their best to conceal the indications of the group's passage with gravel from the bed of the wadi.

During the day, the sky slowly covered with high clouds, veiling the sun. Happily, the temperatures also rose steadily so that by the middle of the afternoon one could be comfortable without extra clothing. In the camp, Ekur-zakir continued to regain his strength. The men only spoke in low tones to avoid being heard by passers-by. At one point everyone was alarmed because one of the horses became a bit unsettled and started neighing excitedly. It turned out that two horses were irritated with each other. Eventually the disturbance with the horses caused a dromedary also to get a bit unruly, but finally, they all calmed down when one of the servants spoke kindly to them and even gave them a few handfuls of grain. It was of enormous importance that the animal sounds not betray the presence of the group to anyone passing on the road.

A servant also found a pool of water about another 50 yards up the wadi about 200 yards away from the road. Finally, it was decided to lead the animals there so they could drink and to leave them there under surveillance until the group was ready to for their departure. At that distance, it was improbable that the animals would be heard from the road.

Guards were posted about 75 yards from the entrance of the wadi, halfway to the camp. One of them could just see the road in the distance, as he hugged the ground behind a rocky outcrop beside the dry watercourse. The men had their bows ready for action. They only spoke to each other in hushed tones.

One caravan of about 100 heavily loaded dromedaries and 15 men passed the wadi going south in the morning. Later toward noonday, a local shepherd with a flock of 15 to 20 sheep was spotted in the distance beyond the road in the direction of the sea. The shepherd stayed for a while and then he led his flock a little further up the valley toward the north. By mid-afternoon, he and the sheep had disappeared.

In the late afternoon, a few hours before dark, a detachment of 20 cavalrymen appeared coming down the valley from the north. The guard who was posted as a sentinel indicated to all the guards to be even quieter and motioned for Callisthenes to come up beside him. From behind the rocky outcrop on the side of the dry watercourse the two men watched the detachment of soldiers in the distance. As they approached the wadi, the soldiers did seem to be looking for something or someone.

A couple of the soldiers advanced about 25 yards up the wadi and Callisthenes motioned to his team of guards to be ready at any instant to shoot a barrage of arrows. Finally, during a short exchange of words, one of the soldiers motioned toward the ground with his hand and shook his head. The two men turned their horses around and returned to the road. The soldiers said a few words to the officer who peered up the wadi as if to just make sure that his men had done a good job, then he signaled to the others to follow him. The entire body of mounted soldiers rode off toward the south in the direction of the Masada fortress.

Callisthenes said to the sentinel, "Keep a good watch. Their departure could be a deceptive effort on their part, to make us think that they do not believe anyone is here. I am not certain that we have seen the last of those men."

As night fell, Callisthenes led most of the guards back to the camp. However, he sent the remaining shepherd guide and a guard to explore the terrain further south near the sea. The horses and camels were brought back from the watering hole 50 yards further up the wadi.

Ekur-zakir seemed to be in much better physical condition. In addition to the extended period of rest, Illis-Kutul had prepared a type of herbal medicine which seemed to help Ekur-zakir. It was evident that he would be able to travel.

Calling the group together, Callisthenes addressed everyone, "I am still concerned that there may be a patrol near the fortress. It would not be surprising that there will be a checkpoint there, with possibly a hidden group of soldiers. We need to be exceedingly careful. I have sent the guide on ahead with a guard to explore the ground between the road and the shore of the great salt lake. We may try to use another path and avoid the main road for the first part of the night."

When the scouting party returned, the men informed Callisthenes that it would be possible to advance along the shore of the lake. That would be the easiest terrain. The shore was fairly uniform. There were not any great physical challenges or barriers. The wadis toward the south spread out considerably into sandy flat deltas before entering the lake.

Unfortunately, the clouds were obscuring much of the moon's surface, but the moonlight was still abundant. They could still continue on horseback with relative ease. About a half-hour after the scouts had returned the entire column descended the wadi, crossed the road and proceeded toward the lakeshore about a quarter of a mile away. Sometimes the group had to walk, but as they headed toward the lake shore, they were able to remount. They all continued advancing as silently as possible.

After a few hours, Callisthenes called for a halt. Now in the far distance toward the west north-west, the men could see the outlines of the Rock of Masada. They had passed the fortress, but they were still not well positioned, and they were not hidden. They would have to continue moving through the night. The group remounted and continued until the increasingly obscured moon began to set several hours later. Callisthenes and a few others had gone on ahead looking for another spot where they could rest for a few hours. They were now ten miles south of Masada. They followed a wadi up toward the road. Ekur-zakir was doing well, but then drops of a light misty rain started to fall. In the coming hours, sometimes the cold rain caused the men to be chilled to the point of shaking.

Month X - Tebētu / Tevet - Day 10   Wednesday morning - Jan. 7, 1 BC

An hour after dawn, the group was able to find a bit of shelter under the edge of a cliff in the upper part of a wadi to the right of the main north/south road. The rain fell harder now, and a bit of water had started to flow in the watercourse. The rainfall was good news for Callisthenes because the rain would cover their tracks at least up to the wadi. For the servants, the rainfall posed problems because they were trying to keep the gear and food dry.

The animals were taken about 25 yards further up the valley to a place which had more room, where a small stream bed joined the main wadi. There a servant and one guard stayed with the animals. Except for two men that Callisthenes placed toward the main road 50 yards away the other men huddled as best they could under the cliff edge. They were generally able to stay dry, but they all worried that if the rain continued for a prolonged period the water in the wadi could eventually become a torrent. That could spell disaster for the entire expedition.

Physically, Ekur-zakir was not doing well. He was noticeably weak and was not very interested in eating. Iqisa and several servants managed to encourage him to take some nourishment. Sometimes he merely appeared to stare off into space, but mostly he tried to sleep. For everyone, Ekur-zakir's health became a major preoccupation. Iqisa was becoming alarmed, and some of the servants whispered among themselves that Ekur-zakir would probably not survive the journey back to Babylonia.

The rain continued throughout the entire morning and afternoon, and the men sometimes trembled physically because of the cold and damp conditions. There was not any let-up, the rain fell without ceasing. The water in the stream bed became a rushing stream about a half foot deep. From time to time, the men on watch near the road and those tending to the animals were relieved by others.

A Painful Separation

Month X - Tebētu / Tevet - Day 11   Wednesday evening - Jan. 7, 1 BC

At nightfall, there was no sign that the rain would stop, but happily, there was some light because of the waxing moon which was nearing fullness. Toward midnight, the rain began to stop, and some holes appeared in the cloudy canopy above. Occasionally, between the showers, the moon shined through from the west.

When the rain completely stopped, and the clouds began to disperse, Callisthenes spoke to the astronomers about the necessity of leaving immediately. The men all agreed that the situation was perilous. They were only 10 miles south of the Masada fortress. If they waited until dawn, there was a good possibility that patrols of soldiers might become active. If the group could put another five miles between them and the fortress, it might be best. They could wait until the following night and travel in the moonlight, but one could not be sure that a patrol might be well south of them at that point. There was also the serious possibility that the weather could again deteriorate.

About an hour was necessary for the baggage and the men to be made ready. It was decided that one of the lighter servants would also ride with Ekur-zakir to assure that he did not fall off his horse. Slightly less than half the night remained before moonset. Callisthenes took the lead, but he left half of his guards at the end of the caravan in case of unexpected visitors from the rear.

At first, the men walked with their animals back to the main road, and then the journey south began again. Sometimes the animals had difficulties in muddy pools of water, but the column covered about a mile and a half during the first hour. After that, there were places where the road was not well built or had been damaged by heavy rains earlier in the year. The condition of the road slowed the group considerably. By moonset, they had covered about seven miles. However, without the moon, it was necessary to stop. The star MUL.BABBAR was shining high in midheaven and toward the southwest during their travels. It was almost like a guardian watching over them.

A few hours before sunrise, Dilbat [6] rose in the east. Within an hour of the moonset, the skies were noticeably brightening in the east. Fairly quickly the column restarted its journey. By mid-morning, they had put another five miles between the group and the Masada fortress. They were now about 22 miles south of the fortress. However, it was at this moment that tragedy struck.

During a pause, Ekur-zakir descended from his horse with the help of his servant. A few others had also dismounted, but the pause was not intended to last long. However, moments after Ekur-zakir's feet hit the ground he grabbed his chest and remained standing only by holding himself up against his horse. Steadying himself, he could not remain standing and shortly afterward he fell to the ground. Immediately everyone dismounted, and the servants brought Ekur-zakir over to one side beside the road. His chest was obviously in great pain. Within minutes, it became clear that Ekur-zakir's heart was failing.

Iqisa seated himself beside his father and tried to comfort him in his arms. However, Ekur-zakir himself spoke, "I will not be able to go any further. I am sorry, I will not be continuing. The end has come for me."

Iqisa attempted to contradict his father, but the old man made it clear that he did not want to hear it.

Addressing Iqisa, Ekur-zakir continued, "Before we began this journey, I spoke to your mother and told her that I had doubts that I would survive the trip. My premonition has been vindicated. You will need to bury me here in this desert."

Gasping for his breath, Ekur-zakir added, "My life is full, I was able to see this famous Messiah, whose coming was announced in the heavens. Who would have dreamed of such a thing? Now I will meet his God. In these last few days, I have looked at the mountains toward the east. Somewhere in those mountains the Jewish prophet Moses is buried. Now I will join him in the soil of this desolate place."

Looking at Eliab and then toward Iqisa, he continued, "But, I believe in the resurrection of the dead. One day my bones shall be knit back together. I hope that all of you will join me on that day."

---

6 Venus (Nogah in Hebrew).

Seizing his last strength, Ekur-zakir raised his head briefly and looked hurriedly around the group. His vision focused briefly on each man: Iqisa, Eliab, Illis-kutul, Suen-magir, Hormizdah, Nikolaus, Callisthenes, Alexis and the others.

Then closing his eyes, and in his growing weakness and fragility Ekur-zakir said, "Goodbye my son, goodbye my friends, I hope to see you again one day."

After a few more moments he breathed his last and was gone. Iqisa sat holding his father's lifeless head and shoulders in his lap for a long while, and most of the group was stunned by what had taken place. Some of the men wept. Hormizdah collapsed on the ground, but he urged the others not to be concerned after two servants came to his aid.

After about a half hour, Callisthenes approached the remaining Magi and spoke to them about the gravity of the situation.

He said, "We will need to evacuate this place as soon as possible. It is not safe to stay here even for a few hours. It is certainly possible that one of Herod's patrols could be looking for us. They may have already reached our last campsite. Their potential nearness puts us in a dire predicament. It will be obvious that a group consisting of possibly twenty men as well as horses and dromedaries has spent some time in the wadi. They will be able to see our fresh tracks coming from the wadi, and they may launch themselves after us with all speed. Even now, there could only be 10-12 miles between us and one of Herod's patrols. We will need to bury Ekur-zakir as soon as possible and continue our route."

Everyone agreed, and Illis-kutul and Eliab were named to speak to Iqisa who was still sitting on the ground yards away, seated and holding his father's lifeless body. Within an hour the men had prepared a shallow grave just out of sight on the west side of the road. There they placed Ekur-zakir's body and covered it over with many rocks. The oldest astronomer's horse was riderless as the group mounted their horses and Callisthenes led them on toward the south. Iqisa, Eliab, and the others looked back briefly as they moved forward. The situation seemed surreal. They had lost almost two hours of travel time, but above all, they had also lost their leader and friend. Iqisa and some others sometimes wept, and tears continued to flow, but everyone tried to restrain their emotions. They were in great danger. They had to move on.

Further north at the wadi campsite,[7] a well-armed army patrol of twenty men on horseback was examining the traces left by the men and animals from the group of wise men. The patrol had left Masada at the first light of dawn and taken the road to the south. Their leader was on an urgent mission. Find and arrest the Babylonians and then bring them to the king. Leaving the camp, the commander gave the signal to hasten the pace. It was evident that the men had left the campsite just after the end of the rainfall.

A Narrow Escape

Although the road was more and more like a wide path, the men advanced reasonably well. The road weaved in and out between some rocky outcrops and the sea. In some places, the available space narrowed to between 20 and 50 yards. Callisthenes deployed two men who served as a rear guard. From time to time, the men stopped at a more elevated section of the road where they could find a good vantage point and looked back toward the north to see if someone might be following the group.

By mid-afternoon, the wise men arrived at the far southern portion of the Dead Sea. About a half mile away on their right, a tiny village surrounded by several date palms indicated that there was an abundant water source. However, the animals already had been able to take some water from the streams which were flowing down toward the sea because of the recent rains. The entire party continued to advance under Callisthenes' direction.

Having reached the southern end of the sea the men proceeded due east across the plain of sand and rocks. At this point the road became a simple path. It was no longer a road. One of the guards, looking back, saw the rear guard riding furiously about a half mile behind. He yelled

---

7 Nahal Bokek (Ein Bokek) about 10 miles south of Masada.

the news to Callisthenes, who then raised his voice to a shout, urging the men to do as much as possible to double their pace. "We need to go as fast as possible. We will go as fast as the dromedaries can go under their burdens." The column picked up speed even while the rear guard approached to within about one-third of a mile.

Within a quarter of an hour, the rear guard had caught up with Callisthenes. Riding beside him the men gave their report. "A column of soldiers of perhaps 20 men is advancing from the north beside the sea. They are moving quickly and will probably overtake us within an hour or so."

The column continued to move forward. In about another quarter of an hour, Callisthenes saw what appeared to be a type of boundary stone obelisk in the distance, perhaps 400 yards away. It could just be made out among the scrubby desert plants which covered the horizon.

Callisthenes said to himself, "That must be the boundary of the Arabian kingdom of king Aretas. If we can get on the other side of the boundary Herod's men will be hesitant to cross."

Again raising his voice, he said, "Look, up ahead across the plain there is the boundary stone of King Aretas of Petra! Keep up the pace! We need to at least get beyond the boundary stone!"

The column continued moving forward, pushing the horses and especially the dromedaries to their limits. As the men arrived about 100 yards from the boundary stone, one of the men who had participated in the rear guard looked back to see the army patrol about 500 yards away and approaching at a gallop. He yelled the news to Callisthenes.

Having been alerted, Callisthenes shouted, "Just a little more effort. We must pass out of Herod's dominions!"

At the boundary stone, Callisthenes urged the wise men and the servants to continue with all haste. At the same time, the Greek mercenary deployed his Parthian archers about 35 yards beyond the boundary stone across the remnant of a road. The men remained mounted, but they fixed arrows to their bows.

Only a few minutes later, the army patrol arrived about 10 yards away from the boundary obelisk, and the commander held up his hand indicating the patrol should halt. Callisthenes and his eight mounted guards remained on horseback in the distance.

The Greek raised his bow and launched an arrow at the boundary stone. Seconds later, everyone saw and heard the sharpened shaft hitting the obelisk. The arrow fell to the ground beside the boundary stone. After a moment of silence, the Jewish commander got down from his horse, walked over, and picked up the arrow. He looked back across the sandy and rocky expanse of the open space toward Callisthenes' guards. Then in Aramaic, he cried out, "Good marksmanship, we are impressed. I see it is a Parthian arrow of excellent quality."

Callisthenes cried in return, "Yes, we have many more, but you can keep that one as a souvenir of our meeting."

The army commander laughed heartily, and all of his men grinned, although some of them even chuckled as well.

Then the commander yelled back, "I think one arrow will be enough."

After looking toward Callisthenes straight-faced for a few moments as if to affirm his manhood, the commander slowly turned, approached his horse, mounted, and raised his voice in the hearing of all.

"We will go to the village and see if the inhabitants can host us for the evening meal. Tomorrow we return to Masada."

Looking once more at Callisthenes, the commander then turned his horse and prodded it, while vocally urging it to greater speed. Soon the entire group of soldiers turned and began to move back toward the west toward the village indicated by the palm trees about a mile away.

Callisthenes and his men remained stationary, watching until the soldiers had covered most of the distance to the village.

He then said to his men, "Well, apparently the reputation of Parthian marksmanship is enough to dissuade the soldiers from being too foolish. I think they have had enough warning. Let us go now and join the others."

Then their nine horses turned together toward the east. The guards could see the column of astronomers and servants perhaps a mile away at the limit of vision. As the late afternoon sun was quickly sinking in the west, Callisthenes and his men rejoined the column. While the entire group slowed its pace, Callisthenes still urged them to continue to advance even after sunset.

Month X - Tebētu / Tevet - Day 12 — Thursday evening - Jan. 8, 1 BC

The column went on, first in the twilight and then in the moonlight. Advancing up the slope on the east side of the plain, the men found another stream that still had plenty of water. They allowed the animals to drink their fill. The column then continued for another hour. As the group reached the first rocky outcrops of the mountains southeast of the boundary marker, they stopped for the night.

Meanwhile back at the south side of the Dead Sea, the army commander was well fed and lodged. The next day, he and his men returned to the Masada fortress, and the day following he sent one of his men with a message for the king along with the Parthian arrow. His message read something like the following:

> *"We followed various indications of a large group of men on horseback accompanied by dromedaries. We could see their traces all the way to the boundary of King Aretas' kingdom south of the Sea of the Arabah. These men must have been the group we were looking for because on the ground near the boundary stone we found the accompanying Parthian arrow. The arrow had not been muddied by the rain the previous night, so apparently, it had been left by the men from the east. It did not seem appropriate to me to continue to pursue the men into the neighboring Nabataean kingdom."*

The commander knew better than to give all the details of the incident at the boundary obelisk. The king did not need to know everything.

Month X - Tebētu / Tevet - Day 13 — Friday morning - Jan. 9, 1 BC

The next morning, after having successfully avoided Herod's soldiers, the entire group of wise men, servants, and guards gathered together to discuss the return journey in more detail. Callisthenes directed the meeting. Based on Callisthenes' advice, the group decided to travel on to Petra, the capital of King Aretas IV. Arriving there, they would equip the expedition with everything necessary to make the return journey to Babylonia through the northern Arabian desert. Then by mid-morning, the group had entered the rocky mountains of Nabatea.

Jericho

Month X - Tebētu / Tevet - Day 13   Friday morning - Jan. 9, 1 BC

About 100 miles to the north of the Magi, in the morning hours, Herod had the leading men from across the country assembled in the large city theater in Jericho. There were possibly 300 men present from all parts of the kingdom, and each one was wondering what might happen during the following hours.

The eastern gates of the city theater came open to the sound of trumpets, and a military contingent of about 200 men marched in and was deployed around the 300 leading men. Others entered and were positioned by the stage on one side, which was well decorated with banners.

Then more than 40 of the conspirators who had destroyed the golden eagle at the temple were brought in bound in chains and accompanied by other soldiers. Many of the prisoners were bloodied. They had obviously been beaten severely. The men were placed in the semi-circular area between the theater stage and the first rows of the leading Jewish men.

After a few more minutes, the king also arrived in the theater in a covered litter accompanied by more soldiers. Herod had much difficulty standing, but he was able to lay on a couch provided for the occasion, propping himself up with his arm. Herod intended to address the crowd. After catching his breath, summoning all his strength, he spoke with the strength that one would expect of a retired general.

Herod enumerated the good deeds that he had undertaken on behalf of the country and its leading men. He pointed out what a vast work and responsibility that had been for him to rebuild the temple.

He said, "Do you not see, I was able to leave a mark by my reconstruction of the temple. I did this in contrast to the Hasmoneans who had power during the hundred and twenty-five years and who were not able to perform any great work for the honor of God. I had hoped I had left myself a memorial through this magnificent building, and procured for myself a reputation after my death."

Herod paused for effect and then began his discourse again. After a few moments, Herod cried out, "Please know that these men have not waited to insult me, even during my lifetime. In broad daylight, and in the sight of the multitude, they insulted me by destroying what I had dedicated to God. They pulled the golden eagle at the temple down to the ground and desecrated it."

The king continued speaking for many more minutes and finally at the end of his discourse, one of the leading men of Jericho rose and affirmed that the men had indeed insulted the king and should be punished. In reaction, fearing the king, all the other Jewish leaders, with one voice cried out that Herod should punish the men for what they had done.

It was at that moment that the king again spoke to the accompanying soldier and their commanders saying, "The two leaders of the insurrection, Matthias, and Judah, who led the men in destroying the golden eagle above the gate of the temple, will be executed by being burned alive. They will be put to death before the others. Then their 40 co-conspirators will also be burned to death after the fire has consumed the ringleaders."

Hearing the sentence, a few cried for mercy because of their families, but Herod pretended not to hear. The king left the theater with a fanfare of trumpets and under heavy military escort. The assembly was dismissed, and the prisoners were taken outside the city where piles of combustible materials were being prepared for their burning.

A considerable number of people gathered outside the city walls to see the punishment of the conspirators. It was now the middle of the afternoon. Even some of the noblemen who had been summoned by the king stood on the ramparts. Each prisoner was tied to a pole surrounded by a stack of wood and brush. At the signal of the military commander, a fire was lighted under both Matthias and Judas. For about a quarter of an hour they endured the flames with much self-control but in great pain and suffering. Finally, it was evident that they were no longer living. Several people who were among their loved ones wailed with grief as they watched the scene.

Soon afterward, soldiers spread out among the prisoners and the flames began leaping up all throughout the entire group of prisoners. Screams of agony filled the air. A vast multitude of people stood peering toward the macabre scene, but many left after a short time. The sight was too hard to bear. The odor of burning flesh filled the air as a cloud of dark smoke settled over the city. The cries stopped after about a half hour. Many of the inhabitants and several of the leading men of the nation sat weeping on the ramparts. They had seen a sight which no man should ever witness.

In the evening, further southeast in the foothills of the mountains east of the Dead Sea, the full moon rose to illuminate the entire desert. The Magi and their entire company had decided to cease traveling at night. There was no longer any need to travel in the darkness, the dangers associated with Herod's soldiers were now well behind them.

At the beginning of the evening, Suen-magir reminded the group that according to the almanac an eclipse of the moon was to take place during the night. The eclipse began about midnight and continued for a few hours. The moon, in midheaven, turned a dark red color and at times was dark gray and almost black.[8] Some night birds ceased making any noise as totality began.

The men were always in awe of these events. However, observing the event in the wilderness of Arabia far from home, made the eclipse especially memorable. A few clouds occasionally obscured the face of the moon, but otherwise, the skies were mostly clear. The totality of the eclipse ended about four hours before dawn.[9]

---

8 Total eclipses can vary in color. They will probably be red, but they may be shades of black as well.

9 The ancients could measure time at night by the rising and setting of constellations. Every two hours a typical Babylonian constellation would set in the west while another one would rise in the east. Each hour the starry sky

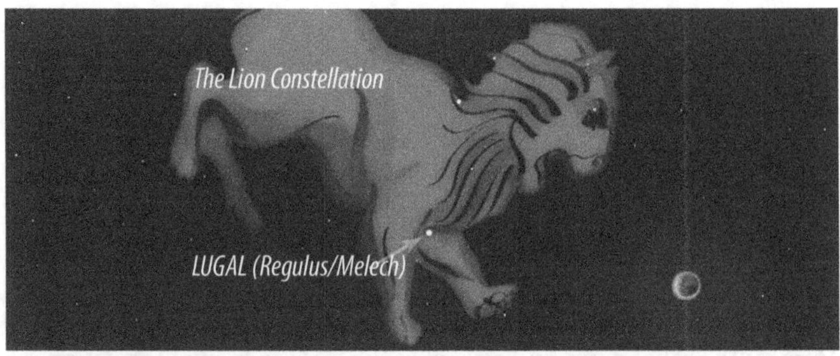

The wise men, their servants, and the guards had no idea that in Judaea the eclipse was seen as an omen against the reign of Herod the Great.[10]

In the early morning, three days after the men were burned in Jericho, the report of the Jewish commander who had followed the Magi arrived at the king's quarters. The commander knew better than to bring the news himself. He sent a soldier with orders to give the message to the king's secretary and then to immediately leave the palace. The commander had given good instructions because he realized that the king would be enraged. When Herod read the report from the cavalry commander, it took him two hours to calm down. If the messenger or the commander had been in his presence, he might have been killed through the kings' orders.

---

moves toward the west at about fifteen degrees. Each Babylonian constellation along the path of the sun and moon measured 30 degrees.

10 The lunar eclipse is mentioned in Josephus' *Antiquities of the Jews,* 17.6.1 through 17.6.4, Sections 146-167.

It is possible that the Magi would have seen the full moon rising over the Jordanian mountains as they left Judaea. This is an actual picture of the mountains seen from the Israeli side of the Dead Sea.

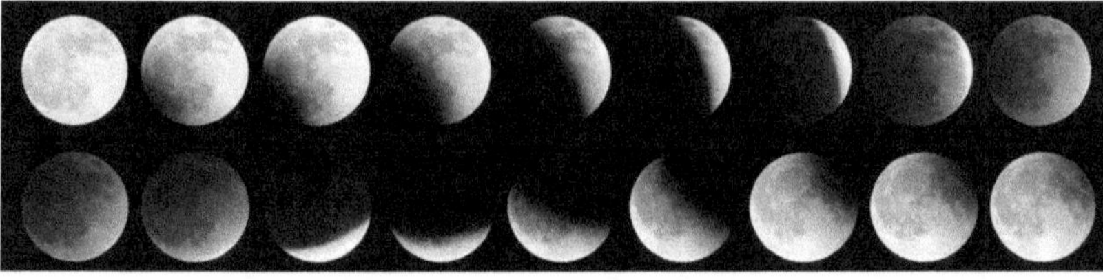

A Massacre Ordered

Finally, after a few days, Herod decided how to respond to the flight of the Magi and the still hidden messianic king in Bethlehem. In the early afternoon, on the 17th of Tevet[11] Herod sent the following message to the commander of his Gallic mercenaries.

Herod the King to Rufus the Commander of the Gallic cohort,

There is an urgent task which needs to be accomplished in Bethlehem. Prepare your cohort of soldiers[12] and 150 cavalry from the royal guard and lead them to my properties near the Herodium fortress beside Bethlehem. I will inform the commander of the cavalry to be ready to follow your orders. You can spend the night camped on my properties just a few miles from Bethlehem.

The next morning on the 21st of the month,[13] cavalrymen should surround Bethlehem as soon as the first light of day appears in the east. The cavalrymen are to block all the exits of the town (include the area up to a mile from the town in all directions). No one is to be allowed to leave. The cohort of infantry is to follow the cavalry on foot at first light. They should arrive at Bethlehem and also surround it within an hour.

When the infantry has completely surrounded Bethlehem you are to send soldiers to visit each lodging. If there are any male children in any home that are less than two years of age, I order you to put them to death. There are to be no exceptions. You must make a thorough and complete search of the town and the hamlets nearby. There is a messianic plot concerning a child who is destined to try to seize the throne in Judaea. Know that your action will stop this treasonous effort. Report to me in person when you have completed the mission.

Herod the King

---

11 January 14, 1 BC

12 About 500 to 600 men.

13 January 18, 1 BC

The Escape to Egypt

Month X - Tebētu / Tevet - Day 21   Evening, January 17, 1 BC

Several days after the wise men made their visit, Joseph had a remarkable dream. In the dream, Joseph was sitting in his house when suddenly the door opened, and a light brilliant light flooded the room. An angel clothed in white cloth and shining silver armor entered the house with a drawn sword in his hand.

He looked determinedly at Joseph in the face and said to him. "I have come to warn you. You all are in danger. Herod is going to try to kill the young child. You are to arise immediately and take the child and his mother to Egypt. The Lord has provided for your needs of your entire family through the gifts of the Magi. Arise now and flee. Do not delay. The danger is imminent."[14] And then with those words, the dream ended.

Joseph, waking from his sleep almost immediately, sensed the urgency of the angel's words. He arose, and in the darkness saw some embers from a cooking fire from the evening meal. Happily, since the night was not far advanced, there were still a few embers. Joseph was able to use them to light a lamp. Mary also woke as she heard Joseph moving about and saw the lighted lamp.

She said, "Why are you up carrying a light? You may awaken the child. It could be hard to get him back to sleep."

Joseph said quietly, but with conviction, "The child very well may awaken, but it will not matter. The Lord sent an angel to warn us. We are to flee from Bethlehem immediately. Herod is going to try to kill the child. We must not remain here even until dawn. It is urgent that we leave Bethlehem within the coming hours as soon as the moon rises to give us light."

"Prepare the things that we will need, food, clothing, things for the child, all of that. I will prepare the two donkeys; we can take some of our belongings. I will place dried fruit, grain and other food on the donkeys. You will probably need to walk for much of the way. I can sometimes

---

14 Matthew 2:13-15

carry the child on my shoulders, and we can occasionally place him on the back of the donkey while we support and steady him. I will also make other arrangements. I am going to leave a note and some funds for my cousin, he can take care of certain details for us. Soon there will be enough light from the moon so that we can travel several hours in the darkness. That will enable us to go perhaps 5-6 miles or farther from Bethlehem. Then at dawn, we will continue."

Mary interrupted, "But Joseph where are we going? Samaria, Galilee, and Nazareth are in Herod's dominions. Where can we possibly hide?"

Joseph said, "Mary, we are not staying in Herod's dominions at all, we are going to Egypt. The angel has instructed me to do so. We must go."

In a couple of hours, everything was ready. Mary, the child, and the donkeys, now being gathered just outside the door, Joseph shut the door of the house, grabbed a rope for one of the donkeys and handed it to Mary. Then he took another rope for the other donkey in his hand. He told Mary also to pass the child to him. Joseph placed the still sleeping Jesus on his shoulders and began to walk.

Happily, the moonlight was now abundant toward the southeast. Joseph, Jesus, Mary, and the donkeys moved along relatively silently as they left Bethlehem. Arriving near his cousin's home, Joseph placed his prepared message on the doorstep under a rock. Within another ten minutes, the couple and their child were moving through olive groves and fields on the road out of Bethlehem toward the southwest.

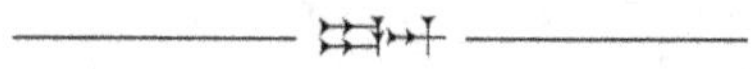

Hours later, a while after dawn in Bethlehem, about twenty-three male children less than two years of age were taken from their parents and were slaughtered within yards of their homes. In many cases, the parents saw their sons executed before their eyes. They could hardly believe what was happening. The king's men entered each dwelling place and searched the whole town. When they found a young male child, they asked the parents and other witnesses concerning the age of the children. All the male children less than two years of age were put to death according to the orders of the king. The incident left the entire town profoundly shocked, eventually causing several mothers and older people to die from grief.

"Then what had been spoken through Jeremiah the prophet was fulfilled: 'A voice was heard in Ramah, weeping and great mourning,

Rachel weeping for her children, and she refused to be comforted because they were no more.'" [15]

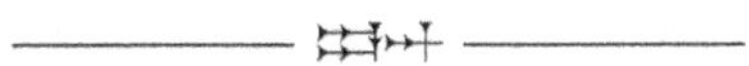

Within ten days, Joseph, Mary, and Jesus reached Pelusium on the Mediterranean coast at the far eastern edge of the Nile delta in Egypt. Joseph decided to go much further. The couple eventually established themselves in a small Jewish community at Heliopolis on the east side of the Nile at the extreme southern part of the river delta. The town was just northeast of Memphis near the pyramids. There the Romans had placed a legion in a citadel named the Babylon Fortress. Joseph thought it was odd that the gifts of the Magi had allowed the family to live within a short distance of a fortress, whose name possibly had its origins with Babylonians who had aided in the conquest of Egypt under the Persian Cambyses II. [16]

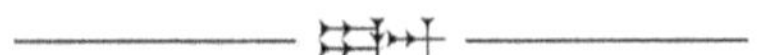

After Herod died, an angel of the Lord appeared in a dream to Joseph in Egypt and said, "Get up, take the child and his mother and go to the land of Israel, for those who were trying to take the child's life are dead."

So he got up, took the child and his mother and went to the land of Israel. But when he heard that Archelaus was reigning in Judea in place of his father, Joseph was afraid to go there. Having been warned in a dream, he withdrew to the district of Galilee, and he went and lived in a town called Nazareth. So was fulfilled what was said through the prophets, that he would be called a Nazarene. (Matthew 2:19-23) [17]

---

15 Jeremiah 31:15, cited in Matthew 2:17-18.

16 The Persian conquest of Egypt happened in the 520s BC.

17 Text from the NASB. This passage gives a reasonably clear indication that Joseph and Mary had been established

The Magi Arrive Back in Babylonia

After leaving Petra in the Nabatean kingdom, over two months were necessary for the group of Magi, the servants, and the guards to regain Babylonia. The journey was long. A few times they were in significant peril in the deserts after they left Petra. Near Duma, the men had been trapped in a sandstorm for two days. Finally arriving not far from the Euphrates River and practically within sight of their homes, the men narrowly avoided a group of brigands. Through Callisthenes' quick thinking the trap set by the robbers was avoided, and the men returned safely home.

In the desert, Illis-kutul had several serious discussions with Suen-magir about the future and the possibilities of a new marriage. Although things were not said in an overt manner, Suen-magir came to understand that Illis-kutul might be referring to Kallisto. He began to hope.

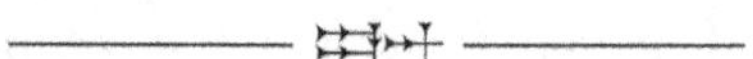

A few days after his arrival in Borsippa, Eliab mounted his horse and went to his father's home. As he arrived at the plantation, the wind was blowing in the date palms as usual. Some workmen were tending to a small irrigation canal as he passed. They waved to him and he waved back. He could see the family house in the distance. Riding up to the porch, he quickly dismounted and walked under the porch. As he neared the door, he remembered the text carved in the great beams making up the lintel and the doorposts. He stood for a few moments and reread the text. He thought to himself,

---

for a longer period in Bethlehem. Joseph would not have desired to return to Bethlehem if their family home had been in Nazareth. It was only after the trip to Egypt that the decision was made to settle the family in Nazareth. Apparently, this only happened because of a dream. Luke's text is accurate when it indicates that "after they had done everything according to the law, they returned to Nazareth. However, he does not tell the entire story. Luke repeatedly tries to show that people involved in the story of the Messiah were good Jews who were abiding by the precepts of the law. However, Luke skips over the incidents which caused their flight to Egypt. He may have done this knowing that Matthew had already told the story. See Luke 1:1-4. Several people had written accounts about the life of Jesus before Luke composed his gospel. Luke apparently avoided repeating parts of Matthew's account.

"Indeed to him shall be the obedience of the peoples."

And he also remembered the phrase from the Psalm,

"His throne shall be established before me like the sun. It shall be established forever like the moon, and the witness in the sky is faithful."

Eliab thought, "Yes, God has also been faithful. He has kept his word." For Eliab, the adventure of the star and the young Messiah had begun there under the porch of his father's home about decades previously.

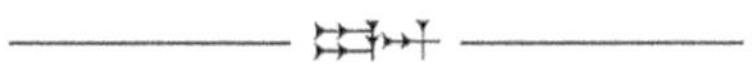

About a month after the group had returned to Babylonia, Eliab received a letter from his cousin Joram who lived in Jerusalem.

Opening the letter, Eliab trembled with anticipation because he was so interested in getting news from Judaea. In the letter, Joram told the story of how there had been the incident in Jerusalem concerning the golden eagle at the temple. The men who had done the deed had later been put to death.

But the worst news concerned the children at Bethlehem. King Herod had sent an entire cohort of infantry [18] and cavalry to surround Bethlehem and part of the immediate area. The slaughtering of the children had happened on the 21st day of the month, 14 days after the group had fled Bethlehem. Eliab's cousin also gave some details about the deaths of the children. Eliab related this to the entire group who had made the journey. They were much grieved to think that some if not all of the young children whom they had met during their investigations were now dead.

They wondered for a moment if the child-king had escaped. However, they all concluded very quickly that the young Messiah had undoubtedly escaped in some manner. It was practically inconceivable to the men that the child would have been killed. His coming had been announced through the stars and accompanied by a strong presence of angels.

How could he have possibly have died? It seemed unlikely to Eliab and

---

18 About 500-600 men.

the others. Eliab's cousin also sent word that Herod had died about four weeks after the wise men had visited the palace.[19] The king had died at Jericho in great pain and suffering. The people did not mourn his passing.

A large part of the population believed that the eclipse of the moon had foretold Herod's doom.

Two months after returning to Babylon, a letter came to Eliab from Malachi. He wrote about how the entire town of Bethlehem had been devastated by the massacre of the children. The killing of the children had hugely affected Malachi as well. Some of the people who worked for Malachi were personally touched. Through Shelumiel's intervention Malachi had contacted the shepherds and they, in turn, went to see if the child had survived.

Questioning Joseph's cousin, the men learned that Joseph had experienced a vivid dream the night before the massacre. The family had fled from Bethlehem in the later part of the night. Apparently, they had gone to Egypt. That was all that Malachi and Shelumiel had been able to learn. God had protected the child. Malachi speculated that the Magi's gifts had helped the family to finance the journey and pay for their accommodation in Egypt.

Unanswered Questions

Six months later, Eliab still had some questions. In discussing things with Iqisa, both men realized that some passages of Scripture about the Messiah seemed strange and they could not quite discern the exact meaning of the texts. Iqisa related his experience of reading in Isaiah

---

19 One of the traditional dates for Herod death has been the second day of Shebat. In 1 BC this would have taken place on January 28/29.

while the men had been in Bethlehem. Back in Babylonia, they read the passage together and discussed it. However, they still were not sure what to think about it.

Daniel's prophecy was also a problem. They had met the young Messiah and even believed that the child had escaped Herod's massacre. However, there was a passage in the book of Daniel which troubled both Eliab and Iqisa concerning the Messiah. The great prophecy of the 70 'sevens' in Daniel had been a key in establishing a date for the Messiah's coming. The prophecy had also been important in revealing the mystery of the star.

One day at home, Eliab took up the scroll of the book of Daniel and read the text.

"Seventy 'sevens' have been decreed for your people and your holy city, to finish the transgression, to make an end of sin, to make atonement for iniquity, to bring in everlasting righteousness, to seal up vision and prophecy and to anoint the most holy place (the Most Holy One in some translations). So you are to know and discern that from the issuing of a decree to restore and rebuild Jerusalem until Messiah the Prince there will be seven 'sevens' and sixty-two 'sevens'; it will be built again, with plaza and moat, even in times of distress."

The city had definitely been rebuilt. Eliab had been there. He had seen it with his own eyes. Herod's temple was even more glorious than anything which the refugees from Babylonia could have ever imagined.

But there were other ominous aspects of the prophecy.

"... and the people of the prince who is to come will destroy the city and the sanctuary. And its end will come with a flood; even to the end there will be war; desolations are determined. ..."

The city and the sanctuary would be destroyed. He remembered how he had thought about that text as he stood before the great gate of the temple several months before. But the passage about an apparent end for the young Messiah was particularly alarming.

"Then after sixty-two 'sevens' the Messiah will be cut off and have nothing ..."

Eliab wondered, "How could this be? What did it mean for the Messiah to be 'cut off and have nothing?' And what were these 62 'sevens'?

They could not be the same as the other 62 'sevens' which had just ended, could they? The 62 'sevens' of years had been the clues to understanding the time of the Messiah's appearing. But were the two periods the same?

Eliab wanted to explore this with Iqisa and Illis-kutul in particular. Perhaps if the three men worked together, they might be able to find a solution to the enigma.

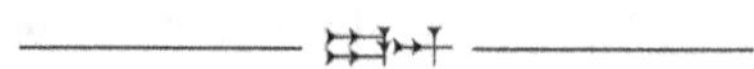

A week later, Eliab was in the notary office in Borsippa. Iqisa was the new head of the notary office. However, he only was beginning to fill the role and enter into the legacy left by his father. The young man would have many challenges in the coming years. When the morning's work was done, Eliab sat down with Iqisa. Eliab had already invited Illis-kutul and Suen-magir to join them.

Eliab explained how he was still very puzzled by the prophecy saying, "You both are well aware how the prophecy of the seven 'sevens' and the 62 'sevens' was key to understanding the timing of the Messiah's coming and in identifying the star."

"However, the text which follows the Messiah's coming is very particular. It speaks of him being 'cut off and have nothing' at the end of a period of 62 'sevens.' Somehow it does not seem to me that this is the same period of 62 'sevens' which we explored earlier. The Messiah came at the culmination of 62 'sevens.' We experienced this. He is not going to be 'cut off' immediately after he has been born."

"But I am wondering how this could happen. Another period of 62 'sevens' cannot be in years. While by a miracle the Messiah could live as long as some of the ancient patriarchs it does not seem reasonable to think that the Messiah alone will live 434 years before being 'cut off and having nothing.' Yes, somehow this child seems to be associated with the resurrection of the dead, but is Daniel's text saying the Messiah will live for hundreds of years before the general resurrection?"

"Here in the prophecy, it appears that he will possibly die. Otherwise, I do not know how to interpret the words. I do not know how one could otherwise interpret the 'being cut off and having nothing.' But how does it serve God's purposes for the Messiah to be 'cut off and have nothing'?

It does not make sense to me at this point."

Iqisa, Suen-magir, and Illis-kutul were not sure how to respond for a moment. Then Illis-kutul had a bit of inspiration.

He said, "Leading up to our journey to Judaea we had noticed literal years connected to the Sabbatical year series. Our calculations allowed us to fix the general date for the Messiah's coming. Then we saw some literal weeks. There were two periods of seven 'sevens' and 62 'sevens' which symbolically brought to mind the prophecy and which were associated with the star. But, I want you to remember something. Perhaps we should think about periods of lunar months as well. Suen-magir, you are a specialist concerning the heavens and especially the calendar. How many years are implied by 62 times seven lunar months?"

Suen-magir did not have to think very long, he said, "That is 434 lunar months. Well, The total of 235 lunar months is the basis of our calendar. That represents 19 lunar years. Of course, twice that would be 38 years or 470 lunar months. If one removes three complete years of 12 months each from 470 lunar months that leads us to 434 lunar months which is 35 years."

"I ask you all, What if the Messiah's 'being cut off and having nothing' is related to an event 35 years after his birth? Or could it even be 35 years after his conception?"

Illis-kutul then looked at the men for just a moment and then continued his explanation.

"As we saw there was a celestial link to the heavens and Jesus' conception. So if his coming is related to his conception then the 'being cut off and having nothing' could very well refer to events 33 years from now at about the time of Passover. That would be the Seleucid Era year 343 and the Arsacid Era Year 279."[20]

Eliab said, "Well, for my part I will be about 70 years old in 33 years if we count the 434 months from the Messiah's conception."

Illis-kutul said, "And I will be over 80. But Iqisa you will only be about

---

20 AD 33. Many scholars think that Jesus was crucified and raised from the dead on in the first week of April in AD 33. His death would have been on April 3, AD 33 and his resurrection on April 5, AD 33. There were probably 434 (62 x 7) lunar months from the time of Jesus' conception in 3 BC until the time of his death and resurrection.

the age of your father. Who knows? Perhaps you will live to know about or even witness some of these events?"

Iqisa replied, "Well, whatever these texts mean and whether or not we will live to know anything about the fulfillment of the last series of 62 'sevens,' I believe that ultimately the Messiah's reign will endure. As it is written in the Psalms, a passage that we all know,

> *'Once I have sworn by My holiness; I will not lie to David. His descendants shall endure forever and his throne as the sun before Me. It shall be established forever like the moon, and the witness in the sky is faithful.'*[21]

---

21 Psalm 89:35-37 NASB

Supplements

"I am God, and there is no one like Me, declaring
the end from the beginning, and from ancient
times things which have not been done."

"Saying, 'My purpose will be established, and
I will accomplish all My good pleasure.'"

(Isaiah 46:9b-10)

Appendix 1
The Prophetic Background
of the Messiah

Appendix 1 Contents:

These prophetic texts are provided as a supplement to the texts in Chapter 1 "Prophecies of the Messiah." They are also partly in a novelized format.

The Star and Scepter

On the Mountains of Moab, Before 1400 BC

This famous text found in Numbers 22-24 is included in this section of *MUL.BABBAR: The White Star over Bethlehem,* because it is often referred to concerning the star of Bethlehem. Numbers 24:17 briefly mentions a star, but not an ordinary star. Some of the early Church Fathers thought of the prophecy as an explanation for the star over Bethlehem. The reader can make up his own mind by examining the prophecy in context. However, the author does not believe that Balaam's prophecy has anything specifically to do with either a natural or supernatural star over Bethlehem. Instead, the star in the prophecy was a human being. Major aspects of the prophecy were fulfilled in the life of King David, who became a bright shining leader for Israel about 400 years after the prophecy was given. David was the star, Jesus was a "son of David."

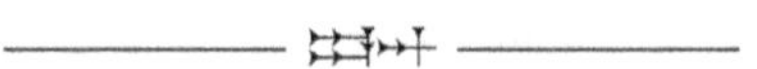

Balaam, a middle-eastern wise man and soothsayer was invited by Balak, the king of Moab, to curse the multitude of Israel which had come out of Egypt. This happened not long before they entered their promised land. Balak took Balaam to a few different high places on the mountains overlooking the plains of Moab and the Israelite camp. Several times he tried to curse the people, but he finally realized that the multitudes below were blessed of God and nothing could be said or done against them.

When Balaam saw that it pleased the LORD to bless Israel, he did not go as at other times to seek omens but he set his face toward the wilderness. And Balaam lifted up his eyes and saw Israel camping tribe by tribe; and the Spirit of God came upon him.

He took up his discourse and said, "The oracle of Balaam the son of Beor, and the oracle of the man whose eye is opened; The oracle of him who hears the words of God, who sees the vision of the Almighty, falling down, yet having his eyes uncovered,

How fair are your tents, O Jacob, your dwellings, O Israel!

"Like valleys that stretch out, like gardens beside the river, like aloes planted by the LORD, like cedars beside the waters.

"Water will flow from his buckets, And his seed will be by many waters, and his king shall be higher than Agag, and his kingdom shall be exalted.

"God brings him out of Egypt, He is for him like the horns of the wild ox. He will devour the nations who are his adversaries, and will crush their bones in pieces, and shatter them with his arrows.

"He couches, he lies down as a lion, and as a lion, who dares rouse him? Blessed is everyone who blesses you, and cursed is everyone who curses you."

Then Balak's anger burned against Balaam, and he struck his hands together; and Balak said to Balaam, *"I called you to curse my enemies, but behold, you have persisted in blessing them these three times! Therefore, flee to your place now. I said I would honor you greatly, but behold, the LORD has held you back from honor."*

Balaam said to Balak, "Did I not tell your messengers whom you had sent to me, saying, 'Though Balak were to give me his house full of silver and gold, I could not do anything contrary to the command of the LORD, either good or bad, of my own accord. What the LORD speaks, that I will speak'? "And now, behold, I am going to my people; come, and I will advise you what this people will do to your people in the days to come."

He took up his discourse and said, "The oracle of Balaam the son of Beor, and the oracle of the man whose eye is opened, the oracle of him who hears the words of God, and knows the knowledge of the Most

High, who sees the vision of the Almighty, falling down, yet having his eyes uncovered.

"I see him, but not now; I behold him, but not near; A star shall come forth from Jacob, A scepter shall rise from Israel,[1] And shall crush through the forehead of Moab, and tear down all the sons of Sheth.

"Edom shall be a possession, Seir, its enemies, also will be a possession, while Israel performs valiantly. One from Jacob shall have dominion, and will destroy the remnant from the city."

And he looked at Amalek and took up his discourse and said, "Amalek was the first of the nations, but his end shall be destruction."

And he looked at the Kenite, and took up his discourse and said, "Your dwelling place is enduring, and your nest is set in the cliff.

---

1 The author does not believe that this prophecy of the star refers to Jesus, but rather to King David. According to 2 Samuel 8:1-15 David accomplished verses 18-19 of Balaam's prophecy. While 2 Samuel 24:17, ("A star shall come forth from Jacob"), was often used even from the early Christian centuries concerning the star of Bethlehem, among the Jews it was seen as being a reference to David the king (and by expansion, David's descendant, the Messiah). It is very clear that the passage refers to a person. The 'star' was to come forth from the people, "from Jacob." The text itself does not refer either to a natural or a supernatural star. It refers to a bright, illustrious, royal, military leader who would "crush through the forehead of Moab, and tear down all the sons of Sheth." The prophecy was fulfilled through David:

2 Samuel 8:1-15 reads as follows:

Now after this it came about that David defeated the Philistines and subdued them; and David took control of the chief city from the hand of the Philistines. He defeated Moab, and measured them with the line, making them lie down on the ground; and he measured two lines to put to death and one full line to keep alive. And the Moabites became servants to David, bringing tribute.

Then David defeated Hadadezer, the son of Rehob king of Zobah, as he went to restore his rule at the River (Euphrates). David captured from him 1,700 horsemen and 20,000 foot soldiers; and David hamstrung the chariot horses, but reserved enough of them for 100 chariots. When the Arameans of Damascus came to help Hadadezer, king of Zobah, David killed 22,000 Arameans. Then David put garrisons among the Arameans of Damascus, and the Arameans became servants to David, bringing tribute. And the Lord helped David wherever he went.

....

*So David made a name for himself when he returned from killing 18,000 Arameans *(some texts read 'Edomites') in the Valley of Salt. He put garrisons in Edom. In all Edom he put garrisons, and all the Edomites became servants to David. And the Lord helped David wherever he went.*

So David reigned over all Israel; and David administered justice and righteousness for all his people.

In accordance with the last line in the text above, it should be noted that the prophesied descendant of David, the Messiah, was to "execute justice and righteousness on the earth" (Jeremiah 33: 14-18).

"Nevertheless Kain will be consumed; How long will Asshur keep you captive?"

Then he took up his discourse and said, "Alas, who can live except God has ordained it?

"But ships shall come from the coast of Kittim, and they shall afflict Asshur and will afflict Eber; so they also will come to destruction." [2]

Hearing the prophecy, Balak was furious and loudly uttered several foul oaths and swore violently. Balaam found himself extremely weak and stumbled as he finished his words. Finding a large boulder a few feet away, he sat down wholly astounded and buried his face in his hands for several minutes. Then looking up again with tears in his eyes, he stared in wonder toward the multitude of Israel on the plains below.

Finally, Balaam turned to the king once more and said, "I assure you there is nothing which one can do against this people. They are blessed. One shall certainly arise from their number who 'shall crush through the forehead of Moab, and tear down all the sons of Sheth,' one from among them will have dominion over the whole region. However, rest assured King Balak, this will not happen in your days. It may not take place for several hundred years, but it will undoubtedly come to pass just as I have spoken."

Then Balaam arose and took his staff. Strengthening his pace by leaning on the wooden staff and finding his servants nearby, they all departed. Balak, after looking down at the multitude of Israel again, uttered another repulsive oath. He then spit on the ground with contempt as he turned and went his way.

---

2 Then entire cited text is from Numbers 24:1-24

Micah - Prophet from Moresheth in Judaea

Before 700 BC

But as for you, Bethlehem Ephrathah, Too little to be among the clans of Judah, from you One will go forth for Me to be ruler in Israel. His goings forth are from long ago, from the days of eternity." Therefore He will give them up until the time when she who is in labor has borne a child. Then the remainder of His brethren will return to the sons of Israel. And He will arise and shepherd His flock In the strength of the Lord, in the majesty of the name of the Lord His God. And they will remain, because at that time He will be great To the ends of the earth. This One will be our peace.[1]

The prophet Micah lived in Judaea roughly from 750–700 BC during the reigns of Yehotam, Ahaz, and Hezekiah. Micah came from Moresheth, which appears to have been in the hills in south-central Israel between the Judaean Mountains and the coastal plain. Micah prophesied that a ruler would come out of Judaea and notably from Bethlehem in the land of Ephrathah.

In a passage in Genesis 35:16-19 we read:

---

1   Micah 5:2-5a

Then they journeyed from Bethel; and when there was still some distance to go to Ephrath, Rachel began to give birth and she suffered severe labor. When she was in severe labor the midwife said to her, "Do not fear, for now you have another son." It came about as her soul was departing (for she died), that she named him Ben-oni; but his father called him Benjamin. So Rachel died and was buried on the way to Ephrath (that is, Bethlehem).

Ephrath was the second wife of Caleb, and mother of Hur (1 Chronicles 2:19). It is believed that Ephrath lent her name to the town of Ephrath or Bethlehem. See 1 Chronicles 2:50,51 4:4, where Ephrath gave birth to a man named Salma who was the father of a man named Bethlehem. In biblical times Ephrath meant "the fruitful." Bethlehem meant the "house of bread."

Boaz, the Judaean and Ruth the Moabitess were associated with Bethlehem (Ruth 1-4). This couple became the parents of Obed, who was the father of Jesse, the father of David, the king.

The Forerunner

Judaea

Sometime in 4 BC

In the days of Herod, king of Judea, there was a priest named Zacharias, of the division of Abijah; and he had a wife from the daughters of Aaron, and her name was Elizabeth. They were both righteous in the sight of God, walking blamelessly in all the commandments and requirements of the Lord. But they had no child, because Elizabeth was barren, and they were both advanced in years.

Now it happened that while he was performing his priestly service before God in the appointed order of his division, according to the custom of the priestly office, he was chosen by lot to enter the temple of the Lord and burn incense. And the whole multitude of the people were in prayer outside at the hour of the incense offering.

And an angel of the Lord appeared to him, standing to the right of the altar of incense. Zacharias was troubled when he saw the angel, and fear gripped him. But the angel said to him, "Do not be afraid, Zacharias, for your petition has been heard, and your wife Elizabeth will bear you a son, and you will give him the name John.

"You will have joy and gladness, and many will rejoice at his birth. "For he will be great in the sight of the Lord; and he will drink no wine or liquor, and he will be filled with the Holy Spirit while yet in his mother's womb. And he will turn many of the sons of Israel back to the Lord their God. It is he who will go as a forerunner before Him in the spirit

and power of Elijah, 'to turn the hearts of the fathers back to the children,' and the disobedient to the attitude of the righteous, so as to make ready a people prepared for the Lord."

Zacharias said to the angel, "How will I know this for certain? For I am an old man and my wife is advanced in years." The angel answered and said to him, "I am Gabriel, who stands in the presence of God, and I have been sent to speak to you and to bring you this good news. "And behold, you shall be silent and unable to speak until the day when these things take place, because you did not believe my words, which will be fulfilled in their proper time."

The people were waiting for Zacharias, and were wondering at his delay in the temple. But when he came out, he was unable to speak to them; and they realized that he had seen a vision in the temple; and he kept making signs to them, and remained mute. When the days of his priestly service were ended, he went back home. (The paragraphs above are from Luke 1:1-23)

After these days Elizabeth his wife became pregnant, and she kept herself in seclusion for five months, saying, "This is the way the Lord has dealt with me in the days when He looked with favor upon me, to take away my disgrace among men." (Luke 1:24-25)

In those days Mary arose and went with haste into the hill country, to a town in Judah, and she entered the house of Zechariah and greeted Elizabeth. And when Elizabeth heard the greeting of Mary, the baby leaped in her womb. And Elizabeth was filled with the Holy Spirit, and she exclaimed with a loud cry, "Blessed are you among women, and blessed is the fruit of your womb!

And Mary remained with her about three months and returned to her home. (Luke 1:39-42 and 56).

Now the time came for Elizabeth to give birth, and she bore a son. And her neighbors and relatives heard that the Lord had shown great mercy to her, and they rejoiced with her. And on the eighth day they came to circumcise the child. And they would have called him Zechariah after his father, but his mother answered, "No; he shall be called John." (Luke 1:57-60)

...

And his father Zechariah was filled with the Holy Spirit and prophesied, saying,

"Blessed be the Lord God of Israel, for he has visited and redeemed his people and has raised up a horn of salvation for us in the house of his servant David, as he spoke by the mouth of his holy prophets from of old, that we should be saved from our enemies and from the hand of all who hate us; to show the mercy promised to our fathers and to remember his holy covenant, the oath that he swore to our father Abraham, to grant us that we, being delivered from the hand of our enemies, might serve him without fear, in holiness and righteousness before him all our days.

And you, child, will be called the prophet of the Most High; for you will go before the Lord to prepare his ways, to give knowledge of salvation to his people in the forgiveness of their sins, because of the tender mercy of our God, whereby the sunrise shall visit us from on high to give light to those who sit in darkness and in the shadow of death, to guide our feet into the way of peace." (Luke 1:67-79)

* Historical Note

According to Church tradition John the Baptist was born in the later part of the month of June, six months before the birth of the Messiah in either December or January. According to the timeline followed here, John was born in the summer of 3 BC. Jesus was born either in December of 3 BC or January of 2 BC.

It is not possible to establish the date of John's conception through the scheduling of the priestly services in the temple. We do not know if Elizabeth's pregnancy followed Gabriel's announcement to Zachariah by a matter or weeks or months. Gabriel only said, "And behold, you will be silent and unable to speak until the day that these things take place, because you did not believe my words, which will be fulfilled in their time." The phrase "which will be fulfilled in their time" does not indicate that Elizabeth would be pregnant immediately after Gabriel made his announcement.

Appendices 2-10

Appendices 2-6 Content

Appendix 2: Mystics, Fiction, Prophecy, and Reality

The biblical account of the wise men and the star written by the Apostle Matthew is trustworthy. However, many details of the story are missing. This book seeks to fill in some of the gaps and give a more detailed explanation of the star. Matthew's account has had many interpreters over the centuries. The most widely held idea concerning the star is that the object observed by the wise men was completely supernatural. Many modern Christian apologetics ministries take this approach. The author believes that the star was a natural object, which was involved in a series of uniquely symbolic events focused on royalty. Whatever view that one may adopt concerning the star, there are also many unspoken assumptions which one brings to Matthew's story. Amazingly, even the most literal interpretations of Matthew's account involve profound assumptions which may or may not be accurate. The author seeks to follow Matthew's text faithfully, while introducing a whole new set of assumptions, which are detailed in Appendices 2 through 5.

At present, Christmas cards, artworks, films, and theatrical presentations often shape our understanding of Matthew's text more than the passage itself. Relatively few people ever seriously ask questions like the following:

Who were the Magi, and how many of them arrived in Bethlehem?
How did the wise men identify the messianic star?
When was the star visible?
How bright was the star or was it bright at all?
What was really unique about the Messiah's star?
Was the star a supernatural or a natural object?

Was the star a heavenly sign or a visual guide?
Did the wise men visually follow a star or are we merely misunderstanding Matthew's intended meaning?

Many Christian interpretations of Matthew's account make the wise men seem more like mystics than serious astronomers. However, our knowledge of the ancient near-eastern astronomers has exploded in the last 150 years. Several thousand pages of ancient near-eastern cuneiform astronomical texts still exist that can be dated from the seventh century BC to the first century AD. (Some even more ancient documents exist as well.) The cuneiform tablets reveal a highly developed statistically and mathematically based understanding of the heavens. Such technical capabilities were often undreamed of by many of our Christian forebearers when they thought of the Magi.

This book is an effort to make Matthew's account come alive in the ancient context, making the story more real and less mystical. The story of the wise men and the star has majestic depth. The glory of God is on full display in the heavens through the heavenly signs which announced the first coming of the Messiah. Many of the symbolically royal celestial signs involved events which were at the heart of Babylonian astronomical theory and practice.

The star that came to be positioned over Bethlehem was a sign concerning the Messiah. The star was not a visual guide. The star informed the wise men about the coming of the Jewish Messiah. The star did not guide the men visually to the Messiah. Appendices 3 to 5 give further understanding of the author's approach to the biblical text.

Who were the Magi? It is notable that in the Greek Septuagint text of the Old Testament, the word "magi" only appears in the book of Daniel (1:20; 2:2, 2:10, 2:27; 4:7; 5:7, 5:11, 5:15). These passages refer to Babylonian, not Median, or Persian magi. It would seem entirely reasonable that Matthew had this connection in mind when he wrote about the "men from the East." Babylonian astronomical science was highly developed by the first century BC. However, hardly anything is known about Median, Persian, or Zoroastrian astronomy with any real certainty before about AD 250. The supposed Zoroastrian material which does exist in Greek texts is overwhelmingly Babylonian in nature. It is probable that most of the Magi who went to Bethlehem, if not all, were Babylonians.

The interactions of Babylonian astronomical science, the Jewish community in the Parthian Empire, and the Jewish Scriptures can explain why the Magi arrived in Judaea seeking the King of the Jews in the last years of the first century BC.

The material presented in this book is in the form of a historical novel. Very many of the circumstances and events have been imagined and are only speculative. However, the astronomical events indicated in this book did take place. The author has explored these events and their possible interpretations in more detail in his other books on the subject.

The Ancient Promises

Chapter 1 of the novel is composed of various stories related to some ancient prophecies of the Messiah. However, a few words are important to put the initial prophetic section in perspective.

The wise men came seeking the King of the Jews. We do not know all of their thoughts concerning this messianic king. However, based on prophetic Scriptures they may have thought of this new supreme ruler as someone who would change the world and bring in a reign of righteousness on the earth.

Many of us have become so accustomed to thinking of the Messiah's kingdom as being somewhere in the heavens. Certainly, those who die in the faith will be received into the presence of God for a time in a heaven realm. However, the apostles and the early believers were looking for "new heavens and a new earth in which righteousness dwells" (2 Peter 3:13). Looking for a righteous king who would reign over the world was a central part of the Jewish messianic belief before the birth of Jesus (Jeremiah 23:5-6). The early Christians believed firmly in the resurrection of the dead and the establishment of God's kingdom on earth (Acts 3:12-21, 17:30-32, 23:6 and 26:1-29).

Many of us have misunderstood passages like John 18:36. When Jesus said, "My kingdom is not of this world," in reality, he was saying "My kingdom does not come from here below (from this world), and neither does it use the methods of this world." His kingdom comes from above, but it is for this world. Therefore, Christians pray as Jesus taught, "May your kingdom come, and your will be done on earth as it is in heaven."

The wise men were looking specifically for the king of the Jews. Whatever their ethnic or religious origins, they came to Judaea seeking a righteous king who would rule over the earth (Daniel 7:9-28).

We can only understand the true nature of the messianic king and his kingdom by looking at the Jewish Scriptures. The biblical Magi who visited Bethlehem would have received most of their perspectives about the Messiah through Jewish people and the Hebrew Scriptures. Multitudes of Jews had lived in Mesopotamia, Media, and Persia since the time of the Assyrian and Babylonian exiles in the eighth and sixth centuries BC. The eastern Jewish population numbered at least several hundreds of thousands at the end of the first century BC.

The biblical texts were widely distributed in the sizable Jewish community living in the Parthian Empire. The Hebrew Bible (Old Testament) was available in a written Greek translation called the Septuagint (often abbreviated as the "LXX"). In addition, some oral Aramaic translations of the Hebrew texts may have been available (the Targums). Many of the Babylonian and Iranian astronomers in the first century BC would have spoken Greek. All of them would have spoken Aramaic, which was the common language in the western part of the Parthian Empire.

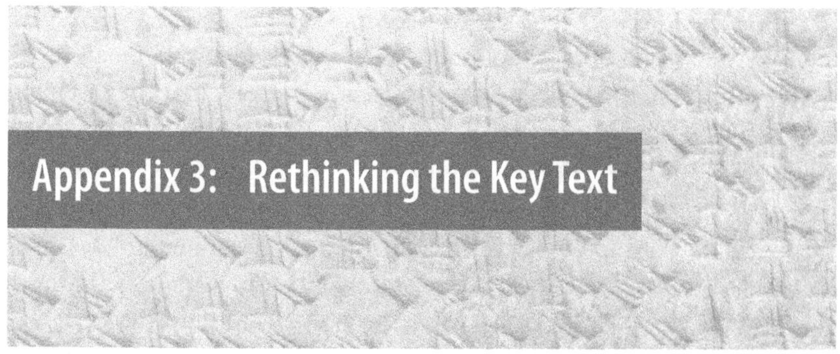

Explanations of the Star of Bethlehem rise and fall based on the following text in Matthew 2:9:

"After hearing the king, they went their way; and behold the star, which they had seen in the east, went on before them until having arrived, it stood over the place where the Child was."

This passage has been interpreted to mean that the star went visually in front of the wise men from Jerusalem to Bethlehem. The Eastern Church Fathers thought that the wise men had visually followed the star all the way from the East to Judaea and then on to Bethlehem. However, these ideas may not be what Matthew had in mind. In fact, the traditional interpretation of the text of the star as a visual guide may be profoundly in error.

One way of understanding Matthew's text would be to look at other passages in Matthew, which use the same keywords. Matthew uses the Greek verb, προάγω (proago), meaning "to precede / to go ahead of," in other passages in his gospel. In Chapter 14:22-25 we read:

"Jesus made the disciples get into the boat and go ahead (προάγειν) of Him to the other side, while He sent the crowds away. After He had sent the crowds away, He went up on the mountain by Himself to pray; and when it was evening, He was there alone. But the boat was already a long distance from the land, battered by the waves; for the wind was contrary. And in the fourth watch of the night, He came to them, walking on the sea." (See also the parallel passage in Mark 6:45.)

Jesus sent the disciples "on ahead" of him. However, he did not follow their boat as if he were following a beacon or guide. Jesus went in a different direction up onto a mountain. He only arrived at the boat much later. In this text, the verb "proago" is used to indicate that the disciples were on their way to a particular place. Later Jesus eventually met them on the lake. The disciples were in the process of "going on ahead" of Jesus to another destination.

During the last supper, Jesus made the following statement: *"But after I have been raised, I will go ahead of you* (προάξω) *to Galilee"* (Matthew 26:32, see also Mark 14:28). After Jesus was raised from the dead, an angel appeared to some of his followers and said to them: *"Go quickly and tell His disciples that He has risen from the dead; and behold, He is going ahead of you* (προάγει) *into Galilee, there you will see Him..."* (Matthew 28:7, see also Mark 16:7).

It is clear that the disciples did not follow Jesus visually to Galilee in the same sense that one usually thinks about the wise men following the star. Jesus indicated that after his resurrection he was going to arrive in Galilee ahead of the disciples. On their way to Galilee, the disciples were not taking visual and directional guidance from Jesus. The disciples arrived chronologically in Galilee after Jesus already had arrived there. Jesus "preceded" them there.

In Matthew 21:9, during Jesus' triumphal entry into Jerusalem, we read ... *the crowds that went before* (προάγοντες) *him and that followed him were shouting, "Hosanna to the Son of David! Blessed is he who comes in the name of the Lord! Hosanna in the highest!"* The atheist Aaron Adair insists that this passage means that the crowd was leading Jesus, thus indicating that Matthew 2:9 also means the same thing (Adair, 2013, Chapter 7).[1] However, in this case, Jesus was not being guided or looking to the crowd for guidance, he was entering the city while some people preceded him. Jesus knew the way to the city gate, and the crowd did as well. They were all on the road together. The crowd was indicating very clearly that they were accompanying the Messiah, not guiding him. They were welcoming him into the city. (See also the parallel passage in Mark 11:9.)

In the parable of the two sons in Matthew 21:31, which follows the triumphal entry, Jesus speaks of *"the tax collectors and the prostitutes go into* (προάγουσιν) *the kingdom of God before"* the chief priests and elders

---

1 Adair, Aaron. 2013. *The Star of Bethlehem: A Skeptical View.* N.P.: Onus Books.

who are questioning him. The verb is in the third person plural, present, indicative, active, indicating they were at that time "entering into the kingdom." Here Jesus is not indicating that the tax collectors and prostitutes serve as guides visibly going on ahead of the others. He is saying that they are chronologically entering the kingdom in advance of the rulers, who themselves may not enter in at all. Jesus' next statement underlines this, *"For John came to you in the way of righteousness, and you did not believe him, but the tax collectors and the prostitutes believed him. And even when you saw it, you did not afterward change your minds and believe him."*

In addition, in the book of Acts the verb προάγω (proago) is used in 12:6, 16:30, 17:5 and 25:26 in the sense of bringing or leading someone out before authorities in legal proceedings / investigations. All these passages use the verb proago, but in the specific context involving prisoners being brought or led out before authorities. In each case, the verb usage is different from considering the star as a visual guide that supposedly led the Magi.

From the preceding paragraphs, it becomes evident that the traditional view of assuming that the star was a visual guide that led the Magi directly to the messianic child in Bethlehem is very questionable on exegetical grounds. None of the other passages in Matthew's Gospel, which use the verb "to go before / to precede," carry a meaning of someone or something going on in advance as a guide, visually leading someone else to a destination. In both Gospel of Matthew and Mark, the verb "proago" is used to refer to someone arriving at a place chronologically before someone else would arrive there. The idea of leading or guiding is not at all present.

It is also important to note that if the traditional perspective concerning the star is correct, then the mystery of the star becomes completely impossible to understand. For example: If a supernatural star preceded the wise men from Jerusalem to Bethlehem and eventually settled over a particular house, then what was the star in the East? How would the Magi have associated the star with the Messiah while they were in the East? If the star was a visual guide for the astronomers, then how, when, and why did the wise men decide to follow it? Was the star in "movement" even while the men were in the East? The traditional view actually creates a whole series of questions, which it leaves unanswered.

An Alternate Interpretation of Matthew 2:9

The words, "and behold the star, which they had seen in the East, went on before them," are not referring to the star visually going before the Magi as a visual guide between Jerusalem to Bethlehem. Instead, the phrase is designed to send the reader back several months in the past to the former situation in the East. Matthew was seeking to relate the Magi's experience in the East to their later experience in Judaea. In the East, the star had been a sign concerning the Messiah. Later it also became a sign over Bethlehem.

It was "from the East" that the star "went on ahead of the Magi." The star "preceded" the men to the skies above Judaea from where the Magi had been before. They had been in the eastern lands, most likely in Babylonia in modern Iraq. The eastern Church Fathers thought that the star went visually on ahead of the wise men from the East. However, the text does not say that the star went visually ahead of the wise men. Matthew was not indicating anything about the star going ahead of the men as a directional guide. Rather, the star was simply waiting for the men when they arrived at Bethlehem itself, having "preceded" them there. It was in Bethlehem itself (not on the way there) that the men had a new experience with the star, while it "stood" over the place where the child was located.

In Matthew 2:9, the star "went before" until "having arrived," "it stood." The imperfect "went before" took place previous to the two aorist verbs "having arrived" and "it stood," both of which indicate completed action. Following the order of events in the text, the Magi's renewed "seeing" of the star in Matthew 2:10 may have happened only after the men had already arrived in Bethlehem itself. If one reads the text in this way, Matthew was affirming that the star, which previously had been seen in the East, was somehow remarkably present in the skies above Bethlehem when the men finally arrived in the town. From this perspective, Matthew was never referring to the star as a visual guide that played a role during the journey.

"Seeing the star" also had to do with a renewed appreciation of the star's symbolic significance over Bethlehem, not just visibly seeing an object. The star could have been visible every night for weeks previously, but without any specific renewed messianic symbolism. In Bethlehem, the men "rejoiced exceedingly" because of the meaning they attached to the star, not because they expected it to lead them anywhere. The star was not a guide, it only functioned as a sign, both in the East and over Bethlehem.

A Possible Scenario: While the wise men were in their homeland, the star gave symbolic indications that the Jewish Messiah had been born. After having received the star's message, the wise men went to Judaea. During their expedition, the men journeyed during the daytime as ordinary travelers would have done. The way to Judaea was well-known. They were not looking to the star for visual guidance because the star's purpose had been to give a message. The star was a sign concerning the Messiah's coming. It was not a guide. Over a period of months, the star came to be positioned well above the men's heads during a portion of each night. In the days before the Magi arrived in Bethlehem, the star was near to the zenith in the nighttime skies above Bethlehem. The star rose in the east each night and then climbed above of the heads of the wise men as part of the regular rotation of the earth.

When the Magi finally arrived in Bethlehem (having traveled there in the daytime), they unexpectedly concluded that the star had again become a celestial sign concerning the Messiah. This realization happened at night in Bethlehem itself when the Magi saw the star in specific symbolic circumstances. In this manner, the star "preceded" the men to the skies above Bethlehem. Essentially it was waiting for them when they arrived. Similarly, decades later, Jesus also "preceded" the disciples to Galilee after his resurrection and then the men saw him there. It is clear that the disciples did not visually follow Jesus to Galilee after his resurrection. Likewise, the Magi never visually followed the star anywhere.

The wise men finally discovered the young Messiah and his parents through doing a careful search. They then presented their gifts in the private setting of Mary and Joseph's home. The wise men's visit happened well after the birth of the child (following his circumcision, etc.). Joseph desired to return to Judaea after taking his family to Egypt. However, Joseph was afraid to go there because of Archelaus who was reigning in the stead of his father Herod (Matthew 2:21-23). Joseph wanted to return "home" to Bethlehem, indicating that he had established his family in Bethlehem for a longer period, not just during the census. The family only went to Nazareth as a result of a dream that took place as Joseph was debating about which course of action to take following their journey to Egypt.

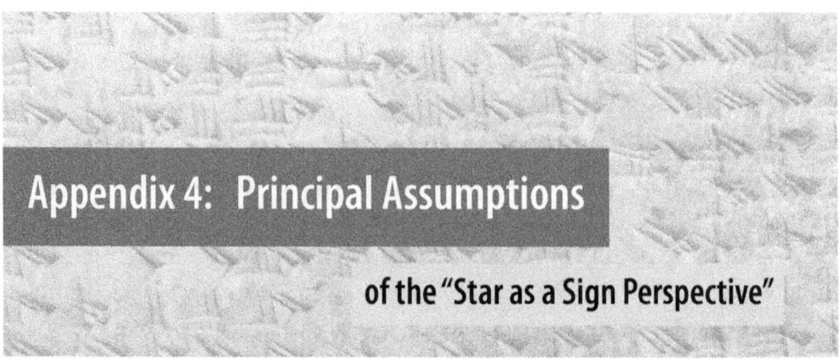

Appendix 4: Principal Assumptions

of the "Star as a Sign Perspective"

• The star was a sign connected to the Messiah's appearing. It informed the wise men of the Messiah's coming.

• The wise men never visually followed the star anywhere at any time. The star never became a directional guide. Its role was to inform, not to guide.

• Time and reflection were necessary for the wise men to understand the star's message.

• The star became symbolic in a context involving other stars and planets as well as the sun and moon.

• The star was a natural celestial object. However, God's remarkable ancient planning was a striking aspect of the star's appearing. The celestial royal signs surrounding the Messiah's coming seem to have been arranged since the time of creation.

• The star was not the brightest celestial object. It never had a tail. The star was not overly spectacular while it was manifest in the East or above Judaea.

• The star was symbolically significant, but it did not indicate the specific day or time of the Messiah's birth. The star announced the coming of a messianic king. Above Bethlehem, the star affirmed the Messiah's presence in the town.

• The wise men went to Bethlehem and did a careful search in order to find the Messiah's family. They did not need the star to give them directions to arrive at the place where the young child was located. Finding the child through a thorough search was possible. Supernatural guidance was not necessary. However, the Magi did need to be informed that the Messiah had come. That was the star's primary role.

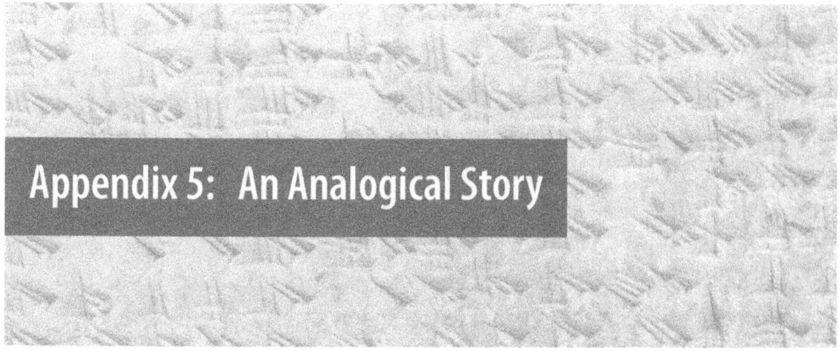

"The Lamp Repairman and the Great Sale"

This story illustrates the interactions between the star and the wise men. It is meant to be both amusing and instructive.

In a certain very large city, there were three friends, Balty, Mel and Casimir. They lived on the far eastern side of the city. One day they went for a walk and saw another friend named Starry Bob, who was a lamp repairman, high above the ground on a ladder repairing a street lamp. Although Bob was far up in the air on his ladder above the ground, there was a lively conversation for several minutes. Toward the end, Starry Bob yelled down to his three friends, "There is a great sale taking place in the massive supermarket named Walden's Superstore on the other side of town." He continued saying, "It is not to be missed, I encourage you to go and find all the good deals."

The three friends continued on their way. Having taken their friend's advice to heart, they walked speedily toward the west, toward the massive store. At one traffic light, a car stopped, and the mayor stepped out. The three friends were a bit embarrassed, but the mayor greeted them kindly and asked them where they were going in such a hurry. They all responded to the mayor together, "We have heard from a friend about a great sale at Walden's Superstore. We are hurrying to get there." The mayor responded, "I too have heard about this great sale. "Could you be so kind as to send me an SMS if you see something really interesting?"

The mayor gave them his personal phone number and the men went on their way.

At the massive store, there was a considerable crowd in several lines. The men started asking others in the waiting line where the best deals might be located. And behold, unknown to Balty, Casimir and Mel the lamp repairman Starry Bob had another job repairing and installing lamps at Walden's Superstore. Starry Bob took his truck and gone on before his three friends to install an essential new light bulb just inside the main entrance of the store. He preceded them there by at least a half hour.

Finally, getting through the main entrance, Balty, Casimir, and Mel saw a high folding ladder standing almost over the entrance. Looking up, the three men saw Starry Bob, who just happened to be looking down as they entered the store. Starry Bob yelled down, "I told you it would be a fantastic sale, see the crowd!" At that moment, Starry Bob connected the new light. Then everyone could see clearly to find the best deals. Mel, Balty, and Casimir, being a bit superstitious, took it as a sign that they had made the right choice in coming to the store.

Commentary: The Magi's star gave a message and preceded the wise men to Bethlehem in a similar manner to what is described above. The star functioned as a messenger and sign. It did not guide or lead anyone to Bethlehem. The star preceded the Magi from the East to Bethlehem chronologically, getting there in advance of the men on the ground. However, it was not visually leading them to the town or the very spot where the Messiah was located. The star was not even visually in front of the men during their travels. Upon the Magi's arrival in Bethlehem, above the small Judaean town, the star manifested itself again as a sign concerning the Messiah. The star never led anyone anywhere. The star was a signal, a sign concerning the Messiah, not a directional indicator or guide.

Appendix 6: Dating the Reign of Herod the Great

For centuries, there have been problems with specifically dating the birth of Jesus. Even the year of his birth remains a subject of debate. Ancient dates are not necessarily easy to calculate. The present calendar terms BC, and AD were only adopted many centuries after the birth of Jesus. Some errors were made in the date calculation process. Therefore, we now have the odd situation of indicating Christ's birth in the years "BC" instead of in a more logical phrasing "in the year of our Lord" (Anno Domini) AD 1.

In the early centuries of the Christian era, Christian scholars like Clement of Alexandria, Tertullian, Julius Africanus, Hippolytus of Rome, Origen, and Eusebius of Caesarea believed that Jesus was born sometime during the 41st or 42nd year of the reign of Augustus Caesar (3 BC or 2 BC). While the Church Fathers sometimes may have been mistaken, they also deserve respect. They may have more to offer us than we would expect.

For various reasons, many Bibles, commentaries, and godly preachers in the last four centuries have used a 4 BC date for the death of Herod the Great. This dating was first proposed by a Polish monk named Laurentius Suslyga in AD 1605. Suslyga's ideas were founded on a series of logical assumptions, but some of his ideas have been seriously called into question in recent decades. If one makes different assumptions about the period of Herod's death and the birth of Jesus, then the chronology takes on another aspect. One's initial assumptions do heavily influence all the dating schemes concerning Herod's reign.

The suggested spring 4 BC date for Herod's death has led many people to search for the famous Bethlehem star in the years previous to 4 BC. Several serious astronomical propositions have been put forward concerning the star in the years from 7 BC to 5 BC. However, a 4 BC date for the death of Herod does not solve all the historical problems. It may create several other serious historical, factual and biblical difficulties. Some of our sources of information also apparently contain errors, which could lead one to false conclusions.

There is significant evidence that Herod was named king of Judah in 39 BC instead of 40 BC as is often assumed. Herod supposedly reigned for 37 years. If Herod were named king in 39 BC, then his death in 4 BC would seem somewhat doubtful. There are only 34.5 years between the early fall of 39 BC and the spring of 4 BC. According to the Gospel of Matthew Jesus was born before Herod the Great died. If one can establish the dates for Herod's death, then it is possible to give estimated dates for the birth of Jesus, the manifestation of the star, and the visit of the wise men.

It has been largely assumed in academic circles that the dates of the reign of Herod the Great are well established. One usually finds Herod's 37-year reign indicated from 40 BC to 4 BC with his 34-year reign in Jerusalem commencing in 37 BC after the defeat of his rival Antigonus. It also appears very clear that Herod's sons and heirs dated their reigns from either 4 or 3 BC. For the vast majority of scholars and the general public, the 40 BC to 4 BC dates remain solidly in place, and such dating is often called the "best scholarship" on the matter.

However, in 1966 W. E. Filmer proposed a different timeline which placed Herod's death in early 1 BC, not long after a total eclipse of the moon during the night of January 9-10 of that year. In addition, Filmer believed that Herod's reign began in the latter half of 39 BC with his nomination as king by the Roman Senate. Filmer also proposed that Herod conquered Jerusalem in the fall of 36 BC and not in the summer or fall of 37 BC as is often indicated by various authorities.

In order to establish his timeline, W. E. Filmer proposed that Herod's sons had backdated their reigns. There are some reasons to think that this may have happened. Some scholars have thought that Filmer's ideas were definitively answered by articles written by Timothy Barnes (1968), P. M. Bernegger (1983) and Harold Hoehner (1989). For various reasons Jack Finegan (1998), Ernest Martin (1991) and Andrew Steinmann (2009,

2011) among others followed Filmer's line of thought in establishing their chronologies concerning the beginning and the end of Herod's reign. The present author has concluded that Herod did die in 1 BC. The following paragraphs indicate various reasons why we should rethink the timeline.

Alternate Assumptions About the Chronology of Herod's Reign

1) A central piece of evidence for the dating of Herod's reign involves three coins which supposedly date the Syrian governorship of the Roman leader Publilius Quintilius Varus. It is without question that Herod died when Varus was governor of Syria. We know this from the writings of Flavius Josephus. The so-called "Varus coins," supposedly date the Syrian governorship of Publius Quintilius Varus from 7/6 to 4 BC.

It has been known for a long time that dating Varus' governorship with the coins from 7/6 to 4 BC poses a chronological problem. This was pointed out by the Oxford scholar, Edward Greswell (among others), in the 1830s. The typical approach to dating the coins causes Varus to become governor a year or more too early to match Josephus' account of events toward the end of Herod's life. Greswell discusses this in more than 50 pages of text and notes as part of his book, *Dissertations Upon The Principles And Arrangement Of An Harmony Of The Gospels*. This chronology problem has never been adequately addressed by the proponents of the 4 BC date for Herod's death in the more than 300 years since the coins surfaced. Most people do not even realize that there is a problem. Greswell himself believed that Herod died in 4 BC, but he did not think that the coins were connected to Varus. Greswell thought that Varus had only become governor in 5 BC and not a year or so earlier as indicated by the coins.

It has usually been assumed that the coins are dated from Augustus' victory at the Battle of Actium in 31 BC (the years 25, 26 and 27 of the Actian Era). However, Edward Greswell believed that the coins were dated from the first year of Julius Caesar's reign (dictatorship) in 49/48BC, the beginning of the so-called "Caesarian Era." In Greswell's opinion, the famous "Varus coins" actually referred to an almost unknown Varro (Varo) in 25-23 BC (The years 25, 26 and 27 of the Caesarian Era). Varro's governorship is described in Josephus' works: (*Antiquities* 15.10.1 and *War* 1.20.4). It seems that all the coins from Antioch were dated by the Caesarian Era down to about 14/13 BC or perhaps later.

Greswell thought that Varro (Varo) might have been written as OUAROU by the team at the Antioch mint as "the form most convenient or most agreeable to the genius of their language." A shorter name also would have been easier to inscribe on the small coins (d. 20 mm). Greswell was convinced that the coins were related to Varro because of the coincidence of dates, which renders the coins and the dated chronology coherent and compatible. In his opinion, this coincidence "was beyond the power of mere chance to have produced." [1]

Since the so-called "Varus coins" can be dated with Caesarian dates (from 49/48 BC), then they could actually be coins appertaining to Varro (Varo) in the 25/24 to 23/22 BC. For more information see Hutchison, *The Lion Led the Way,* pp. 80-82 and Appendix 19 pp. 320-332 (There are 12 pages on the coins alone).

The entire dating scheme for the Roman governors of Syria from about 12 BC to about AD 6 depends on the dates of four coins. There are no monuments, inscriptions or other artifacts which date the governors. (Please note: it is not even known if Gaius Caesar replaced the governor of Syria in AD 1 through AD 4 - Schürer acknowledges this himself.) While one can find neat lists of dates concerning the Roman governors of Syria in books and online, in truth, there are a lot of unknowns concerning the dates and even the lists of governors for the period in question. For example, in the words of one historian: "The dates of the governor Sentius Saturninus' administration of Syria are commonly given as 9-6 BC, or circa 8-6 BC, and with less assurance as 10/9 BC to 7/6 BC with question marks." After citing this list of dates, the historian N. Kokkinos, goes on to state his belief that the correct dates were 12-8 BC.[2]

---

1 Edward Greswell, *Dissertations Upon The Principles And Arrangement Of An Harmony Of The Gospels,* Second Edition, In Four Volumes. Vol. I. Oxford University Press, Oxford 1837). 466-529. His arguments are developed in the later part of the passage on pages 528-529 in particular, although the entire text sets the background for the discussion.

2 Nikos Kokkinos, "The Honorand of The Titulus Tiburtinus: C. Sentius Saturninus?," (© Dr. Rudolf Habelt Gmbh, Bonn) Aus: Zeitschrift Für Papyrologie Und Epigraphik 105 (1995) 32.

(For further insights see *The Lion Led the Way, Third Edition* pages 78-104 and 298-332.)

From this author's perspective, Varus was probably governor of Syria from about 2 BC to about 1 AD, not from 7/6 to 4 BC. Sentius Saturninus preceded him as governor possibly from about 5 to 2 BC. Much of one's perspective depends on how one dates these so-called Varus' coins.

2) Good arguments can be made that Herod's heirs backdated their reigns to 4 BC following the king's death in early 1 BC.[3] It is entirely possible to date the execution of Herod's Hasmonean heirs to 4 BC instead of the usual 7 BC postulated by many scholars. There were several political advantages for Herod's heirs in repudiating the joint-reign of the Crown Prince, Antipater, with their father through backdating coins (Josephus, Anitquities of the Jews, 17.2.32 and 17.5.96). Backdating the reigns of Herod's heirs could have vindicated the unjustly executed Hasmonean brothers over Antipater, who had conspired to put them to death. The dead Hasmonean brothers remained exceedingly popular. An impostor, claiming to be one of the brothers who had somehow escaped death, was widely acclaimed as Herod's true heir after the king's death, and he gained a wide following. Only Augustus' intervention stopped the masquerade (Josephus, *Antiquities of the Jews*, 17.12.324-338; Filmer, 1966, pp. 283–298; Hutchison, 2015, pp. 96-101, see a passage answering Barnes - pp. 298-301).

3) The archaeological teams currently working in Bethsaida have rejected the ideas advanced by Suslyga, Kepler, and Schürer (among others) concerning the renaming of Bethsaida as Julias.[4] In the early 1600s, this was a key concept in re-dating the death of Herod to 4 BC. Laurentius Suslyga and Kepler thought that Philip the Tetrarch had renamed the town in honor of Julia the Elder, the Emperor Augustus' biological daughter. He had supposedly done this before her disgrace in 2 BC, thus proving that Philip was already Tetrarch at that date.

The archaeologists working at Bethsaida now believe that Philip renamed the town in about AD 30. It was renamed after the adopted

---

3   Filmer, W. E.."Chronology of the Reign of Herod the Great," Journal of Theological Studies, ns 17 (1966), pp. 283–298).

4   Josephus, *Antiquities* 18.2.1 and *War* 2.9.1. Bethsaida was situated on the Sea of Galilee where the Jordan River runs into the lake. It was the home of some of Jesus' disciples.

daughter of Augustus, his wife Livia, after her death in AD 29.[5] Livia received the name Julia as part of her being adopted into the Julian family in Augustus' will in AD 14. This would explain why the name Julias persisted for generations. It was used by Pliny the Elder in his book *Natural History* (c. AD 77) and by Ptolemy in his *Geography* (c. AD 150). If the city had been renamed for the deeply disgraced daughter of the emperor in 3 or 2 BC one would expect that a different name would have been chosen at some point (or that the name would have simply been forgotten). Certainly, most, if not all, of the archaeological teams working at Bethsaida would still affirm a 4 BC date for Herod's death. However, their own stance concerning the renaming of Bethsaida as Julias calls into question one of the main original arguments for the 4 BC date for Herod's death. See *The Lion Led the Way* pp. 86-88.

4) According to Josephus, the Parthian supported coup d'état which forced Herod to flee to Egypt and then on to Rome took place near the time of Pentecost in the late spring. Following the most widely currently accepted view, Herod fled to Egypt and Rome where he was named king by the Roman Senate in late 40 BC. But details on Herod's return to Judaea are sketchy in the traditional view.

While Emil Schürer and others have been very imprecise about the dating of the Roman campaign to reconquer Syria when Herod was named king by the Roman Senate, some ancient authors were far more precise.[6] Plutarch explicitly says that the campaign to reconquer Syria (and Judaea) took place after the Pact of Puteoli (Misenum). Cassius Dio says something similar. The agreement/pact of Misenum was signed in the summer of 39 BC. Roman military units were already in Judaea before Herod arrived back in Ptolemais (Acco, Israel) from Rome after having been named king of Judaea by the Roman Senate. This indicates that Herod was named king of Judaea in the fall of 39 BC, regardless of the consular dates usually cited to indicate the beginning of his reign in 40 BC.

If Herod was named king in late 40 BC and he arrived in Galilee and

---

5 Frederick M. Strickert, *Philip's City: From Bethsaida to Julias,* (Collegeville, MN: Liturgical, 2011), pp. 163-188.

6 Even Emil Schürer simply slides over the topic. See Israel Shatzman, *The Armies of the Hasmonaeans and Herod: From Hellenistic to Roman Frameworks,* (Tübingen: Mohr, 1991), p. 151 and note 85.

Judaea in the fall of 39 BC, one could ask what he had been doing for more than nine or ten months following being named king. He left Italy within seven days of having been named king of Judaea. Did he spend 9, 10, or 11 months in Athens or Rhodes while his brother, bride to be, mother and sister were besieged at Masada? It hardly makes sense. Herod immediately went to their rescue when he arrived in Galilee and Judaea. In addition, we read that the Romans on site in Judaea had pretended to want to help Herod's relatives at Masada before Herod ever arrived back in Galilee from Rome. They had done this in order to extract bribes from Antigonus, who was besieging Masada.

What was Herod doing? Why did he not accompany the Romans when they initially arrived back in Judaea? We read that Anthony even sent a man expressly to instruct the Roman generals to help Herod when he arrived back in Galilee / Judaea. If Herod had spent 9, 10 or 11 months in Athens or Rhodes, had he not communicated with the Roman generals who fought their way to Galilee and Judaea?

The stormy weather, which Herod encountered on his way from Egypt to Rome before he was named king of Judaea, was probably the sometimes violent, fair-weather "Etesian Winds," in July or August of 39 BC. The storms were not in late 40 BC as it is often imagined (Josephus, Antiquities, 14.14.2-3) (Hutchison, 2015, pp. 94-95).

Herod did not wait in Athens or Rhodes for 9, 10, or 11 months. He arrived back in Galilee and Judaea as quickly as possible after his nomination as king in Rome. He arrived after the Roman army was already on site in Galilee and Judaea. Herod was named king in the fall of 39 BC. Before Herod arrived back in Galilee and Judaea the Roman army had already arrived in the area.

The consular dates usually used to establish the beginning of Herod's reign in 40 BC were apparently mistakes made by Josephus or errors introduced by well-meaning copyists/editors at a later date. If Herod began his kingship in the fall of 39 BC, it is evident that he did not die in 4 BC (Josephus indicated that Herod reigned 37 years). See The Lion Led the Way, pp. 78-88 and Appendices10-14, pp. 266-279. See also notes 20a and 20b on page 320, as well as note 8 on pages 297 and 298.

The remarkable series of mostly discreet celestial events briefly described in this book is probably without equal in all of history as an indicator of a clear celestial message concerning kingship. The simple fact that this series of events is so precise and so clear should lead scholars to reexamine the timeline of Herod's reign.

Another Aspect of the Dating Issue

Problems surrounding the dates of Quirinius' governorship of Syria and the census in Luke 2:1-5 can be resolved by an alternate translation of Luke 2:2, which reads: "This census took place before the time when Quirinius was governor of Syria."[7] It has also been suggested that the passage can be read, "This census took place before Quirinius was governor of Syria."[8] Quirinius' census in AD 6/7 was mentioned because it was well-known and had been particularly painful for the Jews. The Zealot movement against Rome owed its origin to Quirinius' census. The alternate translation of Luke 2:2 sets the census at Jesus' birth apart from the one under Quirinius (Wright, 1993, pp. 88-89 and Brindle,1984, pp. 43-52). See Luke 2:2 in The Kingdom New Testament by N.T. Wright; Orthodox Jewish Bible (OJB); New International Version (NIV) in a note; English Standard Version (ESV) in a note; Holman Christian Standard Bible (HCSB) in a note.[9]

Conclusion

Perhaps some of the dating questions need to be dusted off. I have the definite impression that most people who hold to the 4 BC date for Herod's death usually do so because it is the "accepted best scholarship."

7 Translation of Luke 2:2 : N.T. Wright, *The Kingdom New Testament: a Contemporary Translation of the New Testament* (Kindle Version). HarperOne, 2011.

8 Harold W. Hoehner, *Chronological Aspects of the Life of Christ.* Zondervan, 1981). p. 21-22.The passage cites work done by A. J. B. Higgins, "Sidelights on Christian Beginnings in the Graeco-Roman world,"The Evangelical Quarterly, XLI (October, 1969), 200-201.

9 N.T. Wright, Who Was Jesus? (Grand Rapids, Mich.: Eerdmans, 1993), 88-89. A summary of the different ideas about this passage is in Wayne Brindle, "The Census and Quirinius: Luke 2:2," JETS 27/1 (March1984) 43-52.

The German scholar Emil Schürer admits that such a translation is possible. Emil Schürer, Géza Vermès et Fergus Millar, The History of the Jewish People in the Age of Jesus Christ (175 B.C.-A.D. 135), (Edinburgh: Clark, 1973), p. 421.

However, few have ever explored the issues in detail. Good scholarship can be improved from time to time. Perhaps the "best scholarship" needs to be reexamined.

As the British historian and theologian, N. T. Wright has written: "Much of our knowledge of the ancient past is based on titbits of information." I find this statement to be especially applicable concerning the period in question. Relatively little information is available about the period and what is available can be interpreted in various ways.

Alexis - Ekur-zakir's chief servant who facilitated the logistical and practical side of the Magi's epic journey to Bethlehem along with a group of servants.

Callisthenes - A Greek mercenary who was hired for the protection of the wise men during their travels; He worked with a team of eight guards.

Eliab - A Babylonian Jew who worked as a notarial scribe for Ekur-zakir.

Elkanah - A principal priest in Jerusalem who facilitated the visit of the wise men.

Ekur-zakir - The chief astronomer in Borsippa in Babylonia. He was also a notary and several other astronomers were involved in his business.

Herod the Great - King of Judaea, Samaria, Galilee, Perea, and regions east of the Sea of Galilee from 39 BC to 1 BC.

Hormizdah - A Zoroastrian astronomer and wise man who was in the service of Larvandad the Rab-mag.

Illis-kutul - Originally from Uruk, Illis-kutul was a very intelligent astronomer. His wife Sarpanit and daughter Kallisto play minor roles in the novel.

Ispubarza - The wife of Ekur-zakir.

Iqisa - The son of Ekur-zakir. Iqisa was also a Magus, a Babylonian astronomer.

Joseph - The adoptive father of Jesus and husband of Mary.

Larvandad - A Zoroastrian Rab-mag, the chief wise man in the Parthian Empire. He spent most of the year in Ctesiphon at the royal court.

Malachi - A businessman in Bethlehem who did projects for Herod the Great and whom the king called upon to host the Magi.

Mary - The mother of Jesus.

Musa - She was the queen of the Parthian Emperor Phraates IV and the mother of Phraataces who would become the ruler of the Empire following Phraates IV's death.

Nikolaos - A Babylonian Greek astronomer who had spent time in Rome and Athens. He was a bit skeptical of heavenly signs and astrological forecasting.

Selebum - A Babylonian astronomer who was seeking to profit financially from celestial events.

Suen-magir - As a young astronomer and notarial scribe, who has known heartbreak, Suen-magir struggles with alcohol and prostitutes. However, he finds help through the God of Abraham.

Shelumiel - This man was the head servant in the household of Malachi, the businessman in Bethlehem.

Theron - A spy sent by Herod to keep watch on the Magi in Bethlehem.

Uzziel - Joseph's cousin who receives the couple in Bethlehem during the census declared by Augustus.

Appendix 8: Kings/Emperors and Daniel's Prophecy

In Chapter Two Eliab and Iqisa counted backwards to arrive at the dates of Cyrus' reign. However, this table gives the counting in a forward manner. The Sabbatical dates in this chart are those of Ben Zion Wacholder. The Sabbatical year dates proposed by Benedict Zuckermann would have been one year earlier.

The Prophecy of Daniel 9:24-25

"Seventy 'sevens' [1] *have been decreed for your people and your holy city, to finish the transgression, to make an end of sin, to make atonement for iniquity, to bring in everlasting righteousness, to seal up vision and prophecy and to anoint the most holy place. So you are to know and discern that from the issuing of a decree to restore and rebuild Jerusalem until Messiah the Prince there will be seven weeks and sixty-two weeks; it will be built again, with plaza and moat, even in times of distress.*

---

1 The word "sevens" is often translated as "weeks." The word should be understood as "units of seven."

Years BC	Name of King or Emperor
559-530	Cyrus II (the Great)
533/532	49 years begins
530-522	Cambyses II
522	Gaumata the Magus
522-486	Darius I (the Great)
486-466	Xerxes I
485/484	49 years ends
484/483	49 years begins (Jubilee)
466-465	Artabanes
465-425	Artaxerxes I
436/435	49 years ends (Jubilee)

49 years

7 X 7 years (7 Sabbatical Cycles)

Persian Rulers

49 years (A Jubilee Sequence)

7 X 7 years (7 Sabbatical Cycles)

Years BC	Name of King or Emperor
465-425	Artaxerxes I
435/434	434 years begins (62 X 7)
425-424	Xerxes II
424-423	Sogdianus
423-404	Darius II
404-359	Artaxerxes II
359-338	Artaxerxes III
338-336	Artaxerxes IV
336-330	Darius III

Persian Rulers

330-323	Alexander
323-316	Philip
316-312	Antigonus
312-280	Seleucus I (founder dynasty)
280-261	Antiochus I Soter
261-246	Antiochus II Theos
246-225	Seleucus II
225-223	Seleucus III
223-187	Antiochus III
187-175	Seleucus IV
175-164/3	Antiochus IV Epiphanes
164/3-162	Antiochus V
150-145	Alexander Balas
145-141	Demetrius II Nicator

(Greek) Seleucid Rulers

434 years

(62 Sabbatical Cycles)

c.171-138	Mithridates I Philhellene
c.138-127	Phraates II
c.127-124	Artabanus I
124-88	Mithridates II
90-80	Orodes I
70-57	Phraates III
57-54	Mithridates III
57-38	Orodes II
38-2	Phraates IV
2/1	434 years ends (62 X 7)

Parthian Rulers

This is a selected bibliography. Much more material could be cited. The author is not necessarily in agreement with all the works in this list, but he has found the reference material to be helpful. Some books and papers in this bibliography could easily be placed in two or more categories.

Ancient Mesopotamian Astronomy and Astrology

Evans, James. *The History and Practice of Ancient Astronomy.* New York: Oxford University Press, 1998.

Gray, Jennifer, Mary, Knightley (2009) *A Study of Babylonian Goal-Year Planetary Astronomy.* Durham theses, Durham University. Available at Durham E-Theses Online: http://etheses.dur.ac.uk/101/

Hunger, Hermann and David Edwin Pingree. *Astral Sciences in Mesopotamia.* Leiden: Brill, 1999.

Hollywood, Louise, and John M. Steele. "Acronycal Risings in Babylonian Astronomy." Centaurus 46.2 (2004): 145-62.

Kasak, Enn and Veede, Raul, "Understanding Planets in Ancient Mesopotamia," Electronic Journal of Folklore ISSN 1406-0949. Available at: http://haldjas.folklore.ee/folklore/vol16/planets.pdf

Kelley, David H., and E. F. Milone. *Exploring Ancient Skies an Encyclopedic Survey of Archaeoastronomy.* New York: Springer, 2005.

Koch-Westenholz, Ulla. *Mesopotamian Astrology An Introduction To Babylonian And Assyrian Celestial Divination.* The Carsten Niebuhr Institute Of Near Eastern Studies, Copenhagen: Museum Tusculanum Press, 1995. Electronic Version from Academia.com

Neugebauer, Otto. *The Exact Sciences in Antiquity.* 2d ed. New York: Dover Publications, 1969.

Ossendrijver, Mathieu. *Babylonian Mathematical Astronomy Procedure Texts.* New York, NY: Springer, 2012.

Rocheberg, Francesca. "Babylonian Astral Science in the Hellenistic World: Reception and Transmission." Ludwig-Maximilians-Universität München 4 (2010): 1-11.

Rochberg, Francesca. *In The Path Of The Moon Babylonian Celestial Divination And Its Legacy.* Leiden: Brill, 2010.

Rochberg, Francesca. *The Heavenly Writing: Divination, Horoscopy, And Astronomy in Mesopotamian Culture.* Cambridge: Cambridge University Press, 2004.

Sachs, Abraham, and Hermann Hunger. *Astronomical Diaries and Related Texts from Babylonia.* Wien: Verlag der Österreichischen Akademie der Wissenschaften, 1988, 1989, 1996, 2001, 2006, 2014.

Sachs, Abraham Joseph & Walker, Christopher B.F., "Kepler's View of the Star of Bethlehem and the Babylonian Almanac for 7/6 B.C.", Iraq, 46 (1984), 43-55.

Swerdlow, N. M.. *The Babylonian Theory of the Planets.* Princeton, N.J.: Princeton University Press, 1998.

Heliacal Risings and Settings

Purrington, Robert D. "Heliacal Rising and Setting: Quantitative Aspects." Archeoastronomy, no. 12 (JHA, xix 1988)

Robinson, Matthew. "Ardua et Astra: On the Calculation of the Dates of the Rising and Setting of Stars." Classical Philology, Vol. 104, No. 3, July 2009. pp. 354-375.

Robinson, Matthew. "Ovid, the Fasti and the Stars." Bulletin of the Institute of Classical Studies©, vol. 50 (2007). Avaialble at: www. http://discovery.ucl.ac.uk/6901/1/6901.pdf

Schaefer, Bradley E., "Astronomy and the Limits of Vision", Vistas in Astronomy, Volume 36, pp 311-361, 1993.

Chronology / Calendars

Anderson, Steven D.. *Darius the Mede: A Reappraisal.* Grand Rapids: Steven D. Anderson, 2014.

Beckwith, Roger T.. *Calendar and Chronology, Jewish and Christian: Biblical, Intertestamental and Patristic Studies.* Leiden: E.J. Brill, 1996.

Brindle, Wayne. "The Census And Quirinius: Luke 2:2." JETS 27/1 (March1984) 43-52.

Filmer, W. E.."Chronology of the Reign of Herod the Great," *Journal of Theological Studies*, ns 17 (1966), pp. 283–298)

Finegan, Jack. *Handbook of Biblical Chronology Principles of Time Reckoning in the Ancient World and Problems of Chronology in the Bible.* Rev. ed. Peabody, Mass: Hendrickson, 1999.

Greswell, Edward. *Dissertations Upon The Principles And Arrangement Of An Harmony Of The Gospels. Second Edition, In Four Volumes. Vol. I.* (Oxford University Press, Oxford 1837).

Hoehner, Harold W.. *Chronological Aspects of the Life of Christ*. Grand Rapids: Zondervan Pub. House, 1978.

Schürer, Emil, Géza Vermès, and Fergus Millar. *The History of the Jewish People in the Age of Jesus Christ (175 B.C.-A.D. 135)*. Edinburgh: Clark, 1973,1987.

Steinmann, Andrew. *From Abraham to Paul: a Biblical Chronology*. St. Louis, MO: Concordia Pub. House, 2011.

Judaism / Jewish History

Amaral, Joe. *Understanding Jesus: Cultural Insights into the Words and Deeds of Christ*. New York: Faith-Words, 2011.

Edersheim, Afred. *The Life and Times of Jesus The Messiah*. New York: Randolph and Co.; London, Longmans, Green, & Co., 1890.

Johnson, Paul. *A History of the Jews*. London: Weidenfeld and Nicholson, 1987.

Neusner, Jacob. *A History of the Jews in Babylonia, Part I, The Parthian Period*. Wipf and Stock Publishers, Eugene, Oregon 1999.

Dates of Christmas / Birth of Jesus

Beckwith, Roger T.. *Calendar and Chronology, Jewish and Christian: Biblical, Intertestamental and Patristic Studies*. Leiden: E.J. Brill, 1996.

Duchesne, Louis. *Origines du culte chrétien ... Cinquième édition, revue et augmentée*. Paris, France: Ernest Thorin, 1889.

Finegan, Jack. *Handbook of Biblical Chronology: Principles of Time Reckoning in the Ancient World and Problems of Chronology in the Bible*. Rev. ed. Peabody, Mass.: Hendrickson Publishers, 1998.

Steinmann, Andrew. *From Abraham to Paul: a Biblical Chronology*. St. Louis, MO: Concordia Pub. House, 2011.

Talley, Thomas J. . *Origins of the Liturgical Year, 2nd ed.* Collegeville, MN: Liturgical Press, 1991.

Steinmann, Andrew. "A Chronological Note: The Return Of The Exiles Under Sheshbazzar And Zerubbabel (Ezra 1–2)," JETS 51/3 (September 2008) 513–22.

Strickert, Frederick M. *Philip's City: From Bethsaida to Julias*. Collegeville, MN: Liturgical, 2011.

Star of Bethlehem

Allison, Dale C. *Studies in Matthew: Interpretation past and Present.* Grand Rapids, MI: Baker Academic, 2005. pp. 17-42 (star as an angel).

Barthel, Peter, and George Van Kooten, eds. *The Star of Bethlehem and the Magi: Interdisciplinary Perspectives from Experts on the Ancient Near East, the Greco-Roman World, and Modern Astronomy.* Leiden: Brill, 2015.

Several other books could be cited in this section, but these two were particularly useful to the author.

Ancient Writers / Historians

Josephus, Suetonius, Appian, Cassius Dio, Diodorus, Livy, Plutarch, Velleius and others were consulted extensively online through the Perseus site and in other formats.

Josephus, Flavius, and William Whiston. *Josephus: the Complete Works.* Nashville, TN: Thomas Nelson Publishers, 1998.

Many of the astronomical images in the interior are from the Stellarium program. The author wishes to thank the Stellarium developers for the possibility of using images from their open source application.

The author highly recommends this application to all who are interested in either ancient or modern astronomy.

The Hebrew text in the background at the beginnings of major sections of the book is from the prophetic text in Genesis 49.

The chapter titles have a Babylonian astronomical document in the background. This is from a cuneiform tablet fragment giving daily position of the moon for the Seleucid year 118 (193-192 BC). From the Oriental Institute Museum, of the University of Chicago. Attribution: By Daderot (Own work) [CC0], via Wikimedia Commons.

Other credits:

Page 451: Enuma Anu Enlil Tablet 56 Louvre Museum [CC BY-SA 3.0 (https://creativecommons.org/licenses/by-sa/3.0)], via Wikimedia Commons
https://upload.wikimedia.org/wikipedia/commons/3/3e/Babylonian_Astrology_Treatise_-_Louvre%2C_Near_Eastern_Antiquities_in_the_Louvre%2C_Room_3%2C_Case_15_-_AO_6540.jpg,

Page 452: British Museum [CC BY-SA 3.0 (https://creativecommons.org/licenses/by-sa/3.0) or GFDL (http://www.gnu.org/copyleft/fdl.html)], via Wikimedia Commons
https://commons.wikimedia.org/wiki/File%3AVenus_Tablet_of_Ammisaduqa.jpg

Page 453: Top photo: Attribution: Author Anagoria https://creativecommons.org/licenses/by/3.0/deed.en.
Bottom photo: Metropolitan Museum of Art [CC0], via Wikimedia Commons   https://commons.wikimedia.org/wiki/File%3ACuneiform_tablet-_commentary_on_Enuma_Anu_Enlil%2C_tablet_5_MET_DP-442-002.jpg

Enuma Anu Enlil Tablet 56 about the observations of planets

See photographic credits page 448.

Above: A close-up view

The MUL-APIN, mentioned in the previous pages, would have been written on tablets similar to these containing the *Enuma Anu Enlil,* which is another very ancient document in the Babylonian omen catalog.

See photographic credits page 450.

Venus Tablet of Ammisaduqa from the *Enuma Anu Enlil* - Tablet 63

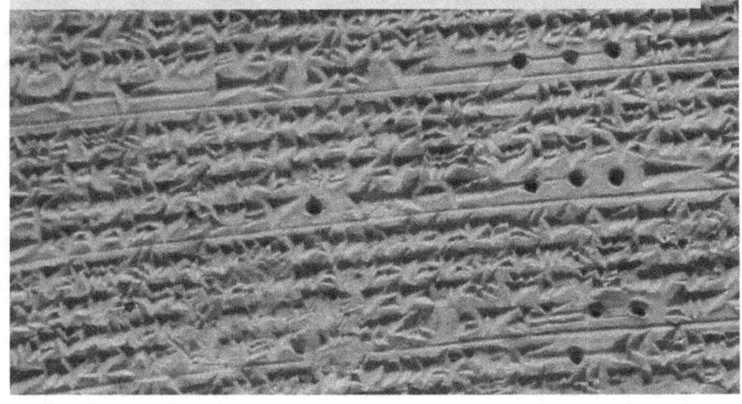

Close-up

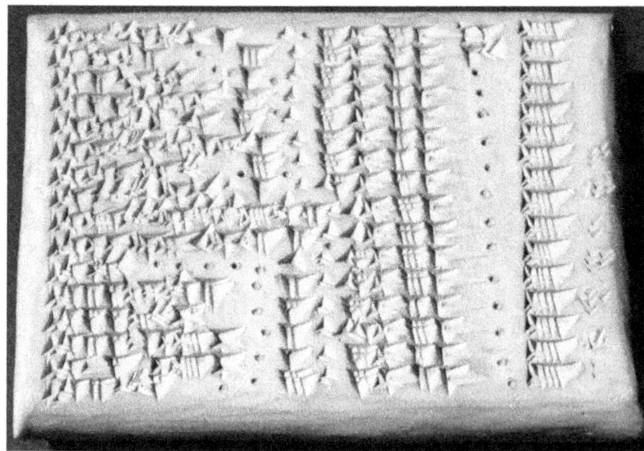

Star list with distance information, Uruk (Iraq), 320-150 BC, the list gives each constellation, the number of stars and the distance information to the next constellation. Special exhibition "Beyond the Horizon - Space and Knowledge in the Old World cultures" at the Pergamon Museum.

See photographic credits page 450.

Fragment of a Cuneiform tablet- commentary on Enuma Anu Enlil, Date: late 1st millennium BC.

See photographic credits page 450.

A tablet giving the rising times for the constellation Scorpio during the first month and also the ninth through the tenth month.

Illustration: Fragment of a tablet giving the daily motion
of the sun for the Seleucid year 124 (187/186 BC).
This image is from the Oriental Institute Museum, University of Chicago. (Public Domain - By Daderot (Own work) [CC0], via Wikimedia Commons)

Illustration above: A lunar ephemeris with the dates of the full moons for a period of two years. Oriental Institute Museum at the University of Chicago.

Below: A tablet fragment giving daily position of the moon for the Seleucid year 118 (193-192 BC) From the Oriental Institute Museum, of the University of Chicago.

Both photos: Attribution: By Daderot (Own work) [CC0], via Wikimedia Commons.

Appendix 11: MUL.BABBAR's Cycle and Daniel 9

Passover (March 30/31, 3 BC)
First Fruits Offering (April 1/2, 3 BC)
(1st Day of the Omer Count)

7 x 7 = 49

49th day of the "Counting of the Omer"
Close lunar conjunction with Regulus
(May 19/20, 3 BC)

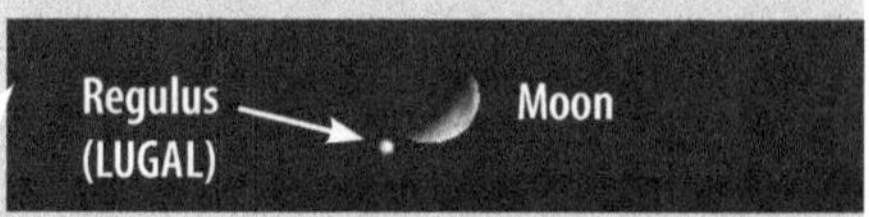

Penecost ("The Feast of Weeks")
50th Day (May 20/21, 3 BC)

(Pentecost makes a separation between the two periods of "sevens.")

1st Day of Counting the 62 "sevens"
(May 21/22, 3 BC)

69 Days
(7 + 62)

Gamma Phase of Jupiter
(July 29, 3 BC)

62 x 7 = 434

Omega Phase of Jupiter
Day 434 of Counting the 62 "sevens"
(July 28, 2 BC)

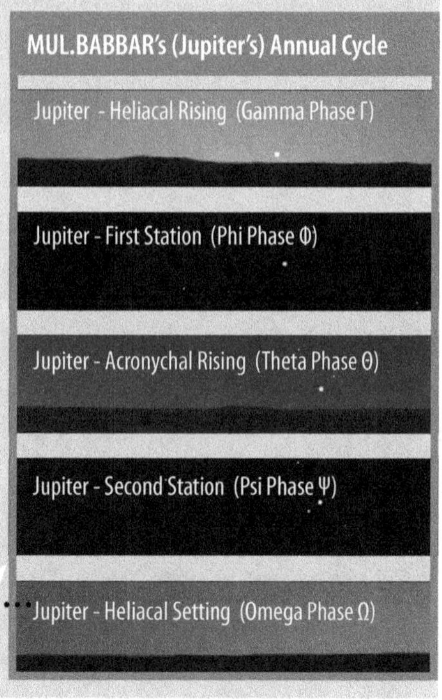

www.ingramcontent.com/pod-product-compliance
Lightning Source LLC
Chambersburg PA
CBHW050454160726
48003CB00001B/5